SWEATER DESIGN
IN
PLAIN ENGLISH

OTHER BOOKS BY MAGGIE RIGHETTI

Knitting in Plain English
Crocheting in Plain English
Universal Yarn Finder

Sweater Design

IN

PLAIN ENGLISH

Maggie Righetti

Original sketches by Maggie Righetti
Redrawn by John Yates

ST. MARTIN'S PRESS   NEW YORK

Design by Susan Hood
Illustrations by John C. Yates
Photographs by Carolyn Foster

Library of Congress Cataloging-in-Publication Data
Righetti, Maggie.
    Sweater design in plain English / Maggie Righetti.
        p.   cm.
    ISBN 0-312-05164-6
    1. Knitting—Patterns.   2. Sweaters.   I. Title.
TT825.R53   1990
746.9′2—dc20   90-37513
                                                    CIP

First Edition

10   9   8   7   6   5   4   3   2   1

Contents

Acknowledgments

I would like to acknowledge and give special thanks to the following people without whom this book would not have been possible:

To Ruth Gordon, then of Chino, California, who first taught me to chart and draft patterns for knitting.

To Ruth Rohn, of Burt Lake, Michigan, the advanced knitting instructor for the American Professional Needlework Retailers/The National Needlework Association teacher certification program, who sharpened my skills.

To Eileen Summerville, for her invaluable help in discussing color in Chapter 10.

To Victoria Kearney, for generously sharing her great knowledge of knitting machines.

To Patty Flowers, for the support and assistance she so ably provided.

To the following members of the Atlanta Knitting Guild who graciously and generously shared their problems about designing sweaters with me in order that I might address and solve these problems for knitters everywhere: Susan Bumbarger, Susan Coe, Joyce Culpepper, Debra Davis, Elizabeth Fenn, Margaret Horton, Betsy Laundon, Linda Mac Donald, Yvonne Morris, Jan O'Neill, Shirley Robb, Whit Harris Robbins, and Betty Wallace.

Especially to my editor, Barbara Anderson, who encouraged and allowed me to change the format of this book in response to the input of the members of the Atlanta Knitting Guild mentioned above.

And to the following yarn companies and their representatives who so generously supplied both yarn and suggestions to make up the model garments in the lessons in Part II: Elinore Bernat and her assistant, Linda Thibault, of Bernat Yarn and Craft Corporation; Mary Ann

Blackburn of DMC Corporation; Mayme Saunders of Coats & Clark "Redheart" ® Yarns; Gabrielle Spellman of Unger Yarns; Ernie Dandeneau and his assistant, Carol Crawford, of Brunswick Yarn Company; Julia Patterson of Reynolds Yarn Company; Sue Matson of Susan Bates, Inc., USA distributor for Patons Yarns; and Richard Powers of Plymouth Yarn Company.

I wish to apologize to all of my male readers. In writing this book, I have often used the pronoun *she* because I feel that *he/she* or *s(he)* is cumbersome. In no way do I mean to imply that men cannot, should not, or do not knit. Quite the contrary!

Introduction

Sooner or later every knitter says, "I want to make a sweater just like that one, except for . . ." She knows what she wants to change and what she wants the finished article to look like, but she doesn't know how to do it. She needs a way to get there from here. She needs to know the magic.

If you have ever found yourself wondering how to adjust, alter, or design a pattern for a knitted article, it is for you that I have written this book. I have stumbled and fumbled through all of these situations myself, making mistakes and learning as I went along. I want to spare you the frustration I felt, and give you the benefits of my painful journey through the land of increases and decreases, cast-on and picked-up stitches, ripping back and redoing. I want to share with you the experience and knowledge I have acquired designing, so that your journeys through the same land may be rewarding, enjoyable, and above all creative.

The magic of sweater design is that there is no magic. There is just common sense, a knowledge of how the human body is put together, an understanding of the way knitted fabric gives and stretches and pulls, and easy fourth-grade arithmetic. Nothing more. Nothing complicated.

Still, there is a magic to sweater designing in that the simple arithmetic actually works. There is a magic in getting just what *you* want, the way *you* want it. And there is a magic in the feeling of pride and accomplishment in doing something for yourself, and doing it well.

The premise of this book is to give the reader the necessary tools to select and design enjoyable knitted garments, to enable the reader to know in advance how each garment will look and feel on the intended wearer before making any investment of time or money.

This book will take you through that nonmagic of common sense, understanding both the human body and the fabric and, using a few numbers, into the *real magic of creating*. Whether you have never designed before or are an experienced artisan, this book will lead you, gently and with humor, step by easy step, to make your dreams and desires come true.

In deciding how best to present this material, I have chosen to divide it into three parts: Part I tells you the vital facts you need to know *before* you can begin to design any garment. (My advisory knitters from the Atlanta Knitting Guild feel that this is the most important part of the book.) It deals with information found in no other book about sweater design—the way the human body works, the difference that the choice of fiber makes, how knitted fabric and different pattern stitches behave, and how color changes apparent size. Part II will guide you from planning the simplest kind of sweater to creating and/or altering more complex designs. It explains not just how to plan the garments and how much (or how little) ease is necessary, but also the good and bad points, the pitfalls and drawbacks, the wearability and comfort of each type of design. By the time you have completed Part II, you will have learned how to design all the common forms of sweaters. You will have learned, as well, how to pick and choose separate parts, and mix and match different elements of the designs to create the kind of garment you want—a sweater that will look good, even great, on the intended wearer.

Part III, the Appendices, contains conversion tables, charts of standard measurements, and an index—all the reference tools you need at your fingertips.

You may be introduced to this book as a class text by your knitting instructor, where the classroom sharing of experiences with others will be rewarding. If you prefer to learn on your own, you will find that this book is complete, uncomplicated, and clear enough to be your only teacher. Working alone or in a class, it is not necessary to know how to knit to learn how to create the directions for perfectly fitting, unique, and attractive handmade garments. Some fine sweater designers do not know how to knit!

It is my sincere hope that by walking step by step through the learning lessons in this book, your innate creativity will find freer expression. More than that, I hope your self-confidence and self-esteem will be raised to the level where you aren't afraid to tackle any knit design project, and make it uniquely your own.

PART I

Before You Begin

1

Overcoming Your Fear
of Failure

When I began to write this book, I invited members of the local Atlanta Knitting Guild to share their problems about designing sweaters so that I could better solve *your* problems. I have been designing sweaters for twenty-five years, and I had forgotten the problems of beginners. What these knitters told me was that the actual designing and the numbers involved were the smallest part of their problems. By far their greatest fears were of criticism and of failure!

That statement took me quite by surprise.

I've always been a creative person, putting the old, tried, and true into new and different uses and combinations, using the unexpected for the obvious. As a child, Mother used to criticize me for making "ridiculous" clothing combinations, "strange" arrangements of the furnishings in my room, and "peculiar" combinations with foods.

As a young bride, some members of my husband's family criticized the way I kept house and cared for my children. I cooked my turkey breast side down to keep the white meat moist. "But it is not traditional to do it that way even if the white meat is moister," they said. "White meat is supposed to be dry and stringy." Also, I changed the babies' diapers in the bathroom on top of a chest of drawers I put there, which also contained their pajamas. "But it is wrong for you to do it because no one else does it that way," they said.

When we lived in a small farming town in Southern California, the local gossips wagged about me often. "Do you know what that Mrs. Righetti did? She bought a brocade tablecloth at a flea market and made a dress out of it and actually wore it to the chamber of commerce annual dinner! Her husband makes enough money; she could afford a new dress. There's just no understanding some people!"

Creativity, innovation, and nontraditional ways of solving problems are feared by noncreative, uninnovative, and traditional people. It causes them apprehension and consternation. They cope with their fear by criticizing people who do things differently.

If nothing can ever change, nothing can ever get any better! If you don't create new ways to solve old problems, you'll always be stuck with the old problems.

There are many critical people in this world. (They may even outnumber the supportive ones.) Depending on the environment you live in and the thought patterns of the people who surround you, you must expect to be criticized for creativity, for solving your problems in a unique way, and for making innovative changes *whether or not your efforts are successful*. Your own family members, and people in small towns or small groups especially, can be the absolutely worst nay-sayers against doing anything different or new.

Criticism and the fear of criticism are real concerns that one must simply learn to deal with. We could free ourselves of criticism by not being creative. There is an old adage that tells us: "To avoid criticism: Say nothing; do nothing; feel nothing; be nothing." But since you are reading this book, I don't think that you are the kind of person who can BE a nothing.

One of the best ways to get over the effects of unwanted criticism is to consider why it was made. What was his/her reason for criticizing instead of congratulating? Did the person feel inferior and incapable of doing what you did? Did he lack the know-how to create? Was the criticism made out of jealousy? Or was it the fear of anything new or different? Might critical remarks have been made because the person was afraid that you were venturing into new territory where he or she feared to go? Was she afraid she would be left behind, loosing you as a part of her world?

When you understand the nature of criticism, that it is easier than craftsmanship and creativity, you will have given yourself a sturdy coat of wax so that the raindrops of unkind and uncalled-for remarks will simply and quickly roll off you like a thunder shower off a freshly polished car.

(A side benefit of understanding the nature of criticism is that it will allow us to stop criticizing others, and to start handing out compliments, freely and openly, whenever and wherever we encounter creativity and craftsmanship.)

The *fear* of failure is something quite different. Unlike criticism, which comes from the outside, the fear of failure comes from within.

The fear of failure is different also because it has two very separate and distinct parts. One part is that the sweater will be a flop. The other part is that if the sweater is a dud, there will be unhappy repercussions because of it.

The fear that the object we are going to create won't be any good—that the sweater itself will be awful—is an honest concern. We have all seen completely disastrous sweaters. We don't want to make one. We want a good-looking and well-fitting garment that we will be proud of, but we fear that the project will be a costly mistake, a waste of money, time, and effort.

This part of the fear of failure can be paralyzing. To the group of Atlanta knitters that I talked with, the fear of making a fiasco was a tremendous burden, a much bigger problem than figuring out the number of stitches to work with. They were afraid that they would spend a lot of money on yarn, go through the bother of designing, spend precious time knitting, and then end up with a mess. They were afraid that the finished sweater would not look good on the intended wearer, that in the end it would be unwearable and a complete loss. Some were so afraid that they said they would never attempt to design their own sweaters.

Other knitters said that if they had more information they would not be so afraid. They asked me to answer all kinds of questions about designing sweaters, not just about the arithmetic of doing it, but the dos and don'ts of making up a good design. They felt that understanding the rules about clothing the human body would help prevent errors. If they could know what things to consider, beside just the numbers of doing it, their fears of failing would be lessened. And my friends in Atlanta are absolutely right. You do have to know about the human body, about how knitted fabric behaves on it, about what color does to shape, what will and what will not work if you are going to create something wonderful. This is what the material in Chapters 2 through 17 is all about—minimizing the possibility of ending up with a flop. I am confident these chapters will relieve your anxiety.

There is a second part to the fear of failure beyond the fear that the sweater will be a dud. It is the fear of the reactions that an imperfect finished garment will elicit from both ourselves and others.

No one wants to appear foolish or stupid. We all need approval—from the self and from others. If we do not hear ourselves and/or others saying that what we are doing is worthwhile, we cannot function. And how can we get approval if what we make is no good?

Long ago, before we were six or seven or eight years old, we received messages from people around us telling us how to view both ourselves and the world. These "old tapes" were put into our heads as truths and we believed them. Even after we have grown up, they play over and over deep inside us saying, we cannot expect approval if we make a mistake; others will laugh at us and ridicule us if what we make is a dud; we must be perfect in everything we do; failure marks us imperfect people; if we are not successful, we are no good; if we fail, we will lose the love and respect of people we care about.

In some of us, these old tapes play so loudly that we find ourselves unable to take any risks at all. We may feel that if whatever we contemplate doing cannot be guaranteed to come out perfectly, there is no point in doing it. We cannot abide the thought of failing. And the fear of failing keeps us from trying new things; we stay in the same unhappy, noncreative place living with the same old problems.

We cannot change the tapes in the heads of other people. We can, however, change the tapes in our own heads. It isn't easy; it takes a lot of effort and courage but it can be done.

Let me help you to put a new set of tapes in your head. Repeat after me: "Relax, it is okay to make mistakes. Even experienced designers make mistakes." As a professional, I know that not everything I create will be a sensation. This is the nature of innovation. I realize that the less than perfect project was a lesson. I analyze why it didn't work and what would make it better, and I try again. It is okay to have mishaps if we allow ourselves to realize they are a part of our lives. Now I take failure in stride and just go back to the drawing board and start over.

All is not lost if the sweater you design is not at first perfect. There is a chapter in my book *Knitting in Plain English* (New York: St. Martin's Press, 1986) that explains how to make simple alterations that can improve error-caused problems. And if everything else fails, you can almost always rip it out. You wouldn't be the first knitter to rip out a sweater!

It is not mistakes that we need to fear. Mistakes are not our undoing. It is the *fear* of failure that is the horror. The fear itself is the terrible monster stalking in the dark. I do not think that you are going to make a failure. In this book I do everything possible to show you how to avoid mistakes that could cause failure, and to help you to instead create wonderful, beautiful, unique, perfectly fitting sweaters.

2

Avoiding Costly Mistakes

No one in her right mind wants to make costly disasters. Avoiding them is usually just a matter of thinking ahead and of being aware. Strangely though, forethought and awareness can easily slip through our fingers. We can be momentarily captivated by a special look, color, or texture and our better sense can be quickly overrun by impulsive desire. Sometimes hasty decisions turn into magical creations. More often than not, spur-of-the-moment choices and less-than-thought-through purchases become unhappy mishaps.

It is sometimes easy to convince ourselves that if we follow prepared commercial instructions we will avoid making costly mistakes. "Somebody else has already made it up and there is a photo of it. So if I do everything exactly as the instructions say, it should turn out all right." Sorry, folks, it doesn't always work out "all right."

Following the published patterns of others is no guarantee that you will not make a disastrous mistake.

Over and above the problems that may be caused by the intended wearer not having the same "standard" measurements that the designer used in making up the directions, printed patterns don't always work out as hoped. You need to understand that pattern leaflets printed by yarn companies are published simply to help sell their yarn. When you buy the specified yarn, the company makes a profit. Yarn companies don't necessarily care if the sweater itself is wearable or if the consumer is happy with the results. (Some firms have never read *In Search of Excellence* and are just out to make a quick buck. The fact that many yarn companies have gone out of business in recent years says something about the lack of interest in satisfying customers.)

Patterns from magazines are often no better. Have you ever seen an editorial comment under a photo that says, "This design is not recommended for people who weigh over ninety-eight pounds," or, "The neckline of this sweater exposes bra straps"? Magazines do not tell the bad points of a design. Moreoever, in the magazine publishing business, an "advatorial policy" is quite common. In everyday language this means, "If you will advertise in our magazine, we will feature your products editorially." In practice it means that the sweaters featured in magazines often come directly from the yarn companies.

Publishers of both pattern leaflets and magazines deliberately photograph garments in a way that minimizes the bad points of the design. The entire first chapter of my book *Knitting in Plain English* discusses how design flaws are concealed in photographs. On your own, you need only spend a week in any yarn shop listening to customer comments and complaints to verify that what I'm saying about printed patterns is true.

As I said before, the information in Chapters 2 through 17 will help you to avoid a bungled mess. But there are other ways in which you can fortify yourself against errors.

TALK TO OTHER KNITTERS

Communication with other knitters is one of the best ways to avoid disasters. Be bold. Leap over your shyness. Talk to other knitters.

I can count on the fingers of one hand the knitters I have encountered who were unwilling to talk and share experiences with me. And I have been knitting for forty years! Wherever you find another knitter—at a committee meeting, in the lunch room at work, in waiting areas of airports—smile, extend a greeting, and strike up a conversation. Even if you don't have your knitting with you there is nothing to stop you from saying, "Hello, I'm a knitter, too. What are you making."

It is amazing what you can learn! It is amazing how many costly mistakes you can avoid! "This Blooper's 'Glop-Glop' is the most miserable yarn I have ever worked with," and that may be what you had planned for your next purchase. "I absolutely adore this sport-weight wool put out by Winners. When it is worked up, it is lovely. It is a dream to work with; the stitches just fly; and it washes wonderfully," and you had passed it by because it looked lifeless sitting in its skein.

JOIN A LOCAL GUILD

Please don't limit your conversations with other knitters to chance encounters. Join a local knitting guild. Beginners and "old hands" alike can belong to the benefit of all. Knitters getting together regularly, even on an informal basis, learn lots from each other. Seeing and touching the items in progress is much more rewarding than looking at colored pictures in magazines. Members applaud one another in successes and support one another in slipups. Ask around to find out if there is such a group near where you live.

If there is not one in your area, start a local guild. You can make your guild anything you want it to be. It can be an informal "kaffee-klatsch stitch and bitch" in someone's home with no officers and no dues. Or it can be a structured affair in a rented room with a stated purpose such as that of the local guild I belong to: "The Atlanta Knitting Guild has been formed solely for the purpose of get-togethers of people who truly *love* the art of knitting. We hope to share, learn, extend, and stretch our skills through each other and outside speakers." Yarn suppliers will usually help you get your guild going by letting you put up signs and notices of meetings in their stores. Local newspapers will often help you by publishing notices of your meetings. Perhaps you can even get a feature editor to attend, photograph, and write a story about one of your meetings or some of your members. Such an article may entice other knitters and would-be knitters into your group.

JOIN THE NATIONAL GUILD

Join the national organization The Knitting Guild of America. Their address is Box 1606, Knoxville, TN 37901 (phone: 615/524-2401). Though TKGA hasn't been in existence for long, it has done much to raise people's awareness of both knitting as a fine art/craft and knitters as artisans/craftsworkers. Attend their annual conventions and regional seminars, where you can take classes from nationally renowned instructors. While you are there you will have endless opportunities to chat with other knitters, comparing notes and getting new ideas.

ASK QUESTIONS

Get to know the shopkeeper at your local friendly yarn store. Don't be shy; pick her brain. Ask about the experiences other knitters have had with the yarn sold there. Will it keep its shape? Does it stretch or shrink? Do the strands split easily? What kind of needles work best with it? Have any of the store's customers made up this pattern? Did they have trouble with it? Did they like the finished result? Most local businesses are sincerely interested in customer satisfaction because if they aren't, they won't stay in business.

TRY JUST ONE SKEIN

Before you buy gobs and gobs of a particular kind and color of yarn, buy one skein and make a swatch. Some specialty yarn shops have opened skeins for you to experiment with. Others will let you open a skein from the shelf and try it out. (When you are finished, if you do not choose to buy it, unravel the swatch, wind up the yarn, and stuff it back in the center of the ball.)

There is no substitute for making a swatch. Only when you make the individual stitches and form a square of them can you know how the yarn will behave and how it will look in the finished sweater.

If that one skein of yarn doesn't behave well, or if it doesn't give the appearance you are looking for, there is no sense in buying any more of it. You will have avoided a costly mistake.

Even the money you spend on single skeins may not be lost. You may want to use the yarn later to trim some other garment. One lady in our guild who does a lot of knitting for bazaars and charities combines her own and other people's odd-ball stuff to make hats and slippers. I know of several knitters who make crazy-quilt afghans of squares from leftover yarns.

BE AWARE

Looking at leaflets and magazines cannot give the full impact of what a sweater is and does. You need hands-on experience. Every retailer who has garments for sale expects shoppers to try them on. Even if shopping is not your hobby, even if you detest it as I do, go into department and specialty stores and try on finished knitted garments. Slip into both handmade and commercially made sweaters to find out what they will look like *on*. A human body is where they will ultimately be displayed, not on a shelf or on a hanger.

As you work through the chapters in Part II, pay special attention to the remarks about the disadvantages of each style. If the drawbacks are pertinent to you, you will have avoided a costly error by not making the garment.

LOOK AROUND

Start noticing the differences in the way human bodies are put together. Later in this book I'll devote a whole chapter to the ways people are shaped, but start looking now. If you've never had a life drawing class you may not realize how differently bodies are put together. You must know the body shape of the intended wearer. It would be a costly mistake to knit a turtleneck sweater for a man whose neck is exceedingly short.

"KNOW THYSELF"

This command has existed throughout history and in every culture. And yet, though it is easy to say, "Yes, yes, I know who I am," few of us really do know ourselves; nor do we take our knowledge into consideration when making purchases. Let me tell you a story about myself.

One time I was preparing to go on vacation. I knew I would be traveling for many long hours in the car and would need something to knit when not looking at the scenery. I charged into a shop and bought the first afghan kit I saw. It took only a day and a half of knitting in the car to realize I had blundered. I disliked the colors and they didn't suit any room in my house. Moreover, I absolutely hated making miles and miles of straight strips of the same pattern stitch over and over. I knew myself well enough to know that my fingers needed to be busy; I did not know what colors were repugnant to me, and I did not know myself well enough to realize how easily I became bored. (The kit was donated to a senior citizens' recreation center for its crafts program just as soon as I got home.)

Part of knowing ourselves is being able to assess honestly our personality and lifestyle. Before you start to knit a new project, ask yourself if you really enjoy working with that color and doing that type of stitch and design. Do you like complicated/challenging or relaxing/ repetitive designs? (If you can't abide finishing the thing, it will have been an expensive disaster.)

Ask yourself where and when and how many times the garment will be worn. If you knit a heavy wool ski sweater for yourself and you live in Florida and never go north in the winter, it will be a waste of time, money, and effort. If you spend hundreds of dollars for yarn to make an angora coat for a granddaughter who's a tomboy, it might be an expensive disaster. This is not to say that it is not worthwhile to knit a special garment for a special occasion. This is to say that honest assessments and careful choices are a part of living fully and living well.

3

Getting New Ideas

Everywhere and anywhere we look, great ideas are waiting to be plucked. Our past experiences, our surroundings, and where and how we live are all sources of ideas from which to create the sweaters we desire. The ideas of others upon which we can build and new ways of solving old problems are sources of innovation. It is all just a matter of being aware, and being aware of new ideas is a state of mind. It is a pervading attitude of "Look what they did! They used this for that." "Isn't that an attractive, though unusual, combination!" "What if . . ." "I wonder what would happen . . ." "Suppose I were to put this next to that. Would they both be enhanced?" "If I could just change . . ."

Ideas are all around us. We just have to make ourselves be aware of them.

In this chapter I'll be telling you some of the places where ideas can be found, but it is up to you to be aware of the ideas when you encounter them.

START WITH YARN AND FIND THE RIGHT "LOOK"

Some of my knitting buddies are "yarn-aholics." They are always acquiring yarn. It seems to beckon and cry out to them from store shelves and yard sales, on vacations, and in advertisements, "Take me with you! Take me home!" Over and over my friends do take these yarns home until they have closets full of their acquisitions.

In no way am I condemning these collectors. I couldn't; I used to be one of them until the day I moved from an eight-room house into a three-room apartment! Never again have I collected yarn!

Sooner or later the day will come when for whatever reason, other yarn collectors, too, must clean out the closets. They will then ask, "What in the world am I going to do with this gorgeous green mohair I picked up in Australia?"

Often they ask me and I reply, "Did you ask the yarn what it wants to be?"

"What do you mean 'Ask the yarn'? Yarn can't talk."

I reply, "Oh, yes it can! You just have to open your ears and listen. Make a cup of coffee, grab your stash of needles, and find a quiet corner. With a likely size needle cast on about twenty stitches and work in stockinette stitch for several rows. If the yarn screams and yells, 'No, no! Those needles are too small, they are choking me,' change to needles a couple of sizes larger and purl a ridge row to mark the change. If, after a few rows, the yarn then says, 'Uh-uh, now you've overdone it, babe, I'm all strung out and I can't pull myself together,' it is time to switch to an in-between size.

"Work a while in stockinette and ask the yarn how it likes the plain smoothness of the stitch. It may purr in response, especially if it is an elaborate novelty yarn. Or, if it is a rather plain yarn, it may jump up and down and demand, 'Fancy me up; I look absolutely blah and dead this way. I want to be lace.' Let the yarn have its way! Try a lace pattern for a couple of repeats. It won't take the yarn long to respond, 'Yes, yes, but more (or fewer) open places, please.'

"Perhaps the yarn will say, 'Yuck! This is terrible. I've changed my mind. I want to be cables with moss stitch instead.' Follow its suggestion. On that same swatch keep on going and try several different widths of cables changing the number of rows between twists until the yarn sings out, 'Yes, this is what I want to be.'

"Sometimes, particularly if the stuff is multicolored or tweed, the yarn will cry with sadness, 'I looked so pretty in the skein (sob) but on my own, worked up, I need help! I need a bright (dull) companion to spark my colors (sob). I'm so lonesome. Please go find some plain yarn to be ribbing (or trim or accent) so that I can live up to my promise.'

"Maybe the yarn will plead, 'I really like being plain stockinette stitch, but do you think you could use a bit of contrast to make a plaid (or cable or stripe) so I will stand out more?'

"Listen to the yarn and try what it suggests!"

The next time my friends see me, they say, "Maggie, I thought you were a complete nut, but you are right. Yarn does talk; all you have to do is listen. The green mohair from Australia says it wants to be plain stockinette with glossy light bitter green silk ribbing for accent. But now I don't know what style to make it."

"What did the *swatch* say about that?" I will respond.

"It didn't say anything!"

"Did you ask it?"

"Of course not, swatches don't talk— Ah, I bet you're right about that, too— I bet they do! But how do you ask a swatch what shape and style it wants to be?"

"Does the swatch shout out to you, 'I'm bold and bulky, flamboyant and flaunting?' or does it quietly sing, 'I'm simple and sweet and demure, traditional and classic'? The swatch knows that if it appears wider than it measures it should become a loose-fitting casual sweater. The swatch also knows that if it looks narrower than it measures, it wants to be a more closely fitting garment. Can you imagine the effect of a glossy perle cotton trying to pass as a rugged outer garment? The swatch will never lie to you.

"Separate the part of the swatch with the pattern stitch and/or companion color that you (and the yarn) have selected. Pin it up on a plain surface across the room so you can see it by itself. I tack it to the off-white wall in my kitchen while I go about preparing supper. Occasionally I glance up at it. Sometimes the swatch is slow making up its mind, pondering, 'Shall I be a superlong cardigan, or shall I be an extrawide pullover?' But more often than not, before the greens are washed for salad it will call out across the room, 'Put that stuff down. Come here. I know what I want to be. I have decided that I shall become a glamorous, long-sleeved, close-fitting, evening sweater to wear to cocktail and dinner parties this winter! I will make every other sweater there absolutely green with envy.' Even if you protest that *you* don't go to cocktail parties and don't need that kind of sweater, the swatch may insist. 'But your daughter-in-law does; make me for her; you have lots of other bags of yarn in the closet that you can make up for yourself!' And how can you argue? It is true. You do have lots of yarn; you're a yarn-aholic."

The next time I see the knitter with the green mohair from Australia, she will say, "The swatch said it wanted to be an oversize boatnecked pullover. It insisted on dropped shoulders set off and accented by an inch and a half of ribbing in the same silk used for the other trim. It is almost finished and I'm so pleased. But, Maggie, people look at me funny when I tell them that the yarn told me what it wanted."

You don't have to tell others that the yarn talked to you; just call it *inspiration* and let it go at that.

START WITH A "LOOK" AND FIND THE YARN

Pure inspiration is what some people do use. There is no other way to explain it. These people "see" a finished work in their "mind's eye" before they ever start. It is the way the minds of many artists and composers function. These individuals often perceive the world in a very different light from other, less naturally creative people. Beethoven "heard" the Ninth Symphony in his head and then just transcribed it to paper. Michelangelo "saw" figures trapped in marble and simply released them. I often "see" a completed sweater in my head. I can even throw it up in the air, rotate it all around, and view it from all angles.

When I have "seen" it from every direction, and am pleased with it, I grab a pad and a pen and quickly sketch it out. My problem then is to find a yarn that will make the "vision" come into reality. I trot myself out to the local yarn suppliers and search their shelves. When I happen on a likely yarn, I make a swatch. Either the knitted square matches the picture in my head or it doesn't. If it doesn't, on I go until I find one that does. After a suitable yarn is selected, it is an easy matter to draw out diagrams of the pieces necessary to make the design work and to fill in the numbers. We'll talk about how to do that in the chapters in Part II. Here we are talking about where ideas come from.

Buried deep within you, this kind of inspired creativity may be waiting to be uncovered. You may not even be aware it is there. To discover if it is hidden in you, try this easy exercise. When you are all alone, try sitting comfortably in a quiet place. Half close your eyes. Let your mind wander to a happy time, then take yourself into the future. Imagine yourself happily knitting something that you really want. Pretend to look down and see what color it is. Then look out behind your half-closed eyelids and try to "see" the completed sweater. Don't give up if the exercise doesn't give you full satisfaction the first time. Try it again and again at other times and in other places. Who knows? There may be a creative genie lurking inside you just waiting to be set free. If not, don't feel discouraged. Reasoning, analytical people can design wonderful garments, too! Read on.

DESIGN A GARMENT TO SOLVE A PROBLEM

I often solve design problems by "interviewing" myself. Here's the internal conversation I had when trying to plan my winter sweater wardrobe.

MAGGIE THE KNITTER: I need some long-sleeved pullover sweaters.
MAGGIE THE DESIGNER: How heavy do you want them to be?
KNITTER: Lightweight but warm; not heavy or bulky.
DESIGNER: That means sport weight or fingering yarn.
KNITTER: Sport, not fingering. There are too many hours spent in knitting up fingering yarn.

DESIGNER: How do you intend to clean these sweaters you are going to knit?

KNITTER: I won't be doing dirty work in them; they won't need cleaning every week; I don't mind an occasional hand washing.

DESIGNER: Then wool is okay? Wool is warmer than acrylic, you know.

KNITTER: Yes, but not Shetland wool or mohair. I find they're itchy and I can't stand going around all day scratching. I'm not fond of cashmere because it tends to pill and ball. I'd love camel's hair, but I can't afford it. Merino would be nice if I could find it and it wasn't too expensive. Lamb's wool would be great, too.

DESIGNER: So you've decided on sport-weight wool sweaters. Are you going to use smooth classic worsted, boucle, or novelty yarn?

KNITTER: The last couple of things I've knitted have been done with boucle and novelty yarns. I'm ready for a change. I'm ready to go back to smooth classic worsted.

DESIGNER: What are you going to wear with these sweaters?

KNITTER: Plain cotton shirts and plain wool slacks or blue jeans.

DESIGNER: A bland sweater with a bland shirt and bland pants is going to make a very blah outfit. Do you think you could put some design into it?

KNITTER: That is a good idea. But I don't want to do a Fair Isle. Not that I don't adore knitting them. I do! It is just that they make a sweater that is too warm for Georgia because of all the strands carried at the back.

DESIGNER: Well, how about some bold intarsia with knit-in graphics?

KNITTER: No, that has to be done flat, back and forth. I prefer knitting in the round as much as I can.

DESIGNER: Stripes then?

KNITTER: Yea! And I could use the old "slip an occasional stitch on the first row of a color change" technique to keep the stripe lines from being hard and firm. I could vary the width of the stripes and just throw in new colors when I felt like it.

DESIGNER: Okay, that's settled; what about style? I gather a turtleneck is out; do you want a crew or V-neck?

KNITTER: I prefer a crew neck; it seems warmer to me. Not a high, firm one though, but rather a loose and sloppy one that lets the collar of the shirt come up and show around the neck.

DESIGNER: What do you want to do about sleeves? I know they're going to be long, but do you want them set in, raglan, or coming from a yoke?

KNITTER: Hey, I didn't say just one sweater, I said I needed several sweaters. I could make one with set in sleeves, one raglan, and one from a yoke. The first one can have a yoke down about two-thirds of the way to the armhole, and then become a raglan at the underarms.

I think they fit better that way. I can make it round from the neck down and throw in some short rows around the back of the neck to make the front portion drop down a bit.

DESIGNER: What about color?

KNITTER: I've had a color analysis and of the colors that suit me, I like the bright, warm, happy ones. It is strange how the colors one likes usually blend with each other. If I'm going to be doing three sweaters in various stripes, I could just select two main body colors and then some other compatible tones and shades for striping. I can use the leftovers of one sweater for the next. All will be flattering colors and all will be different.

DESIGNER: So that is what it will be: a set of three long-sleeved crew-necked pullover sweaters. They will all be made of sport-weight smooth classic wool. Each will be in patterns of stripes of compatible colors, but varying in width, order, and spacing. The first one will be yoked.

Just by holding a conversation with one's self to solve a problem, the design of a sweater will emerge. If you don't choose to acknowledge and solve your own problems, they will probably go unsolved.

REDO AND REMAKE OLD SUCCESSES

We can all recall a favorite, treasured sweater that either disintegrated from use or was lost along the way. Once upon a time, in the years when I was inundated with rearing children and didn't have time to knit, I purchased a mohair cardigan sweater. I know now that it was made of an ombré yarn, but then all I knew was that it was warm and soft, every color and no color and could be thrown over any kind of outfit for an extra bit of warmth to run out and fetch the children or hop in the car and go get a loaf of bread. I loved it. Alas, allergies reared their nasty heads and I could no longer wear it. I gave it to a dear friend who had no problems with red bumps and itching. She treasured it and wore it until it died. Someday soon I'm going to remake that much-loved sweater.

Was there such a beloved sweater in your life or in the lives of your loved ones? An old golf sweater that was devoured by moths? A favorite pullover lost in a stuffy airport waiting room? The knitted lace blouse you loved but outgrew? Do you long, as I do, for a remake? Well, make it over again. You may wish to update some of the details, but you can re-create the essence. I'm certainly not going to remake that cardigan in mohair, but there are good synthetics that simulate the effect. Styles and needs may have changed and you may choose to omit the hood and attach a collar instead, add or subtract a pocket, perhaps change the number of buttons, but your new creation can still be a re-creation of a treasured sweater. Only a foggy memory will limit you.

UPDATE CLASSIC DESIGNS AND BRING THEM INTO TODAY'S WORLD

Good ideas of the past continually pop up and ask to be gathered in. Let me share with you three examples of classic design ideas of our grandmothers that have a place in today's world.

The Atlanta guild has had an ongoing philanthropic project of knitting hats and slippers for elderly convalescent patients at a local hospital. When a recent delivery was made, the nurse in charge thanked our members profusely and then requested we also knit "something to keep the shoulders of the wheelchair patients warm. Sweaters won't do. Just something light to slip over their shoulders and upper arms." We were stymied until someone remembered as a child seeing an old grandmother wear a "shrug." We dug into ancient knitting books searching for patterns and directions. We found that a shrug is just a rectangular piece of knitted fabric perhaps 16 to 20 inches wide and 45 to 55 inches long gathered in at the narrower ends with ribbing, which become sort of sleeves. It covers the back, shoulders, and upper arms without the cumbersomeness of a real sweater. Now this old "good idea" has been revived and we are making shrugs not only for patients at the hospital but also as bed jackets and for gifts.

Loveliness never stays long out of style. There is a resurgence of interest in the gossamer-fine wool lace Shetland shawls of the last century—gorgeous when they were introduced in the past, equally lovely and practical in today's world of low thermostat settings. Again knitters sought out antique instruction books in order to re-create them. One creative knitter I know was leafing through a contemporary European doily book when it struck her that the instruction for a circular knitted lace doily would serve very nicely as directions to make a shawl if only she changed the gauge and the yarn. And finding an appropriate yarn is the only problem that the knitters I know have encountered in remaking and bringing Shetland lace shawls into today's world.

I said earlier that ideas are a matter of awareness. When you watch television and movies are you aware of the sweaters the performers wear? Watching the movie *The Great Gatsby* made me aware of the incredibly beautiful and practical sweaters people wore in the twenties and early thirties. Though I don't play the game, I re-created the white tennis sweater with blue and red cables to wear in the spring and fall. I also made a replica of the shawl-collared longish tweed coat-sweater. I got the ideas by being aware of what was being shown on the screen.

Please be aware of the sweaters the personalities on the screen are wearing. You are free to say, "Oh, I really like that. That color would be horrible on me, but in a sky blue it would be divine." You also have the license to say, "Oh how ghastly. What a travesty of knitters' skills! If the sleeves were changed from leg-o-mutton to simpler ones, it would be a lovely thing to have."

Treasured garments don't have to be restricted to ones that came out of our past or ones that we owned. They can come out of a past that existed before we were born, from classics. One of the definitions my dictionary gives for the word *classic* is: "Having lasting significance or recognized worth." It would be a shame to pass up such treasures.

VISIT MUSEUMS AND CRAFT SHOWS

Though I am no longer a yarn-aholic, I have become a museum devotee. Museums of fine art, local history, agriculture, culture, textiles, and natural history not only tie me to those who have gone before but also allow me a great appreciation of the creativity and inventiveness of our forebears. Museums are filled with examples of how problems of clothing the human body have been solved: gloves without fingertips to keep working hands warm; nightcaps to prevent heat loss while sleeping in chilly rooms; quilted and embroidered jackets and vests (a matador's jacket sent me into ecstasy!); and sweaters, beautiful, glorious sweaters. You find them in paintings of English country life, in pen-and-ink drawings of weary soldiers returning from battle, in block prints of peasants huddled around a fire. Everywhere you look in a museum you can see ideas that you can adapt to your own knitting repertoire.

But don't limit yourself to formal museums alone. I adore exploring country fairs and craft shows. It is not only in the great cities of our East and West coasts that wonderful ideas are born. Unknown local craftspersons give birth to them, too. Indigenous handworkers create great new concepts. I go to fairs and craft shows to become aware of them.

GO WINDOW SHOPPING

Though Betty, my secretary, and I get along very well and agree on many things, we are at complete odds about shopping. She loves to wander for hours in the finest shops and stores gathering ideas for clothing and decorating. These bazaars are marvelous places to gather ideas for your knitting. Not only will you be aware of the newest colors, shapes, and designs, but you will also be able to try them on. Trying on in the stores and deciding that the garment in question is not for you is a whole lot better than spending hours knitting something up only to discover that you don't like it at all. If you, like Betty, adore shopping, by all means take advantage of this storehouse of goodies.

LOOK IN CIRCULARS AND CATALOGUES

Almost every day my postman brings me a new catalogue printed in wonderful colors on glossy paper. These shopping treasure maps are filled with wonderful ideas of things to buy or put on your "want list" and of items to knit. It was in such a catalogue several years ago that I encountered the concept of making afghans of cotton yarn. Using cotton for a body throw would never have occurred to me. Seeing the idea in a catalogue made me say to myself, "Why not!", and opened up new vistas.

Department store circulars and fliers are another good source of ideas. Often the newest and best designs appear on their pages as much as eighteen months before they hit other markets.

SUBSCRIBE TO MAGAZINES OR GO TO THE LIBRARY

Knitters of today are fortunate to have such an abundance of magazines about the craft available to them. As you take your weekly trip through your favorite supermarket, make it a habit to detour to the magazine section. The next time you are in a large bookstore with a good magazine section, take a few moments to familiarize yourself with knitting publications. Certainly I am not suggesting that you subscribe to *all* of them. Different periodicals are slanted toward different kinds of knitters. Only by looking them over can you decide which periodical is directed toward your style. (Both *Threads* and *Knitters* have excellent articles for creative knitters.)

People on tight budgets may want to see if their local library or senior citizens' center can subscribe. That way the magazines can be enjoyed by other knitters in the community as well as by you.

You may never want to make any of the sweaters you see in these publications *exactly as they appear* in the photos. But they can be a source of ideas for you to redesign for yourself.

BORROW AND ADAPT THE IDEAS OF OTHER KNITTERS

Other knitters are a great source of ideas. Perhaps the most informative part of our local Atlanta guild meetings is the time we spend in "show and tell." Members usually *show* their latest creations by wearing them to the meetings. They also hold up and *tell* about their current projects. As they do, you can almost see the minds of the other knitters at work. "I really like that neck treatment; I'd like to do that with the pink yarn I'm going to work up next." "I would never have thought of that color treatment; I don't want to make a pullover in fine yarn like she did, but wouldn't those colors be stupendous in a heavier cardigan." Cooperative, positive, and friendly minds nurturing and inspiring one another furthers creativity.

INCREASE YOUR AWARENESS

Ideas are all around us. If we don't see them, it is only because we are not aware. The more we cultivate our awareness, the more ideas we will see. Others can only point the way to where ideas may be found. *Nurturing* our perception and *seeing* those ideas is our own responsibility.

4

Understanding the Nature of Yarn

HOW SWEATER DESIGN DIFFERS FROM DRESS DESIGN

Even before I learned to knit at age fourteen, I was already making my own clothing. I was not a genius or a child prodigy; it was simply that young girls growing up impoverished in the Great Depression and World War II either learned to sew or went without clothing. By my late teens I was altering and making changes in commercial dress patterns and designing my own clothing.

It was much later that I learned to chart and design for knits. Coming from my background as a seamstress and dress designer, I was aghast at the way sweaters were planned and designed. The first thing that struck me was that

the rules for designing sweaters of knitted fabric are completely different from those for garments of cloth. You cannot use dress pattern shapes and methods because hand- or home-machine-knitted fabrics differ from woven fabric. You have to divorce your mind from thinking about patterns for cloth and learn a whole new way of thinking in order to design for hand- and home-machine-knitted fabrics.

Though there are differences between hand- and home-machine-knitted fabrics, and those differences must be accounted for, the general rules for charting sweaters remain the same for any fabric knitted at home.

Before we can begin to think about sweater shapes and the number of stitches needed to knit them, we need to understand the nature and personality of knitted fabrics. The following section describes some of the personality quirks of all home-knit fabrics. Go get a square of woven cloth and a favorite home-knit sweater out of the drawer and fondle them as you read these paragraphs so that your fingers and eyes, as well as your mind, can comprehend what I'm saying.

UNDERSTANDING THE NATURE OF KNITTED FABRIC

There is a *forgivingness* to knitted fabric. To illustrate, make a fist, insert it behind a single thickness of the sweater fabric, and gently but firmly push your clenched fist toward you. Notice how, with just a little pressure, the fabric molds and conforms to the shape of your fist. If, instead, you push hard with your fist, the fabric may become extended and pushed out of shape; *but it still gives; it does not rip or stop your fist!* This is what I mean by forgivingness. Now try the same thing with your cloth square. Notice the firmness of the cloth and the resistance it has against your fist.

Now look at the shoulder seams and where the back neck stitches have been picked up on the sweater. The stitches of the shoulder seams may take up more or less space depending on how they were bound off and how the seam was made. The stitches of the back neck may be spread out or scrunched together according to the way the ribbing stitches were picked up. This, too, is forgivingness.

Forgivingness means that, unlike woven fabrics, home-knit fabrics give and take a lot. You don't have to be nearly so exact and accurate with knit measurements as you do with gabardine or oxford cloth or crepe. The knit fabric will adjust and forgive you. Cloth won't! Many of the shaping details that must be used with cloth simply aren't necessary with knit fabric.

On the woven cloth square, making sure that the threads run straight from top to bottom and from side to side, place your right hand in the upper right-hand corner, and your left hand on the lower-left corner. Pull your two hands apart in a catty-corner stretch. This upper-right-to-lower-left stretch of the cloth fabric is called "bias". Now try the same maneuver with your sweater fabric. Put your right hand on the left shoulder of the sweater. Put your left hand on the opposite side near the bottom of the sweater and pull gently. Notice the difference!

Knit fabric has almost no catty-corner stretch. Unlike woven cloth, it has little or no bias.

This means that knit fabric will not, cannot, "hang" or "drape" in the same way that cloth does. Exact replicas of cloth garments cannot always be made in knit clothing!

Check the stretchiness of the woven cloth square. Place one hand on the top edge and the other hand on the bottom edge. Now pull hard. The cloth doesn't stretch much, does it? Pull from side to side and see what happens. Not much. Woven cloth doesn't have much stretch at all, except on the bias.

Now check the stretchiness of your home-knitted fabric. Grab the top of the sweater with one hand and the bottom with your other hand. Pull. Notice the incredible lengthwise stretch. Pull the sweater from side to side and notice the difference.

Most home-knit fabrics stretch a great deal lengthwise. They do not stretch so much crosswise.

Of course different fibers and pattern stitches will have different characteristics. We will discuss them in a later chapter. But by and large, most knit fabrics get larger lengthwise, not only with a pull of your hands, but also with gravity. For this reason, it's best to store sweaters flat and never hang them. If they are hung up, behind your back, while hiding in your closet, gravity will sneak in and stretch them down. Did you ever wonder why sweaters usually have a firm ribbing on the bottom and around the wrists? It is because left to its own devices, the sweater will grow longer. The bottom and wrist ribbings help make the garment cling to the body to form a "resting place" so that the sweater will not stretch.

You may be thinking, "Yes, but if I give the finished sweater a good blocking, that will prevent it from stretching."

Blocking the sweater will NOT stop the lengthwise stretch. No thing yet devised by man stops gravity!

This lengthwise stretchiness of knit fabrics determines how sweaters *must* be designed. I can laugh now at my inexperience and lack of knowledge as a beginning knit designer. (At the time it was too painful to laugh about.) Once I designed a stockinette stitch cape for a very lovely lady. It was gorgeous the day she finished it. Every time she wore it after that, it grew a little longer. It started out at her knees. It ended up near her ankles. The tremendous weight of a flared and swirling cape combined with the lengthwise stretch of the knitted stitches caused it to grow until it was unwearable. I never again attempted to duplicate in a knit a garment planned for cloth. I became convinced of the necessity of ribbing to hug the body at the bottom of a garment to make a resting place so that the garment would not grow longer. (If I can spare some other knitter this kind of disaster, the whole purpose of writing this book will have been served.)

SAG AND DROOP

Some designs that are wonderful in cloth just won't work with knits because

all home-knit fabric will sag and droop. Once on the human body, a horizontal line will not stay true and straight.

This fact is true whether that horizontal line is a cast-on, a bind-off, or a stripe. *Square necks in knits usually don't stay square.* No amount of reinforcing and lining will make them do what *you* want.

Home-knit fabric has wonderful qualities, many of them unique, but don't expect it to act like cloth.

HOW HAND-KNIT FABRICS DIFFER FROM HOME-MACHINE-KNIT FABRICS

Everything I've said in the section above applies to both hand- and home-machine-knitted fabric. With hand-knitted fabric it is more so. With home-machine-knitted fabric, it is somewhat less so. Fabric worked on a home-knitting machine is slightly more firm and slightly less forgiving than hand-knitted fabric, but it still in no way resembles woven cloth.

Let me give you a few specific examples to clarify this point.

Plain, straight stockinette stitch skirts are a disaster when hand-knitted. They conform to every lump and bump of the body, cupping under the derrière and getting longer and narrower with every wearing. Made of home-machine-knitted fabric, if the tension is tight enough, such skirts can be wonderful successes.

Covered form buttons turn out well with machine-knitted fabric; the knitter just turns the tension down tight to get a firm fabric. Hand-knitters simply cannot get the tension tight enough to keep the form from showing through.

A dressy overblouse in a fingering or sport-weight yarn with a lace edging around the bottom instead of ribbing is almost always a delight when home-machine-knitted. Hand-knitters run a risk. Unless the bottom lace forms a resting place against the body, the garment may not be prevented from elongating.

It depends on the tension and the gauge, but by and large home-machine-knitted fabrics are a bit firmer and less forgiving than hand-knit ones. Nonetheless, neither will ever behave like woven cloth or even commercially machine-knit fabrics.

HOW PATTERN SHAPES FOR KNITS DIFFER FROM CLOTH SEWING PATTERNS

SEAM ALLOWANCES

The most striking difference between pattern shapes for cloth and knitted fabrics is that

patterns for knits have no seam allowance.

Unless the material is intended to be finished in a special way, cloth garment patterns must allow for an excess of fabric outside the seam. The material will fray and tear out if a seam allowance is not there. Not so with knitted fabric. Both the vertical and horizontal edges are "finished off" as the piece is knitted. No fraying is possible. Only one half of each edge stitch is required to make vertical seams. Only the cast-on or bound-off horizontal edges must be hidden in horizontal seams.

For knitted garments, a seam allowance would be a waste of yarn. Not only that, but the excess fabric would add unnecessary weight. And weight is always a problem with knits.

PATTERN LAYOUT SHAPES

The next thing the designer notices is that

with knits, the back and front sections are usually the same width.

Even for men's clothing, patterns for woven cloth are usually bigger for the front than for the back. With a few exceptions, making the front wider than the back is not necessary for knits.

Remember the "forgivingness" we talked about before? This "front and back the same width" is an example of forgivingness in action.

The same thing is true about lengths.

From shoulder to bottom edge, the front and back of a sweater are usually the same length.

In Chapter 6 we'll discuss the exceptions, the special situations when it is necessary to add either front length or width.

FRONT AND BACK ARMHOLES

When I first began to design for knits, I could not understand why

back and front armholes are shaped identically.

Having sewn cloth, I thought it would be necessary to indent the front armhole more than the back armhole. Not so! It is that same old forgivingness again. When a sweater-wearing person's arms move forward, the knitted fabric scrunches together a bit in the front, and at the same time the knitted fabric expands a bit in the back. No armhole differences are needed for knits.

SLEEVES

For sleeves also, forgivingness comes into play. Before I understood this unusual characteristic of knitted fabrics, I could not comprehend that elbows did not need to be taken into consideration. I thought that either the two edges of the underarm sleeve seam must be made differently or that a dart would be required to allow for the bending of the elbow. But no:

For knitted garments, both sides of sleeves are made in exactly the same way. No elbow darts are necessary.

The knitted fabric will conform to the movement of the arms all on its own.

Experience has taught me, however, that there is a slight hitch to this business of "both sides of the sleeve being shaped the same." It is true that both sides of the sleeves are shaped in the same way, but because of this,

sleeves cannot be made the length the measuring tape says they should be. Sleeves that go below the elbow must have additional length.

Sometimes I'm rather dense, and it took me a long time to get it all sorted out. Though for years I carefully measured sleeve lengths and knitted them accurately, the sleeves of my sweaters were always a bit too short. If I had opened my eyes and thought about it, it would have been clear. Since there is no allowance for elbows, and since the knitted fabric does bend with and conform to the shape of the body, all this forgivingness and movement takes up extra length from the sleeve. We'll discuss this in more detail in the chapter about taking measurements. I just wanted to mention the fact here while we were talking about the forgivingness of knit fabric.

PLACEMENT OF V-NECK OPENINGS

The first time I made a V-necked sweater, I was dumbfounded by the instructions for the front of the garment. They told me to begin to shape the neck opening *at the same time* that I bound off the stitches for the underarms. "Whoa, Maggie," I said, and went to get out a dress pattern from the sewing cupboard. On the paper dress pattern the V-neck began several inches *above* the underarm shaping. Well, I didn't want to make a costly disaster, and even though I had very little knitting experience, I was certain that the knitting directions were incorrect. I began the neck opening two and a half inches above the underarm bind-off. The sweater turned out not to be V-necked at all; the instructions were not wrong; I, as a former seamstress, was.

The forgivingness, stretchiness, and body-conforming qualities of home-knitted fabric allows completely different placement of openings than with woven cloth.

THE ABSENCE OF OPENINGS AND GUSSETS

A turtleneck cloth blouse requires an extra opening for the head. A turtleneck pullover sweater does not. You may have to put in a zipper or a buttoned shoulder placket, or make the blouse button down the back. You do not have to do anything to the home-knit turtleneck garment. The stretchiness and forgivingness of the knit fabric will accommodate the size of the human head, close the opening as soon as the head is through it, and fit appropriately around the neck.

Seamstresses frequently use gussets at the underarm of all-in-one cap-sleeved garments so that if the wearer raises his arm quickly, the fabric will not tear, nor the seam split. Knitters don't have to worry about such occurrences. The forgivingness will accommodate the movements of the human body.

DOUBLED FABRIC IS A NO-NO

There is another area in which sweater designing is radically different from pattern pieces intended for cloth clothing. Weight in knits is always a problem. Therefore

there is usually no doubling of fabric. Lapels, collars, cuffs, and front edging bands are made of a single thickness to avoid extra weight and the resulting possibility of sagging.

Turn-back lapels on a coat, jacket, or cardigan can add an elegant touch. But with knits, it takes extra care to design them. They should not be made double thick; one layer of fabric will do nicely. The fact that they will turn back and the fact that few knitted fabrics look the same on both sides means that the knitting must be reversed along the fold line. It can be done either by making separate pieces and seaming them together, which is usually the best solution for machine-knitters, or by plotting the fold line to allow the hand-knitter to make the part that will turn forward the reverse of the other stitches so that both the outside front of the jacket and the outside of the lapel look the same. (Some professional knitting designers do not realize this problem and do not think ahead to solve it. Even in commercially printed knitting instructions, one sometimes runs across jackets where the foldover lapel is simply the back side of the jacket fabric.)

Collars for knit garments do not have to be double thickness as cloth collars are. The doubling would just require extra yarn and make extra weight. A single thickness of knit fabric is sufficient.

The front bands of cardigan sweaters is another instance where doubling of the fabric is not necessary. Here also doubling would cause weight and bulk that knitters don't need. It is necessary, however, to take special care in selecting the *pattern stitch* for cardigan front bands. I'll discuss it more in the chapters about the characteristics of pattern stitches and the designing of cardigans.

Of course there are exceptions to this rule about not doubling fabric. The words *never, every,* and *always* were not in the Good Lord's vocabulary when the universe was created. These words are man-made and, like man himself, they aren't always honest.

FORGIVINGNESS DOESN'T ALWAYS SOLVE EVERY PROBLEM

While it is true that the forgivingness of home-knitted fabric allows most lumps and bumps to be smoothed over, there are places and occasions when the gentle kindness of the fabric we knit just won't cover all situations. The most obvious exception is the heel of a sock. Forgivingness won't cover a heel successfully. Special care must be taken and extra shaping must be done. Some human bodies have special needs that forgivingness won't gloss over. Very large breasts, hunch-backs, and big "beer bellies" are among such special needs. To compensate, darts will sometimes be required. We'll talk more about when and where it will be necessary to place these darts later. Here, where we are talking about the differences in designing for cloth and for homemade knits, I need to say that *darts are made differently*. In working with cloth, fabric is folded, a seam is made over the unwanted wedge, and the excess cloth is cut off. Knitters don't do that. They simply do not knit the unwanted wedge in the first place. No folding. No sewing. No cutting. No waste of yarn.

Vertical darts, for areas where abrupt changes in width are desired, are made on the sides of an imaginary line with decreases or increases.

Horizontal darts, for areas where special length is needed, are made with short rows.

KNITS NEED LESS EASE ALLOWANCE

Patterns for cloth garments need to make an allowance for "ease," for extra width. It is a must. If the cloth pieces were made exactly the same size as the body parts they are intended to cover, the body could not move or even expand and contract with breathing. Either the cloth would rip or the person would expire. Dressmakers and designers know this and allow for ease in planning the pattern pieces. When a would-be sweater designer comes from a background of dressmaking, as I did, she is aghast at the lack of ease allowance in sweater patterns.

The forgivingness of the home-knit fabric compensates for much ease allowance.

When I first began to design sweaters, I absolutely could not accept what my teacher/employer told me about how little ease allowance was necessary. "You've got to have room to breathe," I argued silently. Behind her back, I would sneak in a few inches of extra width here and there "for good measure." I did not (i.e., refused to) understand the forgivingness of knits. Of course, once the garments were on the intended wearer's body, they were too big. The boss took me gently in tow:

"Only a small amount of ease, of added extra width, is ever necessary. The fabric will expand and contract with the body," said my teacher. "Often no extra width is necessary at all! In fact," she added, "on some types of garments made with certain kinds of yarns, the garment must be planned to be TWO INCHES NARROWER than the actual body measurement. The forgivingness of the fabric will make the sweater conform to the body and it will fit perfectly."

"Won't it look vulgar?" I asked.

"No," she said, laughing. "It will not look like a 'sweater girl' advertisement of the forties. It will look perfectly fitted, not too tight, not too loose."

It took a lot of stubborn trial and error on my own to prove to myself that she was absolutely right.

The only problem with many home-knit sweaters is that they are too wide. Very simply stated, they are planned with too much ease allowance.

Please, please, do not just quietly believe what I say. Argue with me; prove it for yourself. Ask someone to stand in front of you holding their favorite purchased pullover sweater. Measure the person's chest with a tape measure. Lay the sweater on a table and measure its chest width. Now have the person put the sweater on and see for yourself if it fits. Ask the person if it is comfortable. Only then will you really begin to understand how little ease allowance is necessary for sweaters. True, some extra width may be desirable, but not a great deal, not nearly so much as for cloth garments.

I once read a review of several books about designing knitting patterns. The reviewer, obviously familiar with designing for cloth, kept complaining, "They don't tell you how much ease allowance to plan for!" She did not know that there are no hard-and-fast rules for adding extra moving-and-breathing width for sweaters. The books did not, could not, say how much ease allowance was necessary.

The amount of ease required depends upon just how much forgivingness there is to the swatch of the chosen yarn and the pattern stitch selected.

Unfortunately, those books she reviewed did not inform her about the forgivingness of home-knitted fabric, or tell her what a difference the pattern stitch makes. She was left in the dark. You are not.

This subject of ease will come up again in the chapters about measurements, about fiber-fabric-fashion, and in the design plans themselves in Part II.

DON'T LINE KNITS

Inexperienced knit designers often think that they can avoid the differences of designing for home-knit fabrics by adding cloth linings. Rather than learning and understanding how knits differ from cloth, they think that if they just design the same way they do for cloth, and then add a lining, all will come out okay. It usually doesn't work. Cloth linings for knitted garments do not prevent the knitted fabric from doing its natural thing.

Knits are going to stretch, droop, and sag. Cloth linings are no protection against it.

The answer is to design sweater patterns with a full understanding of home-knitted fabric.

5

Understanding Body Shapes

I'm glad there was a span of years in my life when, while my sons were in high school, I had some free hours in the middle of the day. I spent those hours in self-indulgent, disciplined, rapturous painting. I began this personal journey into art by going to the local art/craft supply store and purchasing a handful of tubes of paint, a few brushes, a couple of framed canvases, some linseed oil and turpentine, and a rickety easel. I read one paperback book on "How to Paint" and sat down, or rather stood up, to do it. I gathered a few artifacts from around the house and painted a still life. After a couple of those, I moved my easel outside and painted landscapes. After a couple of those, I happened upon a lovely, ancient, lined, and gray woman in the supermarket, and I knew that all I ever wanted to paint was portraits.

Painting people was much harder for me than painting still lifes and landscapes. I couldn't do it on my own; I needed instruction. So I began to take classes in portrait painting. The teacher taught well and I learned fast. I loved it; I adored doing it; I got completely lost in it. Soon I wanted to paint more than just the faces of people. I wanted to show the way they held their bodies, what they did with their hands, whether they sat upright or slouched. To do this I had to know where their necks came from, the way their arms fitted into their shoulders, and how elbows worked.

Like most of us, I had no idea what the human body was like, so off I went to life drawing classes. It was an experience I have profited from in many ways. If you have never been privileged to attend a life drawing class, let me share with you some of what I learned about this wonderful movable machine—the human body. This information may totally change the way you go about designing sweaters.

Most of us are familiar with Leonardo da Vinci's drawing of a man

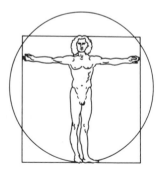

5.1 Leonardo Da Vinci's man in a circle with outstretched arms

33

5.2 The body resembles a series of tapered cylinders, with the head a domed tube with the front (jaw) longer than the back.

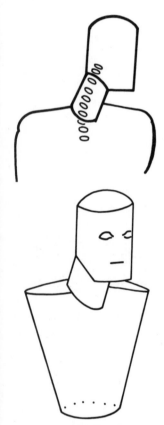

5.3 The front of the neck (throat) sits much lower on the torso than does the back of the neck.

in a circle. (See Figure 5.1.) It is a magnificent work of art, but there is more to the human body than the drawing reveals.

The human body is not just two dimensional, not just up and down and sideways. There is real depth to it. More than just a stick figure, the body is a series of tapered cylinders. In fact, there is an exercise in life drawing classes in which the human body is depicted just that way. Let me walk you through this exercise, body part by body part. We're going to be making a Tin Man just like the one in the *Wizard of Oz*. If you can remember him, you've got the idea.

Children making their first drawings often represent the human head as a ball. That is an oversimplification. The head is really shaped more like a round tube. (See Figure 5.2.) The top of the tube is domed. (In the *Wizard of Oz*, the Tin Man wore a hat, so you didn't see the dome.) The bottom of the tube is cut off straight at the jaw in the front, and then a sharp cut is made on both sides from the edge of the jaw to the center back where the neck enters it. The back of the head is not nearly so long as the front.

In designing for knits, we are not so much interested in the head itself as in the way the head, neck, and shoulders join one another. This is of utmost importance.

The neck can be considered a tube that begins inside the head and moves down at a peculiar angle to fit into and join the torso.

Find these places on your own neck while we are talking about them. Put one hand on the center of the back of your neck. Move your hand upward until you feel the base of the skull. Now make a circle with your fingers and you will locate a sort of "arch" where the neck enters the head.

To represent the torso, we need to start with a cylinder that is smaller on the bottom than it is on the top. Leaving the bottom round, we need to flatten the top of the cylinder somewhat. Down into the middle of this flattened top portion we'll attach the neck. But, ah, necks do not just sprout out from the top of the torso.

Knit designers must always remember this! If we don't, the wearers of our sweaters will never be comfortable.

The back of the neck rests against the center back of the top of our flattened, tapered cylinder, but the front of the neck sits at an angle on top of the front of that cylinder.

Pictures will say it better than words. Putting the head, neck, and torso together, we get something that looks like Figure 5.3. In the drawing the neck is shown longer than it really is, so that you can better see the way these body parts are put together. In the real world, most people have much shorter necks. But it is not the length of the neck that I am talking about here. It is the fact that the front of the neck sits much lower on the torso than does the back of the neck.

Find out where your neck sits on the front of your torso. With your hand, feel the center front of your neck where it moves into your chest. In the exact center, you will notice a small depression and on each side of that hole, you will feel a right-angle-shaped bone. (See Figure 5.4.) If a sweater designer does not account for this fact of life, the wearer will squirm and wriggle and probably take the sweater off, perhaps permanently. When we get to the point where we are taking measurements and then actually designing garments, we'll talk again about the differences of neck lengths in people.

Continuing to draw our cylinder body, let's put a tennis ball at the top outside edge of each side of the torso. This represents the shoulder ball joints.

To locate the shoulder-bone tips on your own body, stand in front of a mirror. Bend your right elbow up and place your fingertips on the front of your body about an inch below the slope line of your right shoulder. Do the same with your left arm and fingertips. Move your fingertips gently in a circle between your arm and your torso. Your fingers will find a bony prominence on each side. These are your shoulder-bone tips. (See Figure 5.5.) Notice that they are not on the outside of your arms, and rather surprisingly they are not so far apart as we usually think of shoulders as being.

Now we attach to the tennis balls two long tapered cylinders for the upper arms and two more tennis balls and tapered cylinders for the elbows and forearms. (See Figure 5.6.) (We could continue with the hands and also describe them as tapered cylinders, but that would be of interest only to glove makers and jewelry designers.)

I hope you've stumbled onto a couple of very important points about how the human body works. In contrast to da Vinci's drawing,

the arms do NOT spring straight out from the sides of the torso. They hang from the tennis balls attached to the upper sides of the torso! Shoulders do NOT extend from outer end of tennis-ball joint on one side to outer end of tennis-ball joint on the other side. In designing, we cannot include the arms in with the shoulders. They are separate parts.

Moreover, few of us walk around with our arms outstretched as we go about our daily life. Our arms *hang down* in normal activities. Not straight down, but in a curved-to-the-front way.

It would be a snap to design a sweater for da Vinci's man. A front and back each straight up and down, a straight-across neck slit, and flat-topped sleeves fastened to slits between the front and back. And

5.4 On either side of the center of the neck is a right-angle-shaped bone (clavicle).

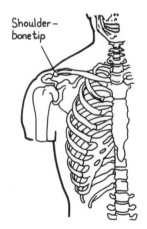

5.5 The shoulder-bone tip is not on the outside of the arm.

I'm sure you've all seen this very sweater in all the glossy sweater design magazines. Slick photos can make it look good, but it really isn't very comfortable or wearable.

The designer of the sweater for the da Vinci man also supposes, as I did before I took life drawing classes, that the arms are attached *from within* the torso instead of hanging from those tennis-ball-like joints outside the torso. You and I now know that this is not true, and will be able to design our sweaters accordingly.

We are now down to the hips. Though it is not an exact representation, let's flatten a short tube a bit, fit the torso into the top of it, and call it the hips. How big a cylinder we choose will depend upon whether we are making a figure of a man or a woman.

This is the only place where there are structural bone differences between males and females. Hips are wider in women, and narrower in men. The hip circumference of most men is smaller than that of their chests. Most women are pear-shaped, with larger hips than chests. If we refuse to recognize this difference, we'll never have comfortable clothing.

We could go on creating our shaped cylinder human body, putting another set of tennis balls inside the hips, hanging from them thighs, knees, lower legs, ankles, heels, and feet, but all this is not really important because I don't intend to discuss the designing of pants in this book.

But please remember all these things I'm saying here about the tapered cylinder human body. They will come up again and again in specific examples as we design garments in Part II. Clothing for the human body must conform to these tapered cylinder shapes.

THE BODY MOVES AND HAS A PERSONALITY, TOO

The human body is more than just tapered cylinders. It is not static; it moves and bends and lives and breathes. Knees flex, arms rotate in all directions, elbows bend up and down, shoulders hunch forward. As an exercise in appreciating the body's range of motion, look at Figure 5.7 and then, in your mind's eye, place a sweater on each of the forms. I don't care what kind of a sweater you choose, just so it will move with and cover the body. Gives you a whole new perspective, doesn't it? The bowler needs a sweater that will allow his arms to move freely. The ballplayer reaching for a high pop fly needs a sweater that won't ride up

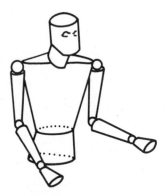

5.6 Think of the body as tapered cylinders connected by ball joints.

5.7 The human body moves! Imagine the particular sweater needs for each of these sports: bowling, baseball, and golf.

and bare his midriff. The golfer needs a sweater that allows for the swing of the shoulders. He needs a sweater that is long enough to cover his body as he follows through after hitting the ball.

Clothing must allow for movement. Life wouldn't be any fun if all we could do was just sit around in a straight jacket. The designer needs to know what the wearer will be doing when he wears the sweater, what movements he will be making. Will he be reaching for boxes on a top shelf or sitting quietly at the symphony? But there is more to the human body than movement. The sweater must fit the personality, too. Each body is inhabited by a person, a unique and special individual. Our sweaters must take that into consideration, too. Designs must be appropriate to lifestyle, age, size, body type, and personality.

Let me tell you a tale of two knitters. My friend Susie is an avid knitter. She is tall, big boned, and presents a dramatic appearance. Young, vital, and energetic are words that describe her. She moves quickly and resolutely. Bold and flashy designs flatter her body and her personality. Her lifestyle takes her to work in offices where she must look businesslike. She is a big supporter of the Atlanta symphony, attending committee meetings as well as the performances themselves. (She likes to really dress up for those occasions.) Susie wears lots of loose and floaty skirts and dresses. I have never seen her in slacks or jeans. Her sweaters must be suitable to wear with skirts and dresses and suits. Her garments must be a statement of her exuberant, outgoing personality—bold colors, flamboyant designs, exaggerated shapes. Blouse lengths are ideal for her as are overlong cardigans. Hip-length sweaters cut her body (and skirts) in an unflattering place and make her look like a potato sack.

Another friend of mine is also an avid knitter and, being retired, has lots of time to devote to it. A sweet and gentle person, Mary is fine boned and petite, conservative and intellectual. Because of a health condition, Mary wears only slacks—cotton in summer and wool in winter. I have never seen her in a skirt or dress. She no longer drives after dark, and her excursions are limited daytime shopping, casual lunches with friends, and trips to the library and matinees. Mary likes current styles, colors, and shapes. But bold and flashy is not now, and never was, her style. Her sweaters must be suitable to be worn with slacks. Hip lengths look great on her. Her five-foot-one-inch frame would be swamped in an overlong cardigan. Bright and colorful intarsia is not for her.

Certainly Susie and Mary are at extreme ends of the age, lifestyle, size, and body type spectrums. Neither is *better* nor *worse* than the other. There is no ideal body, age, personality, or size. Every person, every body God ever created is exquisitely lovely, and no two are the same.

NORMS AREN'T NORMAL

One of the things my "advisory panel" of Atlanta knitters asked me to do in this book was to explain how to handle the designs for sweaters for people whose bodies do not fit into the usual "standard" size measurement ranges "Maggie, if our bodies were 'standard,' we wouldn't have to design our own garments!" Some of them thought there was something wrong with *them* because their bodies did not fit preset norms. I hastened to tell them, and I'm telling you

some of the preset norms and standardized measurements used to create clothing are WRONG. Some "professional" sweater designers have never looked at the way the human body is put together or how it moves.

For instance, earlier in this chapter we talked about human hips and how most men have a smaller hip measurement than chest measurement, and about how most women have a larger hip measurement than chest measurement. *The only human beings who have chest and hips the same size are infants, toddlers, and ninety-eight-pound fashion models.* Yet across the board, sweaters are designed for straight-up-and-down torsos. Pick up any set of knitting directions. Look at the instructions for the back. After the ribbing is completed and the pattern stitch is set up, it will say, "Work *even* to underarms." And only fifteen-month-olds are *even* from hip to chest! Yes, there is forgivingness to the knitted fabric. Yes, it will stretch. But only so much. Only a few inches. If a man has a 46-inch chest and 36-inch hips and you make a sweater to fit his chest, there is going to be a lot of extra fabric flopping in the breeze around his hips. If a woman has a 34-inch bust and 42-inch hips and you make the sweater to fit the chest, it is going to be too tight in the hips. If it is a cardigan, it will hang gaping open in the front.

It is not a personal flaw if your chest and hips are different sizes. It is a flaw in the designer and the designer's pattern if the difference is not taken into account.

My Atlanta knitters breathed a sigh of relief when they found this out. "No wonder my husband wouldn't wear the sweater." "No wonder that cardigan looks awful on me." When designing for themselves, knitters can easily avoid this flaw.

Now the problem becomes deciding when to let forgivingness take care of the problem and when to make adjustments in the shaping to account for differences in circumferences.

When a tape measure around the body says there is a difference of more than four inches between the hips and the chest, something usually needs to be done about it.

Some knitters make adjustments if there is only a 2-inch difference. Of course, the style of the sweater, the fiber, and the pattern stitch used will affect the decision. But when you decide to make a change in the total body width from the hips to the chest, it is a very simple matter to either increase or decrease stitches at the side seam. You will be led through planning several such shapings in Part II.

HOW TO HANDLE THE DEMANDS OF SPECIALLY SHAPED BODIES

I absolutely refuse to call them flaws. I'll admit that there are special situations with some human bodies that require extra thought and care to allow clothing to fit properly, but I cannot say they are defects. I'm talking about things like Big and Beautiful People (of whom I am one), Amply Endowed Women, Dowager's Humps, and Barrel Tummies. These shapes are not usually glossed over by the wonderful forgivingness of knitted fabric. Special techniques, often simply adding short rows, are needed to make extra fabric to cover these parts of the body. You will find more about this in both Chapters 6 ("Getting the Right Measurements") and 14 ("A Refresher Course on Common Knitting Techniques"), and in Part II as we design special garments.

6

Getting the Right Measurements

THE THREE GREAT LIES OF KNITTERS

When knitting instructors and designers from around the country get together at national meetings, they talk about "The Three Great Lies of Knitters." We laugh uproariously and share the most recent versions we have heard from our patrons. The lies are these:

1. "I am a size 34."
2. "I always knit to gauge."
3. "You don't have to explain anything to me; I know all about knitting."

It is the first Great Lie that concerns this chapter. The variations on it that knitting designers and instructors hear go like this:

"You don't have to put a tape measure around me, I always wear a medium. If the sweater doesn't fit, you can refund my money."

"My bra size is 42 double D, but I'm really not very big chested; you don't need to measure me. I'm sure a 38 will fit. It takes less yarn to make a size 38, and you can block it for me if it needs to be larger." . . . "Oh, really, but I'm sure *you* can block mohair."

"My grandson is, eh, ah, I don't know what size he is. He's ten years old, and sort of big for his age. About this tall." She waves her hand up and down. "I'm sure if you design this special school insignia sweater for him in a regular size it will fit just fine."

"How big is my husband? Well, he's just ordinary husband sized."

"My son is s-o-o-o tall. Why, he could have been a great basketball player if he had wanted to. Well, no, I haven't measured him in twenty years, but when he was fifteen he was almost six feet tall."

And it is through our tears that we knitting designers are laughing. The remarks we hear are funny, but the results of believing the lies can be disastrous.

MEASUREMENTS ARE A MUST

You must take accurate measurements if you want your knitted garments to fit. Guesswork often leads to great mishap and grief.

Most designers who do custom work do so insisting on an actual real live body to take measurements from. No "abouts" or "sort ofs" or "ordinary size" estimates are allowed. It is often because of the lack of a living body from which to take measurements that many designers refuse to do custom work; it is not because they do not know how to create the designs.

The first way to measure is to follow the advice of authorities who say, "Measure every possible thing on every body you knit for and keep impeccable records of these numbers together with the dates they were taken and the weight of the person." Meticulous and well-organized people enjoy doing this and always seem to be able to *find* that record when needed. Some of the rest of us have difficulty with our filing systems and can never seem to locate the paper on which all these measurements were written.

The second way to take measurements comes from a different school of design. "Take only the measurements you need for the particular garment." This theory rests on the fact that things change, life changes, and so do human bodies.

Though the distance between the shoulder-bone tips of adults WILL NEVER CHANGE, everything else about any human body MAY change from year to year.

My way of doing things is to take only the measurements I will need for a particular garment. I am a gregarious soul and enjoy people contact. I like the idea of an excuse to get together with the intended wearer to take measurements anew if and when another garment is to be made. *Growth, gravity*, and *gained weight* can be taken into consideration over a cup of coffee or a glass of iced tea.

If, however, some adult you frequently knit for lives across the country, you may have to make a permanent record chart of measurements, updating it when holiday get-togethers are possible.

A TIRADE AGAINST "CONSTANTS"

In some "How to Design Sweaters" books you find the following:

"Constants are numbers or factors that are *always* required in designing knitted garments. Memorize them, and you will always design perfect-fitting sweaters."

"All shoulders should be sloped one inch from neck to armhole."

"Bind off one inch of stitches at the beginning of every armhole shaping."

"The hips should always be measured seven inches below the natural waistline."

"Always add four inches of ease to the chest measurement for a cardigan, multiply by gauge and cast on that number of stitches."

"The following are the constants for neck shaping; they never change: . . ."

Hen's teeth and fish fur! There are no heaven-mandated nor man-decreed "constants" in designing sweaters for every type of body.

How many inches a shoulder needs to be sloped depends upon the shape of the shoulders of the wearer, not a mythical number. How much bind-off shaping needs to be placed at the beginning of armhole shaping depends upon the difference between shoulder width and front chest width. The hips need to be measured at the point of their greatest circumference *wherever that may be.* For a cardigan, adding only four inches to the chest measurement of a person whose hips are six inches wider than her chest simply will not cover the situation. The neck width varies with the body type.

As you begin to understand the basic body types discussed below, you will soon understand why "universal constants" do not work!

Get it out of your head here and now that there are universal constants in designing sweaters. It all depends upon what you want to achieve and for whom.

We are not making assembly-line/one-size-fits-all/wear-it-whether-it-suits-you-or-not model-"T" cars. We are making individualized one-of-a-kind custom-fit fine garments!

As we work our way through the garment designs in Part II, we will discuss desired amounts of ease to add depending on the body type, fiber and fabric used, the style of the garment, and the usage of the sweater.

Basically there are two distinct ways to take measurements from the human body to determine the proper widths for a garment:

1. Measure the actual body size snugly and squarely with a tape measure, write that measurement down on paper and then add (or subtract) the desired number of inches of ease. I usually use this method for bust or chest measurements.
2. Hold the tape measure slightly away from the body and decide how big you want the garment to be at that place. For instance, when I am determining how big around to make a sleeve at the upper arm, I hold the tape measure out from the body and say, "It looks to me like thirteen inches will be about right for the sleeve width of this sweater."

It is not always an either/or decision as to which of the two ways to measure you must use. You can use a combination of both to suit yourself.

WHERE AND HOW TO TAKE A FEW BASIC MEASUREMENTS

All body types and/or designs will need these measurements:

Actual Underarm Depth: Have the intended wearer stand and hold her arms at her sides. From the back of the person, tuck a long straight knitting needle under one armpit. (See Figure 6.1.) Move the needle up as high as possible so that it rests snugly at the joining of the arm and body. Now drop a tape measure from the nape of the back of the neck at the point where you want the top of the sweater to end and the ribbing/trim to begin. Eyeball a line straight across from the knitting needle to the tape measure to determine how long the armpit is (in inches). Write down this number.

A plus number for ease will always have to be added to this actual body underarm depth measurement. If you do not add extra ease length at this point, the armholes and shoulders of the sweater will be too tight.

Note: When planning sleeveless sweaters for women to be worn without an underblouse, be aware of the height of the bra in relation to the actual underarm depth. I may be old-fashioned, but I do not like to see a bra showing through a gaping armhole.

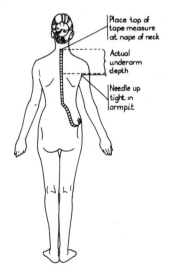

6.1 How to measure underarm depth

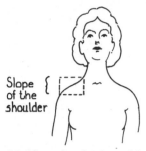

6.2 Measuring the slope of the shoulder on a figure with sloping shoulders

6.3 Measuring the slope of the shoulder on a figure with square shoulders

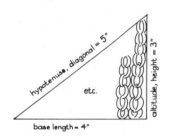

6.4 Triangle with a base of 4″, altitude of 3″, hypotenuse of 5″ on top of a piece of stockinette stitch fabric

Shoulder Slope: This is a necessary measurement, and I need to insert it at this point, but I cannot fully explain it until the next section where we discuss body types. For now I want you to imagine, superimposed on the body, a rectangle that begins at the joining of the neck to the upper torso, goes out across the air to an imaginary vertical line from the tip of the shoulder bone, down to that tip, straight across the body to a point directly below where you started. Notice how the human shoulder divides this rectangle into two equal triangles. (See Figures 6.2 and 6.3.)

Again I have to take exception to other knitting authorities. Many diagrams of how to measure shoulders for sweaters show a tape measure resting along the top of the shoulder from neck to shoulder-bone tip. This diagonal measurement is of no value, and is in fact misleading. The experts who tell you to do this have forgotten their high school geometry.* This sloping line from neck to shoulder is the hypotenuse of a triangle. We do not want to know how long this diagonal line is. What we need to know is how much the shoulder drops vertically in what horizontal distance. We need the length of the base and the height of the side of the triangle. We need the straight-across horizontal distance from the side of the neck to the shoulder tip and we need the up-and-down number of inches that the shoulders are lower than the neck joining. You will see the rectangle and the triangle in action in the section on body types. (See Figure 6.4.)

Write down the horizontal distance between the shoulder and neck, AND the distance that the shoulder is lower than the neck.

Bust or Chest Circumference: Where we take it depends upon whose body we are measuring.

For Women. Women's breasts are somewhere between the shoulders and the waist. The exact placement varies a great deal with body type. We need to measure the chest wherever it is the largest around, wherever the greatest circumference is. We need to note where this largest chest measurement is in relation to the actual arm depth—the same as or lower than. Amy's largest circumference is 3 inches below her armpit. Judy's is at her armpit. Mine is in between at 1½ inches below my armpit.

For Men. Obviously men's chests don't present the same problems as do women's. It is safe to measure about 1½ to 2 inches below actual underarm depth.

*The Pythagorean Theorem: The sum of the squares of the sides of a right-angle triangle equal the square of the hypotenuse. Or, $a^2 + b^2 = c^2$.

In either case, for both men and women, do not let the measuring tape droop down in back. Keep the tape horizontal to the floor. Pull it snugly, but don't squeeze all the breath out of the person. Write down the number. At a later time ease may or may not be added to (or subtracted from) this actual body measurement. Also, the circumference will be divided in two, one-half for the back and one-half for the front. (An exception will be made for very large-breasted women. The front of their sweaters may be made somewhat wider than the back.)

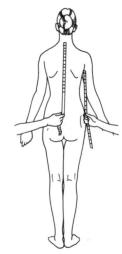

Desired Overall Length of Garment: (*Note:* Before you decide on the overall length of the garment, be sure that you have read Chapter 11, "Choosing the Most Flattering Design for the Wearer.") *1.* Place the top of the tape measure at the neck *at the spot where the upper trim will begin.* Let the tape fall free toward the floor. Press your thumb against the tape at the place on the body where you want the bottom of the sweater (including trim) to be. (See Figure 6.5.) Write down this number. Make a note of what kind of trim will be used on the bottom of the sweater—a hem, ribbing, crochet, or whatever—*and that the length of the bottom trim will be subtracted from the body fabric-stitch length.*

6.5 How to measure overall length of garment

2. To double-check, take an underarm length also. Drop the tape 1 to 1½ inches from the knitting needle in the armpit depending on whether the person is tiny or huge. Again press your thumb against the tape at the place on the body where you want the bottom of the sweater to be—the same height from the floor as the measurement taken from the back. Write down this number. Again note how much of the total will be taken up by the bottom trim. Note whether a sleeve will be sewn into the armhole or if allowance for other trim will have to be subtracted. This will give you an extra checkpoint as you knit.

This "desired length" will determine if you need to take a waist, tummy, or hip measurement. If the sweater will cover or rest on any of these points, you will need to know how big around the area is.

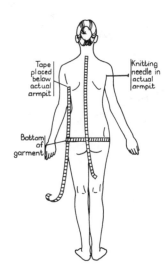

Circumference of Body at Desired Length of Garment: This measurement is taken wherever *you* wish the bottom of the garment to be. (See Figure 6.6.) Write down this number. At a later time, ease may or may not be added to (or subtracted from) this actual body measurement. Also, the circumference will be divided in two, one-half for the back and one-half for the front. (Exceptions: barrel-chested persons and amply endowed women.)

6.6 How to measure circumference at bottom edge

Shoulder-Bone Tip to Shoulder-Bone Tip Across the Front: Standing face to face with the intended wearer, place your right hand on her left

6.7 Taking a shoulder tip to shoulder tip measurement

shoulder and your left hand on her right shoulder. Now poke and feel with your thumbs until you locate the bony shoulder tips. They are not at the outside of the arms; they are not at the rib cage; they are in between the two! Now place your tape measure and record the horizontal distance between these bony tips. (See Figure 6.7.)

Once adulthood is reached this measurement never changes. The distance between the tips of our shoulder bones never gets any wider, whether we weigh ninety-eight pounds soaking wet or drive the needle of the bathroom scales off the dial. This measurement varies only a little bit between a size 6 and a size 16 female. It is the basis of knitting designer/instructor Ruth Rohn's paraphrase of Norrell's statement, "Every woman is a size 8!" Just because our bosoms and waists and upper arms get bigger around does not mean that our shoulder tips ever get farther apart!

This is a good time to take note of where the front neck bones lie in relation to the shoulder tips. The shoulder-bone tips may be higher or lower than the front neck bones. You'll understand this point better as I discuss body types in the next section.

Back Neck (or Garment) Width: In taking this measurement there are many considerations.

1. The wearer will have to be able to get his or her head through the neck opening. Does the person have a large head? Is the person a child? Children's heads are larger in proportion to their bodies than are the heads of adults. Extra width ease must be added for pullover garments for persons with large heads. If they can't get into the sweater, they can't ever wear it.
2. The style of the garment. Is it a cardigan? Does it have a neck placket or a zipper opening? For these types of neck openings, no extra width allowance need be added.
3. Will this sweater be worn over another garment? I like to wear long-sleeved button-down-collar shirts under my knit pullovers. For the collar to show around my face I want an extrawide neck. Many people in cold climates like to wear cotton turtlenecks under heavy sweaters. These garments, too, need wider than usual necklines.
4. How do you plan to finish the neck edge? With ribbing? How much, ¾ inch or 1¼ inch? A ribbed turtleneck usually sprouts from a wider width than a crew neck. Perhaps you plan only a single row or two of crochet, which will take up hardly any width.
5. *For women, never make a neckline wider than the distance between undergarment shoulder straps.*

To take a neck width measurement, stand behind the intended wearer. Place a tape measure horizontally across the *back* of the neck in the area that will be taken up by the neck opening *not including any trim or ribbing*. Don't wrap the tape all the way around the person's neck. (You're measuring only for a sweater, not a noose.) For a woman's boatnecked pullover you may want to measure the distance between shoulder straps. (See Figure 6.8.) For a child, you may decide the neck opening should be one-third of the width between the shoulders.

SOME SPECIAL BODY TYPES AND/OR DESIGNS WILL NEED THESE

Hip Circumference: Forget this business that "Hips are measured 7 inches below the natural waist." Fiddlesticks! Hips are measured wherever they are the widest. How do you find the widest place? You make a circle out of your tape measure holding it securely with a thumb and forefinger. Then, keeping that circle horizontal to the floor, move it up and down the body until it comes to rest at the widest area between the waist and the knees. You may have to make that circle larger or smaller to find the proper measurement. You'll understand this better in the section on body types that follows.

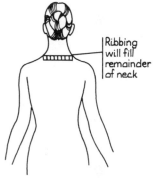

Ribbing will fill remainder of neck

Waistlines: Some of us have them and some of us don't. They are almost nonexistent in children under ten. Some of us have waistlines that are readily identifiable. That makes it easy; if you can see it, you can measure it. Some of us have waistlines that are bigger than our hips. That makes it more difficult to know where to measure. The rule of thumb is to move a generous hand span to the side of the navel then poke and push until you find the bottom of the rib cage and the top of the pelvic bone. Halfway between these two places, measure for a waistline, even if none is there.

6.8 The top illustration shows measuring the distance between shoulder straps, for a woman's boatnecked pullover.

The lower illustration shows measuring the back neck.

Waistline measurements are necessary only when 1) the waistline is larger than the chest; 2) the waistline is larger than the hips; or 3) when the waistline is going to be the bottom of the sweater.

When I plan a waistline-length sweater I like to add 1 inch of length ease between the underarm and the waistline *and* then make the bottom ribbing extend down below that.

Tummy: Each of us has one, but on some of us they protrude and on some of us they don't. Making a decision about whether or not it is necessary to take a tummy measurement will depend on whether or not the wearer's tummy protrudes and how far. I have a decidedly round and protruding tummy, and it is the same circumference as my hips.

This information is critical when I make myself a skirt, but not important at all when I make a simple hip-length pullover.

On most women, measure 2 inches below the natural waistline.

For men, measure wherever the greatest width is.

However, if a man or a woman has a "potbelly," the tummy measurement may be at the waistline, or even above it.

Sleeve Length: First decide what length sleeves you are measuring for: short-short; midway between the shoulder and the elbow; just above the elbow; just below it; or all the way to the wrist. Where and how you measure, and whether or not to add length ease, are determined by how long the sleeves are intended to be.

With the back of the intended wearer toward you, place the end of the tape measure high into the armpit. (See Figure 6.9.) Then drop it down *the same number of inches that you dropped down the armhole depth.* Make a note that the measurement begins at that depth down from the armpit. Now run the tape down the underside of the arm to the desired finished length *including the finishing trim.**

If the sleeves are going to extend beyond the elbow, I always add 1 inch of extra length allowance to take into consideration the bending of the elbow and the forgivingness of knitted fabric as it meanders over lumps and bumps. (I spoke of this in an earlier chapter.)

Write down the number and note how much trim length will be subtracted from it. The length of the sleeve cap will vary according to the design of the sweater. We'll discuss this when we get to individual sweater and sleeve designs.

Sleeve-Width at Underarm: This measurement is taken at whatever point is the widest place between the armpit and the elbow. As I said earlier, I am much happier taking this width *including ease.* I form a circle with my tape measure and ask the wearer, "How wide do you want this sleeve to be?" I pull in a bit to shorten the circle, "Like this?" Or widen the circle and ask, "Like this?" (See Figure 6.10.)

Wrist: Since ribbing (which is elastic) is often used at the wrist, I usually take the measurement at a point ½ inch toward the elbow from

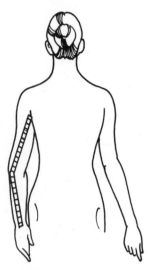

6.9 How to measure sleeve length

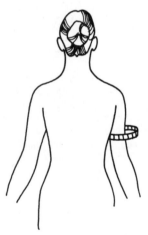

6.10 How to measure sleeve width at underarm

---

*I know that this is a diagonal measurement, the hypotenuse of a triangle, but for sleeves it works. (For shoulders it does not.)

the two prominent wrist bones. I used to measure around those wrist bones themselves, and when I did that I made the wrist ribbing too loose. It is not necessary to add any ease allowance for wrist bands because we want them to fit tight.

A FEW BASIC BODY TYPES

What body measurements are necessary and where on the body they should be taken depend, in part, on what the basic shape of the body is. Naturally, they also depend upon what type of garment you are going to create. What we are looking for are the widest, narrowest, longest, and shortest parts of the body so that we can plan our garment to cover them adequately. Let's look at a few basic shapes.

THE TRIANGLE

Think of a triangle; think of a swan gracefully swimming across a pond. A long slender neck, gently sloping shoulders, lovely round and full hips and thighs are the hallmarks of a triangular figure. (See Figure 6.11.) Notice how the bones that mark the base of the neck are often located *higher* than the shoulder tips. If you can't see them immediately, feel for them as described in Chapter 5. Notice that there is often a gradual increase in the width of the body from the waistline to the place where the thighs join the torso.

The following additional measurements are usually needed for triangular bodies:

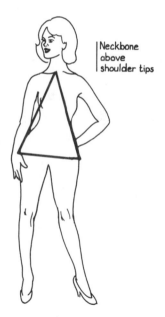

Neckbone above shoulder tips

- Shoulders are _____ inches above or below front neck bones.
- Bust or chest is _____ inches above or below the armpit.

THE RECTANGLE

Think sturdy and strong, think square and well built, think of the Greek warrior gods and goddesses and their human counterparts, the Adonises and Amazons we sometimes see on the street. The short and often wide neck rests on square shoulders. (See Figure 6.12.) The rib cage is almost straight up and down—it tapers only a little. The hips are either the same size as the chest or somewhat smaller. Notice how the outer tips of the shoulders can be higher than the neck bones. Rectangular-shaped women may have a decided waistline; rectangular men may not. Usually neither rectangular-shaped men nor women have a prominent derrière.

6.11 The triangular body (neckbone is usually above shoulder tips)

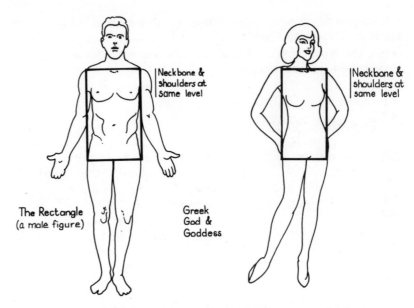

6.12 The rectangular body (neckbone and shoulder bones at same level)

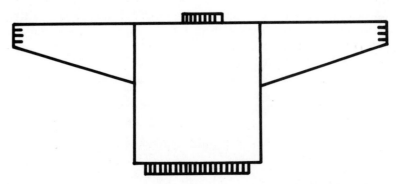

6.13 The "T" Sweater (no shoulder shaping; chest and hips same size)

This is the body that most sweater designers create for, yet which few of us have!

Notice in Figure 6.13 that there seems to be the same number of stitches at the hips as at the chest, indicating the same measurement. No armhole shaping, no shoulder sloping, no sleeve cap. On Adonises and Amazons, this design works okay. On the rest of us, it doesn't.

Things to consider in measuring a rectangular figure:

- Are the bones at the base of the neck higher or lower than the shoulder-bone tips?
- Is there any shoulder slope? How much?
- Is there a natural waistline?
- Which is larger, hips or waist?

THE OVAL

Think opera singers and teddy bears and Cabbage Patch dolls. Think hot apple pie and dumplings. Think soft and round and warm. This body shape is often determined as much by genetics as by overeating, for you see it in underfed Third World populations as well as in the overfed United States. (See Figure 6.14.) You will see it almost equally in both men and women. Sometimes oval-shaped men are called barrel-chested or potbellied, but I don't like either of those terms.

Notice that many oval-shaped people have trim ankles, very slender legs and thighs, and small derrières. Often they wear small shoes.

For the oval body shape, be sure to measure not only the back length of the garment *but also the front length.* The front length is measured by letting the tape measure drop from the joining of the neck and shoulders over that protruding front to the desired length. (See Figure 6.15.)

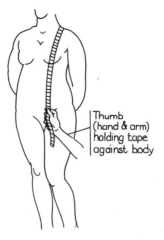

Thumb (hand & arm) holding tape against body

6.15 Take front measurements for the oval-shaped body.

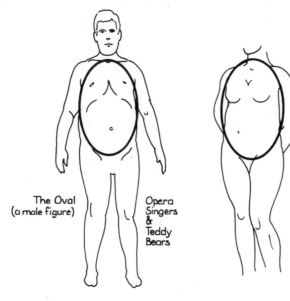

The Oval (a male figure)

Opera Singers & Teddy Bears

6.14 The oval-shaped body

If the front length is longer than the back length, some short row shaping may be necessary to cover that "barrel tummy."

Take the following into account when measuring an oval figure:

- Does the "barrel" extend all around to include the back, or is it just in the front?
- Where is the largest circumference of the torso? Bust, waist, tummy, or hips?
- Is there a waistline?
- Are the bones at the base of the neck higher or lower than the shoulder-bone tips?
- How wide is the neck?
- How long is the neck?

THE "V"

In almost every romance novel the hero has a "V"-shaped body (and he is usually "V"ictorious in the end). Whether his hair is sun-bleached blond or dark with soft curls, his shoulders are extraordinarily wide and (of course) strong. They taper to a small waist and narrow hips.

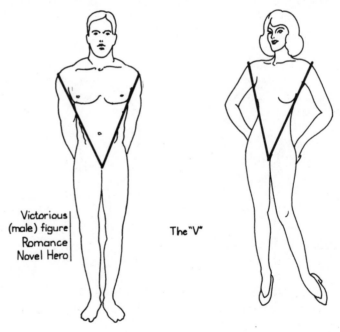

Victorious (male) figure Romance Novel Hero

The "V"

6.16 The "V"-shaped body

His "tush" is tiny. His thighs are long and lean. Though the romance writers don't tell you about it, he has a terrible time trying to buy a suit, for he needs a 44 tall coat jacket and a 36 pant.

But the V-shaped figure is not limited to males. It appears in women also. They, too, have a difficult time purchasing clothing. Their shoulder width requires a much larger size than their hips do. Thank goodness that jackets and skirts and slacks are often sold as separates. (See Figure 6.16.)

For men and women alike, "standard sized" garments simply do not fit. The sleeves are too short; shirt tails are never long enough; and often when they find the proper shoulder width, the neck is too wide.

Things to consider in measuring a Victorious figure: Be aware that the distance from nape of neck to waist may be somewhat long.

- The arms may also be an inch or so longer than normal.
- How much, if any, do the shoulders slope?
- How wide and long is the neck?
- How much narrower is the waist (and hip) than the shoulders?

THE PERFECT HOURGLASS

Think "36-24-36." Think of the pin-up girl and the dream of every soldier in World War II. Think of peasant blouses, cinched waists, and gathered dirndl skirts. Few women have the perfect hourglass figure, but it is not mythical; it does exist. (I've never seen it in a man, however.) These are the women who can wear the straight pencil-slim skirts and, when buying separates, wear the same size on both top and bottom. (See Figure 6.17.)

When measuring the perfect hourglass figure, consider that you may find it necessary to add an inch or so of short-rowing to the front of the garment to form a bust dart.

I wish I had a hard-and-fast rule about when bust darts will or will not be required. It would be nice if I could say, "measure the bust, measure the chest just below (or above) the bust, and if the difference is X number of inches or more, you will need a bust dart. Sorry, but the marvelous movable human body-machine doesn't follow those kinds of rules.

You must learn to eyeball the figure. Ask yourself, are the breasts lemon- , orange- , grapefruit- , or cantaloupe-sized? The "forgivingness" of knitted fabric will accommodate the lemon-, orange-, and sometimes the grapefruit-sized breasts. It will not

The perfect Hourglass

The Pinup Girl

6.17 The hourglass-shaped body

ripple over and cover cantaloupe- and some grapefruit-sized breasts. Ask yourself also about the style of the garment. Will large breasts make it hike up in the front? If it is a waist-length sweater, will large breasts cause a compensating blousing just above the waist at the underarm that will give the wearer a dumpy, potato-sack appearance? Whether or not to put bust darts in a woman's sweater is a matter of learned judgment.

Decide whether or not a bust chart will be necessary and make a note of it. A 1-inch-long bust dart will often do wonders for the sweater of a "perfect hourglass" figure *if the design of the garment will allow it.* Bust darts can interfere with striped, plaid, argyle, and some intarsia designs.

If you decide that a bust dart is necessary, measure the distance between the points of the breasts. (This presupposes that the woman is wearing the bra she will wear under the sweater.) You will need to know this in order to keep the darts from extending into that area.

Also, if you decide to put in a bust dart, you should take a front measurement from the shoulder-neck joining over the nipple to the waist or the bottom of the garment depending on the style. This measurement is necessary to determine how many rows long the dart must be.

THESE MEASUREMENTS ARE REQUIRED FOR ANY FIGURE THAT CALLS FOR A BUST DART!

Top-heavy
Hourglass

Gibson Girl

6.18 The top-heavy hourglass body

THE TOP-HEAVY HOURGLASS

Think of the Gibson Girl of yesteryear. Think of the Yiddish words *zaftig maidle*, which mean healthy, buxom young maiden. Think of pink-cheeked young German maidens carrying heavy trays filled with steins of beer at Oktoberfest.

In this case, the hourglass is definitely top-heavy; it is bigger on top than on the bottom. As an hourglass it would not keep good time, but as a human form it is very much desired. (See Figure 6.18.) Things to consider in measuring the top-heavy hourglass figure:

• Bust darts will almost surely be required. (Refer to previous section about taking measurements for bust darts.)

- How much wider is the chest measurement than the hips?
- Will any width need to be decreased from bust to hips?

THE BOTTOM-HEAVY HOURGLASS

Think of the Renaissance painters Rubens and Titian. Think of the full, round mounds of hips of the nearly nude reclining figures in paintings in museums all over the world. Think of heady perfume and velvet fabrics. Think of golden pears ripening on the windowsill, for often the roundness is of total circumference.

But these Rubenesque figures are not necessarily limited to women; men can have this shape, too.

The bottom-heavy hourglass figure, though very lovely to look at, does pose some pertinent problems in dressing. How do you show off those smooth round hips without letting them overpower the whole figure? (See Figure 6.19.)

Things to consider when measuring for the bottom-heavy hourglass figure:

- Is the roundness found in the front as well as in the back?
- How much larger are the hips than the chest?
- How much decreasing will have to be made between the hips and the chest?
- How much do the shoulders slope?
- Are the neck bones higher or lower than the shoulder tips?

6.19 The bottom-heavy hour-glass body

A TIFFANY DIAMOND

Think of a perfect gem. Think rare and precious. The Tiffany diamond figure is the Dolly Parton look. These women have narrow, often sloping shoulders, usually a tiny waist, and narrow almost nonexistent hips. A size 6 blouse in back, and a size 16 blouse in front. (See Figure 6.20.)

Women who have Tiffany diamond figures almost always have to resort to custom-made clothing (made by a fine seamstress with a knowing hand).

Things to remember in measuring a Tiffany diamond figure:

- *You will not divide the chest circumference by two, half for the front and half for the back, as is usually done with sweaters!*
- You must measure the chest in two parts: 1) regardless of how high or low it is, from underarm to underarm across the largest area of the bosoms, and, 2) at the same height from the floor from underarm to underarm across the back.

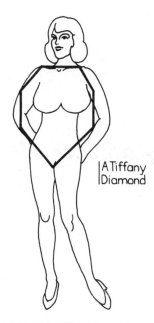

6.20 The Tiffany-diamond–shaped body

Note the height of that chest measurement in relationship to the armhole to know where to place the short-row bust dart that *must* be added.*

- As with the barrel-stomach figure, check the front garment length as compared to the desired back garment length. It may be as much as three inches longer.
- You must also measure the hip in two parts, for you will want the side seams to run perpendicular and not slant to the front at the bottom. Because of this, you will probably need to decrease stitches at the front side seams to bring them down to hip size.

BIG AND BEAUTIFUL

"Big and beautiful or, as some might call them, grand and glorious bodies do have special design requirements.

There are two kinds of grand and glorious people. One type is a true Amazonlike race of people. These people are perfectly proportioned; God simply designed them on a larger scale than the rest of us. There is a couple that I often play bridge with, both of whom are over six feet three inches tall, both of whom are truly beautiful people, just larger than the rest of us. In designing for these people, the numbers are bigger, but the relationships between the numbers are the same as in smaller people.

There are others of us who are also big and beautiful, but our size has more to do with an excess of calories than genetics. We are usually bigger around—in the arms, in the thighs, in the bust, waist, and hips—but we are no taller than ordinary folk. For us there is a difference in the relationships between the numbers. Because our shoulders may still be a size 8, and our bust a size 18, we will have to get rid of an awful lot of stitches between the two places.

START SQUINTING

As you go around doing the things you usually do each day, whether at work, the supermarket, at school or play, learn to look at human bodies through squinted eyes. Take a step back from the lady ahead of you in the checkout line. See if you can superimpose one of the foregoing geometric figures over her body shape. Squint at your children, your

---

*Make a note that you will need to make many more underarm bind-off stitches on the front than on the back to get the width down to the narrow shoulder measurement.

special other, your fellow workers. Almost all people will fit into the nine shape categories described in the previous paragraphs. Soon you'll be a pro at recognizing the basic body shapes and will then know where to place your measuring tape.

NEVER GIVE IN TO THE FUDGE FACTOR

Definition of the Fudge Factor: I will stop eating fudge and will have lost ten or fifteen pounds by the time this sweater is finished. Therefore, I can make it a smaller size.

Optimism is an exemplary characteristic of human nature. Without hope we cannot exist and, of course, we all hope for the best. My best would be to lose ten or fifteen pounds, but I am a faster and more reliable knitter than I am a dieter. It would be foolish for me to give into the Fudge Factor. I hope I will lose the pounds, but I'm not betting on it. If I do lose the weight, I can always take in width at the side seams and make the garment narrower. Or I can give it away and proudly make another in a smaller size. As surely as I *depend* on the hoped-for happening, I will gain instead of lose weight.

GOOD FRIENDS ARE SOMETIMES HARD TO FIND

"A friend is someone to whom you can pour out your heart, wheat and chaff together, who will gently blow away the chaff and return to you the wheat."
—Ancient Arabic Proverb

The best way to get correct and accurate body measurements for yourself is to have a trusted and loving friend help you. A friend who will not criticize or ridicule you with remarks like, "Glory be, Maggie, you sure are big around the behind." A friend in front of whom you are not embarrassed to strip down to the garments you will wear with the new sweater—same bra, same undergarments, same shoes. A friend who will, without comment, hold the tape measure snugly and squarely where it should be and give you an accurate reading.

But, for many of us, good friends never seem to be available at 2 A.M. when we have the peace and quiet to work out the design particulars of a garment for ourselves. Then we must do it for ourselves.

A mirror will tell you when you have placed the tape measure in the right place. Turn slightly and the mirror will assure you that you have not let the tape measure slip down in the back. A tape measure placed snugly and squarely, but not tightly, around your body will tell you how big you really are. Honesty will keep you from cheating yourself.

There are two measurements, however, that you cannot take for yourself. They are the actual underarm depth, and the length at the back from nape of neck to bottom of garment. It is often possible to start a garment without these two numbers. When the wee small hours of the night have passed and someone else is around, you can fill in those measurements.

A REVIEW

There are no universal constants in designing sweaters.

There is no set amount of ease to add.

Body measurements need to be taken at different places on different body types.

The object is not to follow some set of rules.

The object is to make a comfortable, good-looking, well-fitting garment.

Thank goodness knitted fabric has that wonderful characteristic of "forgivingness." It covereth a multitude of our errors. It maketh up for our inaccuracies. Even if we goof up a bit on measurements, forgiveness is at hand.

7

Achieving the Right Marriage of Fiber, Fabric, and Design

I'm sure that every knitter has, at one time or another, knitted something that he or she was not altogether pleased with, or something that was a downright and total disaster. More often than not, there was nothing wrong with the knitter's skills and techniques.

Most failures occur because of an inappropriate choice of yarn for the design.

Whether the yarn for the sweater was chosen by a professional designer, a shop owner, or by the individual knitter, it is likely that a bad marriage of fiber, fabric, and fashion caused the problem. Ignorance of the way these three factors work together is an invitation to a disaster. This chapter will help you learn some rules of the road of fiber-into-fabric-into-fashion to enable you to match up the right fiber with the right design.

The content of the FIBER and the style of the yarn will determine what kind of FABRIC you get and may dictate the kind of FASHION design you can achieve.

   FIRST RULE OF THUMB: You cannot tell what a yarn will do until you make a swatch.
   Yarns glued to swatch books and sitting in skeins on shelves *lie!* You cannot tell the truth about a yarn just by looking at it. It will not tell

the truth about itself. It must be formed into stitches and swatches to find out how it will behave.

We talked about swatches earlier in Chapter 3, "Getting New Ideas," and we will discuss them again in Chapter 13, "Getting the Right Gauge." If it sounds to you like I'm harping on swatches, it is because I am.

SECOND RULE OF THUMB: The more ELABORATE the yarn, the SIMPLER the pattern stitch and the design MUST be.

COROLLARY: The SIMPLER the yarn, the more ELABORATE the pattern stitch and the design MAY be.

Novelty, specialty, nubby, multicolor, textured, eyelash, rustic, and *slubby* are all words used to describe what I mean by *elaborate* yarns. They are yarns that are spectacular and stand out on their own. These yarns are usually so dynamic in themselves that they overpower any fancy or textured fabric pattern stitch that you may choose to work them in. Cables don't show up. The yarn-over holes and corresponding decreases of lace are lost to the eye. Seed stitch or Gansey (Guernsey) patterns are impossible to discern in the finished garment.

Often "good old plain and simple" stockinette stitch is the best way to work these elaborate yarns. However, please be aware that with nubby or slubbed yarns, the majority of the bumps will end up on the *wrong* side, the purl side, of the fabric. The "bumps on the wrong side" phenomenon is even more pronounced on home-machine knit fabrics than on hand-knit ones. All of those lovely lumps, for which you paid so dearly, may hide out of sight on the back side of stockinette stitch. Turning the fabric around and using it as reverse stockinette may or may not always be the best answer. Reverse stockinette stitch, which is discussed in Chapter 9 along with other pattern stitches, has built-in problems that prohibit many types of clothing from being made from it. If you want all those bumps to show, choose a style within the limitations of reverse stockinette stitch.

Because elaborate yarns can be so dynamic and dramatic in themselves, the design of a sweater made from them needs to be simple and plain. The shape of the garment and the way the parts are put together also need to be "good old plain and simple." For instance, a welt or extra fold of fabric at the shoulder-body joining would 1) not show up, 2) be especially thick and heavy because of the nubs and slubs, and 3) use up expensive yarn to no purpose.

At the opposite end of the scale, smooth, classic worsted yarns cry out and plead for fancy pattern stitches, gloriously twisted cables, lovely laces, and textured stitches. And since details and elements such as sleeves and plackets and joinings will be conspicuous, they can be as elaborate and fancy as you choose.

A FEW TERMS USED TO DESCRIBE YARNS

To gain a keen understanding as to what happens to yarn as we knit it into fabric for our garments, we need to know a few common terms that are used to describe yarns.

Loft: The amount of air trapped inside a yarn. How much empty space there is between both the fibers themselves and the strands that are plied or twisted together to form the yarn.

It is very simple to find out how much *loft* there is in a yarn. Simply pinch it. Place a piece of the yarn between your thumb and forefinger and pinch. If the yarn collapses and then pops up again, as with a strand of worsted-weight wool, it has a *high loft*. If the yarn does not compress, as a strand of crochet cotton does not, it has a *low loft*.

Garments made of yarns with high loft hold their shape. Garments made of yarns with low loft tend to sag and bag.

Low-loft yarns can be knitted into wonderful garments; just don't expect them to look like ski sweaters made of wool.

Resilience: The ability of a yarn to stretch out and snap back. Yarns with good resilience have an aliveness to them. Yarns without resilience are more passive. They just sit there and look at you limply. Sometimes the word *memory* is used to denote a yarn with good resilience.

It is easy to tell if a yarn has good resilience. Give it a tug and find out if it stretches and snaps back. Place a four-inch-long strand between the thumbs and forefingers of your hands. Pull your hands slightly apart and then move them together again. If the yarn did not expand and then contract, it is nonresilient. If the yarn stretched out and then bounced back to its original length, it is resilient. One-hundred-percent animal-fur fibers are resilient. Fibers made from 100 percent plant material are nonresilient.

This may be why a sweater design that worked so well in wool was a complete failure in linen.

The stitches in items made of nonresilient yarn will not "seat" themselves and the fabric will stretch. The less stretch-and-snap-back to the yarn, the more stretch to the finished knitted fabric.

It is important to realize that nonresilient fibers do not in themselves stretch. The stretchiness of the fabric is caused by the fact that the stitches never firmly cuddle up to their neighboring stitches and continually move around and rearrange themselves.

Silks, cottons, linens, ramie, and rayon are nonresilient plant fibers. Because fabrics made of these yarns will stretch, garments made of them must be planned to be THE SAME AS OR SMALLER THAN ACTUAL BODY WIDTH!

Ribbings made of nonresilient yarns will not be elastic without help. In a later chapter remedies for ribbing made of nonresilient yarns is discussed.

Now, can you see why a sweater design that turned out so wonderfully in resilient wool can be a complete disaster in silk? One yarn was resilient the other was not.

Worst: Twist. Except for "roving" yarns, all yarns are worsted or twisted. Worsting makes the strands cling to one another and hang together. It also makes the strands stronger and gives them better wearing quality.

But not all yarns have been twisted the same amount. To find out how much worst has been put into the yarn, simply untwist it. Some yarns are twisted so lightly that they tend to disintegrate as you knit with them. Other yarns are so highly worsted that they will twist back and loop on themselves as the strand goes from the skein to your fingers for working. It is important to know about worst because

the more times a yarn is twisted, the more durability it will have. The less a yarn is worsted, the sooner it will get shabby looking.

I once made a coat out of a very expensive novelty yarn that had large untwisted blobs of fiber in it. What a disaster that was! The unworsted baubles began to disintegrate on the second wearing, and by the fifth, the coat was an eyesore.

But a good thing can get out of hand and be overdone. A friend of mine made a sweater of a very highly worsted (twisted) yarn. The knitting of the thing was a hassle because the yarn continually twisted back upon itself, looping and knotting. As the fabric came off her needles, she was aware that it had a strange twist to the left. "Oh," she said, unconcerned, "that will block out with a little steam." But when the garment was finished nothing could save it from "the corkscrew effect."

Fabrics made from yarns that are twisted too tightly will develop a nasty corkscrew effect. The vertical edges will go off at an angle and will not be straight up and down. Blocking cannot cure the problem. Don't even think of giving the yarn to some other unsuspecting knitter. Throw away the yarn.

Ply: The number of threads that have been twisted together to make up a strand of the yarn. How do you tell what the "ply" of a yarn is? You untwist the strands and count them.

Once upon a time, long ago in the dark ages, this was very important in determining the quality and wearability of the yarn. This is no longer true today with modern spinning methods.

Today, ply does not affect the wearing qualities of a yarn. Neither does it determine the weight of the yarn.

Ply is important today only in the way that it affects the loft of the yarn.

Hairiness: Fuzz. Hairy yarns like to be knitted at a rather loose gauge. When they are knitted tight, hard, and firm, their lovely long, loose strands get pulled into the fabric and can't be seen.

Hairy yarns must be knitted loosely to show off their "fur." Even if the hairy yarn has good resilience, the finished garment will elongate and stretch because of the looseness of the knitted stitches.

Garments made of hair yarns such as mohair and angora need a "resting place" against the body to keep them from stretching to infinity. By resting place, I mean an area of ribbing that will cling to the body to stop the elongation of the fabric. Resting places can be elbows and wrists on the arms, or waistlines and hiplines on the torso.

Felt: To mat down. Naturally fuzzy, fluffy yarns and some acrylics should never be blocked and steamed. They will felt, and become hard and firm. Felt hats and "boiled wool" jackets are examples of *felted* items. Mohair and angora are examples of yarns that will felt. Some man-made yarns will also felt. (Always be sure to check your labels before you make or block a garment.) Felted items have lost their resilience and some of their loft, and become more dense than they were originally. Yarns shrink up and the item becomes smaller when felting occurs.

Yarns that will felt when steamed MUST be knitted to the correct size.

Pill or ball: Unsightly signs of wear. Before you ever buy it, while the yarn is still on the skein, a quick "rub test" will tell you if a yarn will pill and ball. Place four to six strands between your thumb and first two fingers. Quickly and briskly rub those strands. Stop and inspect them. If those strands show signs of wear from this simple movement of your hand, think of what will happen on the finished sweater where the underside of the sleeve will rub against the body. It is not worthwhile to waste your time on a yarn that will pill or ball under *moderate* wear.

Cashmere, like certain man-made fibers (see page 66), will ball and pill. Only ignorance of the nature of the fiber would allow you to choose such a yarn for a sweater that would get a lot of use.

Virgin: New yarn that has never been used before. Not "reclaimed." In recent years, some manufacturers have been using this word to be synonymous with "100 percent wool." This usage is not correct; 100 percent wool means that no other fiber is included (not that the yarn has never been used before).

Unscoured: Yarn from which the lanolin has not been removed. It is water repellant and smells like a wet sheep. "Unscoured" also refers to man-made yarns that have not had the "finish" removed.

KINDS OF FIBER

ANIMAL-FUR

The hides of animals were probably the first type of clothing worn by man. But hide clothing with attached fur had its problems. Among other things it is a bit too warm for wear in moderate weather. It didn't take our ancestors long to separate the fleece from the leather and to use each separately, beginning our long heritage of working with the hair of animals to make our clothing.

Though the word *wool* is usually reserved for the hair of sheep, it technically applies to the fur of other animals as well. These animal fibers are composed of keratin, which is a kind of protein. And all animal fibers have some characteristics in common. To be used, these fibers must first be removed from the hide-leather, cleaned of dirt and sometimes of oil, carded in order to align the hairs, and spun. When spun, all animal-fur fibers are resilient. Each kind of animal fur has its own characteristics, some of which are desirable and some of which are disagreeable.

Wool (sheep): durable, warm, holds shape (some people are allergic)
   Shetland: scratchy
   Merino: smooth and soft
   Lamb's wool: first shearing, less than one year old; like baby's hair, it is smooth, rather fine, and soft

Mohair (goat): scratchy (some people are allergic), sheds, hot
   Cashmere: smooth, soft, poor durability, pills
   Kid mohair: first shearing, less than one year old, like baby's hair
   Angora mohair: (a special breed of goat with soft long hair) sheds, is
      hot to wear

Alpaca: (also spelled alpaga; a South American animal) needs to be
knit up rather tightly

Rabbit: because the hairs are very short, the yarn sheds
   Domestic short hair: scratchy (some people are allergic)
   Angora: (a special breed) sheds, but is so luxurious it is worth it

Camel: great softness and marvelous wear, expensive

SILK

In a category almost by itself is silk, the protein excretion of the silk
worm. Threads and yarns made from silk fibers are nonresilient. It is
interesting to note that often the labels of silk yarns specify "Do not
wash. Dry-clean only." This is not because the silk itself cannot be
washed. Rather it is because the dyes used to color silk are not
waterproof.
   Filament silk: a very long continuous strand that has been carefully
      unwound from a cocoon without breakage.
   Tussah: thread from wild silkworms

PLANT FIBERS

Some plants produce long sturdy fibers either in their stalks, leaves, or
blossoms. These fibers are *cellulose* and according to the way they are
processed usually make wonderful, durable, long-wearing yarns. Plant-
fiber yarns are not resilient.

Cotton: absorbent, can be long or short "staple." The longer the
staple, the more durable the fiber is. *Mercerized* cotton has been dipped
in a caustic acid bath, which improves both sheen and wear.

Linen (flax): long wearing, somewhat brittle. *Ramie;* a natural fiber
that comes from the outer layer of the flax plant, is sturdy and durable.

Rayon: (man-made fibers made of regenerated cellulose of wood pulp
or cotton linters) durable, can be processed to be glossy. *Viscose* is a
specially processed rayon.

BAST FIBERS

Though rarely used by hand- or machine-knitters, there is another class of natural fibers called *Bast,* which includes hemp, jute, and tree bark. These fibers are used in making household items like mats, baskets, and handbags, and for other crafts. Occasionally knitters use them for decorative wall hangings and accent pieces. I've included them here so that the list of kinds of fibers would be complete, but since we are learning to design garments, not wall pieces or table mats, there is really no need to delve into their characteristics.

MAN-MADE SYNTHETIC FIBERS

In the 1930s, as technology advanced, man learned how to create his own fibers. Since the 1950s many superlative advances in man-made fibers have been achieved, and the availability of these man-made fibers has outstripped the natural ones. All have good and bad characteristics, just like "good old natural wool and cotton" have advantages and disadvantages. Trying to list all of the fibers, with their registered trademarks and proprietary names, advantages, and drawbacks would take pages and pages. Listed below are some of the generic terms. Even so, you need to be an organic chemist to understand them.

Acrylic: a man-made fiber (in which the fiber-forming substance is a long-chain synthetic polymer composed of at least 85 percent by weight of acrylonitrile units), it is noted for its bulk, loft, warmth, and woollike characteristics.

Nylon: the generic term for man-made fibers composed of long-chain synthetic polyamides derived from petroleum and coal. It is noted for its high strength, elasticity, and abrasion resistance.

Olefin: the generic term for both polyethylene and polypropine fibers.

Polyester: a generic term for man-made fibers made of ethylene glycol and terepthalic acid. It is noted for crease resistance, minimum care, quick drying, and good shape retention in garment form.

BLENDS

There are no hard-and-fast rules about the qualities and characteristics of yarns that are blends of two or more types of fibers. Depending upon the choices of the manufacturer, you can get the best of all possible worlds or an absolute calamity. You cannot even depend upon the price as a guideline for a good blend yarn. About the only thing I can say is to repeat what I have said in earlier chapters. Buy one skein and play with it. Make a swatch and abuse it. Ask questions. Talk to other knitters.

CONCLUSION

It is true, it is true: "You can't make a silk purse out of a sow's ear." Neither can you make a silk blouse out of fluffy angora. Now that you understand some of the nature of fibers, you are ready to go on to the next part of the equation and learn about the characteristics of the fabrics made of pattern stitches. You will minimize failure by understanding that "the content of the fiber and the style of the yarn will determine what kind of fabric you get and may dictate the kind of fashion design you can achieve."

8

Understanding the Lingo of Knitting

This is a rather technical, complicated, and somewhat confusing chapter. I really didn't want to have to write it, or to expose you to all these definitions and terminology, but I found that there was no way to write the next chapter, "Pattern Stitches and How They Behave," without writing this one first. In order to figure out how to use fancy and textured pattern stitches you will have to know and thoroughly understand these terms.

If this chapter seems too complicated at first reading, gloss over it and don't worry about it. You can design sweaters for years by using only simple stitches like stockinette, garter, seed, and such, without ever delving into multiples, repeats, plus stitches, and odd and even numbers. It is only when you decide that you are ready to get into cables and laces and elegant textures that you will need to know all these terms.

The words *multiple, repeat, plus, selvedge, odd,* and *even* are ones you will need to know and understand in order to design sweaters with elaborate pattern stitches. You will also need to know about graphs and charts because they can make the definitions much clearer and help with the placement of these fancy patterns.

WHAT IS A PATTERN STITCH?

Unless you have been knitting for years and years, you may be saying, "Hey, now, just what does Maggie mean by *pattern stitch?* I know what knit stitches and purl stitches are. I even know about yarn-overs and stockinette stitch, but what does *pattern stitch* mean?"

A pattern stitch means that there is some special arrangement(s) of knits and purls and sometimes yarn-overs, increases, and decreases that the knitter is told to repeat over and over to make a certain texture in the fabric.

MULTIPLES

The special arrangement of things that the knitter is required to do over and over is called a *multiple* or sometimes a *set* or even a *repeat*. For instance, the middle tree in Figure 8.1 is a multiple; "K 1, P 1" ribbing is a *multiple*, or *set*, of two stitches. The multiple or set of stitches will often be set off in asterisks (*) such as "Row 1) P 1, *k 1, p 1*, repeat between *s across." "K 2, P 2" ribbing is a *multiple* or *set* of 4 stitches. A 6-stitch-wide cable with 2 purl stitches in between each cable is a *multiple* or *set* of 8 stitches. This particular cable pattern could be written in two different ways: Row 1 (public side of fabric) *a)* *P 2, k 6*, repeat between *____*; or *b)* *P 1, k 6, p 1*, rpt bet *s. Whether the 2 purl stitches are written together or separated, the multiple is still 8. (2 + 6 = 8, just as 1 + 6 + 1 = 8.)

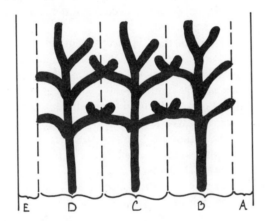

8.1 Three-tree diagram

A. Beginning Selvedge

B. Beginning Plus Stitches. Starting right-hand tree; note there are no overlapping branches on the right side.

C. Multiple Central Motif; note how branches overlap on both sides. Make this multiple as many times as you like.

D. Ending Plus Stitches. Final left-hand tree; note there are no overlapping branches on the left side.

E. Ending Selvedge

PLUS STITCHES

Often an extra or *plus* number of stitches must be added to the end of the first or last multiple of a row to make the edges come out even. Usually the stitches of the multiple are contained within the asterisks, and the *plus* stitches are found at either the beginning or the end of the row, occasionally being split up between the beginning and the end. There are three situations in which plus stitches must be added:

1. One frequent use of plus stitches is to maintain pattern symmetry at each end. In the 8-stitch-multiple cable mentioned above, when making a garment of all-over cables, most knitters would want to add a *"plus 2"* in order to end up with 2 purl stitches at *both* the beginning and the end of the row. This will allow a seam to be made without invading the last cable.

2. A second use of plus stitches occurs particularly in laces when the pattern either begins or ends with a yarn-over. If the multiple in the center has "YO (an increase), sl 1, k 2 tog, pass the slipped stitch over the k-2-tog (which is a double decrease), YO (another increase to compensate for the double decrease)" and the multiple ends with only the first YO, you will have to make only a single decrease at the end in order to keep the number of stitches constant.

An example is found in the "Vertical Openwork pattern V" in the Mon Tricot *1300 Pattern Stitches Booklet.* The multiple is "6 + 2." (Note that in the following Row 1 "wrn to m 1" means "*wool round needle to make one* stitch," and in Row 2 "m 1" is an abbreviation of the abbreviation and means exactly the same thing.)

Row 1) *P 2, k 2 tog, wrn to m 1, k 2*, (the multiple is within the asterisks), rpt bet *s, ending p 2 (the plus stitches).

Row 2) K 2 (the plus stitches), *p 2 tog, m 1, p 2, k 2* (the multiple is within the *s), rpt bet *s across.

3. The third use of plus stitches is to create a selvedge. When working in flat, back-and-forth knitting, if there is a yarn-over at either the beginning or the end of a multiple, it is necessary to add a *plus stitch* to serve as a *selvedge stitch* to make the ends of the rows stay even and straight. (Designers and editors don't always agree; some call it a *selvedge* and others call it a *salvage* stitch, but it means the same thing.) Often charts or graphs of multiples of pattern stitches do not include that beginning and ending selvedge stitch. The designer just assumes that you will know enough to make the plus stitch additions.

Glance again at Figure 8.1. Notice the selvedge stitches at the far-left and right-hand sides. Without these, the trees would run into the side seams.

REPEATS

Besides being synonymous with multiple, the word *repeat* also has another meaning and can easily be confused by knitters, even experienced ones. *Repeat* can also mean the number of rows you have to do to complete a pattern, as in "Repeat rows 2 through 10 for pat st."

From the arithmetic lessons of our grammar school days we need to recall the words *odd* and *even*. *Odd* means a number that cannot be divided by 2, and *even* means a number that is divisible by 2.

Graphs or *charts* can help make the definitions clearer. Charts are symbolized pictures of the way the knitted fabric looks from the outside, the side seen by the public.

All charts are meant to be read from the right to the left. This is just the opposite direction from which you are reading this page. English sentences move across the page from left to right—and from the top of the page to the bottom. Charts move from right to left and from bottom to top.

Most charts will show the beginning selvedge stitch(es) if they are necessary. Then, moving from right to left, they will show the right-hand plus stitch(es) if any are needed. Next they will show *one* example of the multiple itself. Again, moving from right to left, any plus stitch(es) if they are necessary, and last, at the left-hand side any selvedge stitch(es). (Go back and look at the tree chart in Figure 8.1 again.)

This does not mean that the knitter can make the multiple only once. The knitter can work the multiple as many times as desired. It is only in the interest of saving space on the printed page that it appears in the chart only once.

There are three important things for all knitters to remember about charts:

1. The same charts can be used by either flat (two needle, back and forth) or circular knitters. There are differences, however, in how they are read depending on whether the knitter is working back and forth or in rounds.
2. All charts read from the bottom to the top.
3. The first row starts at the bottom right-hand corner and moves along from right to left.

Flat, back-and-forth knitters should remember these additional points:

1. The second row begins one line up from the first row at the left-hand corner and moves along from left to right.
2. Because the flat knitter is working every other row on the backside of the fabric and the graph shows only the front side, on the second row and all other even-numbered rows, the knit and purl symbols are interpreted to be the *opposite* of what they appear. For instance, on even-numbered rows, when the knitter sees a purl symbol she must make a knit stitch instead so that it will appear to be a purl stitch on the public side of the fabric.
3. The third row and all odd-numbered rows begin again on the right-hand side and read from right to left, and the stitches are made exactly as they appear on the chart.

Circular Knitters should be aware of these additional points:

1. Do not begin at the selvedge stitches. Since there are no vertical edges because your piece is a circular tube, you have no need for edge stitches.
2. Depending on the particular pattern stitch involved, you probably do not need the plus stitches either. Because the multiples will bump up against each other as you repeat them over and over, no allowance is made for yarn-overs at the beginning or end of each multiple.
3. You will definitely need to place a marker at the spot where you begin a new round. This is usually at an imaginary side seam. If you don't place the marker, you may not know when to move on to the next row of the pattern stitch.
4. All of your circular rows (actually rounds) read from right to left. (You never have to change purl stitches to knit stitches, or vice versa, as flat knitters do.)

NOTE: *In the charts that follow,*

I means a stitch that will appear as a knit stitch on the outside of the fabric.

— means a stitch that will appear as a purl stitch on the outside of the fabric.

An elongated I *means a stitch that has been slipped on the outside of the fabric and then purled on the inside of the fabric on the next row coming back.*

"O" means a yarn-over.

∧ means K2 tog, a decrease sloping to the right.

∧ means SSK or SKP, a decrease sloping to the left.

∧ means S1, K2 tog PSS0, a double decrease.

But please be aware that not all designers will use the accepted international symbols. Many designers make up their own versions and you must always be sure to refer to their definitions before you begin.

2 × 2 Ribbon

(MULTIPLE OF 4 STITCHES; REPEAT OF 2 ROWS; 2 MULTIPLES SHOWN)

```
Row 2 → — — I I — — I I        ⎫
        — — I I — — I I  ← Row 1  ⎬ repeat
        ‾‾‾‾‾‾  ‾‾‾‾‾‾          ⎭
        multiple  multiple
                 ↑
              Start here
```

Two-Stitch Basketweave

(MULTIPLE OF 4 STITCHES; REPEAT OF 4 ROWS; 2 MULTIPLES AND 2 REPEATS SHOWN)

```
(same as row 4) Row 8 →  I  I — — I  I — —                    ⎫
                         I  I — — I  I — —  ←Row 7 (same as row 3) ⎪
(same as row 2) Row 6 →  — — I  I — — I  I                    ⎬ repeat
                         — — I  I — — I  I  ←Row 5 (same as row 1) ⎭
              Row 4 →    I  I — — I  I — —                    ⎫
                         I  I — — I  I — —  ←Row 3            ⎬ repeat
              Row 2 →    — — I  I — — I  I                    ⎭
                         — — I  I — — I  I  ←Row 1
                         ‾‾‾‾‾‾‾  ‾‾‾‾‾‾‾
                         multiple  multiple
                                  ↑
                              Start Here
```

Herringbone

This is a herringbone pattern made by slipping every 4th stitch on the first row. On the return row that slipped stitch is worked in the usual way. Then, on the next knit row, you move to the left 1 stitch and again slip every 4th stitch, and so on. It is a multiple of 4 stitches and a repeat of 8 rows. In this case 1 selvedge stitch has been added on each edge to avoid having a slipped stitch on the end. By using a selvedge stitch it will be possible to sew an even and neat seam. Therefore the pattern has a "plus 2," 1 for the beginning and 1 for the end of the row.

(MULTIPLE OF 4 STITCHES WITH 1 PLUS STITCH AT EACH END;
EVERY 4TH STITCH SLIPPED, MOVED OVER ONE STITCH ON
EVERY OTHER ROW)

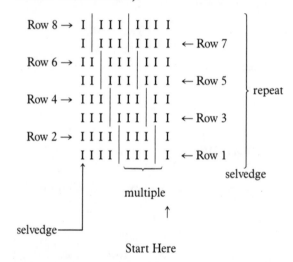

Standard Simplified Instructions would read:

Row 1) K 1 (selvedge st) *sl 1, k 3* (multiple of 4 stitches), repeat from *s across, ending k 1.

Row 2 and all even-numbered rows) Purl across.

Now watch how the multiple within the asterisks moves from the second stitch to the third at the beginning of the odd-numbered rows.

Row 3) K 2 (1 for selvedge stitch and 1 to move the multiple over to the left 1 stitch), *sl 1, k3*, repeat between *s across, ending k 3 (2 for the pattern + 1 for the selvedge).

Sometimes when you are designing a garment with multiples, which may or may not have plus stitches, you must fudge or cheat and add or subtract a few stitches from the number you multiplied out for the width in order to make the pattern stitch multiples come out even and complete. Sometimes it may mean that your finished dimension is ¼ inch to 1½ inches smaller or larger than your chosen number of inches.

Sometimes a selvedge stitch must be added where the multiple begins or ends with a yarn-over, as in this example:

Easy Lace Pattern Stitch with Selvedge Stitches

```
Row 2 →   I I I I I I
               I O / I \ O I   ← Row 1
selvedge      multiple          selvedge
                Start Here
```

CONCLUSION

Don't worry if you didn't absorb all of the information in this chapter the first time through. It isn't easy material. You may never need it, but I do hope that sooner or later you'll get adventuresome and want to create intricate pattern stitch garments. When you do, you'll know where to come to find out what you need to know.

9

Pattern Stitches and How They Behave

"Wish books" are wonderful things. Most of us love leafing through them and dreaming of owning the beautiful items portrayed in the color photographs. But wish books cannot possibly tell us about all of the other factors that will go along with possessing the lovely items they portray. There simply isn't enough space on the page. Besides, if we knew everything involved in owning these things, we might not be interested in having them. The Christmas wish book doesn't tell the child that all of his weekly allowance may have to be spent in continually replacing batteries for the Super Space Station. The seed catalogue does not tell the gardener that certain flowers will have to be sprayed weekly to keep the bugs from devouring the leaves. And I don't know of a book of knitting pattern stitches that will tell you how the finished fabric will actually perform once it is on the wearer.

We know that no knitted fabric will ever act like woven cloth but, according to what pattern stitch is used, some knit fabrics will be very, very "givey," even flimsy, and some will be much more firm. These are the important bits of information that the "knitting pattern stitch wish books" don't tell us. These facts are like batteries for toys and bug spray for plants. And to design sweaters, we need to know them in order for our wishes to come true.

HOW PATTERN STITCHES BEHAVE

In this chapter, I'm not discussing how to make pattern stitches, but rather what happens when you *use* them. Of course I cannot talk about *all* pattern stitches. There are thousands of them! There simply isn't room in this book to discuss all of them, but there are some common family traits that can and need be recognized. Once you know the ways these families act, you can make your choices with better insight.

CHARACTERISICS OF SOME COMMONLY USED PATTERN STITCHES

GARTER STITCH

The simplest of all knitting pattern stitches is *garter stitch*. It is easy to make: Mile after mile, simply knit every stitch of every row, or, if you prefer, you may purl every stitch of every row forever and ever. (If you are working in a circle, knit one round and then purl the next round to make garter stitch.)

Garter stitch has a real advantage in that it lies flat. It does not curl or roll. Every other row becomes a ridge, and it requires more rows to make up one inch of length than stockinette stitch does. Garter stitch is an ideal "thermal blanket" sort of fabric. But,

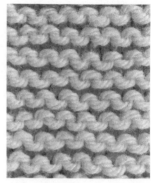

9.1 Garter stitch

as a finished fabric, garter stitch is very elastic lengthwise and VERY expansive widthwise.

If you made a narrow strip of garter stitch 1½ inches and long enough to go around your thigh, you would have a very effective garter to hold up old-fashioned stockings. Probably the first "Ace" bandage to bind sprains and hold splints in place was a very long, narrow strip of garter stitch. The lengthwise elasticness of the pattern stitch allows it to stretch out as it is wrapped, and then pull in firm against the body. The expansiveness widthwise allows it to conform to differences in diameter of the body. And used in the right places, all this is well and good.

Used vertically on the front button bands of a cardigan sweater this is ideal. There is no roll, no curl. (Sometimes it is wise to make a short row after every fourth row to prevent elongation.)

However, used horizontally at the bottom of a sweater, garter stitch absolutely cannot hold the garment next to the body. The silly stuff expands and flies away from the hips. Garter stitch trim on the cuffs or bottom of a sweater is not usually a good idea. The sleeve endings will continually expand, and not only will the sweater not cling to the body for a "resting place," it will flare at the hips and make them look wider.

When a whole garment is made of garter stitch it will expand in both width and length every time it is worn. What starts out to be a size 10 sweater can quickly become a size 16. Even if you measure and multiply correctly, you probably won't be happy with the finished garment after a few wearings.

Garter stitch has a multiple of *1 stitch,* and in flat knitting, a repeat of *1 row.* In other words, it doesn't matter how many stitches wide you make a piece of garter stitch, nor how many rows long you make it.

STOCKINETTE STITCH

The next easiest pattern stitch to make is *stockinette stitch.* Knitters working flat, back and forth, knit across one row to make the outside and purl back on the next row for the inside. Circular knitters simply knit every stitch of every round. Sometimes stockinette stitch is called "flat knitting," or "jersey" or "tricot." (It is usually abbreviated *St st.*)

The outside, the knit side, of stockinette stitch is flat and firm. The inside, the purl side, is bumpy and may have horizontal ridges.

Stockinette stitch fabric will roll to the back along the vertical edges. It will curl to the front along the top and bottom horizontal edges. But most important of all, stockinette stitch will stretch lengthwise and become narrower widthwise.

There is a classic experience that every knitting instructor in the world has encountered. First she teaches a student to make the knit stitch. Next she teaches the pupil the purl stitch. Then she has the student put whole rows of each together to make stockinette stitch. The next week the irate novice knitter will return. "You taught me how to knit, so on my own I decided to make a scarf, and look what happened! It is no good! Just look at this mess! It is not a scarf at all. It is a crummy snake." And sure enough, on its own, the plain stockinette stitch has rolled itself into a tight tube that continually stretches in length. That is the nature of simple, unadorned stockinette stitch.

Stockinette stitch is a versatile and useful pattern stitch. But it cannot be used alone—by itself, without other edgings. All edges—top, bottom, and sides—must be finished off in some way.

If you want a knitted snake, by all means make one. If you want a scarf or a sweater, do something to trim and finish the sides and ends of the stockinette stitch. This is why we usually use about two inches of

9.2 Stockinette stitch

ribbing at hips and wrists, and an inch or so of either garter or seed stitch for open vertical edges.

Stockinette stitch is my favorite to use with elaborate, multicolor, or novelty yarns. I can't see spending the time and effort on a fancy pattern stitch with these ornate yarns because so much is going on with the yarn itself that the carefully made pattern stitches won't show up at all.

For this reason, stockinette stitch is usually the background for Icelandic, Nordic, and Fair Isle color-work sweaters. A fancy pattern stitch would detract from the wonderful impact of the color designs.

Like garter stitch, stockinette has a multiple of *1 stitch* in that the same stitch is repeated endlessly across the row. Unlike garter stitch, however, it has a repeat of *2 rows;* that is, it takes 1 row of knitting across and then another row of purling back to make up the pattern in flat knitting.

STOCKINETTE STITCH KNIT IN BACK LOOP

Sometimes something strange happens to stockinette stitch. Either accidentally or on purpose some knitters make their new stitches into the *back* loop instead of the front loop of the stitches in the previous row. This twists those stitches, and changes the texture and characteristics of ordinary stockinette stitch.

Knitting into the back loop makes the fabric tighter and firmer than stockinette stitch made in the usual way.

9.3 Stockinette stitch in back loop

In an attempt to cope with the stretchy fabrics that result from working with nonresilient fibers, many contemporary knitters are knitting into the back loop on purpose. (When done on purpose it is abbreviated *St st bl.*) And it does work. It does make a firmer, less-stretchy fabric. But the process can also be tedious and time-consuming. I prefer to opt for simplicity and speed, and I cope with nonresilient fibers by making the garment two inches narrower than actual body measurement. Choose whatever works best for you.

Other knitters accidentally make knit stitches in the back loop of the purled stitches of the row below. This happens because they have used a different or unusual method of purling that throws the forward loop to the back of the needle. This, too, makes a firmer and less-stretchy fabric. Knitters who do this have to either accept the firmer stockinette stitch fabric or learn to purl in a different manner.

REVERSE STOCKINETTE STITCH

When a knitter uses stockinette stitch with the flat-knit side on the inside and the bumpy-purl side on the outside, it is called *reverse stockinette stitch*. It is made in exactly the same way; it is just used "wrong" side outside. Knitting magazines, especially European ones, are often filled with designs that call for reverse stockinette stitch *(rev St st)*. Worn by lovely models in attractive settings, these garments look great in the photos. But beware! A funny thing happens to stockinette stitch when it is worn purl-side, wrong-side, out. Please hold a piece of stockinette stitch fabric purl-side toward you and press a fist against it, pushing gently away from you. Notice the resistance of the fabric. Now turn the piece knit-side toward you and again press your fist against it using the same amount of pressure. Notice the difference in the resistance of the fabric; notice how much more it gives way to gentle pressure.

9.4 Reverse stockinette

Beware of garments made of reverse stockinette stitch; they will stretch widthwise and shrink lengthwise.

Think of that superb reverse stockinette stitch Chanel-style suit you saw in the latest French knitting magazine—a narrow skirt topped by a boxy jacket with sleeves ending just below the elbow. In the photo the model was leaning gracefully against a stone lion in a sun-dappled park, looking oh so elegant. The photographer didn't dare let her sit down! If the model did, the skirt would rapidly conform to the shape of her seated rump and, in compensation, would shorten in length. The photographer also must have taken the picture shortly after the model donned the jacket. If he hadn't, the same kind of body conforming and shortening would have occurred with the sleeves, making bulges at the elbows.

Please notice, also, in the photo, the perfect smoothness of the purl-side-out fabric. It shows no horizontal lines. Such smoothness is a dead giveaway that the fabric was produced on a knitting machine. Few hand-knitters can achieve such perfection.

Many hand-knitters make their purl stitches somewhat looser than their knit stitches. There are two ways to find out if you do this: 1) Make a 20-stitch all-purl garter stitch swatch and compare it in size to a 20-stitch all-knit garter stitch swatch. 2) Look and see if there are horizontal lines on the back side of any of your stockinette stitch knitting. My own reverse stockinette stitch is ugly with unsightly lines of looser purl stitches. What is acceptable to me as stockinette stitch is not tolerable as reverse stockinette.

If you are a machine-knitter, or an exceptionally perfect hand-knitter, go ahead and use purl-side-out fabric, keeping in mind the differences in stretch characteristics as you design the garment.

Since reverse stockinette stitch is just plain old stockinette stitch used "wrong" side out, it too has a multiple of *1 stitch*, and a repeat of *2 rows* in a flat knitting.

STOCKINETTE STITCH USED CROSSWISE

When lots of vertical stripes are desired, or when making a dolman sweater from wrist to wrist, stockinette stitch turned crosswise is usually used. This is a favorite technique for either machine-knitters or hand-knitters who do not choose to fiddle with bobbins. There are real advantages to doing it.

Before you try it though, there are a couple of things you must be aware of: 1) A correct measurement of row gauge is critical, because in this case it is row gauge, not stitch gauge, that determines width. 2) Since the lengthwise stretchy characteristics of stockinette stitch is now turned crosswise, unpredictable things happen.

At a recent Atlanta guild meeting I took an informal poll of knitters who had made crosswise stockinette stitch sweaters. Most had solved the problem of accurately measuring the row gauge, and nearly everyone said that the garment fit fine on the first wearing. On repeated wearings, two-thirds of the women had had problems with lengthwise stretch—with the garment growing wider with each wearing. Some other knitters had had problems with the fabric getting narrower so that the sweater no longer reached to the waist after a few wearings.

When asked if they thought these problems were a result of using the fabric sideways or a result of the chosen fiber, there was a fifty-fifty split.

Machine-knitters seemed to have less trouble with the crosswise stockinette, but then we already know that machine-knit fabric is somewhat firmer, tighter, and has a little less forgivingness than hand-knit fabric does.

RIBBINGS IN GENERAL

Ribbings are fabrics filled with vertical hills and valleys. Knit stitches form the hills; purl stitches form the valleys. Any number of knit stitches can be combined with purl stitches to make up ribbing. But regardless of the numbers of knit and purl stitches used, all ribbings have some characteristics in common.

All ribbing will stretch lengthwise, be elastic widthwise, and, when used as an all-over fabric, produce a finished garment that will cling to the body, conforming to (and accentuating) every lump, bulge, and indentation.

On divinely proportioned bodies, ribbed garments look heavenly. A "Knit 5, Purl 5" ribbing on an Adonis or Diana can be a perfect garment. On the rest of us, the ribs tend to separate and stretch over the bosoms and pads of fat, making us look melted-and-poured-into a somewhat too small container. As cardigans, ribbed fabrics get longer and narrower with every wearing. They make slender people look even more skinny and plump people appear even more fat.

Used as trim at the hips, wrists, and necklines, the elasticity and body-conforming qualities of ribbings are plus factors.

Ribbing trim used in these places helps to control the upward curl of horizontal knit edges. It clings to the body and gives the garment a resting place on the body to help control endless lengthwise stretch. Ordinarily, ribbing trim used for this purpose is made on needles that are several sizes smaller than the needles used on the body of the garment. For instance, a #5 needle for the ribbing used with #8 for the body is a common combination for knitting worsted (Class C) yarn. If you want even tighter ribbing, use even smaller size needles.

I *never* use any kind of a ribbing as a front band of a cardigan.

Ribbed front bands will always stretch. They will elongate even if they are knitted separately and made shorter than the sweater front.

Even if I am copying an ethnic garment such as a Norwegian design, I change the front bands to either garter or seed stitch. It may not be authentic, but it results in a better-looking garment. Stretched-out fronts of sweaters may be culturally accurate, but I do not choose to make them.

Though I'll be mentioning it again later as we actually design sweaters, while we are talking about ribbings in general I want you to be aware that planning the use of them usually takes some forethought. I'm a stickler for details—such as the way seams are made and the edges of the fabric that will form those seams.

When figuring out how many multiples of any ribbing will be needed across the bottom of a piece of flat knitting, such as the wrist of a sweater, always remember that the piece must be put

together with a seam. **If you use my method of invisible seam weaving as described in** *Knitting in Plain English,* **you will consume one-half of each edge stitch in the seam. To make the ribbing appear continuous without a visible break, you will need to add an extra stitch to one side.**

For instance, "Knit 1, Purl 1" (1 × 1) ribbing has a multiple of 2 stitches. If you thoughtlessly use an even number of stitches, that is, a multiple of 2, your piece will begin with a knit stitch and end with a purl stitch. One-half of the beginning knit stitch and one-half of the ending purl stitch will be consumed in making a messy looking seam. If you add 1 extra plus knit stitch to the end of the row of the ribbing, you will then be able to use one-half of the first (knit) stitch and one-half of the ending of the last (knit) stitch to make a seam that makes the ribbing look as if it were a continuous circle.

The same holds true for any other pattern of ribbing. If you are making "Knit 2, Purl 2" (2 × 2) ribbing, which is a multiple of 4, you will also have a knit stitch at the beginning and a purl stitch at the ending of the row. Again you have messy seam problems. But simply adding 1 plus knit stitch at the end of the row will clear up the situation.

Even minicable rib, where you "knit the 2nd st but do not remove the needle, k the first st and remove both sts, purl 1," or K 2, P 1, which are both (2 × 1) ribbings, require 1 extra knit stitch at the end of the row to make a pretty seam. And in case you are using a wider cabled rib, if you thoughtfully begin and end it with a purl stitch you'll be prepared to make a lovely joining.

Should you be using some method other than invisible seam weaving as I have described, please count up what portion of how many edge stitches are consumed in making the seam, and add that number to your ribbing. Life can be messy enough on its own without our carelessness adding to it.

Another messy-looking situation to avoid is binding off any ribbing *all knitwise.* Either bind off in pattern stitch, knitwise on the knit stitches and purlwise on the purl stitches, or use an invisible bind-off method.

One more general note about ribbings:

Most designers use a rule of thumb that says, "Use 10 percent fewer stitches in any ribbing than you plan to use in the body section of the sweater. And use 20 percent fewer stitches in the wrist ribbing."

Like all rules of thumb, that percentage system is just a guideline; it is not always "hard and fast and true" and may be broken whenever and however you choose. Obviously, it cannot hold true for gathered and puffed sleeves. Still, rules of thumb can be helpful and save a lot of reinventing of the wheel.

RIBBINGS IN PARTICULAR

As I said in the section above, knit-stitch hills of any width can be combined with purl-stitch valleys of any width to make ribbing. Depending on the ratio of the combination, that is, "how many knits to how many purls," the elasticity will vary.

The elasticity of any ribbing will also vary with the individual knitter. Exactly how much yarn the worker uses up in the changing of the yarn location from back to front and from front to back, as the various stitches are made, directly affects how stretchy the ribbing will be.

Imagine watching a relaxed Mary Jane casually flipping the yarn from side to side when changing from knit to purl. Her ribbing will be much less elastic than the ribbing of the intense Suzie Ann, who firmly and tightly tugs the yarn from back to front and front to back between stitches.

1 × 1 Ribbing

9.5 1 × 1 ribbing

"Knit 1, Purl 1" is the ribbing I most commonly use. (My 1 × 1 is more elastic than my 2 × 2, and my hands adapt to the regularity of the change between knits and purls easily and rapidly.) The appearance of the pattern is unobtrusive and blends well with laces as well as color work and cables. (To my eye, 2 × 2 ribbing appears too bold and masculine for use with delicate lace.)

When making hems in knitted jackets and coats, I make the *underside* of the hem in 1 × 1 ribbing on needles of a smaller size than those used for the body. I use a purl ridge row as a folding line; then I begin working on the body of the garment.

The multiple of 1 × 1 ribbing is *2 stitches*, 1 knit and 1 purl, which is an *even* number. However, if you want to make pretty seams as I suggest in the preceding section, you will want to add *1 plus stitch* to the final product of your multiplication and planning. You will then end up with an *odd number* of stitches. (2 st [multiple per pattern repeat] × 20 [repeats] = 40 + 1 [for seam] = 41.)

2 × 2 Ribbing

When I began to knit in the 1940s, "Knit 2, Purl 2" ribbing was all I ever saw or read about. To be quite honest, it was not until Aran sweater knitting was introduced that I was aware that there was any other kind. Though I was not always happy with my 2 × 2 ribbing because it was not sufficiently elastic, I did not know what to do about it. Perhaps I am very loose and casual about the way I throw my yarn from front to back between stitches, or perhaps I make my purl stitches too loose, but for me, 2 × 2 ribbing is the least elastic of the common ribbings. Make some separate swatches of different ribbing stitches with the same yarn and needles some night while watching TV to find out which ribbing is the most and least elastic for *you*.

Never accept the WORD of any expert without first checking it out for yourself. Your experience may be different from mine, and that is okay. If you don't check out the WORD of experts, you will be stuck with their foibles and fallacies.

9.6 2 × 2 ribbing

Two-by-two ribbing is also more visibly outstanding than 1 × 1 ribbing and to my mind sometimes detracts from the appearance of the chosen body pattern stitch. However, for classic tennis and "Brooks Brothers" sweaters it is a fine and logical choice.

In places where you do not want either a hem or a body-clinging ribbing, two or three rows of 2 × 2 ribbing *made on the same size needle as used for the body* can be an excellent way of finishing a horizontal edge.

The multiple of 2 × 2 ribbing is 4. (2 K + 2 P = 4.) To plan for 2 × 2 ribbing, you will need to have an even number of stitches that is divisible by 4. If you want to make a pretty seam, you will want to add *1 plus stitch* at the end. (4 [stitch multiple] × 20 [patterns] = 80 sts + 1 = 81 sts.) Directions would be written differently depending whether or not you decided to add that extra stitch that I like for seaming.

For an even number of stitches (divisible by 4), instructions would say: "Cast on 80 sts. Row 1) *K 2, p 2*, rep bet *s across. Rep row 1 for pat st."

For an even number of stitches (divisible by 2, but *not necessarily divisible by 4)*, instructions for flat knitting would say: "Cast on 78 sts. Row 1) *K 2, p 2*, rep bet *s, ending k 2. Row 2) *p 2, k 2*, rep bet *s, ending p 2. Rep rows 1 & 2 for pat st."

For an odd number of stitches (a multiple of 4 + 1), instructions for flat knitters would say: "Cast on 81 sts. Row 1) *K 2, p 2*, rep bet *s across, *ending k 1 (the plus stitch*. Row 2) *P 1 (the plus stitch)*, *k 2, p 2*, rep bet *s across. Rep rows 1 & 2 for pat st."

P 1, TWIST 2 K RIBBING

This ribbing has long been a favorite of mine. It is the tightest ribbing that I make. It is also very decorative, and a perfect complement for the sport-weight (Class B) heather wool yarns that I love to work with.

9.7 P1, twist 2K sts ribbing

9.8 2 × 1 ribbing

9.9 ribbing stitches in back loop

Actually it is a minicable and sometimes I call it that. The minicables hug the body and capture and play with light.

For Row 1, beginning on the reverse (private) side, k 1, p 2 across the row, ending with 1 k st (for the seam/selvedge). For the next row, Row 2, on the public (front), *p 1, k the 2nd st, do not remove it from the needle, swing wide around and k the first st, and remove both sts from the needle*, rep from * across, ending p 1 (for the seam/selvedge).

Here, the multiple is 3 stitches, and I always add that *plus 1* for the extra purl stitch on the end to make my seam. Since you don't twist the stitches on the back side of the fabric, this is obviously a repeat of 2 rows.

2 × 1 RIBBING

Lately, I've been experimenting with "Knit 2, Purl 1" ribbing, trying to achieve a firmer ribbing without the decorativeness of the twisted stitches used in the previous example. It is not quite as subtle and feminine in appearance as 1 × 1 ribbing, yet not so bold as 2 × 2 ribbing. Whether or not it will retain its good elasticity through multiple washings and wearings remains to be seen.

By now, you will be old hands at this, try it out for yourself to see what happens to *your* stitches and also know that it is a multiple of 3 sts (1 K + 2 P = 3 on the set-up row) and will need 1 plus st for the seam. The repeat is 2 rows.

WORKING RIBBING STITCHES IN THE BACK LOOP

The first time I encountered natural off-white Aran fisherman sweaters, I was bowled over at their beauty. Of course, I had to find a pattern and begin to make them up for family and friends.

The first Aran pattern I encountered called for 1 × 1 rib, with all the stitches of the ribbing worked in the back loop. And on the first Aran I made, that is exactly what I did. Making the knit stitches in the back loop was a bother, but the effect was lovely. Making the purl stitches in the back loop was a pain, and not worth the effort. On the second Irish fisherman sweater I made, I did only the *knit* stitches in the back loop. No one but an Irish knitter would have known the difference in effect. I certainly knew the difference in effort.

The texture achieved by knitting the stitches of ribbing in the back loop is a very attractive one. But there is a big difference of opinion among knitting experts whether or not KBL (as it is abbreviated) makes a ribbing more or less elastic and firmly holding. The real difference is obviously in the tension at which individual knitters work. To the collection of swatches of ribbing patterns you are making, add two more: one of 1 × 1 ribbing with *every* stitch worked in the back loop, and one with only the *knit* stitches worked in the back loop. Find out for yourself what happens when you do it.

HOW TO MAKE FIRM RIBBING IN NONRESILIENT YARNS

When nonresilient yarns (see Chapter 7) first appeared on the market, manufacturers and designers treated the instructions for making them up into garments just like "good old-fashioned stretch-and-snap-back wools." Individual knitters faithfully followed the given directions and immediately found out that

ribbings of nonresilient yarns need very special attention and precautions to make them elastic and stretchy.

All around the country creative and innovative knitters came up with solutions to make ribbing in nonresilient yarns behave itself and act like all good ribbings should.

My own immediate reaction was to reduce the number of stitches in the ribbing (as compared to the number of stitches in the body) and to use a much smaller needle than I would ordinarily use. (This worked well until I tried to do some ribbing on a #0 needle. I swore under my breath at every stitch of that one. The needles were just too small for my hands!)

Some colleagues tried knitting a translucent monofilament thread in with the nonresilient yarn. It gave an unnatural sheen to the ribbing, which some knitters objected to.

Other knitters preferred to work in a thread of elastic along with the yarn in the ribbing area. It was sometimes difficult to get just the desired amount of stretchiness without making the ribbing too tight.

Some knitters considered working with the elastic thread an unnecessary pain. Instead, after the garment was finished, they threaded the elastic thread onto a tapestry needle and basted four horizontal rows across the backside of the ribbing—one on the bottom, one on the top, and two others, each one-third of the distance between. They then pulled the elastic up to the desired length and fastened it in place.

Knitters also tried adding another strand of yarn or thread to the nonresilient yarn. They tried everything from sewing thread to embroidery floss to fine wool yarn. Sometimes their efforts were successful; other times they either didn't seem to help at all or changed the appearance of the garment.

Some authorities wrote long articles about the differences in elasticity of the different kinds of ribbing pattern stitches and which were best to use with nonresilient yarns. Often they overlooked the fact that different knitters throw the yarn from back to front and front to back with different degrees of tightness. *What is true of the characteristics of the authority's knitting habits may not be true of yours.*

Still others insisted that the simple answer was to use the same number of stitches and the same size needles, but to both knit and purl into the back loop of every stitch.

I honestly do not know what the best answer for ribbing in nonresilient yarn is in all situations and for all types of garments. I can only tell you about these solutions that sometimes work for some people, and then say once more that you never know what will happen with a yarn until YOU make a swatch. Try any or all of the suggestions above.

Good luck! And don't get discouraged.

SEED STITCH

I sometimes describe seed stitch to my students as 1 × 1 ribbing moved over one stitch on every row. At other times I say, "On the first row, set up a K 1, P 1 ribbing. After that, on all following rows, whatever kind of a stitch you see before you, do the opposite."

How the directions for seed stitch are written out in printed patterns depends on whether the designer is using an odd or an even number of stitches. This can cause a lot of confusion for novice knitters, which is why I use the foolproof instructions above.

However there is no confusion about the results that are achieved with completed seed stitch fabric.

Seed stitch lies flat. It does not curl or roll. Because back and front look alike, it is reversible. The fabric has more forgivingness than stockinette stitch, but less elasticity than ribbing. Seed stitch has a great stabilizing influence when used as trim for stockinette stitch garments.

9.10 seed stitch

Now that I am a Continental Pic knitter, and hold the yarn in my left hand, I use seed stitch frequently. When I was an American-style, yarn-in-the-right-hand knitter, I hated making it. I loathed the slowness of flipping the yarn from back to front and from front to back with every stitch.

A word of warning, though. Not all knitters get the same *gauge* with both seed and stockinette stitch. It may be necessary to work seed stitch trim on a *smaller needle* to keep the cuffs, collar, and bottom edging of a garment from flaring.

Whether seed stitch made with the same yarn, on the same needles, will give the same gauge as stockinette stitch will depend both upon how tight or loose the knitter makes her purl stitches and upon how firmly she flips the yarn from front to back and from back to front.

And how do you find out if it is going to be necessary to change needle sizes? You make a couple of inches of seed stitch on the end of your stockinette stitch swatch and find out!

Though technically seed stitch has a multiple of 2 stitches, 1 K and 1 P, and a repeat of 2 rows, one offsetting the other, you can use it over either an odd or an even number of stitches. Also, you don't have to wait for the end of a row repeat to quit making it. However, you do have to be careful that when binding it off, you do so in the sequence the *next row* should be worked.

IRISH MOSS STITCH

Another stitch that I learned to love after I became a yarn-in-the-left-hand knitter was Irish moss, sometimes called double seed stitch. It is really a child of seed stitch, and resembles its parent, but with a character of its own.

9.11 Irish moss stitch

Irish moss stitch has a glorious diagonal texture that captures and reflects light in a marvelous way. It is especially effective in light-colored and heather-toned yarns. (In very dark colors, not enough light is reflected to make the effort of doing the stitch worthwhile.) Like its parent, it lies flat, does not curl or roll, and is reversible. Irish moss is less firm and more expansive than seed stitch. It has some of the "thermal blanket" qualities of garter stitch but without the lengthwise stretch.

Because directions must be written differently according to whether it is worked over an even or an odd number of stitches, I teach it to my students in simple words. "Make 1 × 1 ribbing for two rows. On the third row, move over one stitch and make 1 × 1 ribbing again for 2 rows. There is a multiple of 2 stitches and a repeat of 4 rows."

I have included Irish moss stitch here because I want to save you from some of the disasters I have had with it. The first garment I designed using it as an all-over fabric was a little raglan Chanel-like buttonless jacket for my good friend Norma, years ago in California. The day she finished it, it fit perfectly. She took it home and wash-blocked it, and it stretched widthwise almost four inches. I thought the problem was just some fluke of her knitting or that she had stretched it in the wash-blocking. Then, a little later, I designed another garment for someone else again using Irish moss stitch. The same thing happened. The completed garment stretched widthwise with the first washing.

It is always wise, and oftentimes vitally necessary in designing, to wash and/or block your swatch to find out what will happen to the fabric IN USE.

The more you knit and the more you communicate with other knitters, the more forewarned you will be about what really happens to pattern stitches when they clothe the living, moving human body. I do not know how each and every pattern stitch will behave. (I doubt if anyone has *all* that knowledge.) I do know that Irish moss stitch will expand; I do know that it is necessary to make both a *working gauge swatch* and a *finished wearing gauge swatch*. You will be unhappy with the results of any garment made of Irish moss if you don't make and use both swatches.

CABLES OF ALL KINDS

I like simple, all-encompassing definitions. They allow me to clear my mind of details and get down to the basics of a problem.

The simple definition of all cable pattern stitches is this: a base of ribbing, of any combination of knits and purls, with the stitches on the knit-stitch hills worked out of sequence on certain rows.

Whether there are 2-stitch purl valleys between 4-stitch cabled-knit hills, or 4-stitch purl valleys between 8-stitch twisted-knit hills, or whether the cables are twisted every fourth row or every tenth row, the definition and the behavior are the same.

The biggest problem with all cable stitch patterns is that the twisting of the cables, that is, the working of the stitches of the knit-stitch hills out of sequence, EATS UP WIDTH.

9.12 Four-stitch, four-row back-twist cable

A cabled swatch of knitting worsted will be much narrower than a swatch of stockinette (or seed or Irish moss) made with the same yarn and needles. The stockinette may get a gauge of 4½ stitches to the inch. The cables piece may get a gauge of 6 stitches to the inch. I have heard and read of "constants," such as "Add 1 stitch of width for each cable used," or "Add 1 stitch per inch of stockinette gauge" to compensate for the width-eating character of cables. Nonsense! The only way to tell exactly how much width the cables will use up is to make a swatch of them and measure it.

Not only do cables eat width, they also constrain the widthwise stretchiness and forgivingness that is common to knitted fabrics.

I once made a crew-necked pullover sweater in 4-stitch-wide cables that were twisted every fourth row. Getting in and out of that garment was much more difficult than if it had been made of stockinette stitch because there was so much less widthwise forgivingness to the fabric.

That same 4-stitch, 4-row, all-over-cabled sweater also added visual bulk to the wearer. Thank goodness he was skinny, because wearing that sweater made him look twenty-five pounds heavier. Broader stitch cables twisted at less frequent intervals usually do not have such intense pound-adding looks. In fact, a few wider, less-often twisted cables centered in a narrow band up and down the center front of a sweater can often give a slimming visual effect. The important thing to remember in designing such garments is to increase some extra stitches *only in the area where the cables will be.* This will compensate for the cables' width-eating nature without scrunching or stretching.

Unfortunately, cabled fabrics have many of the same rolling and curling characteristics as does stockinette stitch fabric. Their edges need to be finished off in some way and should never be left to their own stubborn habits.

9.13 Six-stitch, six-row back-twist cable

FAIR ISLE, NORDIC, AND MULTICOLOR STITCHES

Besides the incredible joy of creating a wondrous work of art, there are two clear objectives in making Fair Isle and other multicolor pattern stitches: 1) to get the warmth of two garments with one sweater; and 2) to use up odd bits of leftover yarn.

The second objective is a matter of thrift, which is vital for serious knitters, but it really doesn't affect the character of the fabric, only how much of it we can afford to make.

The first objective, that of getting the warmth of two sweaters in one, definitely changes the nature of the finished fabric. Because yarns not in use for making particular stitches must be stranded across the back of the work, they trap air and add a thermal factor. Now two separate and distinct things happen:

1) The fabric is thicker than that made with one color only. Also, it is not as pliable, nor as body-conforming; and 2) no matter how carefully we watch the tension of the stranded yarn at the back,

there will almost always be less horizontal stretch to these multi-color fabrics. Multicolor pattern stitches usually have less forgivingness than single-color fabrics. Therefore it is usually necessary to add more ease width to these types of garments than to plainer stitch stockinette or Guernsey sweaters.

If the sweater has two distinct areas, for instance, a body and sleeves of plain stockinette stitch and a yoke of Fair Isle patterning, it may be necessary to use larger needles on the multicolor patterns in order to maintain the same gauge throughout the sweater.

One more word of warning about these incredibly gorgeous patterns. Recall the climate where these designs originated, that is, northern latitudes on islands surrounded by cold oceans. It was overcast, damp, and chilly most of the year. The indigenous populations were comfortable in these garments even in midsummer when sixty degrees might seem to be a broiling hot day. Now be aware of the climate in which the intended wearer of your garment lives. Will he/she swelter in it? Will there be only a few occasions when it can be comfortably worn? If the wearer lives in California, Florida, or the sunny South, the answers will be "yes," meaning "no, don't make the sweater even if it looks wonderful."

Machine-knitters using finer weight yarns such as fingering (Class A) and lightweight sport (Class B) do not have this problem with excessive warmth.

9.14 Fair Isle pattern

9.15 Raised eyelet lace

MOSAICS AND SLIPPED-STITCH PATTERNS

Most multicolored mosaics and some slipped-stitch patterns were created especially for knitting machines, which cannot work with two colors on one row, or for hand-knitters who do not enjoy working with two colors at the same time on the same row. (Personally, I avoid mosaics and slipped-stitch patterns because I dislike having to work every row twice—once with color A slipping the stitches that do not call for it and then again with color B on the stitches that were slipped before. I prefer to carry color A in my right hand [American style] and color B in my left hand [Continental Pic method] and make all of the stitches across a row at one time.) Some knitters, however, love working mosaics and slipped-stitch patterns. The object of knitting is to enjoy what you are doing; do whatever *you* enjoy!

I have placed this section on mosaics and slipped-stitch patterns immediately following the section on other multicolored patterns because most, in fact almost all, of the same factors apply—the extra warmth, the possible difference in gauge from stockinette, the same differences in forgivingness. Of course, all the same problems in designing will also occur.

LACES

Laces are fabrics that have yarn-over holes made intentionally with matching decreases to retain the same number of stitches across a row. Depending on how and where the compensating increases and decreases are made, the fabric can be absolutely filmy frothy, like a Spanish mantilla or the pattern of the foam of waves on the beach at high tide, or geometrically patterned like blocks and diamonds separated by rigidly established defining lines.

Laces can cause three problems:

1. They do not make a firm fabric, but that is okay; all knitted fabric does not have to be firm. Just don't expect all-over laces, once they are on the body, to hold fast-and-true straight-across and up-and-down lines.
2. Keeping the pattern in order while making increases and decreases to widen or narrow can be mind-boggling. In the early sixties, knitted lace dresses were all the rage. On the slender models in the glossy knitting fashion magazines, they were gorgeous. On normal, pear-shaped women, they weren't so satisfactory. Making side-seam decreases from hip to bust while staying true to the lace pattern defeated many hand-knitters. (For machine-knitters it is no problem to increase or decrease in lace patterns.) Not to make those side-

seam decreases meant either an overabundance of fabric at the bust or a dress that stretched too tight over the hips and cupped under the derrière. Most hand-knitters are comfortable making laces only when they are working straight up and down. This illustrates what I meant when I said that the fabric often determines the fashion you can make. A shaped lace blouse or dress may be difficult to knit. Hand-knitters desiring lace items are best off choosing straight up-and-down projects.

3. Laces usually have a different gauge than stockinette stitch made with the same yarn and same needles. Where an up-and-down panel of lace is desired in the midst of stockinette stitch, it may be necessary to make the lace separately on smaller needles and then seam it to the stockinette side panels.

The difference in gauge between lace and stockinette can be handled more easily when making horizontal bands of lace. Simply make the lace rows with smaller needles (or tighter machine tension).

Let me share with you a problem I recently had when designing a series of "big and beautiful" sweaters for "grand and glorious gals." I wanted to make a pretty, dressy garment that used a diamond-pattern lace. But understanding the lack of firmness of lace fabric, I didn't want to use lace all over the garment, just on the sleeves and on a panel up and down the center front. That way I could use the softness of lace, get a slimming vertical panel of it, and avoid using it in places that would expand over and accentuate the bosoms of us larger gals. In making the gauge swatches in preparation to designing the sweater, it became apparent that the lace had to be worked on needles two sizes smaller than those used for the stockinette stitch. And the only way to have an up-and-down center lace panel was to make the front in three separate pieces and seam them together.

INTARSIA

The word *intarsia* used to mean making a mosaic worked in wood, like an inlaid wood design of flowers and leaves. Contemporary knitters use the word to mean mosaiclike shapes and designs that are knitted into a fabric. The process often means using bobbins to keep the yarns from becoming tangled while being knitted, and

it always means working flat, back and forth, never in the round.

When you are working back and forth, the yarn for the color change will be at the edge of the area waiting for you. Working in the round, it would be waiting on the opposite side of the area, way out of reach.

9.16 Intarsia

The only important thing to remember when working with intarsia is to twist the yarns when changing from one color to another. That is, throw the old yarn up and to the left and bring the new yarn up from underneath and to the right of the old. This will avoid gaping holes or making two separate pieces of knitting.

If you plan and plot your own unique intarsia designs, you will be wise to invest in *knitter's graph paper*. This special paper takes into account the fact that knitted stitches are rarely truly square. We more commonly make something like 5 stitches and 8 rows per inch, or 6 stitches and 10 rows per inch. Designs—hearts and flowers and alphabets and such—that are plotted on standard graph paper will appear flattened and squashed when translated into knitted fabric. Some knitters insist that the differences don't bother them. They casually say, "Oh, I just throw in one extra row every fourth or fifth row and it comes out okay." I've tried that routine, and I'm far happier with the special knitter's graph paper. That way I know exactly how my design will reproduce.

Some intarsia fabrics not only use areas of different colored yarns but also make those magnificent splotches of color in different pattern stitches. Having read the sections on seed and Irish moss stitches, you are already forewarned about the possible differences in gauge. In very small areas of just a couple of inches, the difference may not be noticeable. In larger areas, it can cause bagging and sagging problems.

In planning intarsia designs, especially free-form and wildly asymmetric creations, be very careful where you locate splotches of color. It is incredibly easy to place brilliant-hued blobs so they resemble striptease dancers' pasties. And I have also allowed important parts of the design to fall near the armpits where they disappear from sight. In the planning stage, it is a good idea to draw a circle with a 3½- to 4-inch radius centered at the armpit and to keep important parts of the design out of that area.

DUPLICATE STITCH

To avoid the aforementioned problems in planning the location of intarsia designs and the problem of working with bobbins, and to make splotches of color on knitted-in-the-round fabric, some knitters resort to using duplicate stitch instead of knit-in intarsia. (See *Knitting in Plain English* for instructions on how to make duplicate stitch.) One or two stitches of duplicate stitch often work out very well. Because it results in a double thicknesses of yarn, however, two unfortunate things will happen if you make large areas of it.

Large areas of duplicate stitch will be much heavier than the rest of the fabric. They will also be much more firm and rigid.

As much as I prefer to do circular knitting, when I want large areas of color I resort to flat, back-and-forth knitting and intarsia made with bobbins.

ARAN FISHERMAN PATTERNS

There are whole books written about the fascinating lore and intricate details of Aran fisherman knit stitches. If they intrigue you and if you love complicated knitting that demands total concentration, by all means explore them.

Just remember that these gorgeous pattern stitches are cousins and second-cousins-twice-removed of cable stitches. Like their cable relatives, Aran pattern stitches that have crossed or cabled stitches will eat width. It will take a much greater number of stitches in any Aran pattern to equal the same width you would get with stockinette stitch or with most any other type of pattern stitch. Exactly how many more stitches can be told only by knitting a swatch of each and every Aran pattern to be used.

Also, because of the twists and turns of the intricate stitch patterns, often more rows will be required per inch. Frequently garter stitch or quaker rib* is used to eat up the extra length in adjacent flat areas.

---

*Quaker rib is made by alternating horizontal bands of stockinette stitch and reverse stockinette stitch.

Because of the extra stitches and rows per inch, Aran garments will use more yarn than a sweater made in stockinette stitch. Be sure to buy extra of the same dye lot before you begin to create your own design.

Not only will there be more stitches across the width of an Aran, but because of all the lovely twisting of stitches and the fact that many of them have been worked out of sequence,

both the finished fabric and the finished garment will have much less widthwise stretch. More body ease allowance must be planned for intricate Arans.

Most Irish fisherman patterns are not reversible, so be careful of using fold-back lapels or turn-down collars when designing your own.

PLAIDS

Plaid fabric is relatively easy for knitters to *make*. The horizontal lines are just stripes of different colors. The vertical lines can either be knitted in or added later by dropping a stitch and then crocheting a chain stitch over that dropped one.

Knitted plaid fabric is much more difficult for knitters to *use* effectively. Remember, early on, I told you that all knit fabric will sag and bag and that horizontal lines may not remain straight across and that the forgivingness of knit fabric will allow it to slither across lumps and bumps like water over rocks in a creek bed?

A knitted plaid sweater may look exquisite—all perfect squares and lines—lying neatly folded in its gift box. Once on the wonderful movable (and bumpy) human machine, it may no longer hold to "all perfect squares and lines." The fabric may stretch a bit here, scrunch a bit there, and conform to the shape of the wearer.

A way to avoid this nasty habit of knitted plaid fabric is to make it at a much firmer and tighter gauge than normal for stockinette stitch, perhaps even knitting into the back loop of the knit stitches to attain a rigid fabric. Of course, making the gauge tighter will necessitate adding more width ease allowance to the garment.

ARGYLES

I will always have a fondness for argyles. They are simply flat, back-and-forth plaid fabrics with the squares made on the diagonal with all colors knitted in, using bobbins. I made lots of argyle socks riding in buses back and forth to high school. A lot of us teenage knitters in the 1940s made them. They were complicated enough to be challenging and easy enough to be successful. By the choice of colors, they can be brilliant and bold or subtle and quiet.

Of course, the knitter has to remember to "throw the yarn" when changing colors to avoid holes, and has to keep her bobbins untangled. But because the plaid is diagonal instead of up and down, argyles don't cause the kinds of sagging problems for the designer that plaids do.

And because the finished fabric is "elaborate," I like to see the design shapes of argyle sweaters kept simple and classic. Pullover vests are an ideal use of argyle patterns. The only problem that I have ever had in designing argyle sweaters was trying to make the side seams match perfectly while at the same time making the sweater the appropriate size for the wearer. I suppose it can be done, that is, getting the perfect gauge together with the perfect size of diamonds to make the underarm seams match perfectly, so as to form a seemingly continuous diagonal design. I must admit, however, that after several attempts, my seamstress training to perfectly match plaids gave way to just happily knitting away and letting the side seams fall however they wished. I became content with the pattern centered in the front and back. Unless you are prepared to sweat blood and tear out your hair, I suggest you settle for imperfect side seams too.

Argyle fabrics usually have no other problems than does ordinary stockinette stitch fabric.

CHEVRONS AND UNDULATING PATTERNS

Fishtail lace, feather-and-fan lace, and ripple afghan stitches are all examples of pattern stitches that have wavy or jagged top and bottom edges. *Undulating* is the fancy word for them, and it means to move up and down.

Please don't destroy the beauty of the upward-and-downward-moving top and bottom edges of these pattern stitches by trying to force straight horizontal top and bottom ribbing, finishing, or seams on them.

Plan your overall design to work with the undulating horizontal edges instead of against them. There are several ways to do this.

Let the bottom move up and down. Make it conform to the body by using a few inches of the same pattern stitch made with smaller needles instead of ribbing. Forcing the pattern to begin above ordinary ribbing can look ugly.

Don't try to make straight-across shoulder seams. Instead, make crosswise gussets to inset into the shoulders seams. Increase and then decrease the edges of the saddle-sleeve-like gussets so that they fit exactly into the undulating shapes of the top edge of the pattern stitch.

One other thing about undulating pattern stitches. Sometimes the

9.17 Feather and fan lace

pattern multiple repeats are quite large. A favorite of mine, feather-and-fan lace, is 12 stitches, often 2½ inches even in sport-weight (Class B) yarn. This can cause real problems when the designer tries to multiply out how many patterns wide she wants a garment to be. Thank goodness most of these undulating pattern stitches are stretchy. For instance, if the designer wants a 36-inch-wide finished garment, and divides that number on her pocket calculator by 2½ inches, the width of each pattern multiple, she will find that she needs to make the sweater 14.4 patterns wide. 14.4? No way. She will have to make it either 14 or 15 patterns wide. There is no in between. Or she will have to fiddle with needle size and gauge. Knowing about the stretchiness of this particular pattern, I'd opt for 14 patterns, 7 for the back and 7 for the front. In a less stretchy fabric a better choice might be 15 patterns. But there is no law that says you *must* use the same number of pattern repeats on the front as on the back. There could be 8 on the front and 7 on the back. The difference between front and back could be made up in the width of the center front neck opening.

Awareness, knowledge, ingenuity, and creativity. These are the factors that can make our lives richer, warmer, happier, and better. I hope this chapter has helped you gain a knowledge of the ways some of the different families of knitted pattern stitches behave when made into garments and placed on the human figure. I hope you are now no longer at the mercy of the glossy photos in "wish books," not knowing that Irish moss stitch will stretch widthwise, that stockinette stitch will transmogrify into a snake, that garter stitch bottoms will magnify the width of hips, and that your gauge in seed stitch may be different from your gauge in stockinette. Just as I wouldn't give a child a new toy without the proper batteries, I wouldn't give you the "how to" of designing a sweater without the knowledge of pattern stitches that must go with it.

10

Choosing the Right Color

A number of years ago, I attended a fashion show of handmade needlework garments. Each woman proudly modeled her original creation. There were hand- and machine-knit garments, crocheted ones, dresses and blouses with gorgeous smocking and embroidery of all kinds, quilted jackets, hand-painted and dyed textiles, even garments of handwoven fabric. Each example was lovelier than the one before and exhibited the fine skills of their maker/wearers.

But while learning all the ins and outs of their handcrafts, these creative women had failed to learn a few simple lessons about color and how it can affect the overall appearance of an item, especially about how color should flatter the wearer. A florid, rosy-cheeked woman wore a wonderful red knit suit that made her look hot and flustered. An olive-skinned, silver-haired woman wore a pale yellow crocheted sweater that made her look washed out and tired. There were lots of inappropriately chosen beiges, sad grays, and army greens that did not enhance the personality or coloration of the wearers. I wanted to cry for these women. They had spent countless hours making their finely stitched garments without having spent a few moments carefully thinking through their color selections.

The choice of an appropriate color is critical to the success of the finished garments.

Before you select the yarn, make a swatch, or even start to dream, be aware of what effect the color will have on the wearer and how he or she will look in the chosen color. Also think about what the color will do to the design concept. A considered selection of color is as important as a careful selection of design.

CONSIDER THE PERSONALITY OF THE WEARER

I have always considered myself to be a bold, flamboyant, rather dramatic person. As a young person, because I was born that way, it never occurred to me that everyone else was not the same. As a young bride I made gifts for family members that they never wore, and I couldn't understand why. Though it fit perfectly, my brother-in-law never wore the bright red plaid shirt I made. A sister-in-law never dressed her child in the bold green print corduroy coveralls I had sewn. It took me quite a few years to realize that not everyone in this world had the same personality that I did and that not everyone felt comfortable in the bright bold colors that I loved.

Allow the personality of the wearer to determine the color of the garment.

Of course there are all kinds and types of personalities in this world. I'm not a psychologist and I'm not about to get involved in a long discussion of the various schools of thought about personality types. For the purposes of this chapter it is sufficient to say that there are two basic types of personality. There are quiet, shy, retiring people and there are more noisy, bold, outgoing people. (Of course there are many subtypes between these two extremes, but making this simple division will get my idea across and start you thinking about color selection in terms of personality.)

Shy people like to blend into the background; they choose not to wear anything that will make them stand out from the crowd. They like unobtrusive colors and small patterns and designs. Beiges, tans, gentle pastels, soft and muted tones are their favorite colors. My quiet, retiring, bookish older son, Tim, never wore the bright red cardigan I knit for him. To this day he says, "But, Mama, I do like any color—as long as it is a medium or dark blue."

On the other hand, flamboyant people like to make bold, dramatic statements that will distinguish them from the crowd. They like flashy designs and big, bright patches of color. They prefer the brilliant colors, reds and purples, sunshiny yellows, shocking blues, and biting greens. My outgoing, gregarious, and daring son, Chris, liked his red sweater and was only sorry that I refused to put purple stripes on the sleeves.

We have no right to (and, in fact, cannot) force our personality type on other persons. Everyone is entitled to wear his own color choices, to make his own statement to the public as to the kind of person he is. Our opinions about ourselves should not be forced upon anyone. I was wrong to try to dress my brother-in-law in a bold plaid. I was wrong to deny Chris his purple stripes.

On the flip side of the coin, we owe it to our integrity to clothe ourselves in the style and color of garment that reflects what we think of ourselves. Don't let your retiring shopping companion convince you. "Oh, my goodness no! Don't buy that awful bright green." Neither should you let an overbearing shopkeeper, trying to rid herself of a nonselling color, convince you, "But, honey, that bright purple tweed is just you all over," if you are not a bold purple person.

But besides personality, individual natural coloration is another factor to think about.

CONSIDER THE SKIN TONE OF THE WEARER

Portrait painters and professional make-up artists have known it for years.

The underlying skin tone of the wearer will tell you what colors will make that person look most alive and vibrant—what color families and tones will be most flattering to the individual.

Some craftspersons have understood the importance of skin color intuitively. Others of us only became aware of differences in skin color a few years ago when the practice of "color analysis" became popular.

There are basically two skin tone types, one is sallow and the other is ruddy.

Sallow means that the basic underlying color tone of the skin is yellowish. Portrait painters will often underpaint skin areas of people with yellow tones, then add flesh tones on top of that to achieve a realistic color.

Ruddy means that the basic underlying color tone of the skin is reddish or pink. To depict these people, portrait artists will often use a red underpainting before they put on the flesh tones.

Yes, it is true that people of different races often appear to have different-color skin, but still there are only two basic *underlying* skin tones. Regardless of whether we are black, Asian, or Caucasian, our skin is either ruddy-reddish or sallow-yellow. I am Caucasian and my skin is sallow. Next to a pink person, I look downright yellow. One of my favorite Atlanta knitters is Oriental, but her skin is ruddy. Next to me, she looks very pink. Colors that flatter her do not flatter me.

CHOOSE THE OPPOSITE COLOR

We usually look our best—most vibrant and alive—wearing the color that is OPPOSITE our underlying skin tone.

If the underlying skin tone is sallow (yellowish), choose colors that have red in them.

If the underlying skin tone is ruddy (red or pink), choose colors that have yellow in them.

This does not mean that there are only two color choices—pure red and pure yellow. Most commercially available yarn colors are magical blends of many tones. There are greens that are yellowish and there are greens that are reddish. The same is true of all the other colors.

Of course it is true that hair and eye color further determine what colors make us look our best, but this does not change the red-yellow opposites rule.

It is interesting to note that almost everyone looks good in aqua-turquoise (a blue-green-white blend) and apricot-coral (a red-yellow-white blend). If you do not know the underlying skin tone of the intended wearer, you can hardly go wrong with those two colors.

Another intriguing fact is that few people look good in khaki and camel, both of which are devoid of red and yellow.

A COLOR ANALYSIS MAY BE MONEY WELL SPENT

Not everyone has an eye for color. Different people perceive color differently. Not everyone can see purple in tree trunks at twilight or the red in a green forest. If you see everything as black and white, everything only as light, dark, or gray, get some professional help.

First, from a bookstore or library obtain a copy of the book *Color Me Beautiful* by Carole Jackson (New York: Ballantine, 1987) to help you determine what colors flatter you most.

If, even with the help of that book, all colors look the same to you, go to a color specialist and pay to have yourself analyzed. The small amount you spend on a color analysis will be saved over and over in not choosing clothing of unflattering colors.

ALWAYS DOUBLE-CHECK

Once you have the "names" of the colors that are flattering to a particular wearer, don't just stop there because what was called "dusty rose" last year may be called something different this year, perhaps "lavender pink." Names don't mean a thing as far as colors are concerned. It is quality of light that is radiated that is important. All reds are not the same. Some reds are yellowish and orangey, some are bluish and violety. There is nothing like checking out the real thing against the real person in real light.

Hold a skein to the face and look in a mirror under natural light. When the color is a good one for the person, a smile will slowly steal across the face, the eyes will light up, and the person will have a look of well-being. (I look positively ill in violet or purple, but put a royal blue next to my face and I appear to get well in a hurry.)

If the shop does not have a mirror, ask a trusted friend which color makes you look best, that is, happiest, most radiant. Then, when you get home, double-check the unopened skein in your mirror for yourself. No matter how finely the stitches are made or how perfect the fit is, you won't look or feel your best if the color isn't right for you.

If the shop does not have natural light, go outside to check the color. Artificial light can do funny things to color. Though the color and hue of both incandescent and flourescent lights have improved in recent years and become more lifelike, good old natural sunshine is still the best source of light.

To some extent, the "use the opposite color" rule can be broken if we carefully add trim, a collar, or a scarf of the *correct* color next to all skin areas, particularly around the face. Of course it is best to choose a flattering color in the first place, but if for some reason we find that we are using yarn that does not enhance the appearance of the wearer, we can modify the disaster by dolling it up. So long as the area near the face reflects a better color, the wearer may look more attractive.

SOME ART SCHOOL RULES ABOUT COLOR

Physicists and painters have long known that "colors" as "things" do not exist at all. What we think of as a color is only an illusion. Colors are really the eye's *perception* and the mind's *idea* of differing qualities of light emitted, reflected, and refracted in a particular range of wavelengths.

Still, while the previous paragraph is really the physical truth about colors, we handworkers can deal with colors as if they were real things so long as we know and use a few simple and eternal rules about the characteristics of color.

"COLOR DOES NOT EXIST IN A VACUUM"

Every color is always influenced by the other colors of its surroundings. *Surroundings* is one of those wonderful all-inclusive words and is synonymous with *environment* and *atmosphere*. What this rule means is that every item in every area is giving off, reflecting, and refracting light all the time. Light from every object bounces around and interacts with every other object.

Color does not exist or stand by itself: it is continually influenced by the other colors that surround it.

Let me give you a real-life example. The walls and ceiling of my kitchen have been painted plain, pure white. When you walk into the room, however, the walls do not appear to be stark white because the cabinets are wood toned and reflect to the walls a warm yellow tone; the floor is red and casts a pinkish glow to the white walls; the windows are uncurtained and the yard outside is filled with green pine trees that reflect green-colored light through the glass. Though the walls of my kitchen were *painted pure plain white*, they appear to be a soft, warm pastel.

Look at the ceiling of the room you are in now. It may have been painted from a can labeled "flat ceiling white," but if the walls are painted blue, it will appear to be a pale pastel blue. If the walls are painted red, the ceiling will appear to be a pale pastel pink. (Look up at the ceiling of all the rooms you go into for the next couple of days and check it out for yourself.)

The same thing is true of the sweaters we design and wear. The color that the finished garment "appears" to be will be influenced by the colors of the slacks or skirt it is worn with, the color of our hair, what color blouse (if any) it is worn over, the colors, of our accessories, and, of course, the color of the room we are in.

"LIGHT IS ONLY LIGHT AS CONTRASTED WITH DARK"

In Chinese landscape painting, if you look closely you will almost always find that the artist has included a human figure. The painter put the person there so that the viewer would have "a frame of reference" with which to compare sizes. The human figure, the frame of reference, allows the observer to know immediately whether the mountain is a small hill or a towering pinnacle, whether the pine tree is an ancient giant or just a seedling.

So, too, with color we need "a frame of reference." To know exactly how delicately pale the pink of a camellia blossom is, we need to see it contrasted with a dark green leaf.

The color brown can be any shade from tan to almost ebony. The only way to realize how dark the brown really is, is to set it up against a light color so that the difference between the two shows up.

"Dark is only dark as contrasted with light." A dark brown tweed sweater will appear to be much darker and richer when it is worn with a winter-white skirt.

"Light is only light when compared to dark." Wear a white lace Shetland shawl over a light-colored dress and it is lost. Wear that same shawl over a dark outfit and you have something spectacular.

"WHITE REFLECTS ALL LIGHT, BLACK ABSORBS ALL LIGHT"

We wear white and light colors in summer because they RE-FLECT light and heat. We wear black and dark colors in winter because they ABSORB light and heat.

And what has this to do with knitting and designing sweaters? A very simple lesson:

Some pattern stitches need to be made of white or light-colored yarn because the beauty of the pattern stitch is in the way it refracts and reflects light.

Cables and Arans are perfect examples of pattern stitches that need to be made of colors that will reflect light. If dark yarn is used to make cables and Arans, the depth of the color will absorb light and it will never get a chance to play and bounce around in the valleys and the ridges of the stitches. Also, the human eye may never be able to see that seed stitch was used on black or dark brown or navy yarn. The differences in the height of the stitches that make seed stitch so lovely may be lost because the light could not reflect from either the heights or the depths.

Tiny people look larger in white, smaller in black. Big people seem more prominent in white; they seem smaller in black.

Of course what I've said about black and white also applies to any very light and any very dark color.

"NEITHER BLACK NOR WHITE IS REALLY A COLOR AT ALL"

When I began to paint with oils, my instructor refused to allow me to have tubes of either titanium white or ivory-black in my paint box. "You don't need them," he said. "But how can I mix colors without them?" I asked. "Neither white nor black is really a color at all. You can make things dark or light by mixing other colors, and the effect will be better without black or white." I still didn't believe him. "Look at the slacks you are wearing," he said. "That supposed black is really a combination of ultramarine blue, Indian red, and raw sienna. It is not ivory-black at all." I mixed those colors on my palette, and sure enough it was true!

"THE KEY TO ALL COLORS IS UNDERSTANDING GRAY"

Soon I was asking, "If black and white are not colors, what is gray?" "Gray is not a combination of black and white. Gray is a *real* color; black and white are not. Gray is always a blend of other colors. The key to understanding all colors is understanding what happens in mixing grays."

Exciting grays occur when three or more distinct colors are mixed together in unequal amounts to make one new color. That new color can be blue-gray, red-gray, green-gray, or any other kind of gray. If you want to find out the dominant color in a particular gray yarn, there is a simple way to do so. Go visit your local paint store. Ask for a handful of paint chips—clean, bright, vibrant ones. At home, put the various colored chips next to the gray yarn. The gray yarn will snap to life when its vibrant parent color is put next to it. And that will tell you the colors that went into making up that gray, and which is the dominant color.

Few items of true unaltered colors are sold in the marketplace. The true primary and secondary colors have already been grayed-down for you by manufacturers. The yarn companies, knowing that you live and purchase in the real world, have altered true colors by adding touches of complementary or contrasting color to the dyes. (Only teenagers seem able to tolerate and like true primary colors.)

"SOME COLORS ARE WARM; OTHER COLORS ARE COOL"

It is as simple as saying, "Red/fire is hot; blue/sky is cool." But it is also more than that; red and blue are not the only examples of warm and cool. An easy way to understand and define warm and cool colors is to look to nature. Look down at the earth; warmth is of the earth; warm colors are soil and sand and rocks; the red clay of Georgia and the golden expanses of wheat ripening in the sun. Look up at the heavens; cool comes from above the earth; cool colors are sky, turquoise sunsets, mauve sunrises, and the endless space of midnight.

At one time, I was designing some needlepoint for myself. I wast trying to make a modern adaptation of a unicorn in a forest surrounded by adoring animals under a twisted arbor of tree branches. I sketched out the design in black and white with pen and ink until I thought I had it just right. I transferred the design to graph paper and began lightly coloring in with colored pencils. Then, when that looked okay, I began to stitch the layout onto canvas. *Something terrible happened.* All the proportions changed once they were stitched with colorful needlepoint yarn. The white unicorn appeared much too big against his deep mulberry background. The tan bunny also seemed too big, and the blue bunches of grapes in the trees appeared to shrink into insignificance.

Color changed the apparent proportions that I had so carefully drawn out in black and white. Warm colors expanded in apparent size; cool colors shrank in apparent size.

A red rose on white background looks larger than it is, because red is a warm tone and warm tones appear to the eye to be larger than they really are.

If you want to look larger, wear warm colors.

A blue flower on a white ground looks smaller than it is, because blue is a cool tone and cool tones appear to the eye to be smaller than they really are.

If you want to look smaller, wear cool colors.

Of course, colors can be mixed, and there are warm blues and cool reds. This is a very simplistic lesson about the basics of color. The rules given above are just generalities and basic concepts. Now that you are aware of some of the very basic concepts of color theory, you can see how color is going to affect the finished look of your knitted projects.

SOME DESIGN AND DECORATING RULES

ONLY BLACK AND WHITE LOOK GOOD IN EQUAL AMOUNTS

Equal amounts of contrasting colors, such as blue and orange, or red and green, play funny tricks on our eyes. The colors will bounce around on the backs of our eyes and, like flashing lights, first one color and then the other will jump out at us.

Equal amounts of noncontrasting colors also play funny tricks. Though they may be used in equal proportions, one color will always dominate and attempt to swallow up the other. If you make the right-hand side of a sweater navy blue and the left-hand side yellow, the left/yellow side will appear to be bigger than the right/blue side. The wearer may walk around looking lopsided! The navy blue will look weightier and heavier than the light playful yellow.

THE PROPORTIONS OF ACCENT COLORS

"Okay, Maggie, if, except for black and white, half-and-half is out as good color proportion, what are some handy rules that will help us spark up and enhance our garments?"

It is best to begin by considering the value of the darkest and/or warmest color.

Say, for instance, that you wanted to make a sweater of five shades, one of which was navy blue. If you make it 60 percent navy and use 10 percent of the other four colors of lighter values, the navy blue will absorb and overwhelm the other colors. The sweater will "read" to the human eye as a navy blue sweater.

The color with the deepest value will dominate.

Okay, so you still want to use the same five colors, but you don't want the sweater to "read" navy blue, you want a sweater that will be a rich blend of your colors. What do you do? You reduce the percentage of the navy.

Like salt, use a little bit of the deepest value to keep it from dominating.

If you use only 20 to 25 percent navy plus a 75 percent combination of all the other colors, you will have a richer blend of the colors, though the sweater will still appear dark.

If you use only 10 percent navy, you will have a lighter sweater "sparked" by dark.

A GOOD COMBINATION

I know that it adds up to more than 100 percent, but a rule of thumb of proportion that I often use is $\frac{1}{3} + \frac{2}{3} + \frac{1}{8}$.

Say, for instance, I want to make a plaid jacket-sweater in the University of Georgia colors—red, white, and black—which are all intense tones. I will use two-thirds red, one-third white, and just a little bit of black. To the eye of the viewer, I will appear to be wearing a red sweater.

Or suppose I want to make a sweater that will "read" to the eye as a green sweater, but I do not want to look like the Jolly Green Giant. In that case, I might use two-thirds green and a one-third total of other colors.

ENHANCING A TWEED OR MULTICOLOR

I'm not the only knitter who has been deceived and disappointed by the way tweeds and multicolors often fail to live up to their promise. What seemed a divine dance of colors in the skein sometimes wilts through the floor when knitted up. To resurrect such yarn, it is often necessary to add an accent color chosen from the tweed. A common mistake is often made. Knitters who have not been introduced to color theory will frequently choose either the predominant color or the secondary color to use as an accent. Those are not the best choices, and usually don't make the dancing begin again.

Often the LEAST-USED COLOR makes the best choice for an accent for tweeds and multicolor yarns.

Remember my friend from Chapter 3 with the green tweed mohair yarn from Australia? She not only chose the least-used color from the yarn, a bitter green, but also elected to change from a dull matte finish to a shiny glossy silk for accent. It was a wonderful choice.

If you feel unsure of your color sense, try many options and see what happens. Make lots of swatches. Often the thing you think of last is the best solution.

PLAYING WITH COLOR GROUPINGS

An artist friend of mine who helped me with this chapter suggested making a hank of colors to carry around in your purse to help you learn about color relationships. "Take it to the grocery store, the dentist's office, into church," she said, "and meditate on it. Cut strands, at least 20 inches long, of a lot of different yarns of different colors—at least four strands of each. Mix up all kinds of colors, group them together, and twist them into a hank. This will give you an idea of what would happen to those colors if they were married into a sweater. If the colors begin to quarrel, pull one or all of the strands of that color out. Don't hesitate; be ruthless; get the offender out. If you desire, replace the culprit with some other color of your choice. Carry the hank of strands around with you until you feel your selection is a marriage made in heaven. Then make a swatch and let the wedded bliss begin."

MAKING A SWATCH

Because "Color does not exist in a vacuum," often we cannot tell how two (or more) colors will "work" together until we actually make interlocking stitches (or stripes) of them in a swatch.

The visual effect that four or five unopened skeins sitting side by side give may not necessarily be the visual effect that the colors will have when the stitches are made side by side.

Once I selected a luscious deep lavender and a gentle pink to work together in a Fair Isle design. Side by side in the skeins it looked as if the colors would sing a song of fairies dancing together. When knitted up, the intensity of the pale purple swallowed up the pink, making it appear to be a pale cream color, and the stitches didn't dance at all. Unless I had tried it out in a swatch, I never would have known. If I had just started knitting the sweater, I would have been sorely disappointed.

BREAKING THE RULES

I've tried hard in this chapter to share some of the things that artists and physicists and psychologists know about color without becoming dry and pedantic. And being limited to only one chapter on color when it is a subject that often takes a lifetime to understand, I've only glossed over some of the very basic facts and rules.

Learn more about the rules, use them, play with them, and don't be afraid to BREAK THEM to help yourself get the perfect effect that YOU want.

Remember that what I've said is true of light and paint pigments. The rules get fuzzy when you are dealing with commercially prepared and dyed yarns. The spinner may have already grayed colors for you; he may have carefully blended the hues and values so that all the colors in a particular line are preharmonized to complement each other.

Go ahead, dive in, have fun, play with color, break the "rules," and use colors that sing songs of joy to you, even if only *your* ears can hear them.

11

Choosing the Most Flattering Design for the Wearer

Today, besides achieving garments that really fit, one of the most important objectives of designing our own sweaters is to make the wearer look the very best possible. That includes enhancing the personality, expressing individuality, and complementing skin color, all of which we have discussed in earlier chapters. But it also means flattering the individual's figure.

No matter what body type or shape or size we are, some designs are going to flatter us more than others, and there is no reason not to always look our best. Looking our best is a matter of understanding which styles look most becoming on which bodies.

THE "IDEAL" FIGURE

When I was a teenager, I had a little booklet that described the "ideal feminine figure" and how to dress to make your own figure look as much as possible like that mythical form. That silly little book did me bundles of harm and a great deal of good. The harm was that I believed I was "flawed and imperfect" because I did not have an "ideal body." The good was that at a very early age, I learned how to portray favorably—to show off becomingly or advantageously—any human body.

"YOU CAN NEVER BE TOO THIN OR TOO RICH!"

Horse feathers! Of course you can be too thin. You can be skinny and anorexic to the point of discomfort, ill health, and death. All the media hype about being thin is just that—unreal mythology—to make people buy specific products.

And, of course, you can be too rich. True, not enough money can make you unhappy, but having too much money can do the same thing. Rich people often live in fear of being used for their money, and of being dishonestly befriended by deceitful and manipulative people. They may also fear their own value as human beings without riches.

Ideal images, thinness, and money have nothing to do with feeling good about yourself and your figure. Those things are just nonsense. Now I'll get off my soapbox and talk about some very simple things concerning design and style concepts, which you can easily use "to portray favorably, to show off to the very best advantage" whatever kind of body you have.

BE COMFORTABLE

When your body is physically uncomfortable you cannot look your best. If your sleeves are dangling in the soup, if you must constantly adjust your bra straps to keep them from showing, or continually pull up or down on your sweater, your looks are not going to be enhanced. And like dogs constantly scratching at fleas, people who are forever itching from irritating yarn are not being favorably perceived. **In order to look good, you must be comfortable.**

If you find that you have made an uncomfortable garment, either alter it or give it away. Suffering is never attractive. Rip out the neck or wrist ribbing and enlarge the openings. Change the sleeves and sew up the shoulder seams. No matter how much the yarn cost, if it irritates your skin give away the garment.

BE APPROPRIATE

Our concepts about youth being the best time of life are changing. We no longer believe that "After thirty, life is all downhill," or "Once you are a mother (or a grandmother), you must dress the part." Paraphrased, those myths told women that after the blush of youth they were no longer desirable or valuable and had to dress dowdy and frumpy.

Still, our sweaters need to be appropriate to our lifestyle, climate, personality, size, body type, and age. I leave it to you to judge whether they suit your own lifestyle and climate. Matching color to the personality has already been covered in Chapter 10. In this chapter we are going to discuss appropriateness to body type and size. Before we do that, however, we need to go back to some simple art school rules about the funny things color and shape do to apparent size.

SOME MORE ART SCHOOL RULES

PLAYING TRICKS WITH THE EYE

Dark and cool colors recede, move away from, and diminish an area.

Light and warm colors move to the front and increase in importance.

These rules give us important information that allows us to visually modify our figures. Let's look at some examples. Which rectangle in Figure 11.1 looks the tallest? The widest? The outer dimensions of all the rectangles are exactly the same, but the choice of lights and darks and the placements of them play tricks on our eyes. Does this apply to designing sweaters? You bet it does.

If you want to increase the apparent width of a figure (and make it look shorter), run a wide area of cool/dark color up and down the center front and border it on each side with equal-width areas of a warm/light color. (See Figure 11.2.)

If you want to decrease the apparent width of a figure (and make it look taller), run a light/warm color up and down the center front and border it with an equal width of a cool/dark color. (See Figure 11.3.)

A narrow band of cool/dark color up the center front will make you appear taller. (See Figure 11.4.)

A narrow band of warm/light color up the center front will make you appear less wide. (See Figure 11.5.)

Just because the drawings in this chapter are shown in black and white, please do not think that I am talking only about white yarn and black yarn. Not at all. These art school rules apply to all warm/cool and light/dark colors. Imagine the sweaters pictured in forest green (dark/warm) and lime green (light/cool), royal and sky blue, navy blue and sunshine yellow, or any set of colors that flatters you!

USING BLOCKS OF COLOR TO BEST ADVANTAGE

A magician on the stage sawing a lady in half is a visual illusion. Where we choose to place horizontal lines will change the illusion of the height of a figure. The height at which we choose to cut ourselves into horizontal parts will make us seem taller or shorter, wider or narrower.

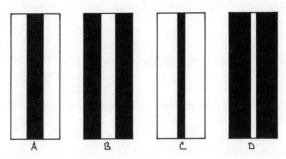

11.1 Side-by-side vertical rectangles: A. looks wider; B. looks narrower; C. looks taller; and D. looks shorter.

⅓ ⅓ ⅓

Figure looks wider with cool/light color on sides & dark/warm in center

11.2

⅓ ⅓ ⅓

Figure looks narrower with cool/light in center & dark/warm on sides

11.3

Emphasizes height

11.4

Diminishes width

11.5

All the rectangles in Figure 11.6 have the same outer dimensions, but look at the difference in appearance!

Figure 11.7, with the horizontal band located just under the bustline as in an Empire dress that might have been worn by Napoleon's Josephine, shows the location that is most flattering to all types of figures.

Figure 11.8, with the horizontal band at the waistline, is the most flattering to women who have pear-shaped figures with hips wider than chests, which is most of us who are not professional models. Why contemporary designers keep on designing for fashion models instead of regular women, I'll never know! When you are in the driver's seat designing your own things, you can assess your figure and create especially for it. And plan what flatters it most, which, surprisingly, is shorter-than-usual sweaters.

Figure 11.9 is great for slender fashion models (who have little or no hips). It places a horizontal line about 7 inches below the waist.

Figure 11.10 makes a marvelous fun statement for young and tall people. A band across the midthigh speaks of dancing and parties, fun and games. The sweater is actually a minidress to be worn alone, or with slacks or tights.

The differences become even more striking when instead of just belting the figure, we change color entirely. Where light/warm and dark/cool color areas are placed makes a difference in the visual impact

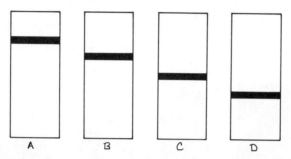

11.6 Where you place horizontal bands will change the illusion of height: A. near bust (good for most figures); B. near waist (good for pear-shaped figures); C. near hip (good for slender figures); or D. near thigh (good for tall figures and young people).

11.7
Band across upper quarter

11.8
Band across upper third (waist length)

11.9
Band across mid-point (hip length) approx. 7" below waist

11.10
Band across lower ⅓ (thigh)

CHOOSING THE MOST FLATTERING DESIGN FOR THE WEARER **117**

our eyes receive, with the lighter area generally appearing larger/wider than the dark area. (See Figure 11.11.)

Figures 11.12 through 11.15 show these rectangles translated into real sweaters on real people.

If you turn the rectangles upside down, placing dark above and light below, you widen the hips. (See Figures 11.16 through 11.19.)

Note that each of the eight sweaters shown is drawn on a pear-shaped feminine figure. Male figures, particularly young ones, usually have chests that are bigger than the corresponding hips. Proportions that look good on photographer's fashion models usually look good on men. Men and models look great cut in half at the hips.

11.11 Variations of light and dark proportions

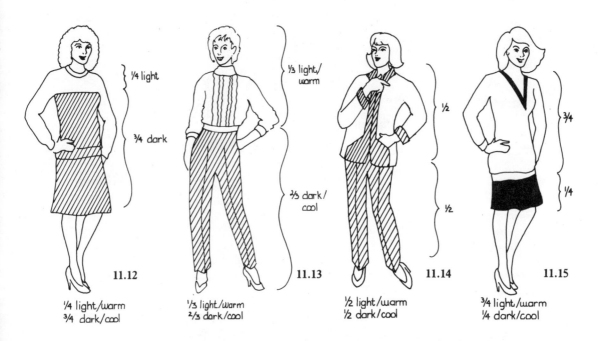

¼ light/warm	⅓ light/warm	½ light/warm	¾ light/warm
¾ dark/cool	⅔ dark/cool	½ dark/cool	¼ dark/cool

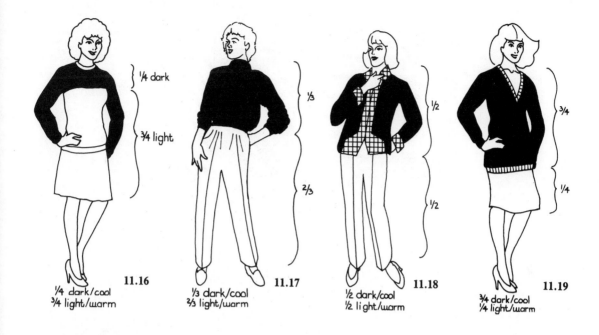

11.16 — ¼ dark / ¾ light
¼ dark/cool
¾ light/warm

11.17 — ⅓ / ⅔
⅓ dark/cool
⅔ light/warm

11.18 — ½ / ½
½ dark/cool
½ light/warm

11.19 — ¾ / ¼
¾ dark/cool
¼ light/warm

USING STRIPES TO BEST ADVANTAGE

Who says knitting has to be big blocks of color? Not me! I love *stripes* and *strips of color shadings*. These, too, follow art school rules. Figure 11.20 shows what happens when we take the same rectangles and play with them. Figures 11.21 through 11.24 show how stripes can enhance or detract from various body shapes.

Because this is a black-and-white book, it is difficult to portray stripes of all one color in varying intensities. Take my word for it, the effect can be glorious. More and more adventuresome knitters are plying their own yarns from thinner strands. Imagine a cardigan-coat subtly striped in varying tones of ocean colors ranging from light warm greens through turquoise and royal to inky purple. By plying many strands of thin green and blue—light, medium, and dark—and purple yarns together, the lines of shading from stripe to stripe could become almost imperceptible so that the effect could be as wonderful as looking down at a tropical sea from an airplane.

CHEVRONS AND "V"S

All diagonal lines do not have to go the same direction. We can divide them in the middle or at any other place and come up with some very interesting designs. (See Figures 11.25, 11.26, and 11.27.)

11.20 Variations of broad and narrow horizontal and diagonal stripes

Equal-width
stripes

11.21

Stripes of
different widths

11.22

Broad-diagonal
widening

11.23

Narrow-diagonal
slimming

11.24

11.21 Broad horizontal stripes widen the figure.

11.22 Narrow horizontal stripes add some width.

11.23 Broad diagonal stripes are bold (and fattening!).

11.24 Narrow diagonal stripes are slimming.

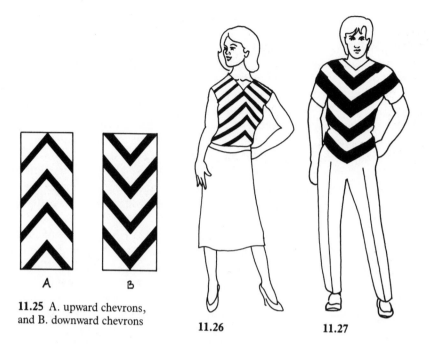

11.25 A. upward chevrons, and B. downward chevrons

11.26

11.27

11.26 Upward chevrons emphasize the face and make the figure appear taller.

11.27 Downward chevrons emphasize the slope of the shoulders and make the figure appear shorter.

Chevrons and Vs can be formed in several ways. You can use *bobbins with flat knitting,* flipping from color to color as you have preplanned on graph paper. Or you can use a *diagonal knitting technique* using whole rows (or rounds) of one color while making a double decrease at the bottom of the V and increasing at the outer edges (or the top of the V) to retain the same number of stitches in each row (or round).

VERTICAL STRIPES

Stripes can run not only across the figure but also up and down.

There are two ways of making vertical stripes in knitted garments. You can knit across in the usual way, carrying one bobbin for each color change and always remembering to throw the old yarn up and over the new to avoid holes (I find this to be a horrible bother), or you can stripe in rows and then turn the fabric sideways. As I noted in the chapter on pattern stitches, when you use knitted fabric crosswise you must have an absolutely accurate *row* gauge, and you must be aware that the cross-turned fabric may behave in strange ways.

From all I've said in the previous sections, please don't think that stripes or diagonals must always be regular, regimented, or rigid. The previous paragraphs were meant only to give you the basic art school rules about what happens when areas of colors are combined and worked side by side. Once you have an understanding of the basics, you can play. The members of the Atlanta Knitters Guild do a lot of playing. They are such a creative and innovative *and thrifty* group of souls that it is a pleasure to go to every meeting just for the "show and tell" part when they display their newest creations. They combine fluffy angora with shiny metallics and glossy silks and simple worsteds into marvelous stripes, diagonals, and chevrons using different pattern stitches for different yarns in ways that delight the eye and boggle the mind. Their comments are always informative: "I had a little of this pink mohair left from something else, so I put a few stripes of it near the neck. It calls the eye to my face and gives it a nice glow"; "I didn't have enough of this yellow to make a whole sweater, so every now and then I put in some stripes of green and orange that I found in an odd-lot bin at Betsy's store. The bright stripes cut my figure in two so that I don't look so tall."

HOW TO FLATTER ANY FIGURE

Now that you know the art school rules about what areas of color do to the apparent lengths and widths of shapes, you can begin to appreciate how to flatter *your* figure.

If you've got it, flaunt it! Always lead the eye to the part of the body that you want to be noticed.

What are you most proud of about your looks? Your friendly and open face? Your luxurious hair? Your sparkling eyes? What parts of you please you the most? Your long slender legs, your tiny waist?

You can lead the eye to areas you want to be noticed with light/ warm colors, with lines, or with shapes.

What is there about your body that you *don't* want people to notice? I'd just as soon others were not aware of my round tummy and full hips! Susan wants to minimize the size of her breasts, and Amy hopes that no one will notice her grand-piano legs.

Always lead the eye away from the part of the body you don't want to be noticed. Remember that dark/cool colors do not hold the eye.

Darken areas you want to "go away." Let them absorb all light and reflect none. Make them plain without any design that might call out to the eye, "Notice me! Notice me!"

Choose clothing that does not STOP at the body point you want to minimize.

To be even more specific about body types, if a person is tall and/or thin and wants to appear to be shorter and/or wider, *cut up the silhouette* with appropriately placed horizontal lines.

If a person is short and/or plump and wants to appear taller and/or thinner, *run vertical lines up and down, with warm-light colors in the center and cool-dark colors at the sides,* and be careful where you cut up the silhouette. One-third/two-thirds is more elongating than half and half.

Now let's refer to the basic body types that we discussed in Chapter 6 and talk about what parts of each one of them we might want to camouflage.

THE TRIANGLE

Though there is nothing "wrong" about it, it is the wide torso-thigh joining that many people want to minimize. That can be done with a waist-length sweater or blouse and a softly gathered skirt. (See Figure 11.28.) A longish hip-length sweater would only draw attention to the wide area we want to ignore. (See Figure 11.29.) Often a belted waist will draw the eyes away from those broad hips. (And be sure that there is enough fabric in skirts or slacks so the wearer doesn't look melted and poured in.)

Concerning the delicate swanlike neck and shoulders, raglan seams and a V-neck would only make them appear more sloping. (See Figure 11.30.) A boatneck would enhance the lovely lines, as would a turtle- or cowl-neck. (See Figure 11.31.)

THE RECTANGLE

These Greek gods and goddesses don't need any cosmetic help—just be careful not to detract from their natural beauty. (See Figures 11.32 through 11.35.)

No shoulder pads please. The shoulders are square enough as they are.

11.30

11.31

11.28 Triangular figures look good in blouse-length sweaters and gathered skirts.

11.29 Triangular figures do not look good in hip-length sweaters over straight skirts.

11.30 Triangular figures do not look good in raglan or V-neck sweaters.

11.31 Triangular figures look good in boatneck sweaters.

11.28   **11.29**

11.32   **11.33**   **11.34**   **11.35**

11.32 Rectangular figures do not look good in blouse-length sweaters and gathered skirts.

11.33 Rectangular figures look good in hip-length sweaters and straight pleated skirts. Colorful designs on top also flatter this figure.

11.34 Rectangular figures look good in raglan and V-neck sweaters.

11.35 Rectangular figures do not look good in boatneck sweaters.

If you add artificial pads, the shoulders will appear to go *up* from the neck to the tip, and look as ridiculous as water running uphill.

On women, watch out for sweaters with flat-across bound-off shoulders. They will accentuate the horizontals of the rectangular figure and won't look feminine. Watch out, too, for dropped shoulders. They move the eyes to the sides and widen the shoulders inappropriately. We are looking to soften and round the figure of the rectangular-shaped woman; we don't want to square her off and make her look shoved in a box.

If a rectangular-shaped woman has a waistline, accentuate it by adding a belt.

THE OVAL

On this body type, it is the tummy, the "potbelly," that cries out, "Please don't notice me." Use a cool-dark splotch of color there. Draw the attention up to the face. (See Figures 11.36 and 11.37.) In cloth clothing this is often done by accessorizing with superlong strands of colorful beads. Knitters can design the attention-getting devices into their pattern.

You may choose to widen the shoulders with horizontal lines across the chest and the sleeves—in the area just above and/or just below the breasts. (See Figure 11.38.) Shoulder pads are an asset, too. (See Figure 11.39.)

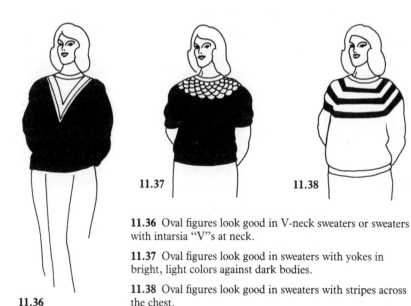

11.36

11.37

11.38

11.36 Oval figures look good in V-neck sweaters or sweaters with intarsia "V"s at neck.

11.37 Oval figures look good in sweaters with yokes in bright, light colors against dark bodies.

11.38 Oval figures look good in sweaters with stripes across the chest.

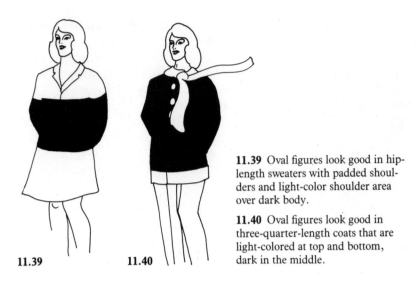

11.39 Oval figures look good in hip-length sweaters with padded shoulders and light-color shoulder area over dark body.

11.40 Oval figures look good in three-quarter-length coats that are light-colored at top and bottom, dark in the middle.

11.39   **11.40**

A look of one-quarter on top and three-quarters on the bottom is also good. In either case, the eye jumps over the tummy area, and it seems to disappear. (See Figure 11.40.)

THE "V"

The "V"ictorious hero of a romance novel needs no modification. Every romantic woman in the world will take the beautiful hunk as he is!

The V-shaped female, however, may need help in order to win. You will want to draw attention away from her wide shoulders; wide and/or swingy skirts are a big help. Strangely enough, the same "accentuate the face" technique that worked so well with the oval figure works superbly for this woman as well. (See Figures 11.41 and 11.42.)

Simply making the sleeves a cool-dark color will appear to narrow the shoulders. On cardigans, a contrasting-color "tuxedo" lapel works wonderfully well for V-shaped women. (See Figure 11.43.)

Beware of dropped shoulders, especially if they are accentuated with any kind of trim such as a different pattern stitch (like ribbing), folded tucks, or color change. They broaden what is already wide. Raglans, however, look great!

Some "V" women are happy with their height and like to leave it as it is or even accentuate it. Others would like to look shorter than they are. You already know how to accomplish these things.

Remember that you may well need to decrease width from the chest to the hips on many male and female "V"ictorious figures.

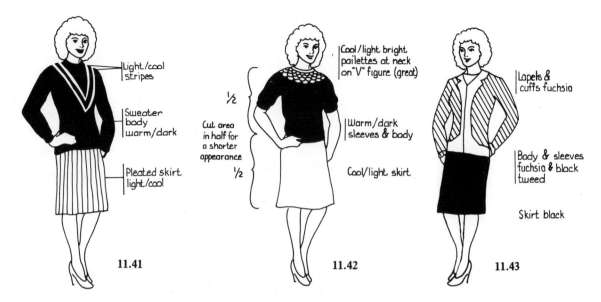

11.41 "V" figures look good in V-necked sweaters or sweaters with light-colored intarsia "V"s at neck and dark bodies.

11.42 "V" figures look good in sweaters with yokes in bright, light colors against dark bodies. Waist-length sweaters and light-colored skirts also enhance the appearance of V-shaped figures.

11.43 "V" figures look good in two-color, tuxedo-front cardigans. Try light-colored lapels and cuffs against dark body and dark skirt.

THE PERFECT HOURGLASS

With the perfect hourglass figure, several adages come to mind:

"If it is not broke, don't fix it."
"Why would anyone want to tamper with perfection?"

These are most certainly true for hourglass-shaped women, but not necessarily for hourglass-shaped men. Hourglass-shaped men will probably want to minimize the width of their hips. They should stay away from loud plaid slacks and abrupt changes of color at the hipline, but those are not necessarily matters of sweater design.

Hourglass-shaped women have delightful "curve and flow" figures and will want to accentuate all the possibilities. Show off that waist by belting it. Knitted or pleated skirts may be more becoming than gathered ones. Likewise, blouse-length sweaters may be more flattering than straight, hip-length sweaters. (Remember, if you throw in a few short rows across the bust you can avoid an unflattering fabric bulge at the sides just above the waist.)

THE TOP-HEAVY HOURGLASS

How the top-heavy, hourglass-shaped woman chooses to look will depend entirely on her image of herself. Some women want to hide their breasts; other women are proud of their femininity and want to make the most of it. You already are aware of the art school rules for minimizing and maximizing.

The narrow hips of this figure are definitely an asset in both men and women. Show them off; draw attention to them.

THE BOTTOM-HEAVY HOURGLASS

The bottom-heavy hourglass, the pear shape, is the figure type that a great majority of women have. Most women with this shape want their clothing to "accentuate the positive and eliminate the negative," that is, to maximize the bust and minimize the hips.

Shoulder pads are often called for because they tend to draw the eye away from wide hips. Also indicated are smooth-textured, subtle-colored, lightweight fabrics to cover the wider hips.

Look what happens when we put a traditional Icelandic sweater on this kind of figure. (See Figure 11.44.) It is a natural, made-for-each-other combination.

THE TIFFANY DIAMOND

The object in dressing a Tiffany diamond figure is to trick the eye *not* to look at the bustline. (See Figure 11.45.)

Another way of accomplishing the same thing is to update a classic Chanel design, knit yourself a suit, and tuck a bright print blouse under it. Be sure to add shoulder pads; make the bottom of the jacket 2 inches below the natural waist; and make the A-line skirt with a natural flare. (See Figure 11.46.)

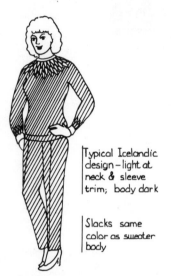

Typical Icelandic design – light at neck & sleeve trim; body dark

Slacks same color as sweater body

11.44 Bottom-heavy hourglass figures look good in Icelandic designs. Use light colors at neck and sleeve trim; dark body with matching dark pants.

EVERYONE IS IDEAL

That booklet I read as a teenager about how to make every feminine body look more like the "ideal" feminine figure had lots of good ideas about color and design that are still valid. Thank goodness other things in that book are passé. Today women of all shapes and sizes feel better about their bodies.

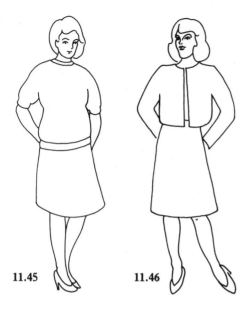

11.45 Tiffany-diamond figures look good in crew-necked hip-length sweaters with sleeves ending just above elbows.

11.46 Tiffany-diamond figures look good in modified Chanel-type knit suits (ending about two inches below waist) with shoulder pads and slightly flared A-line skirts.

11.45   11.46

If we are tall and/or slender, we can be proud of it and emphasize it. If we are short and/or round, we can play up our feminine softness for all it is worth.

Go back now and flip through the drawings of body types in Chapter 6 ("Getting the Right Measurements"), then flip through the drawings in this chapter. Imagine yourself in each of the sweaters shown. Ask yourself, Would I feel physically comfortable walking around in that sort of sweater? How would that look on me? Would that sweater flatter me; would it enhance my looks, portray me favorably, show off becomingly and advantageously my figure type? And, Would I feel like myself if I wore that garment in public?

BE THYSELF

Life is a continuous learning process. Both our bodies and the styles currently in fashion constantly change. Life is a do-it-yourself project. Only you can do your life for you. Try on every type of garment you can. And *remember!*

Be yourself. Be the self that God uniquely made *you* to be. Be the *you* that is under the fear and the mask and the facade. You don't have to have the "ideal" figure or even dress yourself so that you appear to have one. You do have to be comfortable.

12

Estimating the Amount of Yarn You Will Need

"If I design my own sweater, how will I know how much yarn I will need?"

The answer is, you are going to have to guess—not a wild guess, but an intelligent and educated *estimate*. There are many reliable sources that will help you to arrive at the approximate amount of yarn you will require.

ASK YOUR SHOP OWNER

If you are purchasing the yarn from your local friendly yarn shop, ask the salespeople how much is usually required for the size and general type of sweater you choose to make. "Oh, a skein of Gooey-Gooey has lots of yards in it, and most knitters are finding that only five skeins are needed for a small short-sleeved pullover like you want to design." Your shop owner should always have your best interests (and continued business) at heart, and is unlikely to mislead you. Of course, the owner is only human and therefore fallible. If she does make a mistake, it is unintentional.

Good manners dictate that if you did not buy your yarn locally, it would be unspeakably rude to ask the local shop personnel to give of their time and effort to help you with a purchase that someone else had already made a profit on. Respect your local independent yarn supplier. These dedicated (and caring) small-business people are both backbone and flesh of the knitting industry. If you undercut them or are rude or discouraging, they may go out of business and leave you without instructional classes, supplies, accessories, or "hands on" help when you need it most.

If you are not buying the yarn from a local source, then you must look to other avenues for help in estimating how much yarn you will need for a project.

YARN YARDAGE

When I started knitting, yarn was always sold by weight and the amount required was always given in terms of "2 ounces of 4-ply" or "6 skeins of fingering." Usually even more specifically than that, directions would say "2 ounces of Super-Duper 100 percent 4-ply" or "6 skeins of Blooper's SuperFine." That may have been a good thing for the manufacturer, but it left the craft worker up in the air, because

no one ever uses yarn by weight. Yarn is always used by length— the yard or meter.

Now most labels list not only the fiber and weight but the length as well, either in yards or meters. Most yarn stores also have yarn interchange chart books for their own use, and, often, for sale. The yardage of thousands of different yarns is listed. Having this information takes a lot of guesswork out of estimating the amount of yarn you will need for an original design. With a pocket calculator and yardage (or meter amounts) you can:

1. Substitute one yarn for another so long as both are used at the same stitch and row gauge and both have the same resiliency.

With a pocket calculator it is a simple matter of multiplying the number of skeins specified for an existing design by the amount of yardage in each skein to find the total number of yards required. Divide that total yardage by the amount in each skein of the selected substitute yarn to find out how many skeins will be needed.

Example: For a size 36, instructions call for six skeins of one color of Bloopers "Gooey-Gooey," and you want to substitute Wonder's "Slippery" to be used in three colors of equal-width stripes.

$$
\begin{array}{rl}
 & 235 \text{ yards in each skein "Gooey-Gooey"} \\
\text{x} & \underline{6} \text{ skeins} \\
 & 1410 \text{ total number of yards required for size 36} \\
\div & \underline{180} \text{ yards in each skein Slippery} \\
= & 7.8 \text{ total number of skeins of Slippery needed} \\
\div & \underline{3} \text{ equal amounts of three colors} \\
= & 2.6 \text{ skeins of each color of Slippery}
\end{array}
$$

Obviously you cannot buy 2.6 skeins. That figure must be rounded up to 3. To substitute Gooey-Gooey yarn in all one color for Slippery in three colors you must purchase three skeins of each color.

2. *Estimate* the amount an original project will require according to the following Rules of Thumb or instructions for similar garments.

QUICK AND HANDY RULES OF THUMB

My friend and knitting compatriot Evie Rosen of Wausau, Wisconsin, is a long-time yarn shop owner and has a couple of quick and handy rules of thumb:

1. It takes about 1,600 yards of Class B sport-weight yarn to hand-knit a woman's size 40 long-sleeved simple basic slipover sweater at a gauge of 6 stitches and 8 rows per inch.
2. It takes about 1,200 yards of Class C worsted-weight yarn to hand knit a woman's size 40 long-sleeved simple basic slipover sweater at a gauge of 5 stitches and 6½ rows.
3. For the same sweater in a Class D bulky-weight yarn, it will take only about 800 to 850 yards if the gauge is 3½ stitches and 4 rows.
4. Machine-knitters always use more yarn! (This is partly because it is very difficult for them to add new yarn in the middle of a row.)
5. No rule of thumb is always exactly accurate all of the time!

Linda Tobias of Patternworks has assembled these figures on a handy plastic card that fits easily into your purse or knitting bag. Called the "Pocket Yarn Yardage Guide ©" it is available through your local yarn supplier or by mail from Linda at Patternworks, PO Box 1690, Poughkeepsie, NY 12601.

Rules of thumb are good, educated, reliable *guesses*. They are useful in estimating how much yarn you will require for an original project. But, please, if you are 10 or 20 or even 50 yards short on a particular garment, don't come angrily attacking either Evie or me saying, "You said it would take only 1,200 yards to make this sweater and I ran out, and it is your fault." These rules of thumb say "about"; they do not say "only."

If you add a collar or a turtleneck, you'll need more yarn; if you make a cardigan with a front overlap, you'll need more yarn. Should you decide to put pockets into that cardigan, you'll need still more yarn. Of course, if you leave off the sleeves and make an unpocketed pullover vest instead, you'll get by with about one-third less yarn.

LOOK AT PATTERNS FOR SIMILAR DESIGNS

A very easy way to help you arrive at a good estimate is to look through printed patterns requiring the same yarn you have chosen and see how much they call for. If you find instructions for a long-sleeved sweater, and you want to make a short-sleeved version, you will know that it will take about one-sixth less yarn for your project in the same size. If you find directions for a pullover and you wish to make a similar sweater as a cardigan, you will know that an extra skein or two will be required for the front overlap. If a similar design to the one you have in mind calls for "Small: 8 balls; Medium: 9 balls; Large: 11 balls," and you want to make an Extralarge, a size that is both wider and longer, you'll probably need 3 additional skeins. Where did the number 3 come from? Remember, each size is wider and longer than the one before it. Between Small and Medium there is a difference of only 1 skein, but between Medium and Large there is a difference of 2 skeins. To continue at the same rate, it would take an additional 3 skeins for the Extralarge.

RESERVE SOME SKEINS

If you are purchasing yarn from your local friendly yarn shop, they will often set aside an extra skein or two of the same dye lot just in case you happen to run out before your project is finished. Please respect this thoughtfulness on their part by being thoughtful yourself. As soon as you know whether or not you will need that extra yarn, call the store and let them know. Go down and purchase the yarn immediately if you need it, or tell them "Thanks, but no thanks" and allow them to put the set-aside yarn back on the shelf while the dye lot is still current.

NEVER BE AFRAID TO BUY EXTRA YARN

I think that the most disheartening thing that can happen to any knitter is to design an original garment, watch it grow and unfold in front of your eyes just as you had imagined it in your mind, finish the back, front, and one sleeve, and then run out of yarn with 3 inches to go on the last sleeve. Running out of yarn has happened to me enough times that

now I always buy an extra skein or two of yarn just in case! Frequently I will use up an entire skein in making play/experiment swatches while I am waiting for the yarn to tell me what it wants.

Some stores will allow me to return surplus yarn for credit within a reasonable length of time when accompanied by the original receipt.

Even if I know ahead of time that I cannot return the yarn, I purchase extra anyway!

Don't be afraid of having a basket of odd yarn in your knitting closet. One way or another it always gets used. Sometimes I use it in making "proof swatches" while playing with the effects of different colors on a yarn. (I never would have thought to add orange to that dull red mohair if there had not been a surplus skein in the odd-lot basket.) Sometimes I use it for additional color when making "Caps for Kids" or in projects for bazaars and other charities. Often volunteer knitting teachers for Girl Scouts and Girls Clubs clamor for the stuff to use in teaching.

IF YOU THINK YOU ARE SHORT ON YARN . . .

Still, regardless of how carefully you plan ahead, there will be times when you will be short of yarn. Perhaps the amount you bought was all the store had and you just had to have the glorious stuff even if it wasn't enough; perhaps you changed your mind and are using a yarn for a different project than the one it was purchased for. Don't despair. You are creative; you will find a way to solve the problem. There are three well-known ways to overcome an insufficient supply of yarn.

1. Work from the top down. Early on in my knitting career, I encountered the method of making sweaters in one piece from the top down. What marvelous freedom and latitude it gave me! I guess I was always a designer even as a beginning knitter, and making sweaters in one piece from the neck down let me adjust lengths as I went along. (Detailed instructions for designing garments from the top down are included in Part II of this book.) After the division of the yoke stitches was made and the sleeves and body were separated, I would work a while first on the sleeves and then on the body. If I was short on yarn, either the sleeves or the body might end up somewhat shorter than I had originally intended. Once all the body stitches are on one needle, it is easy to determine just how many inches one skein will knit. "Hmm, I am getting 2½ inches out of each skein. I will need to reserve one whole skein for the bottom ribbing. I'm going to run out of yarn, and this sweater will end up being more than a half-inch shorter than I had intended. But that is okay; it is better than running out 3 inches shy of finishing the final sleeve."

2. Make invisible cast-on and work ribbing/trim later. Knitters who do not enjoy knitting in one piece from the top down have an option when they fear running out of yarn. They can use a machine-knitters trick!

Make the sleeves first. (Body length can often be adjusted with no adverse effect but sleeves that are 2 inches too short look ridiculous.) Begin each piece above the bottom ribbing/trim. Cast on with waste yarn at the point where the fashion-fabric stitch begins and work both sleeves. Again casting on with waste yarn above the ribbing/trim, next make the body, adding together the stitches for the back and front(s) so that the body is all in one piece. By the time you have worked up several inches, you'll have an idea of how much yarn will be required to complete the shoulder area. When you know that, you can adjust the length from the bottom to the armhole accordingly. If you do not have enough yarn remaining for the ribbing/trim, you can use either a different dye lot of the same yarn or a different yarn entirely to finish off the sweater.

3. Add stripes, blocks, or pieces of another color. In addition to being a top-down knitter, I am also a stripe knitter. I love the interplay of colors, sometimes set off with raised purl ridges, sometimes with different pattern stitches, which can make an ordinary-design garment into something unique and special. It is an ideal way to go when you haven't enough of one yarn to make a whole sweater. However, it is not the only way to go.

Blocks and intarsia areas of other colors can help to stretch yarn supplies of back-and-forth knitters. Do you know the story of how Caesar salad and its delicious dressing were created? Out of an insufficiency of supplies! The ingredients used were all the chef had on hand. Sweaters as unique and special as Caesar salad is delicious can be created out of an insufficiency of supplies also.

One of our creative Atlanta knitters fell in love with a superb turquoise-with-black novelty yarn. The shop did not have enough of it to make a whole sweater in her size. It did, however, have some of the same type of yarn in black-with-turquoise. Our gal said, "Ah, ha! I'll make the body of the predominantly turquoise yarn and the sleeves of the mainly black. I'll tie the two together by putting open-block plaidlike squares of the opposite color on each." It is a lovely sweater, and just by looking no one would ever know that design arose out of shortage and necessity.

Not only necessity, but shortage and adversity can be the mother of wonderful inventions!

THE ANSWER

"If I design my own sweater, how will I know how much yarn I will need?

You can ask your shop owner, follow rules of thumb, or look at patterns for similar designs. You can reserve some extra skeins or buy extra. If you are worried that you'll run out, you can work top down, or use invisible casting-on, or add areas of other colors.

But the real answer is that you will never know until you make up the sweater. Not to worry, though; educated guesses and creativity will get you through. Using "don't know" as an excuse for not attempting to create unique designs is a quitter's excuse.

13

Getting the Right Gauge

The second great lie of knitters is as follows:

"I always knit to gauge on the suggested-size needles! I always get whatever it says on the label. There is no reason for me to take the time and bother to make a gauge swatch."

The next time someone quotes this horrendous lie to me, I'm going to quote them the second great truth of knitting. That is,

"A person can never know what gauge they will get with a particular yarn and a particular set of needles on a certain pattern stitch until they make an accurate gauge swatch."

Gauge may seem like just a bunch of numbers, but they are very important numbers. Gauge means how many stitches and how many rows per inch (or centimeter) a person is making. Without these numbers, it is impossible to know how many stitches to cast on and work across to get the appropriate width. It would be like trying to build a bridge to the moon without knowing whether you are using little Legos® or fifty-foot steel spans.

STITCH GAUGE TIMES INCHES EQUALS WIDTH

The number of stitches in one inch times the number of inches wide you want the section to be equals the total number of stitches necessary for the width of the area you are knitting.

If you don't know how many stitches *you* are making in one inch, there is no way you will be able to multiply those stitches by the number of inches you want in order to make the appropriate width.

Knitting is unlike any other way of making a garment. When crocheting a sweater, the section being worked lies flat and smooth and can easily be measured to see if you are on target. When sewing cloth, you can take a pair of scissors and cut a section down if it is too wide or sew on another piece if it is too narrow. No such luck with knitting. Knitting doesn't usually lie flat and smooth so that you can quickly see and measure it. Though it is possible to add or subtract necessary width after the section is started, it really isn't very easy. And, yes, it is possible to whack off an area if it is too wide, but that is not always advised. *You are better off making a good, accurate stitch-gauge swatch before you begin.*

ROW GAUGE TIMES INCHES EQUALS LENGTH

The number of rows in one inch times the desired number of inches long you want the section to be equals the total number of rows that will be necessary to work to get the length of the area you are knitting.

Usually, for hand-knitters making sweaters with set-in sleeves and worked in separate sections from the bottom up, row gauge is not critical. However, for hand-knitters making a yoked or raglan-sleeved garment, correct row gauge becomes vital. This is because the number of rows in the yoke or raglan part will determine the length from armhole to shoulder. If the row gauge is off, the armhole depth may be distorted, either strangling the arm or sagging to the waist.

For machine-knitters, row gauge is always of critical importance.

While on a knitting machine, the fabric is distorted and cannot be accurately measured as the worker forms it. This is because the work in progress hangs downward from the needle "frame" and is deliberately weighted to keep the stitches from jumping off the needle bed. Therefore the machine-knitter must work with an accurate row gauge taken from a swatch. She must also chart her patterns in terms of rows instead of inches, so that she will know when the desired length is completed.

NEVER ACCEPT ANYONE ELSE'S GAUGE

All hand-knitters are different. All knitting machines are different in the same way that no two typewriters are exactly alike. All machine-knitters knit differently on the same machine.

The gauge that someone else got with a particular yarn using a particular set of needles or a particular machine at a particular tension does not in any way mean that YOU can or will get the same gauge.

THE SECRET TO MAKING A GOOD SWATCH: PLAN AHEAD

I recall as a teenager laughing at a placard with the words PLAN AHEAD printed on it. It was laughable because the typesetter did not do what the sign instructed others to do. He began placing the letters before stopping to figure out how much space they would take. He ran out of room before he got to the end of the line, so the final letters were not only smaller than the others, but scrunched together as well. The point of the admonition was communicated very well because obviously the typesetter didn't do it.

We knitters run into the same kind of a problem when we grab a skein of yarn, immediately make a swatch of it, and expect to start designing our new garment thirty seconds later. We are doing the same thing the thoughtless typesetter did with the placard. We are not taking time and forethought. A swatch needs time to rest and go through torture and recover before it is ready to give us an accurate measurement.

The secret to making a good swatch is thinking and planning two garments ahead. Just as soon as you begin one sweater, start thinking about the next one. Begin playing with the new yarn, exploring its possibilities, giving it time to have long conversations with you, letting it show you how it will hold up after repeated washings. Then by the time the original project is completed, your new yarn will have given up its secrets and be ready to tell you how it will best be made up.

IMPORTANT THINGS TO REMEMBER WHEN MAKING A GAUGE SWATCH

USE THE CORRECT END OF THE SKEIN

Just like woven corduroy or velvet fabric, all yarn has a nap to it. Run your thumb and forefinger over the yarn in one direction and the fibers lie flat and smooth. Run your fingers over the yarn in the opposite direction and it will feel rough and hairy.

Whether hand- or machine-knitting, always use the yarn in the direction that allows it to run most smoothly through your hands (or carriage), even if it means rewinding the yarn.

KNIT THE GAUGE SWATCH WHEN YOU ARE RELAXED

Our emotions affect the way our muscles work. When we are happy and relaxed, we tend to make easy and relaxed stitches, to move the machine carriage smoothly and evenly back and forth. When we are worried, frustrated, and under pressure, we tend to pull our stitches hard and tight, slam the carriage back and to.

In my early days as a knitting instructor and custom designer, I used to insist that my students and patrons sit down and make a gauge swatch before my eyes. This was a mistake on my part. The tension of having to make a swatch under the watchful eye of an "expert" caused my knitters to tense up, become agitated, and make an inaccurate gauge, one that they would not maintain under more relaxed conditions at home. It did not take long for me to become aware of my error and change my ways. I began to keep my customers thinking and planning one or two garments ahead, and *had them make their swatches at their leisure under relaxed conditions. (This also gave them time to "treat their swatch in the ordinary way," as below.)*

USE THE SAME MATERIALS FOR THE SWATCH AS FOR THE GARMENT

When making a swatch, please don't use someone else's needles or machine, for everything about your swatch must be the same as you intend to use on the garment itself—the same pattern stitch; the same needles (maker and material); the identical yarn, color and all. If you intend to use a motorized knitting machine, you need to make your swatch with the motor running.

I know I'm sounding picky, but Blooper's size 8 shiny aluminum needles may not be anywhere near the same size as Bleep's size 8 wooden needles. Besides, the yarn may drag and hang up on aluminum and simply float along on wood. Mary Jane's knitting machine may be dirtier than yours. A swatch made on yours may get a stitch-an-inch difference in gauge.

Color, too, can make a difference. In the same yarn, darker colors tend to be thicker than lighter colors because the deeper tones have absorbed more dye. Don't expect to get the same stitch and row gauge with white knitting worsted that you get with navy blue.

OTHER THINGS THAT AFFECT GAUGE

Besides our emotions, other things in our physical environment will affect our gauge. Humidity as the yarn runs through our fingers and static electricity as the yarn runs through a knitting machine carriage can affect the number of stitches and rows that we get. The speed at which we work will affect the results of both a machine-made swatch and a hand-made swatch.

But there comes a time when we cannot worry over every possibility, and we just go ahead and make our swatch and plan our sweater anyway.

NOTES FOR SWATCHES IN GENERAL

Recall from Chapter 3, "Getting New Ideas," the concept of letting the yarn tell you what it wants to become by making a long "play swatch" and listening to the reaction of the yarn.

If you try to cheat and eliminate this play/experiment, you will only be cheating yourself and the yarn.

After you have finished the fun-and-games playing, if you have made a long strip of experiments, you can now either free the one you choose from its neighboring swatches or start fresh and make a swatch "for real" from which you will get your accurate stitch and row gauge.

Handy hint: My friend Shirley cuts her beginning cast-on thread extralong. She then ties a series of knots in it—the same number of knots as the size of the needle or the tension setting. Five knots for a size 5 needle; seven knots for a #7 tension setting. This attached string with the knots in it goes through the washer and dryer and blocking (if necessary) and is still there to remind her what size needle she made this particular swatch on. Paper notes or "idiot tags" cannot do that!

FLAT HAND-KNIT SWATCHES

Hand-knitters who intend to make their garment in flat pieces going back and forth have several options in making gauge swatches. One method is to cast on 20 stitches and work in pattern stitch for 20 rows. Another is to multiply the desired number of stitches in one inch by four (6 stitches per inch × 4 = 24). Cast on that number of stitches (24). Work on whatever size needle it takes until you get a swatch that is 4 inches wide.

Neither one of the above methods will apply if you are making a combination of twists and cables, or a lace that has a multiple of 36 + 2 stitches. In that case you must make your swatch at least one pattern width wide, however many stitches that may be.

CIRCULAR SWATCHES

There is a problem with purls: you cannot tell what will happen when no purl stitches are used and the fabric is made with all knit stitches, all going in the same direction. Remember in an earlier chapter I said that many knitters make their purl stitches much looser than they make their knit stitches. If you are going round and round on a circular garment and not making any purl stitches, you won't have the looseness of the purl stitches in your finished piece. A flat-made swatch may not be accurate for circular knitting.

How then can a circular knitter tell what gauge she is going to get before she actually goes round and round?

Elizabeth Zimmermann suggests starting to make a hat first. It is a small round-and-round project and soon you will have gone far enough to measure accurately the overall width and see what your gauge is going to be. She says you can then cease working on the hat and get on with your sweater. Alas, unless you go ahead and finish the hat first, there is no way to tell what washing and blocking are going to do to the gauge.

Jacqueline Fee, in her book *The Sweater Workshop* (Interweave, 1983), suggests making a "sweater sampler" in the round before you begin a sweater. It is a good suggestion because it allows you not only to wash and block but also to try different ribbing, pattern stitches, and color combinations. For myself, I find making a sampler somewhat time-consuming.

I much prefer to make a small flat stockinette stitch swatch using only knit stitches. "How in the world can you do that?" It is easy; think about it for a moment; you can make a flat stockinette stitch swatch without ever making a purl row. Cast on 22 stitches on the circular needle you think you will use. *Break off the yarn. Push all the stitches back to the same tip of the needle where you cast them on. Add new yarn and work across the row. Tie the yarn strand to the strand end from the previous row.* Repeat between the asterisks using a fresh piece of yarn for each row.

My friend Shirley gets a much tighter (more stitches to the inch) gauge without the purls. My neighbor Elizabeth gets a looser (fewer stitches to the inch) gauge without the purls. I get the same gauge, but my back-and-forth knit-and-purl swatch is much stretchier and has much more forgivingness than my all-knit swatch.

If any of the three of us tried to design a sweater without making an all-knit swatch, we would find ourselves in deep trouble.

HOW TO MEASURE HAND-KNIT SWATCHES

Lay the completed swatch with the outside, public side, down on a flat surface. Unroll the curled edges gently with your fingers. Measure across the whole width of the swatch. Divide the number of stitches in the swatch by the width (in inches or centimeters) of the swatch. If you've made a 20-stitch/20-row swatch, you may use a "Gauge-O-Knit."* It is simply a rulerlike measuring device against which you lay your 20-stitch/20-row swatch to read off your stitch and row gauges. The arithmetic is done for you! (Circular knitters who have used the method described above to make a flat all-knit swatch should disregard the *first and last* stitches of their swatch because these edge stitches will be distorted by the yarn joinings.)

This will give you a *working gauge*, against which to check your work in progress. As you work along with your knitting, you will need to check yourself against this working gauge to make sure that your measurements are on target.

MACHINE-KNIT SWATCHES

If your yarn is on a cone that was prepared by the manufacturer, you may actually use it directly from the cone. (That is, unless the "nap" of the yarn happens to be running in the wrong direction to flow easily through your carriage.)

If the yarn is not on a cone, and is instead in hanks or skeins, or outside-pull balls, you must always rewind that yarn into a center-pull ball. As you rewind it, make sure that you cut out all the knots, imperfections, and unintended baubles. These blemishes can get caught up in the carriage feed and cause problems that are as disgusting as pieces of shell in walnut fudge candy.

If you are using a new or unfamiliar yarn, cast on 50 stitches with waste yarn and work several rows with it.

Do not put in "contrasting tag yarn," which is sometimes suggested. The tag yarn will distort the swatch.

Do not put a needle out of work in order to measure between the "dropped stitches." The spaces will distort the swatch.

Now play! Experiment! Using about 2 inches of waste yarn between them, try several different pattern stitches to see what the yarn "likes." (Note that ribbing swatches must be made separately, not as a part of this play/experiment swatch.) After you take this play swatch off the

*Available from your local yarn shop, or contact "Gauge-O-Knit," New Beginnings for Life, Inc., PO Box 1237, Barrington, IL 60010, (312) 381-5448.

machine, cut the different patterns apart in the middle of the waste yarn joinings. Now let the swatches relax. Give them a chance to rest and recover from the trauma you have put the yarn through. That rest period should last at least twenty-four hours, better forty-eight hours. Just as gardeners don't expect a transplanted geranium to recover in thirty seconds, machine-knitters should not expect yarn to recover in the twinkling of an eye.

If you are using a familiar yarn *and* a familiar pattern stitch, cast on 50 stitches with waste yarn. Work an inch with the waste yarn, change to the fashion yarn and work for 50 rows. End your swatch with 1 inch of waste yarn. Remove the swatch from the machine and go do something else—weed the garden, go shopping, or read a good book—leave the swatch alone. Let the yarn relax.

The next day or so you will want to measure a "working gauge." Just as the hand-knitters do, you will need a friendly reminder as you go merrily along that will assure you that you are on target, that the way the piece looks as it comes off the machine is indeed how the swatch looked *before* it was washed and blocked.

Lay the swatch on a flat surface, public side down. Using your fingers, carefully unroll and uncurl the edges.

Measure the swatch from top to bottom, divide the number of rows you have made by the length in inches (or centimeters) for the row gauge, that is, the number of rows per inch (50 rows divided by 6.5 inches = 7.69 rows per inch).

Measure the swatch from side to side, divide the number of stitches you have made by the width in inches (or centimeters) for the stitch gauge, that is, the number of stitches per inch (50 stitches divided by 12.5 inches = 4.0 stitches per inch).

Be sure to record your working gauge!

"TREAT ME IN THE ORDINARY WAY"

A freshly made knitted swatch is not an indication of how the fabric will behave during normal use: washing and steaming and wearing.

If the sweater will be hand-washed and laid flat to dry, hand-wash the swatch and lay it flat to dry.

If the sweater will be machine-washed and machine-dried, do that to the swatch.

If the swatch must be dry-cleaned or steam-pressed and blocked, do that to the swatch.

The swatch may shrink; it may stretch; the yarn may pill or ball; the colors may run. This is the information you need to know in order to design a garment that can be enjoyed.

No one wants a garment that cannot be depended upon through repeated cleanings. If your swatch is for a baby or child's garment, put the swatch through the washer and dryer two or three or more times, just as the finished piece will have to go through the washer every time the child wears it.

Sometimes with some pattern stitches, when you take the swatch out of the washing machine you will find that it is terribly distorted. It may have expanded 4 inches in width and shrunk to only 2 inches in length. This happens more frequently with machine-made swatches than with hand-made swatches. If you have to pull and tug to restore it to some semblance of the original, it is time to stop and rethink your choice of pattern stitch. Do you or the intended recipient really want to have to go through a tug-o-war trying to restore the shape of the garment every time it comes out of the washer?

Even if you have worked with the particular yarn before, and know how it behaves in stockinette, if you are trying a different pattern stitch, be sure to treat it in the way it will be treated as a finished item. We want no surprises.

MEASURE AGAIN

In the same way that you did before, measure the exposed-to-real-life swatch again. This will give you a "finished gauge." These are the numbers that you will work with in creating the pattern for your garment.

YOUR GAUGE MAY CHANGE

As a hand-knitter relaxes and gets into the swing of knitting, it is not uncommon for the gauge to loosen. This is why we have noted and written down both the working and the finished gauges—so that you can continually recheck the total width of the piece as you work on the garment.

If your gauge changes as you knit, change to a different-size needle immediately: a larger one if your stitches shrink in size, a smaller one if your stitches get looser.

DON'T LIE!

Whatever you do, please never repeat the second great lie of knitters. Few people "always knit to gauge on the suggested size needles." Repeating the lie will label you as a phony as quickly and as surely as if you were to say "I am Elizabeth the Second, the queen of England!"

14

A Refresher Course on Common Knitting Techniques

Remember the third great lie of knitters? It occurs as the customer leaves the designer or the store. The salesperson or designer will ask, "Is there anything about these instructions that is not perfectly clear or that you don't understand? Are there any techniques that you need to brush up on?"

And the knitter will reply, "Well, really, I should hope not. I was knitting before you were born. You don't have to explain anything to me; I know all about knitting."

And then invariably the shop owner's or designer's home phone will ring at 11:45 P.M. When answered, there is no "Hello," no "This is Mrs. X. Y. Zee"; just "What in the world do *EOR* and *SSK* mean?"

Since you are going to be your own designer, this chapter is devoted to refreshing your memory about common knitting techniques as well as familiarizing you with the new jargon of knitting designers.

This is a book about *designing* sweaters, not a book about the techniques used in *making* them. What follows is a cursory glance at some things you will have to be familiar with. If you need more help or explanation, I can recommend the following books:

Knitting in Plain English by Maggie Righetti (New York: St. Martin's Press, 1986).
The Handknitter's Handbook by Montse Stanley (London: David & Charles, 1986).
The Principles of Knitting by June H. Hiatt (New York: Simon & Schuster, 1989).
Crocheting in Plain English by Maggie Righetti (New York: St. Martin's Press, 1988).

COMMON KNITTING TECHNIQUES YOU SHOULD KNOW

BEGINNING AND ENDING

Cast On: A way of getting the first row of loops on the needles or the needle bed of a machine. There are many methods for casting on, and I don't have space here to describe and instruct you on each technique. There are advantages and disadvantages to all of the forty or more approaches. Hand-knitters should be familiar with at least *the two-strand method,* a removable type of cast-on, and the over-the-thumb/ single-strand method.

Cast On with Waste Yarn: Although invented by machine-knitters, this technique has many advantages, and there is no reason for hand-knitters not to use it. You *cast on and make your first row(s) with a yarn that you are going to take out later and throw away.*

Bind Off: To permanently get rid of stitches that you never intend to work again.

Beware: Don't bind off neck-area stitches that you will later pick up to finish off with ribbing. Tight bind-offs can kill sweaters.

Your bind-off may be so firm, inelastic, and just plain tight that the intended wearer will never be able to get the garment over his/her head. In the instructions that follow in Part II, neck areas (or areas that will be worked again later) will list the number of stitches and then either the abbreviation *BO* (Bind Off) when appropriate or *TH* for *To Holder.*

Depending on your preference, you have two options with stairstep shoulder shaping: 1) you can very loosely bind those stairsteps off and later seam the back and front together with invisible weaving, or 2) you can short-row the stairsteps and then form a seam by making a *double bind-off.* Some knitters love to throw in short rows at every opportunity; others hate making them. The directions in Part II will show the stairstep shaping and give you the option of making them as you choose.

MOVING STITCHES

Slip Stitches to Holder:

As long as you always slip-as-if-to-purl, you can move any stitches, at any time, to either a commercially made stitch holder or to a double-pointed needle.

I frequently use a double-pointed needle fastened on both ends with rubber tip protectors as a stitch holder. It is as impossible to find yourself on the closed end of a double-pointed needle as it is to forget your own name.

WIDENING AND NARROWING

Note: It is never wise to increase or decrease in the edge stitch. Later, it will be difficult to make a nice seam or pick up in edge stitches that have been increased or decreased. Always knit at least one, preferably two, stitches before making any changes.

Increase Sloping to the Right: KRB; causes the "grain" of the fabric to shift to the right.

Insert the right-hand needle into the right-hand loop of the next stitch IN THE ROW BELOW and knit into that (side) loop.

Increase Sloping to the Left: KF&B; causes the "grain" of the fabric to shift to the left.

With the yarn at the back of the work, knit the next stitch in the ordinary way, but do not remove the old stitch from the needle. Swing the right-hand needle wide around and to the back, and knit into the back loop of the old stitch. Remove the old stitch from the needle.

Increase—Yarn-Over or Wool Round Needle: This increase makes a hole in the fabric. Don't use it in the middle of a fashion fabric stitch unless you want that hole.

Make-1 (French Style) = Blind Stockinette Stitch Increase: Leaves no hole; does not cause the "grain" of the fabric to move either to the right or to the left.

From the back, with the right-hand needle lift the strand that lies before the next stitch and place it on the left-hand needle sloping the same direction as all the other stitches. Knit into the back loop of this strand.

Decrease Sloping to the Left: SSK; as the garment faces you, this decrease is usually used on the right-hand side for raglans and under-arm shaping.

The Slip, Slip, Knit decrease: As if to knit, slip the next stitch to the right-hand needle. As if to purl, slip the next stitch to the right-hand needle. (Two stitches have been slipped.) Insert the tip of the left-hand needle into the fronts of the 2 slipped stitches and knit those 2 slipped stitches together as if they were one.

Please note the new development in the instructions above. It used to be advised to "slip both stitches as if to knit." Recently an inventive knitter found that by slipping the first as if to knit and the second as if to purl, an even better-looking decrease was made.

Decrease Sloping to the Right: K 2 tog; as the garment faces you, this decrease is usually used on the left-hand side for underarm shaping and raglans in particular.

Knit 2 together decrease: Work to within 4 (or desired number) stitches of the end of the row. Through the front loops, knit the next 2 stitches together as if they were one. Knit the remaining stitches.

WORKING IN THE ROUND

More and more knitters are knitting round tubes on circular needles whether the finished pieces are to be flat or circular. Special care must be taken on the first and second rounds to avoid twisting the whole piece, but other than that, the knitting is trouble free.

To avoid the problem at the beginning of making a permanent twist in the work, some knitters cast on and work the first couple of rows back and forth, joining only when there is sufficient fabric to make sure there is no twisting.

Other knitters prefer to work in the round from the start. Use a two-strand method of casting on. Do not use the simple "over the thumb" method because it will be important to have the "bead" at the bottom of the stitches. When all the stitches are cast on, push the beginning and ending stitches toward the tips of the needles, making sure that the "bead" is facing down all the way around and the stitches are not twisted. Pull the yarn across the gap and make the first row as usual.

At the end of the first round, place a ring marker to note the beginning of a new round and double-check that all of the stitches are hanging *under* the needle and that there is no twist.

Making a Steek: If you want your circular knitted tube to end up either as a flat piece (as in a cardigan) or with arm and neck holes in it, you will probably want to make a steek.

A steek is an area of stitches made on purpose to be thrown away. The steek will be cut open down the middle and the garment will be finished along the edge between the fashion fabric and the steek.

For instance, you may choose to make a steek in a Fair Isle vest at a proposed armhole opening. Bind off the underarm stitches in the ordinary way. Continue to work around the garment. On the next round, over the bound-off stitches place markers and cast on 10 stitches for the steek. Make the armhole shaping in the usual way on the body side of the steek. When the knitting is finished, cut open the steek.

How many stitches wide you want your steek to be will depend upon both the yarn you are using and on how you intend to finish the cut-open area. Traditional Fair Isle sweaters made of Shetland wool use a steek 10 stitches wide. The 5 stitches on each side of the cut are rolled under to the back and whip-stitched in place. Ribbing is usually picked up along the fold line. For cardigans I often make a steek only 3 stitches wide. When finished, the two side stitches are sewn (separately) twice on the sewing machine, and the center stitch is cut open. The garment is usually finished with single crochet with the first row made over the machine-stitching.

KNITTING WITH TWO HANDS

Two- and multicolor ethnic designs such as Icelandic, Nordic, and Fair Isle garments are traditionally knitted in the round, usually from the bottom up, but occasionally from the top down. The whole garment is made as a tube even if openings will be cut later. The knitter holds the least-used strand of yarn in her right hand and forms the stitches of that color in the American-British way. (See Figure 14.1.) She holds the other color (or colors) of yarn in her left hand and forms the stitches of that (those) color(s) in the Continental Pic method. (See Figure 14.2.)

With a little practice, anyone can learn to knit with both hands. By working in the round and knitting with yarn in each hand, the knitter never has to drop one color and pick up the other. The yarns automatically wrap themselves and an even gauge is achieved. Also, the knitter does not have to read the alternate rows of the chart backwards and opposite.

MAKING DARTS

Short Rows: If you are going to design and knit sweaters for big-breasted women or potbellied men or women, you are going to have to

14.1 Two-handed knitting: making a stitch the American-British Way

14.2 Two-handed knitting: making a stitch with the Continental Pic Method

know how to make short rows. If you hand-knitters have never encountered this technique before, I strongly recommend that you read the chapter "Shape It Up with Short Rows" in my book *Knitting in Plain English*. In that book I fully and carefully explain how to stop short of the end of a row, wrap the base of the next stitch, turn and go back in the opposite direction, and "catch" the wrap on the final finishing row. Machine-knitters are usually taught to short-row in their intermediate classes.

Never forget the forgivingness of home-knitted fabric. Though horizontal short-row darts are often required and vitally necessary, be careful about overdoing them—don't make them too long! If you calculate that a dart 3 inches long will be required, SUBTRACT AN EASE FACTOR and make the dart 2–2½ inches long instead.

The following instructions for short-row shaping are all-purpose; that is, they work for both the knit and the purl sides of the work, and they work for either flat knitting or knitting in the round. The letter X equals the number of stitches that are left unworked at the ends of the rows. N means the number of short rows that are made.

1. Work to within X stitches of the end of the row or the last marker near the end of the row.
2. As if to purl, slip the next stitch to the right-hand needle.
3. Take the yarn between the tips of the needles to the opposite side of the work.
4. Transfer, as if to knit, that same slipped stitch back to the left-hand needle by putting the left-hand needle in the back loop of the stitch, and then take it off the right-hand needle.
5. Again take the yarn between the tips of the needles to the opposite side of the work.
6. Place a ring marker on the right-hand needle.
7. Turn the piece around and, going in the direction from which you came, work the next 2 stitches, leaving the X stitches on the other side of the marker unworked.
8. Stop. Check your work. There should be a strand of yarn wrapped around the base of the unworked stitch next to the marker.
9. Continue across the row following the instructions beginning at step 1.

When all of the stitches have been short-rowed, to avoid holes in the work, it is imperative that on the next row you pick up the strand that you so carefully wrapped around the base of the stitch at the turning point and work it, together as one, with the turning stitch. You will pick up that strand differently depending on whether you are on the knit or the purl side. If it is the knit side, from below with the tip of the right-hand needle, scoop up the wrapped strand, insert the needle into the stitch in the usual way, and work both strands together as if they were one. If it is the purl side, tilt the work toward you. With the tip of the right-hand needle, pick up the wrapped strand and place it on the left-hand needle. Work both strands together as if they were one.

Short-Row Horizontal Bust Dart for a Pullover: You will need accurate stitch and row gauges. You must have the following measurements: 1) back length from nape of neck to bottom of garment; 2) front length from neck-shoulder joining to bottom of garment; 3) desired width of front of garment; 4) distance between bust points (nipples).

1. Subtract the back length from the front length to find how many inches long the dart should be. Multiply that number by the row gauge to determine how many rows will be used in making the dart. Now we must divide by 2, because a short-row "turnaround" uses up 2 rows.

Example:

    23″ (front length)
  − 20″ (back length)
  = 3″ (of short rows necessary)
  × 6 (row gauge: rows per inch)
  = 18 (rows of short rows necessary)
  18 rows ÷ 2 = 9 turnarounds

2. Add to the distance between the bust points (nipples) an "ease" factor of 2 inches to keep the ends of the darts from ending exactly at the breast points. This will give you the flat width in the center between the ends of the bust darts. Subtract this flat width between the ends of the bust darts from the total width of the front of the garment. Divide this number by 2 (for the right and the left side) to determine how many inches of width on each side you have available for the dart. Multiply this number by the stitch gauge to know how many stitches you have to work with.

Example (see Figure 14.3):

    8″ (width between bust points [nipples])
  + 2″ ("ease" factor)
  = 10″ (flat width in center between ends of bust darts)

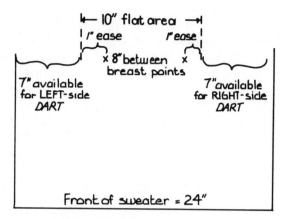

14.3 Calculating the length of a bust dart

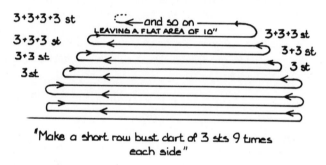

"Make a short row bust dart of 3 sts 9 times each side"

14.4 Calculating turnarounds

```
     24" (width of front of garment)
  −  10" (flat width in center between ends of darts)
  =  14" (width available for bust dart)
  14" ÷ 2 = 7" (width available for bust dart on each side)
      7" (width available on each side)
  ×   4  (stitch gauge: stitches per inch)
  = 28  (stitches available on each side for dart)
```

3. Divide the number of stitches available on each side by the number of turnarounds.

Example (see Figure 14.4):

28 (stitches) ÷ 9 (turnarounds) = 3 stitches each turnaround

Your instructions will say, "Bust dart: short-row 3 stitches each side 9 times."

Short-Row Horizontal Dart for Extra Back Neck Length for a Circular Yoked Pullover: Remember that in adults the front neck sits on the front torso about 2½ inches lower than the back neck does on the back torso. However, because of the forgivingness of knit fabric, usually 1 inch to 2 inches is sufficient length for the dart to do its job and keep the back neck of the sweater from being too low. Depending upon the pattern and design of the sweater, the dart can be placed either in the neck area above the last design or lower on the back, after the sleeves are separated, just before the first design is made. If you place the dart in the neck area, you have the distance all the way around from the right front flat part of the neck across the back to the left front flat part of the neck to work with. If you place the dart lower down, you have the width across the back between the sleeves to work with.

In either instance you will need accurate stitch and row gauges. You will need to know how many inches the front neck is lower than the back neck.

1. Determine how many inches need to be added to the back length. Multiply this number by the row gauge. Divide this number by 2 because a short-row turnaround uses up 2 rows.

Example:

> 2″ (length necessary)
> × 4.5 (row gauge: rows per inch)
> = 9 (rows of short rows necessary)
> 9 rows ÷ 2 = 4.5 (round off to 5) turnarounds

2. Determine how many inches wide the area where the dart can be made is. Decide how much of this area you wish to remain flat (usually as much as the width of the back of the person's neck.) (See Chapter 6 on measurements.) Multiply area available for darts by stitch gauge.

Example:

> 10″ (width available) ÷ 2 (half for each side) = 5″ (width available on each side)
> 5″ (width available on each side)
> × 3 (stitch gauge: stitches per inch)
> = 15 (stitches available on each side for dart)

3. Divide the number of stitches available on each side by the number of turnarounds.

Example:

15 (stitches of width) ÷ 5 (turnarounds) = 3 stitches each turnaround

Your instructions would say: "To raise back neck, short-row 3 stitches each side 5 times."

Short-Row Horizontal Dart for Barrel-Chest or Potbelly for a Pull-over: You will need accurate stitch and row gauges. You must have the following measurements: 1) back length from nape of neck to bottom of garment; 2) front length from neck-shoulder joining to bottom of garment; 3) desired width of front of garment.

1. Subtract the back length from the front length to find out how many inches long the dart should be. Multiply that number by the row gauge to determine how many rows will be used in making the dart. Now we must divide by 2, because a short-row turnaround uses up 2 rows.

Example:

```
    26" (front length)
 −  24" (back length)
 =   2" (of short rows necessary)
 ×   7  (row gauge: rows per inch)
    14  (rows of short rows necessary)
14 rows ÷ 2 = 7 turnarounds
```

2. Decide how much width you want to remain flat in the center of the front of the garment. (This flat area will be determined by the visual shape of the body.) Subtract this amount from the total width of the front of the garment. Divide this number by 2 (for the right and the left side) to determine how many inches on each side you have available for the dart. Multiply this number by the stitch gauge to know how many stitches you have to work with.

Example:

```
    26" (width of front of garment)
 −  12" (width to remain flat in center front)
 =  14" (width available for darts)
14" ÷ 2 = 7" (width available for bust dart on each side)
     7" (width available on each side)
 ×  10  (stitch gauge: stitches per inch)
 =  70  (stitches available on each side for dart)
```

3. Divide the number of stitches available on each side by the number of turnarounds.

Example:

70 (stitches) ÷ 7 (turnarounds) = 10 stitches each turnaround

Instructions will say, "Dart for barrel-chest: short-row 10 stitches each side 7 times."

Short-Row Horizontal Dart for Dowager's Hump: For people with hunched backs the dart to add extra length to cover the hump of the shoulders is made in the same manner as the dart for a barrel chest, except that it is made on the back of the garment instead of on the front.

Short-Row Horizontal Darts for Cardigans: These are figured in the same way as for the horizontal darts above. The only difference will come when you write out the directions for the right and the left side. For a cardigan there will be a corresponding short-row dart on each half of the front.

Vertical Dart Decreasing: There are three occasions when you may need to know this technique: 1) when working from the bottom up, going from a very wide bosom to a very narrow shoulder, or from a flared skirt bottom to a narrow hip and/or waist; 2) on diagonally knit sweaters made in the round to form underarm shaping; 3) on top-down sweaters when you want to go from a chest measurement to a narrower waist measurement either at the underarms or under the breasts.

On the row before, place a marker where you want the dart(s) to be located. On a knit-side row, work to within 2 stitches before marker, SSK, slip M, K 2 tog, continue across row. If desired, you can allow 1 or 2 stitches in the center of the dart to remain plain for a smoother effect.

Vertical Dart Increasing: You may need to know this technique when working from the bottom up if you are planning to increase from waist to chest, or when working from the top down when you choose to increase the bust to hips to accommodate a pear-shaped figure.

On the row before, place two markers, with 2 stitches between them, where you want each of the dart(s) to be located. On a knit-side row, work to the first marker. Make-1 French style, slip marker, knit the 2 stitches before the second marker, slip marker, Make-1 French style, continue across row. This dart allows 2 plain stitches between increases in order to get a smooth effect.

MAKING BUTTONHOLES

The chapter in *Knitting in Plain English* about these pesky openings for fastenings is called "Buttonholes Are Bastards!" And they are. But if you are going to make any kind of a cardigan other than one calling for a zipper, you will need to know how to make them. Please learn at least the "Best (One-Row) Buttonhole" and the "Three-Row Buttonhole."

Best (One-Row) Buttonhole: On the public side, work the required number of stitches before starting the buttonhole.

As if to knit, slip 1 stitch. Between the tips of the needles, bring the yarn to the front of the work and drop it. As if to knit, slip the next stitch from the left-hand needle to the right-hand needle. Pass the first slipped stitch over the second stitch and off the needle. Not using the dropped yarn, bind off the required number of stitches in this manner.

Slip the last loop on the right-hand needle back to the left-hand needle. Turn the work around. (Private side is facing you.) Bring the yarn to the front. At the edge where the buttonhole was started, using the twisted method of casting on purlwise, cast on the number of stitches you bound off plus 1 more.

Turn the work around. (Public side is facing you.) Slip the first stitch of the left-hand needle to the right needle. Slip the final cast-on stitch over this stitch that you just moved. Slip this stitch back onto the left-hand needle (because it has not yet been worked). Work to the end of the row.

Three-Row Buttonhole: Row 1: On a public-side row, work to the desired location of the buttonhole. Yarn-over twice, then knit the next 2 stitches together. Continue across row.

Row 2: Work across to the yarn-overs of the previous row. Purl 1 yarn-over and drop the other off the needle. Continue across row.

Row 3: Work across row to buttonhole. Knit 1 stitch *through the hole* and allow the old stitch to fall off the needle. Continue across row.

SIMPLE CROCHETING

Knitters who do not know what to do with a crochet hook are limiting themselves. I'm not suggesting that you give up knitting and take up crocheting as a hobby. I am saying that you need to know how to handle a hook, for frequently the best way to finish a knitted edge is with a row or two of simple crochet. For instance, the vertical edges where you intend to put in a zipper will behave much better if you work a row of single crochet around the area, putting in a triple decrease at the bottom of the placket.

COMMON ABBREVIATIONS YOU WILL ENCOUNTER IN PART II

A: color **A,** or #1

approx: **approx**imate(ly)

beg: **beg**in, **beg**inning

B: color **B,** or #2

BH: **b**uttonhole

Bl St inc.: **bl**ind **st**ockinette **inc**rease, increase that does not slope to right or left; same as Make-1 French style

BO: **b**ind **o**ff

C: color **C,** or #3

CC: **c**ontrasting **c**olor

cm: **c**entim**e**ters

CO: **c**ast **o**n

cont: **cont**inue

COW: **c**ast **o**n with **w**aste yarn

D: color **D,** or #4

Dec: **dec**rease(ed)(es)(ing)

Dec L: **dec**rease sloping to the **l**eft

Dec R: **dec**rease sloping to the **r**ight

E: **e**very

ea: **ea**ch

EOR: **e**very **o**ther **r**ow

est: **est**ablished

E3R: **e**very **3**rd **r**ow

E4R: **e**very **4**th **r**ow

FF st: **f**ashion **f**abric **st**itch, any fabric pattern stitch other than ribbing or stockinette

Inc KF&B: **inc**rease by **k**nitting in the **f**ront **&** **b**ack

Inc YO: **inc**rease by making a **y**arn-**o**ver

K: **k**nit

K 2 tog: **k**nit **2** **tog**ether; a decrease sloping to the right

KBL: **k**nit in **b**ack **l**oop

KF&B: **k**nit in the **f**ront **&** **b**ack of the next stitch; an increase sloping to the left

KRB: **k**nit 1 stitch in the **r**ight-hand loop of the stitch in the **r**ow **b**elow; an increase that slopes to the right

M: place a **m**arker

MC: **m**ain **c**olor

M-1: **m**ake **1** stitch French style increase that does not slope to right or left; same as blind stockinette stitch increase

mtpl(s): **m**ul**t**i**pl**e(s)

mutl(s): **mul**tiple(s)

p: **p**url
pat(s): **pat**tern(s)
pat st: **pat**tern **st**itch
rem: **rem**ain(s)(ing)
rep: **rep**eat(s)
rev St st: **rev**erse **st**ockinette **st**itch
rnd(s): **rnd**(s) (for circular knitting)
rpt: **rp**ea**t**
sel: **sel**vedge
SKP: **s**lip, **k**nit, **p**ass over; a decrease sloping to the left
SSK: **s**lip, **s**lip, **k**nit; a decrease sloping to the left; *now preferred over SKP;* it makes a better-looking decrease, more perfectly matching K 2 tog
st(s): **st**itches
St st: **st**ockinette **st**itch
St st bl: **st**ockinette **st**itch knit in **b**ack **l**oop
TH: **T**ransfer to **H**older; slip stitches as-if-to-purl to a holder to be worked later
UA: **u**nderarm(s)
wrn: **w**ool **r**ound **n**eedle
×: times (as in repeat 6 times)
&: and (an ampersand on the typewriter)

Examples of designer's shorthand instructions:

dec 1 st ea side EOR 6 × until 12 sts rem & = 4″ from BO

Translation: Decrease 1 stitch each side every other row 6 times until 12 stitches remain and the piece measures 4 inches from the bind-off.

Inc KF&B before & after ea M E4R 8 × until piece measures 8½″ from back neck & 210 sts rem.

Translation: Increase 1 stitch (by knitting into the front and then the back of the existing stitch) before and after each marker every 4th row 8 times until the piece is 8½ inches long from the center back neck and there are a total of 210 stitches.

15

Final Preparation Steps for Designing Your Own Sweater

VISUALIZING YOUR FINISHED GARMENT

You must have firmly planted in your mind the idea that you have the right to control what you make and do. If you do not believe that you are entitled to be a self-determining, self-fulfilling, responsible adult, you are not going to get very far in creating, adapting, and altering your own knitted garments. We all know of children who have doomed themselves to flunking a test in school because they did not think that they could pass it, had the right to pass it or get a good grade on it. These kids *thought* that they were too dumb to make the grade. The fancy phrase for this kind of behavior is "self-fulfilling prophesy." If you *think* that you cannot accomplish something, you will subconsciously rig the situation so that you will surely fail.

If you cannot "see" the finished piece before you start, as Michelangelo "saw" finished forms in his uncut marble, you must still have *an idea of what you want the finished piece of clothing to look like* or a sense of the impression you want the sweater to convey. Once you have clarified these things in your mind—bulky or form fitting, loud or subtle, weighty or zephyrlike—you can begin to make specific plans to create *that* garment.

SKETCHING THE BASIC SHAPE OF YOUR GARMENT

Even if you are not an artist, even if you can't draw a straight line, you must squiggle out a rough sketch of the finished sweater. Even if it is only a kindergarten-style stick figure, draw it out as it will be worn,

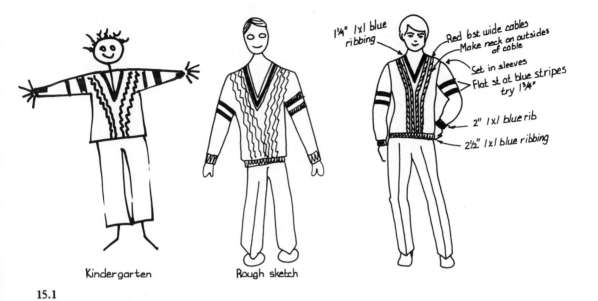

1¼" 1x1 blue ribbing

Red bst wide cables
Make neck on outsides of cable
Set in sleeves
Flat st at blue stripes try 1¾"

2" 1x1 blue rib

2½" 1x1 blue ribbing

Kindergarten

Rough sketch

15.1

with slacks, shorts, or a skirt. If you choose, color in your drawing with crayons or colored pencils. This drawing, however imperfect, will bring to your attention just how and where the sleeves will fit into the body, where the neckline will sit, and where the bottom of the garment should rest. Each of the sketches in Figure 15.1 shows the basics of neck type, sleeve type, detail, etc., for the same sweater.

Though you must start with a rough sketch of the finished garment, this does not mean the completed garment has to look like the original drawing. At almost any point along the way, you can change your mind. An important part of creativity is listening to the yarn and making changes when better ideas pop up.

DRAWING A FLOOR PLAN OF THE DIFFERENT PARTS OF YOUR GARMENT

We are not talking about architects' working blueprints for a grand mansion. We are talking about a rough layout sketch of the individual pieces that you will need to plan and make. These diagrams of the garment parts are similar to dress pattern pieces in sewing, except that you don't need to make them in tissue paper or to cut them out. They don't even have to be to perfect scale. You need only a layout of the shapes of the pieces. (See Figure 15.2.)

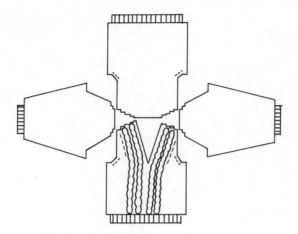

15.2 Layout of pullover with set-in sleeves

ASSEMBLING THE NECESSARY SUPPLIES

A SAMPLE OF THE FINISHED FABRIC

Have in hand a sufficient amount of yarn (or an emergency/contingency plan for what you will do if you run out of yarn) and a completed and thoroughly tortured swatch. This is the *gauge swatch* we talked about in Chapter 13 that has had time to rest, that has been subjected to all the terrors the finished garment will have to endure, and that has had *both a working and a finished gauge* taken from it. Your gauge swatch is your road map.

CLOSINGS

I'm adamant about some things; I'm wishy-washy about others. I absolutely insist on having in hand *zippers, frog closings,* and *any other specialty items* that will be needed *before* I begin to design a garment that will require them. I'm wishy-washy about whether or not I have *the buttons and/or belt buckle* I intend to use on a sweater before I start to design it.

If you have ever been caught, as I have been, with a finished pink sweater, only to find that 22-inch separating zippers are not made in pink and you have no way to close the front, you'll understand my insistence on this point. (I had no more pink yarn with which to crochet a front button band to take the place of the zipper, so I used a dark blue yarn of the same weight to make front bands and added decorative crocheted pockets of the same blue to keep the thing from looking like a mistake.)

Buttons are another matter. It is nice to know in advance how wide to make the buttonholes and the front band (if there is one). But sometimes it's better to make the sweater first (with medium-sized buttonholes), and then take the finished garment to the button counter of your favorite fabric store and let the sweater tell you what it wants. The sweater's choice is not always what you would have chosen before the garment was completed. You can always whip-stitch one end of a too-long buttonhole closed. Besides, with buttons you always have the choice of crocheting covered "bone" ring buttons.

TAPE MEASURE

Trying to design a sweater without a good nonstretchy, reliable tape measure is like trying to raise a baby without diapers—a very messy situation with lots of disasters. A retractable steel tape measure won't do; neither will a 12-inch ruler. A plain cloth tape will stretch and give untrue numbers. You need *a good plastic-coated 60-inch tape* with inches on one side and centimeters on the other.

As I am designing and laying out the number of stitches, I often pull out my tape and double-check myself. "Maggie, you have written down that Susy's shoulder bone tips are 18½ inches apart. Can that really be true?" And I hold the tape up to my own shoulders. "Mine measure 14. She is not that much bigger than I. I must have made a mistake, and will need to double-check before I go on."

A CHART OF THE MEASUREMENTS

You are going to need a filled-in and notated chart of the intended wearer's necessary measurements. Some of these measurements are illustrated in Figure 15.3.

POCKET CALCULATOR

Oh, how I wish we had pocket calculators years ago when I was beginning to design patterns. In those days we carried all the multiplication and division tables in our heads and did our figuring on plain paper with pencils (and made gobs of mistakes!). I still use a lot of plain paper and pencils but all the tables are carried in the head of my handy pocket calculator. In order to remember which number was the sum of what, I jot down the steps, but the actual figuring is done by my magic electronic genie.

If you don't have one, run, don't walk, to the nearest store and buy

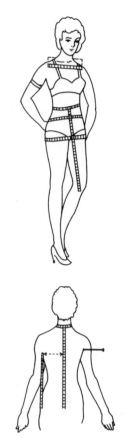

15.3 The above illustrations show a few of the body measurements to be taken with a tape measure.

Body Measurement Record

NAME   DATE   WEIGHT   BODY TYPE

GARMENT STYLE   TYPE OF YARN

ACTUAL BODY   DESIRED GARMENT
MEASUREMENT   MEASUREMENT

——— . . . . Back Neck Width . . . . ———

——— . . . . Slope of Shoulder . . . . ———

——— . . . . . Width Between Shoulder Bone Tips. . . . . . ———

——— . . . . Chest/Bust . . . . ———

——— . . . . Armhole Depth . . . . ———

——— . . . Desired Back Length of Garment from Nape of Neck . . . ———

——— . . Desired Front Length of Garment from Neck-Shoulder Joining . . ———

——— . . . . . Length from Armhole to Desired Length . . . . ———

——— . . . . . . Circumference at Desired Length . . . . . ———

——— . . . . Upper Arm Width . . . . . . ———

——— . . . . Desired Sleeve Length . . . . . ———

——— . . . . Wrist . . . . ———

——— . . . . Waist . . . . ———

——— . . . . Tummy . . . . ———

——— . . . . . Length from Waist to Tummy . . . . . ———

——— . . . . . Hip, Measured at Widest Circumference . . . . . ———

——— . . . . . . Length from Waist to Hip . . . . . . ———

——— . . . . . . Length from Waist to Skirt Bottom . . . . . . ———

Horizontal darts necessary ——————— Vertical darts necessary ———————

Additional notes:

one. It doesn't have to be fancy with logarithms and cosines and exponents; all it needs to do is add, subtract, multiply, divide, and do percentages.

PAPER

It sounds obvious, but it's essential. Sometimes I use yellow legal-size pads and sometimes I use typing paper. The only criteria is that it is erasable and that ink does not run or blur on it. (If you plan to keep a notebook, and I hope you do, choose 8½- × -11-inch paper that can be punched to fit a three-ring binder.)

Whenever I'm plotting difficult diagonals, I use graph paper to double-check my figures. (See Figure 15.4.) For instance, if I am planning an angle for a raglan sleeve and I get into a situation where decreasing "1 st ea side EOR until 4 sts rem" is going to make the armhole depth a grand total of 5 inches deep, and if decreasing "1 st ea side E4R . . ." is going to make that same armhole depth very close to the waist length, I grab some graph paper and plot it out. When we come to sleeve caps and raglan sleeves in Part II, I'll carefully explain how to do it.

Pads of large (11- × -17-inch) sheets of graph paper are available at artists' supply stores and at some office supply stores. I use, 4, 5, or 8 squares to the inch. Any larger than that and I can't fit the area onto a

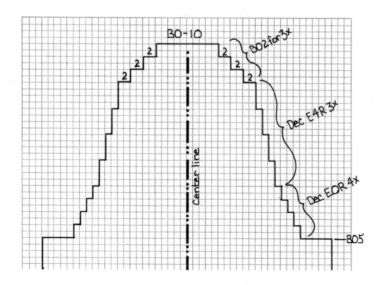

15.4 Using graph paper to proof out a compound angle

single sheet; any smaller than that and my astigmatic eyes rebel.

If you have in mind doing Nordic, Fair Isle, alphabet, or intarsia designs, you are going to want to get yourself a supply of *knitter's graph paper*. Knit stitches are not square in the sense that needlepoint or cross-stitch stitches are square. Knit stitches are almost always shorter than they are wide. Think about it: "Gauge: 4½ sts & 7 rows = 1 inch." or "Tension: 24 sts & 40 rows = 10 cm." There are usually more rows in one square inch than there are stitches. If you plotted a balloon on regular graph paper and then knit it up into your design, your balloon would come out looking somewhat flattened. Special paper with rectangles instead of square squares has been designed for knitters in many different gauges. Knitter's graph paper is available from your local yarn retailer or by mail directly from any of the following:

The Stitching Post, 5712 Patterson, Richmond, VA 23226
Knitech, 914 Warwickshire Court, Great Falls, VA 22066
Schoolhouse Press, 6899 Cary Bluff, Pittsville, WI 54466
Pat's Potpourri, RR 6, Cedar Falls, IA 50613
Gail Selfridge, 1509 Houston Street, Manhattan, KS 66502

SOMETHING TO WRITE WITH

In planning my designs I use *black-, red-, and green-colored pencils or pens*. The black pen marks out the shape of the layout pieces, the floor plan of the garment. Red indicates the number of inches wide and long the pieces are supposed to be at the various locations. When I have multiplied these widths and lengths by the gauge, I fill in the actual number of stitches and rows with a green pen. Using the three colors of pens or pencils makes life easier and less confusing for me. I am less apt to mistake inches of width for number of stitches if they are written in different colors. (It is also an excellent tool for teaching "how-to-plan-knit-patterns" classes. The students catch on much more quickly when I use the different colors.)

THE MOST IMPORTANT ITEM OF ALL

There is one more item you are going to need and that is *a healthy sense of humor*. Sorry, but it cannot be purchased in any store or ordered through any catalogue. If a person is not born with a sense of humor, it can be gained only by looking at the world through yellow glasses that turn everything topsy-turvy. Only by seeing the ridiculousness of being self-important and the absurdity of being injured by trivialities can we learn to laugh at ourselves. As a seamstress I once made a dress that had no opening, no way to get it over my head. In my frustration I could have attacked either the sewing machine, the fabric, or the worth of myself as a person. Instead I chose to laugh at myself. As a knitter I have made sleeves the length of legs and turtlenecks that would strangle any human or turtle. I could have hated myself. Instead I made a big mug of herb tea and laughed at me. (I'm glad to report that herb tea is now available in every supermarket.)

DON'T REINVENT THE WHEEL

Keep a notebook of projects made. Save all patterns, yours and others.

Once upon a time I kept a three-ring binder of all the designs I had created. I used see-through plastic sleeves to protect them, and tucked in photos and swatches along with the instructions as well as notes to myself. "Glorious, but had only one yard of yarn left over." "A real beauty." "Can be worn only in subzero weather while on an iceberg." "Never never again! The lace pattern wasn't worth the effort."★

I no longer keep a notebook. I now have several large metal file cabinets filled with records of designs, both mine and others. If I want a snowflake that will be a perfect hexagon, I don't have to spend hours creating one—reinventing the wheel. I can pull one out of the file cabinet. I don't have to recall how I got that shawl collar to lie so perfectly on Timmy's cardigan. I can pull out the original instructions that I wrote fifteen years ago.

BE WELL PREPARED

Designing, originating, and creating are rewarding activities, but just as you wouldn't expect to be a champion figure skater in your socks without ice skates, you can't expect to chart sweaters in your head without supplies.

★An ideal knitting organizer with transparent sleeves, conversion charts, yarn inventory cards, a foreign language reference, and much more, entitled The Higher Mathematics of Pleating A Cat, by Margaret Heathman and Janine Styre-Stebbins, is now available and can be ordered through your local yarn retailer or by mail from Pleated Cat Enterprises, 2625 Piedmont Road NE, Suite 56-128, Atlanta, GA, 30324; (404) 266-9101. The price is $34.95 + $6 (shipping and handling). Georgia residents, add $2.10 sales tax.

16

Understanding the Arithmetic of Knitting

Please don't let this chapter and the arithmetic it includes frighten you away from designing your own knit garments. After you have read through the simple lessons in Part II it will all make sense to you and will be easy to understand.

We use both multiplication and division in designing sweaters. We multiply by the gauge (the number of stitches and rows per inch) by inches to get the total number of stitches and rows.

$$\begin{array}{rl} 16'' & \text{(desired width in inches)} \\ \times\,4.5 & \text{(gauge: stitches per inch)} \\ \hline = \quad 72 & \text{(number of stitches necessary to obtain desired width)} \end{array}$$

$$\begin{array}{rl} 18'' & \text{(desired length in inches)} \\ \times\,8 & \text{(gauge: rows per inch)} \\ \hline = \ 144 & \text{(number of rows necessary to obtain desired length)} \end{array}$$

We divide the total number of stitches a piece is wide by the number of stitches in the gauge to get the width of the piece in inches.

$$\begin{array}{rl} 72 & \text{(stitches wide)} \\ \div\,4.5 & \text{(gauge: stitches per inch)} \\ \hline = \ 16'' & \text{(the number of inches the piece is wide)} \end{array}$$

Sometimes we have to divide the total number of stitches by the number of stitches in a pattern-stitch multiple in order to juggle and make the patterns come out even. 72 (stitches of desired width) ÷ 5 (pattern stitch multiple) = 14.4. To have complete pattern multiples, we have to either add 3 stitches to make the number 75 or subtract 2 stitches to make the number 70. Which we choose to do will depend upon the stretchiness or firmness of the finished knitted fabric.

A CHEAT SHEET

Even someone like me who has been designing for more than twenty-five years gets tired and confused. I have a card just like the box shown here stuck up on the wall in my workroom. I refer to it when I have any questions.

---

5 × 20 = 100
5 sts per inch × 20 inches wide = 100 sts needed to make 20 inches wide

20 × 5 = 100
20 inches wide × 5 sts per inch = 100 sts needed to make 20 inches wide

100 ÷ 20 = 5
100 sts of width ÷ 20 inches wide = gauge of 5 sts per inch

100 ÷ 5 = 20
100 sts of width ÷ gauge of 5 sts per inch = piece 20 inches wide

---

You might also find it useful to keep a card showing the multiplication tables, as follows.

1 × 1 = 1	2 × 1 = 2	3 × 1 = 3	4 × 1 = 4	5 × 1 = 5
1 × 2 = 2	2 × 2 = 4	3 × 2 = 6	4 × 2 = 8	5 × 2 = 10
1 × 3 = 3	2 × 3 = 6	3 × 3 = 9	4 × 3 = 12	5 × 3 = 15
1 × 4 = 4	2 × 4 = 8	3 × 4 = 12	4 × 4 = 16	5 × 4 = 20
1 × 5 = 5	2 × 5 = 10	3 × 5 = 15	4 × 5 = 20	5 × 5 = 25
1 × 6 = 6	2 × 6 = 12	3 × 6 = 18	4 × 6 = 24	5 × 6 = 30
1 × 7 = 7	2 × 7 = 14	3 × 7 = 21	4 × 7 = 28	5 × 7 = 35
1 × 8 = 8	2 × 8 = 16	3 × 8 = 24	4 × 8 = 32	5 × 8 = 40
1 × 9 = 9	2 × 9 = 18	3 × 9 = 27	4 × 9 = 36	5 × 9 = 45

continued on next page

continued from preceding page

6 × 1 = 6	7 × 1 = 7	8 × 1 = 8	9 × 1 = 9
6 × 2 = 12	7 × 2 = 14	8 × 2 = 16	9 × 2 = 18
6 × 3 = 18	7 × 3 = 21	8 × 3 = 24	9 × 3 = 27
6 × 4 = 24	7 × 4 = 28	8 × 4 = 32	9 × 4 = 36
6 × 5 = 30	7 × 5 = 35	8 × 5 = 40	9 × 5 = 45
6 × 6 = 36	7 × 6 = 42	8 × 6 = 48	9 × 6 = 54
6 × 7 = 42	7 × 7 = 49	8 × 7 = 56	9 × 7 = 63
6 × 8 = 48	7 × 8 = 56	8 × 8 = 64	9 × 8 = 72
6 × 9 = 54	7 × 9 = 63	8 × 9 = 72	9 × 9 = 81

FRACTIONS ARE A NO-NO

Back in the old days when we designed sweaters by working out all of the figures with pencil and paper from multiplication tables carried in our heads, it was simple to do much of the math work with fractions. That was before pocket calculators.

Because electronic pocket calculators cannot handle fractions, we must change all our fractional numbers to decimals or percentages.

In case you've had no need to use them lately and have forgotten the equivalents, some of the more common conversions are listed here:

$\frac{1}{4} = .25, \frac{1}{2} = .50, \frac{3}{4} = .75, \frac{1}{3} = .33, \frac{2}{3} = .66$

Note: To determine the decimal equivalent of a fraction, simply divide the top number of the fraction (numerator) by the bottom number (denominator).

PERCENTAGES

If you have never been involved in creating sweater instructions before, you may be unaware that designers often use simple percentage formulas to determine the number of stitches to be used, increased, or decreased.

For instance, after I determine how many stitches should be in the circumference of the body, I often use an arbitrary figure of 10 percent (or 20 percent in the case of nonresilient fibers) fewer stitches for the bottom ribbing.

When planning upper arm sleeve widths, I prefer to measure the desired circumference of the sleeve and multiply by the stitch gauge to find the required number of stitches. Many designers and knitters, however, prefer to use a percentage system. For instance, they may say that sleeve width at underarm should be 20 percent of total body circumference.

It used to throw me into a conniption fit to try to remember whether to add, subtract, multiply, or divide to find percentages.

To determine what percentage a smaller number is of a larger number, divide the little number by the big number.

The opposite of a percentage is a reciprocal, a fancy word that arithmetic books use to explain the fact that 80 percent *of* a number is the same as 20 percent *less than* the number.

80% *of* 100 = 80 = 20% *less than* 100

It works this way whenever two percentages add up to 100: 90% and 10%; 80% and 20%; 70% and 30%; 60% and 40%; 50% and 50%. It will save you a lot of time, subtraction, and confusion if you understand reciprocals.

I also had problems figuring out what to do to increase and/or decrease a certain percentage of stitches across a row. Then late one night it occurred to me that I could think of percentages in terms of *units*.

Remember this easy rule when thinking of percentages as units:

To increase, add 1 stitch to complete the unit. To decrease, subtract 1 stitch from the unit.

Think of 5% in units of 20.
To increase: *K 19, inc 1 st*, *rep between* *s *across.*
You now have 20 stitches in each unit where before you had only 19.
To decrease: K 18, k the 19th and 20th stitches together, *k 18, k 2 tog*, *rep between* *s *across.*
You now have 19, that is, 1 stitch less than each unit of 20.

Think of 10% in units of 10.
To increase: *K 9, inc 1 st*, *rep between* *s *across.*
You now have 10 stitches in each unit where before you had only 9.
To decrease: K 8, k the 9th and 10th stitches together, *k 8, k 2 tog*, *rep between* *s *across.*
You now have 9, that is, 1 stitch less than each unit of 10.

Think of 20% in units of 5.
To increase: *K 4, inc 1 st*, rep between *s across.
You now have 5 stitches in each unit where before you had only 4.
To decrease: K 3, k the 4th and 5th stitches together, *k 3, k 2 tog*, rep between *s across.
You now have 4, that is, 1 stitch less than each unit of 5.

Think of 25% in units of 4.
To increase: *K 3, inc 1 st*, rep between *s across.
You now have 4 stitches in each unit where before you had only 3.
To decrease: *K 2, k 2 tog*, rep between *s across.
You now have 3, that is, 1 stitch less than each unit of 4.

Think of 50% in units of 3.
To increase: *K 2, inc 1 st*, rep between *s across.
You now have 2 stitches in each unit where before you had only 1.
To decrease: *K 1, k 2 tog*, rep between *s across.
You now have 2, that is, 1 stitch less than each unit of 3.

INTEGERS AND INTERVALS

Numbers are *integers*. Spans of time and space are intervals. Integers and intervals are not the same thing.

A common example is that we live in the 20th century, but the decade is the 1990s. What happened? The "20th century" is an interval, a span of time. The year "1990" is an integer, a number.

year	year	year	year	year	year	year
number	number	number	number	number	number	number
integer	integer	integer	integer	integer	integer	integer
0	50	100	150	200	250	300

+		+		+		+

FIRST CENTURY   SECOND CENTURY   THIRD CENTURY
SPAN/INTERVAL   SPAN/INTERVAL   SPAN/INTERVAL

There is one *less* span than year. The first century is going on *before* the year 100 arrives!

"Oh, come on, Maggie! Why is this important? I don't have to figure out for myself what century we are living in. Newspapers and TV and books will tell me. What has this got to do with sweaters?"

It is important that you understand that points/places/numbers/ integers and spaces/spans/intervals are not the same. This difference will become critical when we get into planning and spacing increases and decreases.

For instance, when we want to increase the sides of a fitted sleeve along the underarm seam from the wrist to make the sleeve get wider for the underarm, there are four ways we could do it:

1. If we wanted to increase a total of 5 stitches, we could increase 1 at the beginning, 1 at the end, and 3 evenly spaced in the middle. (See Figure 16.1.)

This will give you five points/integers but only four spans/intervals. To arrive at this type of spacing you must subtract 1 from the number of increases you wish to make.

For example, if you want to make 5 increases, 1 at the beginning, 3 evenly in the middle and 1 at the end (to get 5 increases and 4 spans): 5 − 1 = 4. Suppose the sleeve is 16 inches long. 16 inches ÷ 4 = 4 inches between increases. Therefore, make an increase at the beginning, 1 every 4 inches thereafter, and 1 increase at the end.

For sleeves, planning your increases in this way makes your ending increase come too late. This makes your last increase-to-gain-width come just at the point you are ready to bind off for the armhole. That is silly! We really need that last increase for the width of the upper arm 2 inches before we are ready to bind off.

2. It would be possible not to increase at the beginning or at the end, but to make 5 increases evenly spaced in the middle. (See Figure 16.2.)

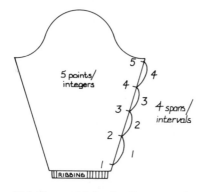

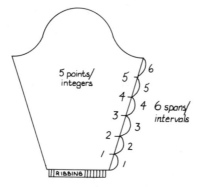

16.1 Sleeve with 5 points/integers and 4 spans/intervals

16.2 Sleeve with 5 points/integers and 6 spans/intervals

This gives you five points/integers, and six spans/intervals. You have one more span than you have increases. In order to get this type of spacing you must add 1 to the number of increases you wish to make.

For instance, if you want to make 5 increases, none at the beginning, 5 evenly in the middle, and none at the end: 5 + 1 = 6 spans/intervals. Suppose a sleeve is 16 inches long. 16″ ÷ 6 = 2.66 inches. Knit 2.66 inches before you begin to increase, increase then and every 2.66 inches thereafter until 5 increases have been made, and then knit 2.66 inches to the end without any more increases.

This is a good way to plan your increases (if your bottom ribbing is wide enough), because the final/top increase is well below the armhole bind-off. You have no lumpy increases at the beginning or at the end.

3. We could make a total of 5 increases with 1 at the beginning and then 4 evenly spaced in between, but not 1 at the end. (See Figure 16.3.)
Notice that this is the first time we get the same number of points and spans!
To figure out how to position this arrangement of increases, we don't have to either add or subtract anything. We just divide our 16 inches by 5.
This is okay, and works out well.

4. We could not increase at the beginning, make 4 evenly spaced increases in the middle, and 1 final increase at the very end. (See Figure 16.4.)

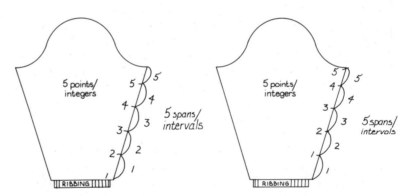

16.3 Sleeve with 5 points/integers and 5 spans/intervals

16.4 Sleeve with 5 points/integers and 5 spans/intervals

Again we have the same number of points and spans, and we simply divide our 16 inches by 5. However, the same thing happens here as in #1 above. You are making your last increase to gain added width at the same point you are binding off to get rid of stitches. It is a senseless thing to do!

To know whether or not it is necessary to change the number of increases by adding or subtracting 1, count the number of SPANS you want to end up with, not the number of increase points.

That way you'll never end up living in the wrong century.

In the examples above, I have discussed making increases—but the same thing is true when making decreases. Either in your mind or on paper, draw out the piece. Decide how many spans you want. Do you want an increase (or decrease) to fall either at the beginning or at the end? Count the spans, and then divide the length by that number.

THE FORMULA FOR DIAGONALS THAT COME OUT CLEAN AND EVEN

Oh, what a joy it is when numbers work out clean and even without leftovers. For instance, it is lovely when you divide 6 into 24 and get a clean answer of 4. When you have 24 rows to work with and want to put 6 spans in so that you get 5 increases, divide 24 (rows) by 6 (spans) and you get 4 (rows between each span), so that you will know to "work 3 rows even, increase then (on the 4th row) and every 4th row thereafter, working the last 4 rows even."

But, unfortunately, when God created this wiggly-wobbly world She didn't bother with numbers, and man-made numbers do not always work out even and clean and exact. You will need instructions for figuring out diagonals when the numbers come out messy.

THE FORMULA FOR DIAGONALS THAT DON'T COME OUT EVEN

These instructions are written as if you were going to plan a V-neck, decreasing for a 6-inch-wide neck opening that is 8½ inches deep on a fabric with a gauge of 4 stitches and 5 rows to 1 inch. When you want to figure out a diagonal increase, simply substitute the word "increase" for "decrease." You can also substitute the word "span" for "decrease" after you have decided the total number of span/intervals you will need.

1. Always allow yourself a certain (few) number of rows to work even after your last decrease in case your row gauge is a bit off. In other words, your last decrease should never come exactly on the spot of the end of the piece.

$$
\begin{array}{ll}
8.5'' & \text{(length of opening)} \\
- \quad .5'' & \text{(allowance in case row gauge is off)} \\
\hline
= \quad 8'' & \text{(length available for decreases)}
\end{array}
$$

2. Find out how many rows are available for making the decreases. Multiply the row gauge by the number of inches the area is long.

$$
\begin{array}{ll}
8'' & \text{(length)} \\
\times \quad 5 & \text{(gauge: rows per inch)} \\
\hline
= \quad 40 & \text{(rows available for making decreases)}
\end{array}
$$

If necessary, round off this number of rows to an even number. *YOU MUST HAVE AN EVEN NUMBER OF ROWS TO MAKE THIS FORMULA WORK.*

3. Determine how many stitches you are going to decrease. Multiply the row gauge by the width of the desired opening.

$$
\begin{array}{ll}
6'' & \text{(width of desired opening)} \\
\times \quad 4 & \text{(gauge: stitches per inch)} \\
\hline
= \quad 24 & \text{(stitches across entire neck opening)}
\end{array}
$$

If this number of decreases is going to be split between the right and left sides, divide by 2, half for each side.

$$
\begin{array}{ll}
24 & \text{(stitches across entire neck opening)} \\
\div \quad 2 & \text{(half for right side, half for left side)} \\
\hline
= \quad 12 & \text{(stitches to be decreased on each side)}
\end{array}
$$

4. Plan one side of the piece of knitting. (The other side will be exactly the same.) Divide the number of decreases desired into the number of rows available. You will probably get a decimal/fraction.

$$
\begin{array}{ll}
40 & \text{(rows available for decreases)} \\
\div \quad 12 & \text{(number of decreases/number of decrease rows)} \\
\hline
= \quad 3.33 & \text{(number of hypothetical rows between decreases)}
\end{array}
$$

Obviously it is impossible to decrease every 3.33 rows. A hand-knitted piece will look best if decreases are made only on public side rows.

5. *Go to the NEXT WHOLE EVEN NUMBER on either side (smaller or larger) of this decimal/fraction. Some of your decreases will be made on the smaller number and some will be made on the larger number.*
   2 is the next smaller whole even number from 3.33.
   4 is the next larger whole even number from 3.33.
Some decreases will be made on every 2nd row (that is, every other row). Some decreases will be made on every 4th row.

6. *Make an equation.*

____ (Total Number of Decreases)	____ (Number of Rows Available for Decreases)
=	=
____ (Smaller Whole Even Number) × ____ (Number of Times Made)	= ____ (Number of Rows Used by Smaller Number)
+	+
____ (Larger Whole Even Number) × ____ (Number of Times Made)	= ____ (Number of Rows Used by Larger Number)
=	=
____ Total Number of Decreases	____ Number of Rows Available for Decreases

7. *Begin to solve the equation by replacing the blanks with known numbers.*
Use a pencil. Write in "temporary" or "try-on" numbers in parentheses so you will know which numbers to erase.
Total number of decreases to be made on each side (from step #3) is 12.
Number of rows available for making decreases (from step #2) is 40.
Smaller whole even number (from step #5) is 2.
At this time we do not know how many times it will be made, nor do we know the number of rows that will be used by the smaller number. Put in a question mark.
Larger whole even number (from step #5) is 4.

At this time we do not know how many times it will be made, nor do we know the number of rows that will be used by the larger number. Put in a question mark.

Our equation looks like this:

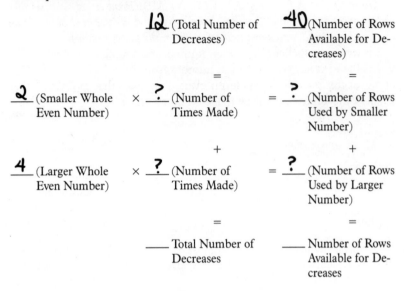

$\underline{12}$ (Total Number of Decreases) $\underline{40}$ (Number of Rows Available for Decreases)

=   =

$\underline{2}$ (Smaller Whole Even Number) × $\underline{?}$ (Number of Times Made) = $\underline{?}$ (Number of Rows Used by Smaller Number)

+   +

$\underline{4}$ (Larger Whole Even Number) × $\underline{?}$ (Number of Times Made) = $\underline{?}$ (Number of Rows Used by Larger Number)

=   =

_____ Total Number of Decreases   _____ Number of Rows Available for Decreases

8. Cancel out and get rid of half of the equation by supposing that all of the decreases will be made at the rate of the smaller whole even number. That is, suppose all 12 decreases were to be made every 2nd row. Multiply the 12 decreases by 2 to find out how many rows would be used up.

> 12 (total number of decreases)
> × 2 (supposing they were all made every 2nd row)
> = 24 (would use up 24 rows; but this is not the final/real number you want to use in the end)

With a pencil, write these numbers into the equation. Put parentheses around both these numbers, 12 and 24, because they are just temporary.

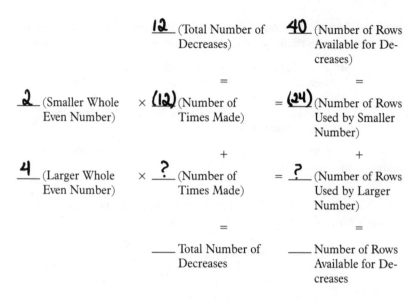

12 (Total Number of Decreases)   **40** (Number of Rows Available for Decreases)

=

2 (Smaller Whole Even Number) × **(12)** (Number of Times Made) = **(24)** (Number of Rows Used by Smaller Number)

+

4 (Larger Whole Even Number) × **?** (Number of Times Made) = **?** (Number of Rows Used by Larger Number)

=

____ Total Number of Decreases   ____ Number of Rows Available for Decreases

To work out the final/real number, find out how many rows would be left over. Take the total number of rows available (40) and subtract the supposed 24 (at the rate of the smaller whole even number) from it.

    40 (total number of rows available)
− 24 (supposed number of rows used at the rate of the smaller whole even number)
= 16 (supposed number of rows left over)

Now divide this supposed number of rows left over (16) in half.

I'm not enough of a mathematician to know why you divide by 2. Just take my word for it that you do!

This will give you the number of times to decrease at the rate of the larger whole even number (every 4th row).

    16 ÷ 2 = 8

You will decrease on the larger whole even number (every 4th row) 8 times. This is a final number. Enter it, without parentheses, into the equation.

9. *Now to find the real number of times to decrease at the rate of the smaller whole even number (every 2nd row).* From the total number of decreases, 12, subtract the number of times decreases will be made at the rate of the larger whole even number (every 4th row), which is 8. You get the

final/real number of times you have to decrease at the smaller whole even number: decrease every 2nd row 4 times.

> 12 (total number of decreases to be made)
> − 8 (number of times decreases to be made at the rate of the larger whole even number)
> = 4 (number of times decreases to be made at the rate of the smaller whole even number)

You will enter this final number, without parentheses, into the equation in the next step.

10. *Prove it out!* Erase the temporary numbers in parentheses from step #8, enter the final numbers, and make sure it all adds up.

<table>
<tr><td>__12__ (Total Number of Decreases)</td><td>__40__ (Number of Rows Available for Decreases)</td></tr>
<tr><td>=</td><td>=</td></tr>
<tr><td>__2__ (Smaller Whole Even Number) × __4__ (Number of Times Made)</td><td>= __8__ (Number of Rows Used by Smaller Number)</td></tr>
<tr><td>+</td><td>+</td></tr>
<tr><td>__4__ (Larger Whole Even Number) × __8__ (Number of Times Made)</td><td>= __32__ (Number of Rows Used by Larger Number)</td></tr>
<tr><td>=</td><td>=</td></tr>
<tr><td>__12__ Total Number of Decreases</td><td>__40__ Number of Rows Available for Decreases</td></tr>
</table>

Decrease every *2nd* row **4** times   uses up **8** rows
+   +
Decrease every *4th* row **8** times   uses up **32** rows
= **12** decs will use up **40** rows

MEASURE OFTEN

Still, regardless of the perfection of your arithmetic, the correctness of the numbers notwithstanding, *the fabric has a magic of its own; always double-check yourself as you create your dream.*

What? Measure every piece and section you knit.

When? Measure after you have worked 2 inches of the fashion fabric pattern stitch.

Where? Measure across the total width of the piece to double-check that you are working at gauge and that the piece is *really* coming out the width you want it to be.

How? Remember that as long as you always slip as if to purl, you can move your stitches anywhere you want as many times as you want. Spread the work out on two straight needles, or on one or more circular needles (ends protected with rubber stoppers, please), or on a ⅛-inch-wide ribbon.

TRY IT ON

Part of creativity is continually stopping and assessing what you are creating. Part of originality is changing your mind as you work, as you see your creation developing before your eyes, and improvising when the dream isn't coming true. An equally large part of making new designs is junking the project just as soon as you see that the garment is not working.

And how do you *know* when the design is not working? *You stop and try it on!*

If you are knitting in the round, either top down or bottom up, it is a cinch to stop at any time and put the garment on the intended wearer. Most of the time you will be right on target and keep going.

If you are working flat, back and forth, just as soon as you have finished the back, hold it up to the intended wearer. After you have completed the front as well, baste the two sections together and slip them on the person. Pin or baste the sleeves in place as soon as they are finished and get the whole effect.

Continually trying on the garment as you go will ensure that your new creation will never go astray.

Keep on going. Don't be frightened. All this complicated-sounding arithmetic is just common sense. Once you see it in use in Part II it will become very clear and easy.

17

Preventing Knitwear Disasters: A Quick Quiz

It is easy to make a garment with obvious design flaws. The catch is that they may not be obvious until the garment is completed. At that point it may take a lot of work to solve the errors. It is also easy to create a new garment *without* obvious design flaws. Usually, a little forethought can prevent these mistakes. That is what this chapter is about, a checklist of flaws to watch for *before* they become apparent.

In Part II, the specific drawbacks of each garment and the body types that it does not suit will be discussed. This checklist chapter deals more in generalities.

_____ *Is the sweater appropriate to the wearer?*

     _____ Personality?

     _____ Age?

     _____ Skin tone?

     _____ Climate?

     _____ Lifestyle?

     _____ Allergy or skin sensitivity?

_____ *Does the wearer have the appropriate clothing needed to wear with this sweater? Will the appropriate colors and styles be available?*

     _____ Blouse?

     _____ Shirt?

     _____ Skirt?

     _____ Slacks or shorts?

     _____ Pants?

_____ Dress?

_____ Outerwear—What kind or color or style of winter coat can I wear over this sweater? (Only a cape will fit over dolman sleeves!)

_____ Will the other clothing have to be custom-made?

_____ Will the right color fabric be available to make other clothing?

_____ *Did you take accurate measurements of the body at the places that will be covered by the sweater?*

_____ *Are these measurements current?*

_____ *Has the intended wearer gained or lost weight?*

_____ Between shoulder-bone tips?

_____ Width of back of neck?

_____ Chest?

_____ Length of garment and circumference at that point?

_____ Upper arm circumference (or sleeve width)?

_____ Length of sleeves?

_____ *Did I make an accurate gauge swatch using the exact same needles and yarn that I will use for the garment?*

_____ Did I get a "working gauge" from the swatch?

_____ Did I wash and dry or clean and block the swatch in the same way I will treat the finished garment?

_____ *Do I have sufficient yarn?*

_____ *Do I have a contingency plan if I run out of yarn?*

_____ *Have I purchased the necessary supplies?*

_____ Zipper?

_____ Buttons?

_____ Frog closings?

_____ Shoulder pads?

_____ Bobbins, markers, stitch holders, cable needles or other notions?

_____ *Does the neckline suit the wearer?*

_____ Will the wearer's head slip into it easily?

_____ Is it too high or low? Does it take into consideration how high or low the wearer's neck emerges from the torso and does it consider the slant of the shoulders?

_____ Does it take into consideration whether the person has a short or a long neck? Slender or wide neck?

_____ Is it too wide; will a woman's bra straps show?

_____ Is it too deep; will cleavage show?

_____ *Are the armholes the right size for the use of the sweater?*

    _____ Will a shirt be worn under this sweater? Did I allow enough room for that shirt?

    _____ Did I make the armholes so deep that it will be difficult to wear an outer garment over the sweater?

    _____ Are the armholes so deep that a bra will be visible?

_____ *Will the length be flattering and comfortable for the wearer?*

    _____ Does the bottom of the garment "cut" the body in a flattering place?

_____ *Have I placed all color changes and highlighting in the most flattering places?*

    _____ Have I avoided placing designs or color patches or pockets over the breasts so that they won't look like pasties on a striptease dancer?

    _____ Have I avoided placing color bands across big hips or bustline so as not to make them more noticeable?

_____ *Have I designed the most flattering bustline for the wearer?*

    _____ Will the design spread over the breasts, making them appear vulgar? If the design is lace or ribbing over large breasts, it will!

_____ *Have I considered whether this sweater will maximize the hipline?*

_____ *Are there any new techniques that I need to learn?*

CONCLUSION

If you can answer each of the foregoing questions satisfactorily, if you can say that you've taken all these points into consideration, go ahead with confidence, pride, and determination and make the garment.

PART II

Doing It—
The Actual Designs

Preface to Part II

In addition to commentary, each chapter in Part II contains a sketch of the garment, a rough layout of its pieces, and a photo of the completed article.

These sweater designs progress in degree of difficulty with each chapter. Each subsequent pattern is built on information learned in the previous example. Even if you don't want to make each garment, start at the beginning and go through the motions of designing each project just for the learning experience. Once you understand all the parts of each garment, you can easily make marriages of any of those parts.

This section begins with sweaters designed to be worked from the bottom up in separate back-and-forth pieces. I am aware that many of you wish to make your garments either in the round or from the top down and, of course, you may do so. However, in my experience in teaching others to design, I have found that students must learn to design (but not necessarily knit) in separate pieces from the bottom up before they can learn to design in the round and/or from the top down. Once they understand the designing process, they can add the pieces together and make it in the round, or they can easily turn the project topsy-turvy and knit in the opposite direction.

Sometimes I take to modern improvements very rapidly. I was sold on automatic clothes dryers from the day after they came out in the early 1950s. But I'm a real laggard about other things. I simply can't get used to the idea of using centimeters instead of inches. In the chapters that follow, I will use inches. Please, if you are more forward-looking and contemporary than I am, use centimeters instead.

18

The "T" Topper

In this chapter you will learn how to:

1. Take accurate measurements;
2. Multiply rows and stitches;
3. Lay out and mark pattern pieces;
4. Write instructions.

THE IDEA

The first garment we are going to learn to design is the versatile "T" Topper for men, women, children, and teenagers. This is the most basic and simple of all sweaters. It is simply two identical T-shaped pieces, one for the back and one for the front, that are seamed together at the underarms and shoulders. It is an excellent beginner's learn-to-knit sweater because of its simplicity and avoidance of shaping techniques. The garter stitch trim is used horizontally on top and bottom, and vertically on the sleeve ends. The neck-opening width for women is determined by the width between bra straps.

The object of this lesson is to learn all the steps necessary to create a garment. Later on we can skip around in our designing and creating; in this first lesson, however, let me lead you through it as if *I* were doing it.

18.1 "T" Topper (yarn supplied by Coats & Clark, Redheart®; knitted by Elaine Wang; modeled by Betty Wallace)

PERSONALIZING THE IDEA

Elaine wants to make a quick birthday gift for her tiny, slender daughter Sophia. The young student attends university in the northeast where the winters are damp and cold. Sophia usually wears slacks and long-sleeved shirts with a sweater over them.

Sophia is a shy and quiet young woman who loves natural warm earth colors—browns and greens and oranges. A solid, plain, heathery-soft orange would be an ideal color to blend with her wardrobe and highlight her dark hair and creamy skin. She likes small, delicate designs; she would never wear anything bright, bold, or dramatic. Both the sweater design and yarn must be simple and unobtrusive.

Since Sophia is a busy student with an active social life and has little time or space for hand-washing and drying flat, Elaine has chosen to make this sweater of machine-wash, machine-dry, 100 percent acrylic.

Elaine hasn't much time to get the sweater finished, so she is going to keep it simple—quick and easy—and the "T" Topper is just that.

Sophia's shoulders are narrow and sloping and added visual emphasis at that point would make them appear wider. Simple cast-on cap sleeves would do the trick, and Elaine will tuck in a set of shoulder pads with

Velcro® fastenings, so that her daughter can remove them if she wishes. It will be finished and in the mail on time.

On her, the sweater will look as it does in Figure 18.2.

Notice how the body type, age, coloring, personality, and lifestyle of the intended wearer have been taken into consideration as well as the knitter's own time schedule and preferences.

FLOOR PLAN OF THE PIECES

First with a pencil Elaine draws the general shapes of the pieces she will need. She arranges the individual pieces in the positions in which they will fit together. Pretending that the side and underarm seams are waiting to be sewn together, she puts the front on the bottom, the back upside down above it, and stretches the sleeves out to the sides. In this way, she can see and make sure that everything will fit together. When the piece layout is perfect, she goes over the final lines with a black pen and erases the extra pencil lines. (See Figure 18.3.)

18.2 Rough sketch of "T" Topper

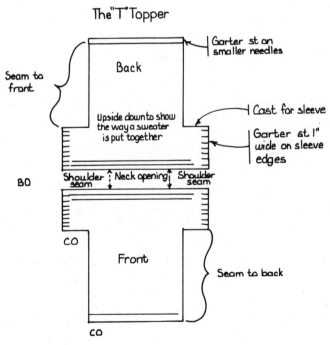

18.3 Layout of "T" Topper

THE YARN AND THE GAUGE

For this learning lesson standard 4-ply smooth classic knitting worsted (Class C) yarn was chosen. The knitter tried #8 aluminum single-pointed needles and was pleased with the look of the plain stockinette fabric and garter stitch for trim. Several rows of garter stitch were added to the swatch before binding off to make sure there was no difference in width between the stockinette and garter stitches. There was not. We measured the gauge.

WORKING GAUGE: 4.5 sts and 6 rows = 1″ on #8 needles

Then the swatch was machine-washed and -dried; it was treated just as Sophia will treat the finished sweater. The washed, dried, and rested swatch told us we were getting

FINISHED GAUGE: 4.58 sts and 6 rows = 1″

The tortured swatch had a stitch-gauge difference of .08 stitches per inch. This was not enough to bother with in this style of garment. (It is not unusual for the row gauge to stay the same while the stitch gauge changes.) The finished gauge is close enough to the working gauge that the knitter will have no problems in checking up on herself as she knits.

In this yarn, a good estimate is that the sweater in a woman's Small (32–34) size will take about 900 yds.

MEASUREMENTS NEEDED

Elaine looks at the floor plan, decides what measurements she will need, and writes them down on a piece of notebook paper. She will need the following:

1. *Desired length from nape of neck to botton edge;*
2. *Circumference of body at bottom edge of sweater;*
3. *Circumference of body at bust (or chest);*
4. *Difference between chest and bottom circumference* (to determine if there needs to be a bust dart or a change in width from chest to bottom);
5. *Desired upper arm width;*
6. *Desired length of add-on sleeves;*
7. *Desired length from underarm to bottom edge* (for a double-check on the figuring);
8. *Width across back between bra straps for neck opening.*

Sophia's college is far away from Georgia where her mother lives, but Elaine has the girl's measurements on hand from a visit last summer. A quick phone call lets her know that Sophia has neither gained nor lost weight. (Elaine didn't tell why she asked, because she wanted the birthday sweater to be a surprise.)

MARKING THE LENGTHS AND WIDTHS ON THE LAYOUT

Reassured that her measurements are correct, Elaine goes back to the layout drawing and starts filling in the lengths and widths in inches (or centimeters) with a red-colored pen:

1. Desired length from nape of neck to bottom edge: The sweater is planned to end about 5″ below the waistline. This will make the length from the nape of the neck to the bottom edge 17.5″. However, because of the boatneck design of the garment, the sweater will not rise up all the way to the nape of the neck; it will end and hang about 2″ lower. *Therefore the overall length of the sweater is 15.5″.*

      17.5″ (length from nape of neck to bottom edge)
   −   2″ (length between nape of neck and top edge)
  = 15.5″ (desired finished length of sweater)

The layout drawing (Figure 18.3) shows that the bottom and top of the sweater are trimmed with garter stitch, 1.25″ at the bottom and 1.25″ at the top.

     1.25″ (Garter st trim at bottom)
  + 1.25″ (garter st trim at top)
  = 2.5″ (total inches of trim)

We need to subtract this number from our 15.5″ of sweater length.

     15.5″ (desired finished length of sweater)
  − 2.5″ (total inches of trim)
  = 13″ (length of St st from bottom to top)

2. Circumference of body at bottom edge of sweater: We don't really know what this is. We do know what Sophia's hips measure, what her waist measures, and what the shape of her body is. Since the sweater is going to rest above her hips but needs to be wide enough to wear over slacks without fitting too snugly, we are going to manufacture the number by subtracting 1″ from her hip measurement.

$$35″ \text{ (actual body hip measure 7″ below waist)}$$
$$- \quad 1″ \text{ (ease subtracted because sweater ends only 5″ below waist)}$$
$$= 34″ \text{ (desired circumference at bottom edge)}$$

This number will have to be divided into two equal parts, half for the back and half for the front.

$$34″ \text{ (desired circumference at bottom edge)}$$
$$\div \quad 2 \text{ (half for back, half for front)}$$
$$= 17″ \text{ (desired bottom width each back and front)}$$

3. *Circumference of body at bust (or chest):* If a sweater is to be worn over other clothing it is traditional to add a bit of width called an ease allowance to keep the knitted fabric from being stretched. *Most designers add too much ease allowance; they forget the forgivingness of knitted fabric.* On this style garment for this tiny person using this yarn and stockinette stitch, *only 1 inch of ease will be necessary.*

$$32″ \text{ (actual body bust measurement)}$$
$$+ \quad 1″ \text{ (ease allowance)}$$
$$= 33″ \text{ (total desired chest circumference)}$$

This number also must be divided by 2, half for the front and half for the back.

$$33″ \quad \text{(total desired chest circumference)}$$
$$\div \quad 2 \quad \text{(half for back, half for front)}$$
$$= 16.5″ \text{ (desired chest width each front and back)}$$

Decimals will make it easier for us to calculate.

4. *Difference between chest and bottom circumference* (to determine if there needs to be a bust dart or a change in width from chest to bottom):

$$34″ \text{ (desired total circumference at bottom edge)}$$
$$- \quad 33″ \text{ (desired total circumference at bust)}$$
$$= \quad 1″ \text{ (difference between chest and bottom circumference)}$$

There isn't enough difference to bother with; there will be sufficient forgivingness in the knitted fabric to cover both the bust and the hips.

Neither bust dart nor change in width is necessary. We will make the bottom width 16.5".

5. *Desired upper arm width:* On a "T" Topper sweater with cast-on sleeves, the armhole is as deep as the sleeve is wide. When deciding how long/wide these sleeves should be, two things must be considered: 1) The distance from the cast-on stitches to the shoulder seam bind-off must be the length of the armhole plus a bit of ease. This amount of ease is not nearly so great as one might think *because when worn, the armhole slides off the shoulder and rests partway down the upper arm.* 2) This same length/width must of course be wide enough for the upper arm plus some ease. Adding the ease is no problem. Keeping the opening small enough is! *Don't make it too big.* Sophia's upper arm measures 10" in circumference. Her armhole depth is 6.5". Adding 4" of ease will solve both problems.

    10" (actual body upper arm circumference)
+   4" (ease allowance for style and because it will be worn over other garments)
= 14" (desired garment sleeve width/length at upper arm)

One-half the width of each of the sleeves will be an integral part of the back on each side of the body and the other half of the width will be an integral part of the front. Therefore we must divide the desired garment sleeve width/length by 2 to arrive at the add-on sleeve width/armhole depth.

    14" (desired garment sleeve width/length at upper arm)
÷   2 (half for back add-on, half for front add-on)
=   7" (add-on sleeve width/armhole depth each back and front)

Now look again at Figure 18.3. The last (top) 1.25" of the back/sleeve is worked in garter stitch in order to become the neck edge. Therefore we must stop making the stockinette stitch 1.25" before we make our final bind-off.

    7"   (add-on sleeve width and armhole depth each back and front)
− 1.25" (top garter st trim)
= 5.75" (length of St st from sleeve cast-on to beginning of top garter st trim)

6. *Desired length of add-on sleeves:* Look again at Figure 18.2. Notice how the sleeves extend down the arms both for warmth and to cover any shoulder seams on the blouse, but end above the elbow. On the

"T" Topper the length of the add-on sleeves depends on how many stitches will be cast on. I have made an arbitrary decision that 4" is an appropriate length to make these sleeves. Note also that of these 4" of cast-on stitches the outer 1" on each side will be worked in garter stitch.

> 4" (length of cast-on for sleeve length)
> − 1" (vertical garter st edge trim to cast on)
> = 3" (length of St st to be cast on)

7. *Double-checking the length from underarm to bottom:* The desired length on this sweater from underarm to bottom is 8". Let's see if it checks out. Out total desired length of the sweater is 15.5". Of this length the upper 7" will be consumed by the armhole/add-on sleeve. Now we must subtract the 7" (of sleeve length) from the 15.5" (total length), which leaves 8.5" between the bottom and the sleeve cast-on stitches.

> 15.5" (total desired length)
> − 7" (add-on sleeve width/armhole depth)
> = 8.5" (remaining length from underarm to bottom edge)

Does it check out *nearly the same* as our original estimate of 8"? Yes, it does. (The half-inch difference will be absorbed by the forgivingness of the fabric.)

Of this 8.5" of length from the bottom edge to the sleeve cast-on, 1.25" will be consumed by the bottom horizontal garter stitch trim.

> 8.5" (length from bottom edge to sleeve cast-on)
> − 1.25" (bottom edge garter st trim)
> = 7.25" (length of St st from top of bottom garter st trim to underarm cast-on)

8. *Width across back between bra straps for neck opening:* 10". This is a simple tape measure length in case the wearer ever decided to wear the sweater without other clothing under it.

With your red pen write in the desired lengths and widths in inches (or centimeters). (See Figure 18.4.)

Only when you know and have written down in the appropriate locations the desired widths and lengths can you begin to figure out the numbers of stitches.

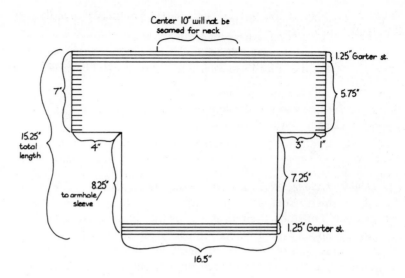

18.4 Actual measurements added to layout sketch of "T" Topper

DOING THE ARITHMETIC

GAUGE: Stockinette stitch—4.5 sts and 6 rows = 1″ on #8 straight needles

It is customary to figure the back of the sweater first simply because the back is usually less complicated than the front. When the numbers for the back are worked out, then the front with its (sometimes different) neck shaping is planned. The sleeves are usually designed last because their shaping is often dependent upon the back armhole shaping. This does not mean that the pieces must be knitted in this same order.

Beginning with the back on the bottom:

$$16.5″ \quad \text{(desired bottom width in inches)}$$
$$\times \quad 4.5 \quad \text{(gauge: sts per inch)}$$
$$= \quad 74.25 \quad \text{(st to cast on)}$$

Oops! There is no way in the world that we can cast on one-quarter of a stitch! We are going to have to change the 74.25 sts to either 74 or 75. Let's arbitrarily choose to round that number off to 74. Using the green pen on your layout at the bottom very close to the 16.5″ write "CO 74″."

Back: Beginning at the bottom CO 74 sts on smaller needles so that trim will be firm.

Next, our piece layout tells us that we have 1.25″ of garter stitch to make.

Work even in garter st until piece measures 1.25″ from CO.

At this point our layout shows plain stockinette stitch to the point where we cast on for the sleeves. Our layout drawing tells us the distance that we are going to make stockinette stitch is 7.25″. We must change to the larger needles we will use for the rest of the sweater.

Change to larger needles. Work even in St st 7.25″ until piece measures 8.5″ overall.

Mark the above information on your drawing with your green pen.

Now it is time to cast on the extra stitches for the sleeves. Look again at Figure 18.4. We have decided that 4″ long is an appropriate length to make these sleeves, of which the outer 1″ will be garter stitch.

$$
\begin{array}{rl}
4'' & \text{(width to be added each side for sleeves)} \\
\times \quad 4.5 & \text{(gauge: sts per inch)} \\
\hline
= \quad 18 & \text{(sts to cast on for each sleeve)}
\end{array}
$$

Look at the layout drawing, Figure 18.4. See the garter stitch at the outer edge of each of the cast-on sleeves? Hand-knitters can work both garter stitch edges and stockinette stitch body on the same needles at the same time. Machine-knitters cannot.

$$
\begin{array}{rl}
1'' & \text{(desired width of garter st trim)} \\
\times \quad 4.5 & \text{(gauge: sts per inch)} \\
\hline
= \quad 4.5 & \text{(sts of garter st)} \\
= \quad 5 & \text{(rounded off to the next whole st)} \\
\\
18 & \text{(total sts to cast on for each sleeve)} \\
- \quad 5 & \text{(sts will be garter st)} \\
\hline
= \quad 13 & \text{(sts of St st to be cast on)}
\end{array}
$$

At the end of the next 2 rows, CO 13 sts, place a marker (to note the following 5 sts are to be worked in garter st), CO 5 sts more. (18 sts cast on ea side and 110 sts rem.)

Mark the above information on your drawing with a green pen.

Now look again at Figure 18.4. The last (top) 1.25″ of the back/sleeve is worked in garter stitch in order to become the neck edge. Therefore we must stop making the stockinette stitch 1.25" before we want the armhole/sleeve/length/width to end, which is the same as 5.75" from cast-on of sleeves. We must change to the smaller needles we used for the bottom trim.

Change to smaller needles. Keeping 5 sts ea side in garter st, work even in St st 5.75". Change to all garter st. Work even in garter st 1.25". (Armhole/sleeve measure 7" from cast-on. Piece measures 15.5" overall.)
Loosely BO.
Work front same as back.

Mark the above information on your drawing with a green pen. Your drawing will now look like Figure 18.5.

FINISHING THE SWEATER

If you will go back to your drawing (Figure #18.5) and look at the directions that are in green ink, that is all the instructions many of you will need to make the sweater. Some people do not like to bother with the written-out instructions and prefer to knit directly from the notated layout drawing.

For other knitters the layout is incomprehensible, and these people prefer to use written directions. If you will now go back and read the

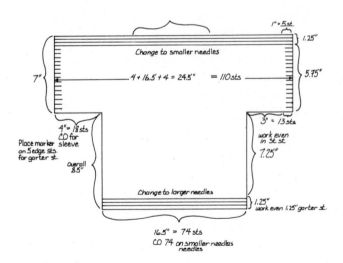

18.5 "T" Topper layout with measurements, stitches, rows, and instructions

bold print in the preceding "Doing the Arithmetic" section, you will have the written instructions for making this garment.

Whether you choose to go to the extra effort of writing out the instruction will depend upon you and the person for whom you are designing. In the next few chapters I will continue to include the written words. After that, when you know how to do it, I'll just use the layout and cut down on the verbiage.

VARIATIONS

You can use either smooth classic worsted or novelty yarn with equally good effect. Likewise, you can use any fiber or blend yarn. In ribbon, the "T" Topper becomes an evening blouse. In cotton or cool silk or linen, it is a summer topper. In wool, acrylic, or mohair, it slides over a blouse or cotton turtleneck for warmer winter wear.

Make it short-short midriff length for a cool summer topper.

Make it extralong (past the crotch) to wear as a warmer-upper over leotards and tights on the way home from exercise class.

Though the example above is designed with cast-on sleeves, the sweater can be made without them. Instead the pullover could be two plain rectangles. Simply follow the plan up to 1 inch before the point of casting on the sleeves. At that location, place a ring marker 5 stitches in from each edge. Work those 5 stitches on both sides in garter stitch to form an edging for the armholes, and don't cast on the extra sleeve stitches. Other than that, finish the garment in the same way.

If you like circular work, you can add the back and front stitches together and work the sweater in the round. At the armholes you can either make a steek (see Chapter 14) to be cut open later or place half the stitches on another (smaller) circular needle to act as a stitch holder and work the back and front separately.

Make colored stripes. You can stripe with two colors in equal amounts or you can let the stripes get thinner and farther apart as you work up. You can use lots of different colors in a striping pattern and have a knock-the-eye-out topper.

Make visual textured stripes simply by changing the pattern stitch occasionally. How about stockinette stitch for 1½ inches, an inch or two of seed stitch, some more stockinette, and then perhaps an Irish moss or Guernsey pebbly stitch. (When changing pattern stitch without changing yarn, I think it looks very effective to throw up a purl ridge★

★A *purl ridge* is one row (or round) of plain stitches that will appear on the public side as a horizontal line that protrudes slightly from the background. If made on the public side, purl; if made on the private side, knit.

to the public side in order to highlight such a change.)

If you want to avoid making a shoulder seam, you can work the back and front flat, that is, back and forth, all in one continuous piece. Bind off only the center back neck stitches. On the next row, immediately cast on the center front neck stitches and just keep on going.

Or you can do any of the above in combination.

CONCLUSION

This is a good and adaptable beginner's sweater *for people with sloping shoulders.* On square-shouldered people the center front neck will either rub the chin or, if the stitch gauge is loose, sag to accommodate the front neck, which will make any added stripes sag correspondingly.

If either the yarn or the knitted fabric is stiff, the sweater may look like a capital letter *T* and stand out away from the body because the shoulders are not sloped. This will be especially true if you do not add the sleeves.

On full-hipped, full-chested, or barrel-chested people this sweater won't look so hot. In fact, it may look terrible.

19

The "Da Vinci Man" Sweater

Drop-Shouldered Long-Sleeved Boatneck Pullover

In this chapter you will learn how to:

1. *Make ribbing come out the right width;*
2. *Plan increases evenly across a row;*
3. *Plan decreases evenly across a row;*
4. *Figure tapered sleeves and read instructions for simple diagonal line increases;*
5. *Design for a rectangular body type.*

THE IDEA

The second garment we are going to learn to design is the sweater we talked about in Part I, the sweater for the man in a da Vinci drawing with his arms outstretched.

This is an easy sweater to design, consisting of two basic pattern pieces—the back, which is repeated for the front, and two identical sleeves. These four sections are seamed together at the sleeve-drop-shoulder joining and at the underarms. Take a pencil and make a sketch of how the finished sweater will look. (See Figure 19.2.)

Because it is so easy to design, the "Da Vinci Man" sweater is encountered in almost every knitting magazine and pattern leaflet. But, as I said in Part I, it fits few people. On the garment itself, the shoulders have no slope to them; there is no differentiation in the neck opening

19.1 "Da Vinci Man" sweater worn by rectangular body type with turtleneck underneath (yarn supplied by Unger; knitted by Shirley Robb; modeled by Danny Darby)

19.2 Rough sketch of Da Vinci Man sweater, with two shades of the same color (light with dark trim)

between front and back; the chest and hips are the same size; the wearer is intended to walk around all day with arms outstretched. God did not design many humans with that kind of body or posture. Nonetheless, I'm going to take you through the steps of creating the Da Vinci Man sweater in its pure and simple form. Later, when you've learned more, you can modify it so that it becomes a comfortable, wearable sweater for the kinds of bodies and posture that most people have.

FLOOR PLAN OF THE PIECES

Please note, in Figure 19.3, that on the back and the front and the bottoms of the sleeves, the ribbing area is indented. *This does not mean that they will be indented on the final garment.* This is just sweater designers' hieroglyphics to alert knitters that there is a different number of stitches on the ribbing than on the body fabric of the garment.

PERSONALIZING THE IDEA

Take into consideration the body type, sex, age, coloring, personality, and lifestyle of the intended wearer as well as your own time schedule and preferences.

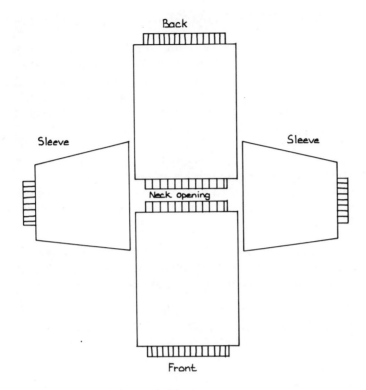

19.3 Layout of Da Vinci Man sweater

Recall a real male in your life, or conjure up a mythical one, because I want you to go through the steps of making sure that you are designing the right sweater for this person.

Your man may be entirely different from my man, but the following is what I came up with:

Body type: Rectangular, 6′ tall, 175 pounds
Age: 20
Sex: Male
Coloring: Skin ruddy and somewhat tanned; hair light brown
Personality: Quiet and retiring
Color Preference: "I like any color so long as it is blue."
Lifestyle: College student, cross-country skier, and winter-sports fan
Knitter's time schedule: Need for Christmas (it is now July); six months is plenty of time
Knitter's preference: Prefers wool. Doesn't mind acrylic. Likes blends. Allergic to mohair and rabbit

THE YARN AND THE GAUGE

This sweater works well in wool, cotton, acrylic, or blend yarns. It can be worn either over a shirt, blouse, or turtleneck, or by itself.

I look in the yarn shops and find Unger's "Aries," a smooth classic standard 4-ply worsted (Class C), a machine-washable blend of 45 percent wool and 55 percent acrylic, in two tones of the same blue. Each 100-gram skein contains approximately 180 yards.

My handy "Pocket Yarn Yardage Guide©" suggests that I will need 1,450 yards for a man's Large (44–46) long-sleeved pullover in worsted weight, but I know that I am knitting for not only a tall person but also an active one and I may need more yarn, so I opt to get extra. Seven skeins of color B, plus two skeins of color A used for ribbing trim should be sufficient.

It is important to know the type, content, and characteristics of the yarn as well as the pattern stitch at this point, because it will affect the style and the amount of ease added.

I play with the yarn, making swatches and, though I would love to go fancy and make Gansy-type patterns, I settle on a twisted minirib-bing and ordinary stockinette stitch because the intended wearer doesn't like anything showy or ostentatious.

WORKING GAUGE: Stockinette stitch—4.5 sts and 6 rows = 1″ on #5 needles.
Twisted minicable rib—4.5 sts and 7.5 rows = 1″ on #4 needles

FINISHED (TORTURED) GAUGE: After machine-washing and -drying the swatch measures the same as above.

MEASUREMENTS NEEDED

1. *Circumference of the chest*
2. *Desired circumference of sweater at bottom edge*
3. *Desired length from nape of back neck to bottom edge*
4. *Desired length from underarm to bottom of sweater*
5. *Desired upper arm width*
6. *Desired length of sleeves*
7. *Desired width of sleeves at lower arm*

1. Circumference of the chest: I get an actual measurement of 43.5″, but will round it up to 44″, then add another 1″ for ease because this is a winter sweater and will be worn over a shirt or cotton turtleneck.

44″ (43.5, body chest circumference, rounded up to whole number)
+   1″ (ease allowance)
= 45″ (total desired chest circumference)

So the desired number circling the chest is 45″. Half will be in the back and half will be in the front.

45″   (total desired chest circumference)
÷   2   (half for back, half for front)
= 22.5″ (width each back and front)

The width of each of these sections will therefore be 22.5″. I mark these numbers on my layout drawing in red.

The ribbing at the bottom and the top will be worked on smaller size needles and will contain fewer stitches than the stockinette-stitch body. Since it is usually a percentage of the number of body stitches, I can wait to include this figure until I know how many stitches there will be on the body (it is easier for me that way.)

2. Desired circumference of sweater at bottom edge: The actual body measurement is 45″—only 1″ different from the chest width. I decide that there isn't sufficient deviation between chest and desired bottom circumference to bother with. This is normal for a rectangular figure. The back and the front will have the same chest and bottom edge width of 22.5″. I mark these numbers on the layout drawing in red.

3. Desired length from nape of back neck to bottom edge: 29″. This is a direct measurement from the intended wearer. You may find this length surprisingly long. Recollect that under "Body Type" a few paragraphs ago, I said that he was tall; under "Lifestyle," I said that he liked active winter sports. Also remember from Chapter 5, "Understanding Body Shapes," I showed you three sketches of human bodies engaged in active sports. Now close your eyes and recall from watching winter sports on TV the movements a cross-country skier makes. I think I can safely assume that my intended user will wear this sweater skiing, and I wouldn't want him to have gaps between the bottom of the sweater and the top of his pants as he glides over the snow.

Because of the habit of Da Vinci Man sweaters to ride up at the front neck and down at the back neck, I am going to subtract 1.5″ from the total desired length of 29″.

29″   (nape of neck to bottom edge)
−   1.5″ (allowance for drop at back neck)
= 27.5″ (desired finished sweater length)

Part of that remaining 27.5" will be consumed by bottom and top ribbing trim. Such a large body requires a lengthy ribbing. I decide on 2.5" bottom ribbing. The ribbing at the top can be a bit shorter. Let's make a 2" top ribbing.

$$
\begin{array}{ll}
& 27.5\text{"} \text{ (desired finished sweater length)} \\
- & 2.5\text{"} \text{ (length of ribbing at bottom)} \\
- & 2\text{"} \text{ (length of ribbing at top)} \\
\hline
= & 23\text{"} \text{ (length of St st fabric between ribbings)}
\end{array}
$$

I mark these numbers in red on my drawing.

4. Desired length from underarm to bottom edge, and *5) Desired upper arm width:* Both of these dimensions must be considered in the same breath when designing a Da Vinci Man sweater. Look again at the way the layout pieces are arranged, and then look at Figure 19.2. From the layout you will quickly realize that

on drop-shoulder sweaters, the desired upper arm width is the same as the total (back and front) armhole depth.

Also you will see that subtracting one-half of the total sleeve top width from the overall length of either the front or the back gives the desired length from underarm to bottom. You can't get one without the other! My own particular rectangular-shaped man works out with weights and his actual upper arm circumference is 17". He will need at least 2" or 3" of ease added.

$$
\begin{array}{ll}
& 17\text{"} \text{ (actual upper arm circumference)} \\
+ & 3\text{"} \text{ (ease allowance)} \\
\hline
= & 20\text{"} \text{ (desired width of sleeve at upper arm)}
\end{array}
$$

The greatest width of the sleeve therefore needs to be about 20". To accommodate this width, the combined back and front armhole depth of the body needs to be at least this same number of inches.

His actual body underarm depth measured as described in Chapter 6 with a knitting needle in the armpit is 9.75", but this isn't really relevant because on the Da Vinci Man sweater there is no underarm shaping, just a flag marker indicating where to attach the sleeves. Moreover, once on the body, the area from the joining of the sleeve to the top of the shoulder hangs off the edge of the shoulders and down along the arm. Look again at Figure 19.2 to prove to yourself that I'm not leading you astray. *On the Da Vinci Man sweater the armhole does NOT always need to be as deep as the actual body depth nor does any breathing room always have to be added to the armhole depth.* I repeat, "There are no constants in designing sweaters." Consider the width of the sleeve at the upper arm, the depth of the armhole, and the amount of length that remains, the length from underarm to top of bottom ribbing.

We will throw all three numbers up in the air and juggle them like a circus performer does balls.

If this sweater were for a sedentary figure, I would be happy making that armhole as short as 9" with a corresponding sleeve top width of 18". However, my sweater user is going to be moving his arms in great sweeping motions as he propels himself over chilly trails. I'm arbitrarily going to make the armhole depth 10", which necessitates an upper arm width of 20" to match the opening.

> 10" (back armhole depth)
> + 10" (front armhole depth)
> = 20" (final upper arm sleeve width)

Because the final upper arm sleeve width is 20", the total (back and front combined) armhole depth is also 20".

20" (upper arm sleeve width) = 20" (entire armhole depth)

Half of this 20" of armhole depth will be on the front, and half on the back.

> 20" (upper arm sleeve width/entire armhole depth)
> ÷ 2 (half for back, half for front)
> = 10" (depth of each back and front armhole)

Look one more time at Figures 19.2 and 19.3. Notice the horizontal band of ribbing across the top of the garment. I have decided that this will be 2" long, and it will be necessary to adjust the length of stockinette stitch on the armhole part of the body down to 8".

> 10" (depth of each back and front body armhole)
> − 2" (ribbing on top of each back and front)
> = 8" (length of St st after beginning of armhole before top ribbing)

For a double-check, figure the length from bottom to underarm as follows:

> 29" (actual body length)
> − 1.5" (drop from top nape of neck)
> = 27.5" (total finished length of sweater body)
> − 10" (armhole depth)
> = 17.5" (length from underarm to bottom edge of sweater)

That number agrees with my original measurement of 27.5".

Mark all these numbers in red on the layout drawings of the body and sleeve.

6. *Desired length of sleeves:* Sleeve length from underarm to bottom at wrist including bottom trim measured 20″ on my tall rectangular-shaped man. Personally, I like a healthy length of ribbing on the bottom of the sleeve so that it can be turned up or down according to the preference of the wearer. I decide on a 2.5″-long ribbing, which will leave 17.5″ of stockinette stitch on the sleeve.

$$
\begin{array}{rl}
20'' & \text{(total sleeve length)} \\
-\quad 2.5'' & \text{(wrist ribbing length on bottom of sleeve)} \\
\hline
=\ 17.5'' & \text{(St st from top of wrist rib to bind-off)}
\end{array}
$$

Mark this number in red on the layout drawing.

7. *Desired width of sleeves at lower arm:* The sleeve width just above the wrist ribbing will need to be 12″. The 12″ is *not* an actual body measurement taken around the wrist. It represents an "average for the size" of the circumference of the lower arm between the elbow and the wrist plus ease. (See Leisure Arts' Standards in the Appendix, page 388.) Sweater sleeves just seem to work better using a measurement like this and then "gathering in" for the wrist ribbing than if the knitted fabric were precisely tapered from underarm to exact wrist measurement.

Mark this number on your drawing in red ink.

The ribbing itself will be worked on smaller-size needles and will have fewer stitches than the stockinette stitch. Again, I will calculate these figures later after I multiply by gauge.

You will notice that I have determined, checked, and rechecked every length and width. Only after all of the lengths and widths are carefully calculated and written on the drawing can we determine the appropriate numbers of stitches.

DOING THE ARITHMETIC

On both my freshly made and my washed, tortured, and dried stockinette stitch swatches, I get the following gauges:

GAUGE: Stockinette stitch—4.5 sts and 6 rows = 1″
Ribbing—4.5 sts and 7.5 rows = 1″

It is now time to get out the pocket calculator and start multiplying. Then, using the green pen, fill in the numbers on our layout. *Body (back and front each):* Multiply the number of inches of desired width (22.5″) by the stitch gauge (4.5).

>   22.5″ (desired width of each front and back)
>   ×   4.5 (gauge: sts per inch)
>   = 101.25 (total number of sts to make each back and front)

No one can make one-fourth of one stitch, so round the number off to 101. 101 is a messy number so round that down to 100. (Back and front are each 100 stitches wide.)

Write this in green ink just below where you show the width by inches. *But this is not the number of stitches that we will cast on for the ribbing.*

FIGURING OUT THE BOTTOM RIBBING

How many fewer stitches will the bottom ribbing have? I personally like to have 10 percent less.

10% less than the total is the same as 90% of the total.

If you are familiar with working percentages on your calculator, figure 90% of 100 = 90.

If you are not familiar with figuring percentages on your calculator, simply multiply the decimal equivalent (90% = .9) times the 100 stitches.

>   100 (number of sts on body back)
>   ×   .9 (equivalent of 90%)
>   = 90 (approximate number of ribbing sts)

The ribbing will be approximately 90 stitches wide. Now let's refine that number. We know that our twisted minicable rib has a multiple of 3 stitches (on the public side, 1 purl and 2 knit stitches). A seam will have to be woven and so we need to add 1 more stitch (a purl stitch) at the end of the row. This makes our multiple 3 + 1.

Let's see how many complete multiples we can get into our (approximately) 90 sts.

>   90 (approximate number of ribbing sts)
>   ÷ 3 (ribbing pattern st multiple)
>   = 30 (number of multiples across ribbing)

Ninety stitches will give us 30 complete patterns across. (We're lucky that it came out even this time. It won't always, and in a later chapter we'll learn to fiddle and fudge until it does.)

Adding the 1 plus stitch to our 90 stitches, we get 91 as the number of stitches to cast on.

Using smaller needles and color A, cast on 91. Work in twisted minicable for 2.5″ ending after completing a private-side row.

Now it is time to 1) increase the number of stitches horizontally across the row to the number necessary for the stockinette stitch body, 2) change the needle size to a larger one, and 3) change the yarn color. *But don't do all on the same row!*

Reason #1: Never change color and pattern stitch on the same row. Unsightly purl beads of the old color will appear on the first row of the new color.

Reason #2: Life is hard enough without adding unnecessary aggravations. Changing to a larger-size needle on the row on which you are also trying to make increases is an extreme aggravation, and difficult to do. Not only does the larger-size needle have to be forced into the stitches, but also increases need to be made.

The exact instructions to do all three things—increase stitches, change pattern stitch, and change color—will be written into the instructions as we go along.

In Chapter 16 we talked about thinking of percentages in terms of units. Recall that it was very easy to think of 10 percent in units of *ten*. To increase by 10 percent meant simply to complete the unit of 10, or "K 9, inc using French M-1 method" across.

With the public side of the piece facing you, and using smaller-size needles, inc'ing 9 stitches evenly across (i.e., approx after every 9th st) make 1 knit row. (100 sts rem.)

Of course, you will count the number of stitches remaining when you are almost across the row and adjust accordingly.

Change to a larger-size needle and color B and purl across to estab St st.

Work even in St st until piece measures 15″ from beg of St st (17.5″ overall). Place flag markers on each side edge of the work to note bottom edge of sleeve joining.

Work even until piece measures 23″ from beg of St st (25.5″ overall).

PLAN DECREASES FOR TOP RIBBING

One of the joys of designing your own sweaters is in changing your mind as you knit along *with knowledge and understanding* so that you get just the effect you want. Standard knitting design practice would be simply to decrease 10 percent of stitches across to 91 stitches and repeat the ribbing of the bottom for 2″. Bind off all stitches. But as your own designer you can do whatever you want. Is the bottom ribbing just exactly the width you wish the top ribbing to be? Too stretchy? Too tight? Too wide? Too narrow? You don't have to repeat the bottom ribbing at the top. You can alter the amounts. Simply count the number of pattern repeats on the already completed bottom and determine how many stitches wide you wish *your* top ribbing to be. In this case, we would multiply by 3 stitches for each multiple and then add the 1 plus stitch for the seam.

However, for the sake of learning, on this sweater let's choose to use 20 percent fewer stitches of ribbing than the body width. Twenty percent less is the same as 80 percent of the number of stockinette stitch body stitches.

```
      .2  (equivalent of 20%, the amount to decrease)
 ×  100   (existing sts on body)
 =   20   (approximate number of sts to decrease)
```

Then we must refine the "approximate number" to make our pattern stitch multiple work out correctly.

```
    100  (existing sts on body)
 −   20  (approximate number of sts to decrease)
 =   80  (approximate number of sts to remain for ribbing)
```

The final stitches that remain must be divisible by our multiple of 3 + 1.

```
    80     (approximate number of ribbing sts)
 ÷   3     (number of sts in multiple)
 = 26.66   (approximate number of patterns across)
```

Round the 26.66 up to 27 and multiply by the number of stitches in the multiple.

```
   27  (desired number of patterns across)
 ×  3  (number of sts in multiple)
 = 81  (number of sts needed to make 27 complete multiples across)
```

Now add in the 1 plus stitch.

```
  81 (number of sts needed to make complete multiples)
+  1 (final st necessary for seam)
= 82 (number of sts after decreasing across)
```

If we want 82 stitches to remain, this will change our approximate number of stitches to decrease from body to ribbing. We need to refine that approximate number of 20 (which was 20 percent of the stitches).

```
   100 (sts on body)
−   82 (desired number of sts to remain for ribbing)
=   18 (sts to decrease from body to ribbing)
```

When making the actual decreases themselves, recall Chapter 16. Think of a 20 percent decrease in units of 5—you are taking 5 stitches down to 4. *Be sure to alternate types of decreases to avoid a corkscrew* as follows: *K 3, k 2 tog, k 3, SSK*. K 2 tog slopes to the right and SSK slopes to the left.

In this instance of wanting an almost, but not quite exact, decrease of 20 percent equally spaced across, omit the first and last decrease on the row to come out with the desired number of stitches.

MULTIPLY THE NUMBERS OF STITCHES FOR THE SLEEVES

The underarm width at the top of the sleeve is 20".

```
   20" (width at top of sleeve)
×  4.5 (gauge: sts per inch)
= 90   (sts of width at top of sleeve)
```

Add this number to your layout diagram. The desired width above the wrist is 12 inches.

```
   12" (width just above wrist ribbing)
×  4.5 (gauge: sts per inch)
= 54   (sts of width just above wrist ribbing)
```

The desired width at the wrist is 8".

There are many ways to figure the desired number of wrist ribbing stitches.

We will discuss only one way in this chapter: multiply desired width in inches by gauge.

```
   8" (desired width of wrist)
×  4.5 (gauge of ribbing: sts per inch)
= 36   (approximate number of wrist ribbing sts)
```

Divide by the pattern stitch multiple to see if it comes out even.

$$
\begin{array}{ll}
36 & \text{(approximate number of wrist ribbing sts)} \\
\div \quad 3 & \text{(pattern st multiple)} \\
\hline
= \quad 12 & \text{(number of patterns across)}
\end{array}
$$

Yes, it does. Now multiply back by the pattern stitch multiple.

$$
\begin{array}{ll}
12 & \text{(number of pattern st multiples)} \\
\times \quad 3 & \text{(pattern st multiples)} \\
\hline
= \quad 36 & \text{(revised approximate number of wrist ribbing sts)} \\
+ \quad 1 & \text{(1 plus st for seam)} \\
\hline
= \quad 37 & \text{(final number of sts to cast on for sleeve/wrist ribbing)}
\end{array}
$$

Mark the chosen numbers of stitches in green on your layout drawing near the number of inches written in red.

Sleeves: With smaller needles and A, CO 37 sts. Work even in rib pat st to 2.5″ ending after completing a private-side row.

Now we have to figure out how many stitches to increase horizontally across from 37 (number of ribbing stitches) to 54 (number of sleeve stockinette stitches). Subtract the smaller number from the larger number.

$$
\begin{array}{ll}
54 & \text{(desired number of sleeve sts just above the wrist)} \\
- \quad 37 & \text{(number of wrist ribbing sts)} \\
\hline
= \quad 17 & \text{(number of sts to increase horizontally across the row at top of} \\
& \text{ribbing)}
\end{array}
$$

How shall we figure out how frequently to make those increases? That is, "make 1 increase after every *how many* stitches?" There are a number of ways to do this, and it can be figured out very accurately, but I prefer to use an approximation of the percentage method that we used for increasing after the back body ribbing. It is not perfectly accurate, but it's quick and easy to do. Recall from Chapter 16 that

to find out what percentage of one number another smaller one is, we divide the big number into the little one.

$$
\begin{array}{ll}
17 & \text{(number of sts we wish to increase)} \\
\div \quad 37 & \text{(number of sts across in which we have to make our increases)} \\
\hline
= \quad .45 & \text{(decimal equivalent of the percentage of sts that need to be} \\
& \text{increased)}
\end{array}
$$

The number .459 is very close to 50 percent. So, if we were to think in units of 3, that is, from every 2 stitches make 1 more to complete the unit of 3, we would come very close to getting our desired 17 increased stitches.

Remembering what we learned before about not changing *both* pattern stitch and color on the same row, we would write:

With the public-side of the piece facing you, and using smaller-size needles, inc'ing 17 sts evenly across (i.e., approx after 2nd st), make 1 knit row. (54 sts rem.) Change to larger-size needle and B and purl across to estab St st.

INCREASING THE WIDTH OF THE SIDES OF THE SLEEVES AND FIGURING TAPERED SLEEVES

Now we must figure and plot the increases on the sides of the sleeves from these 54 stitches of width just above the ribbing to the desired width at the top. (See Figure 19.4.) Recall that you marked down on your layout drawing how many stitches you wished to end up with. The number was 90.

Subtract from the number of stitches needed at the top the number of stitches currently existing on the bottom (just above the ribbing).

```
      90 (sts of width at top of sleeve)
   −  54 (sts just above wrist)
   =  36 (total number of sts to be increased along the sides of sleeve)
```

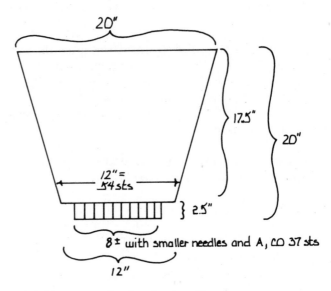

19.4 Sleeve layout showing planning of increases

Next divide the remainder by 2, because half of the stitches will be increased on the right-hand side and half will be increased on the left-hand side.

    36 (total number of sts to be increased along sides of sleeve)
  ÷ 2 (half for right side, half for left side)
  = 18 (sts to be increased on each side of sleeve)

On the Da Vinci Man sweater it is okay to make our increases at the beginning *and* at the end of the length available, because this type of sweater already has a problem with too much fabric under the arms. Therefore we will have 18 increases but only 17 spans. Seventeen is the number we will use in determining the spacing of the increase points. (In a later chapter we will learn to shape sleeve underarm increases in a different way.)

How much length will we have in which to make these 18 increases on each side of the sleeve? When we were figuring the lengths and widths in inches a few pages ago, we decided that there would be 17.5″ of stockinette stitch from the top of the wrist ribbing to the bind-off.

Before we work out the final/perfected plan for our increases, let's do some arithmetic. We have a total of 17.5″ with which to work.

      17.5 (total length of St st of sleeve)
  ×   6 (gauge: rows per inch)
  = 105.0 (maximum possible rows)

Pulling a number out of a hat, if we were to increase every 6th row how many rows would that consume?

    17 (spans between increases)
  × 6 (increase made every 6th row)
  = 102 (rows would be used up for increase/spans)

Hey, this works out just fine! We have a total of 105 rows with which to work out our increases, and only 102 of those rows would be consumed by making 18 increases, 1 on every 6th row. We can fudge with the lengths of the spans at the top and the bottom of our sequence of increases to take up that 3-row difference.

With all of these numbers of stitches and other notations written in, your drawing will now look like Figures 19.5 and 19.6.

Experienced knitters will use the notes and numbers, written in green ink on the diagrams of the garment pieces. I didn't choose green and red ink for the numbers just by chance.

Green is for GO; red is for STOP and check the width with a tape measure.

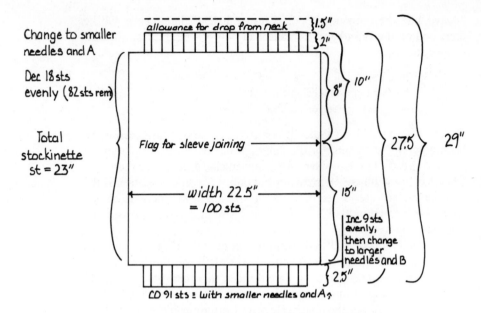

Change to smaller needles and A

Dec 18 sts evenly (82 sts rem)

Total stockinette st = 23"

allowance for drop from neck — }1.5"
}2"

8" 10"

Flag for sleeve joining

width 22.5" = 100 sts

27.5   29"

15"

Inc 9 sts evenly, then change to larger needles and B

}2.5"

CD 91 sts = with smaller needles and A?

19.5 Da Vinci Man sweater with measurements, stitches, rows, and instructions

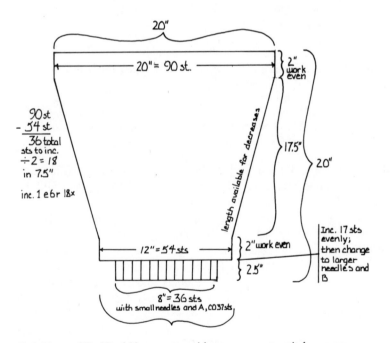

20"

20" = 90 st.

2" work even

90 st
− 54 st
36 total sts to inc.
÷2 = 18
in 7.5"

inc. 1 e 6r 18x

length available for decreases

17.5"   20"

12" = 54 sts

2" work even

2.5"

Inc. 17 sts evenly; then change to larger needles and B

8" = 36 sts
with small needles and A, co37sts

19.6 Sleeve of Da Vinci Man sweater with measurements, stitches, rows, and instructions

Those knitters happier with word-for-word explanations can go back and follow the directions in bold print in "Doing the Arithmetic," pages 208–214.

Note: This is the last time that we will write out all the words. Hereafter, unless I am teaching you a new technique, we will use the green-ink notations only.

VARIATIONS

To accommodate the fact that the front neck is lower on the torso than the back neck, simply making the front of the sweater a bit shorter between the armhole marking flag and the beginning of the neck ribbing, and making the back of the sweater a bit longer in the corresponding place, will allow the back to ride up higher and drop the front lower. A 2" difference in length will usually solve the problem.

After you learn in later chapters how it is done, you can shape the shoulders better with stairsteps.

After you learn in later chapters how to shape sleeve caps, you can alter the design of the sleeves to fit better and avoid so much bulk at the underarms. (See Figure 19.7.)

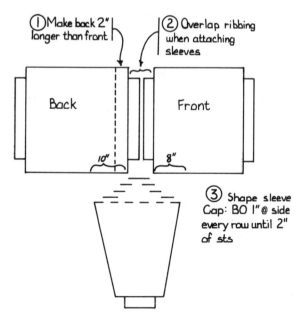

19.7 Layout of modified Da Vinci Man sweater

Add back and front together and work in the round to armhole flag, put in a steek*, keep on knitting up to the top, and cut two openings, one for each sleeve.

The sleeves can be worked from the top down or from the bottom up. Especially if you are working in a striping pattern, going from the top down makes life much easier. The sleeve stripes will always match the body stripes. The sleeves can be worked as separate pieces or, if you don't mind the extra weight while working, after the shoulder seam is sewn, pick up the stitches for the top of the sleeves and work the sleeves down (one less seam to weave).

Use any other type of ribbing.

Stripe with either different colors or yarns. (See Chapter 34, "Creating Your Own Interesting Effects: Stripes, Intarsia, Different-Colored Cables.")

Use the same yarn, but stripe with different pattern stitches, setting off the changes with a purl ridge row.

If working flat, back and forth, use either argyle or intarsia designs.

All of the above in combination (except it is impossible to do argyle or intarsia in the round).

CONCLUSION

As originally designed, the Da Vinci Man sweater has too much bulk at the underarms and rides too low at the back neck and too high at the front neck. It makes no concession for people with different-size chest and hips.

---

*For definition of *steek* see Chapter 14.

20

The Puff-Sleeved
Boatnecked Beauty

In this chapter you will learn how to:

1. *Work with nonresilient yarns,*
    a. *What to do about the ribbing;*
    b. *How to plan any ease allowance;*
2. *Plan when the working and finished gauges are not the same;*
3. *Use a different yarn for ribbing trim;*
4. *Plan for "blousing" ease for waist-length sweaters;*
5. *Increase at side seams from waist to bust;*
6. *Shape body armhole for set-in sleeves;*
7. *Shape sleeve armhole for set-in sleeves;*
8. *Plan puff sleeves;*
9. *Design for a triangular body type.*

THE IDEA

Now that we have mastered the basics of plotting and planning, multiplying and marking, we can begin to learn to do some shaping. Let's begin by learning to shape from a small waist to a larger bust, and let's also begin to make "real" armholes for real people instead of stick figures.

An ideal sweater on which to learn these lessons is the "Waist-Length

20.1 Puff-Sleeved Boatnecked Beauty and gathered skirt worn by triangular-shaped young girl (yarn supplied by Bernat and Phildar; knitted by Betty Wallace; modeled by Lisa Wallace)

20.2 Rough sketch of Puff-Sleeved Boatnecked Beauty

Puff-Sleeved Boatnecked Beauty.'' In the chapter on flattering body types, I drew a picture of it being worn by the swanlike triangular figure. (See Figure 20.2.)

As with the Da Vinci Man sweater, there are only two basic pattern pieces: the front-back and the sleeves. Each piece is made twice to form the four parts of the sweater. (See Figure 20.3.)

FLOOR PLAN OF THE PIECES

Recall one of the drawbacks we found with the DaVinci Man sweater—that the front neck does not drop down low enough. Look at the floor plan and see how this problem can be solved. The length of the back armhole of the sweater is *longer than* the length of the front armhole. This difference in length, *combined with* overlapping the front and back ribbing areas when we sew the sweater together, will make the front neck drop down to a comfortable wearing height without causing the sweater to sag across the upper chest of the wearer.

THE YARN AND THE GAUGE

Body: Bernat "Cajun Cotton," 100 percent cotton, worsted-weight (Class C) novelty yarn, approximately 180 yards per 100-gram ball.

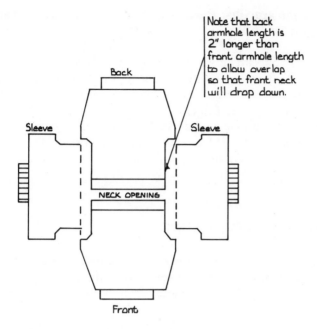

20.3 Layout of Puff-Sleeved Boatnecked Beauty

WORKING GAUGE: Stockinette stitch—5 sts and 7 rows = 1″ on #4 needles

FINISHED GAUGE: Stockinette stitch—4.75 sts and 7 rows on #4 needles

Ribbing: Phildar "Cotton D'Egypte 4½," 100% mercerized cotton, worsted weight (Class C) glossy yarn, approximately 93 yards per 50-gram ball,

WORKING GAUGE: 1 × 1 ribbing—5.25 sts = 1″ (stretched) on #4 needles

The working stitch gauge and the finished/wearing stitch gauge are NOT the same. The working row gauge and the finished/wearing row gauge ARE the same. Washing causes the fabric to expand widthwise, but not lengthwise. It is highly probable that the fabric will stretch lengthwise from gravity after a few wearings. Therefore we are taking the precaution of giving this soft blousy sweater firm body resting places. It will cling securely to

the waist and arm (just above the elbow) with tight ribbing so that any lengthwise stretch will not be a problem.

A total of 750 yards of worsted-weight yarn will be necessary for a size 30 (bust) short-sleeved sweater. Some will be of the ribbing yarn and some of the body yarn. Look at the quickie sketch and notice that there are several inches of ribbing trim at the top of the boatneck. (The finished sweater actually used slightly less than 3 balls of "Cajun Cotton" @ 180 yards, and also somewhat less than 3 balls of "Cotton D'Egypte 4½" @ 93 yards.)

MEASUREMENTS NEEDED

Notice there is no added body ease allowance. Instead, because of the nonresilient cotton yarn selected, width and length to allow for the cotton stretch is subtracted from body circumferences.

1. Bust circumference:

	32″	(body circumference)
−	2″	(allowance for cotton stretch)
=	30″	(sweater circumference)
÷	2	(half for back, half for front)
=	15″	(each back and front)

2. Waist circumference:
  a. Body fabric:

	26″	(body circumference)
−	2″	(allowance for cotton stretch)
=	24″	
+	2″	(ease for gathered blouse effect)
=	26″	(sweater circumference)
÷	2	(half for back, half for front)
=	13″	(each back and front)

  b. Ribbing:

	26″	(body circumference)
−	2″	(allowance for cotton stretch)
=	24″	(ribbing circumference)
÷	2	(half for back, half for front)
=	12″	(each back and front)

3. *Nape of neck to bottom of sweater:*

$$\begin{array}{rl} 18'' & \text{(nape of neck to bottom of sweater)} \\ - \quad 2'' & \text{(sweater will end 2'' below nape of neck)} \\ \hline = \ 16'' & \text{(top of sweater to bottom of sweater)} \\ - \quad 2'' & \text{(length of top ribbing)} \\ - \quad 2'' & \text{(length of bottom ribbing)} \\ \hline = \ 12'' & \text{(approximate length of St st)} \\ + \quad 1'' & \text{(length allowance for blousing effect)} \\ \hline = \ 13'' & \text{(length of St st between bottom and top ribbing)} \end{array}$$

4. *Length from underarm to bottom of sweater:*

$$\begin{array}{rl} 11'' & \text{(length from underarm to bottom)} \\ - \quad 1'' & \text{(underarm ease allowance)} \\ - \quad 2'' & \text{(length of bottom ribbing)} \\ \hline = \quad 8'' & \text{(approximate length)} \\ + \quad 1'' & \text{(for blousing effect)} \\ \hline = \quad 9'' & \text{(length of body St st at underarm)} \end{array}$$

5. *Shoulder tip to shoulder tip across the front:*

On most hand-knit sweaters the shoulders are made too wide! Be sure that you have measured the wearer's body at the point where you wish the sweater body fabric to end and the sleeves to begin.

$$\begin{array}{rl} 13'' & \text{(body measurement where sleeves desired)} \\ - \quad 1'' & \text{(allowance for cotton stretch)} \\ \hline = \ 12'' & \text{(width of back [and front] at shoulder)} \end{array}$$

6. *Actual armhole depth:* 7″ (to nape of neck). See #9 for shoulder slope.

7. *Upper arm circumference:*

a. *Body fabric:*

$$\begin{array}{rl} 9'' & \text{(body measurement)} \\ + \quad 4'' & \text{(approx half of width for puff of sleeve)} \\ \hline = \ 13'' & \text{(width of sleeve St st)} \end{array}$$

Note: the additional width added for puff sleeves is arbitrary and approximate according to the thickness of the fabric and the wishes of the wearer.

b. Ribbing:

$$9'' \text{ (body measurement)}$$
$$-\ 1'' \text{ (allowance for lengthwise cotton stretch)}$$
$$=\ 8'' \text{ (length of sleeve ribbing)}$$

8. Finished desired length of sleeves from underarm:

$$6'' \quad \text{(measurement from body)}$$
$$-\ 1.5'' \quad \text{(bottom ribbing)}$$
$$-\ 1'' \quad \text{(allowance for lengthwise cotton stretch)}$$
$$=\ 3.5''$$
$$+\ 1'' \quad \text{(allowance for blousing effect)}$$
$$=\ 4.5'' \quad \text{(length of sleeve St st from rib to underarm)}$$

9. Shoulder slope: 3″. The nape of neck to actual armhole depth is 7″ (see #6 above); *however,* 3″ of this depth is lost in the slope of the shoulder; *therefore,* the armhole is only 4″ long, to which we must add 1″ of movement ease allowance, making the knitted armhole depth 5″ long.

$$7'' \quad \text{(nape of neck to actual armpit)}$$
$$-\ 3'' \quad \text{(slope of shoulder)}$$
$$=\ 4'' \quad \text{(actual body armhole length)}$$
$$+\ 1'' \quad \text{(armhole ease allowance)}$$
$$=\ 5 \quad \text{(sweater armhole length)}$$

We will add 1″ to the armhole depth on the back to allow for boatneck ribbing overlap at shoulders. Mark these lengths on the layout drawing in red ink.

DOING THE ARITHMETIC

GAUGE: Body, Finished Gauge: St st—4.75 sts and 7 rows = 1″
Ribbing: 1 × 1 (stretched)—5.25 sts = 1″

10. Back and front sweater bust:

$$15'' \quad \text{(from \#1, desired inches of sweater back bust width)}$$
$$\times\ 4.75 \quad \text{(gauge: sts per inch)}$$
$$=\ 71.25 \quad \text{(approximate number of sts necessary for back bust)}$$
$$=\ 72 \quad \text{(rounded to a whole number, final number of sts needed for back bust)}$$

11. Back and front sweater waist:

a. Body fabric

13″	(from #2a, desired inches of sweater back waist width)
× 4.75	(gauge: sts per inch)
= 61.75	(approximate number of sts necessary for back waist)
= 62	(rounded to a whole number, final number of sts necessary for back waist)

b. Ribbing

12″	(from #2b, desired inches of width of ribbing)
× 5.25	(gauge: sts per inch)
= 63	(number of sts necessary for ribbing)

This number (63) is a multiple of 2 + 1. Our planned 1 × 1 ribbing plus an extra stitch for the seam will work out perfectly. Therefore 63 is the number of stitches that will be cast on for the ribbing.

The knitter has had a problem in the past with casting on too tightly. She chooses to cast on with a needle one size larger and then immediately change to the regular size (#4) on the first row of ribbing.

12. Width of shoulders:

12″	(from #5)
× 4.75	(gauge: sts per inch)
= 57	(approximate number of sts at shoulders)

Fifty-seven is an odd number. The other numbers (for body chest and body waist) are even numbers. Let's arbitrarily round this number (57) down to 56. There will be 56 stitches on the body at the shoulders.

13. Difference in waist ribbing width (stitches) and body waist width (stitches):

Remember that this is an unusual situation. Not only are we using different yarns for the ribbing and for the body fabric, but also both of the yarns are nonresilient. In more ordinary sweaters made all of the same resilient yarn it is usual to *increase* the number of stitches from the ribbing to the body fabric.

63	(from #11b, number of ribbing sts)
− 62	(from #11a, desired number of sts of St st at body waist)
= 1	(number of sts to decrease)

That is easy to do. Just decrease 1 stitch somewhere along the row.

INCREASING FROM BODY WAIST TO LARGER BODY BUST

This is the same thing we did with the Da Vinci Man sleeves. We made them get wider from wrist to underarm.

14. Increasing from waist to larger bust:

$$
\begin{array}{rl}
72 & \text{(from \#10, desired number of sts at back chest)} \\
-\ 62 & \text{(from \#11a, desired number of sts at back waist)} \\
=\ 10 & \text{(total number of sts to increase from waist to chest)} \\
\div\ 2 & \text{(half for right side, half for left side)} \\
=\ 5 & \text{(number of sts to increase each side of back and front from waist to chest)}
\end{array}
$$

Go back to your layout drawing and #4 to find out how many inches of stockinette stitch length there will be from underarm to bottom of sweater (minus the ribbing) in which to make these increases. The number we worked out there is 9″ of stockinette stitch.

$$
\begin{array}{rl}
9'' & \text{(from \#4, length of body St st at underarm)} \\
-\ 2'' & \text{(to be left plain after last increase)} \\
=\ 7'' & \text{(available in which to make 5 increases/spans)}
\end{array}
$$

The 2″ to be left plain after last increase does not need to be precise. It can be a little more or a little less. Let's see how it works out.

$$
\begin{array}{rl}
7'' & \text{(available in which to make 5 increases/spans)} \\
\times\ 7 & \text{(gauge: rows per inch)} \\
=\ 49 & \text{(rows available for 5 increases/spans)}
\end{array}
$$

That works out great! It is almost 50, and 50 is divisible by 5. Just round 49 up to 50.

$$
\begin{array}{rl}
50 & \text{(rows available for 5 increases/spans)} \\
\div\ 5 & \text{(number of increases/spans)} \\
=\ 10 & \text{(number of rows on which to make increase)}
\end{array}
$$

We will increase 1 stitch each side every 10th row 5 times.

HOW TO PLAN BODY ARMHOLE SHAPING FOR SET-IN SLEEVES

15. Planning how many stitches to get rid of at the armholes:

>   72 (from #10, number of sts on back/front at chest)
> − 56 (from #12, number of sts on back/front at shoulder)
> = 16 (total number of sts to get rid of between underarm and shoulder)
> ÷   2 (half for right side; half for left side)
> =   8 (number of sts to get rid of on each side)

Deciding how to allocate the stitches to be gotten rid of between the underarm bind-off and the every-other-row decreases made at the underarm is always an exercise of judgment and a juggling act. It is customary (but not mandatory) to bind off 1″ of stitches and then decrease 1 stitch every other row until the total number of stitches have been eliminated. It is also customary (but not mandatory) to contain all the decreases within 1.5″ above the bind-off. BUT THIS IS NOT ALWAYS POSSIBLE OR EVEN DESIRABLE BECAUSE:

Sometimes the number of stitches to be gotten rid of may be greater than can be consumed in a 1″ bind-off combined with 1.5″ of decreases.

Sometimes a pattern stitch such as lace will dictate a bind-off of one whole repeat even if it is more than 1″ wide.

In later chapters, on larger sizes we will bind off as much as 4″ of stitches, and on some body types we will extend our decreases more than 1.5″ above the bind-off.

Thank goodness that on *this* sweater we do not have such a problem. We need to get rid of only 8 stitches each side. We can divide these 8 stitches half and half: half for underarm bind-off and half for every-other-row decreases. To shape the underarm, we will bind off 4 stitches at the beginning of the next 2 rows, and then decrease 1 stitch each side every other row 4 times. (This makes our total of 16 stitches that will be gotten rid of between the chest width and the shoulders.)

FIGURING OUT THE TOP RIBBING

16. Determining the number of stitches for the top ribbing:

Because the ribbing at the top of this boatnecked sweater is made of nonresilient yarn and will be pulled widthwise by the full puff sleeves, an arbitrary decision was made to decrease the width of the ribbing. An out-of-the-hat figure of 10 percent was chosen. (Recall that the reciprocal of 10 percent is 90 percent.)

$$\begin{array}{rl}
56 & \text{(from \#12, number of sts of width at body shoulder)} \\
\times \quad .9 & \text{(decimal equivalent of 90\%)} \\
\hline
= 50.4 & \text{(approximate number of sts to remain for ribbing)} \\
= 51 & \text{(rounded off to a whole number)}
\end{array}$$

Again we are in luck, because this number (51) is divisible by 2 plus 1, which we need for our ribbing.

Use the rules for decreasing 10 percent of the stitches that we found in Chapter 16: Think of units of 10. To decrease 10%: K 8, k 2 tog to make 1 fewer stitch in each unit.

PLANNING SET-IN PUFF SLEEVES

17. Determining number of sleeve ribbing stitches:

In the previous chapter I said that there were several ways to decide how many stitches would be necessary for the arm/wrist ribbing. In this chapter I want to explain a very easy, foolproof way that you can use when you are designing your own sweaters.

Place the ribbing from the bottom of the finished back section piece around the intended wearer's arm/wrist, deciding what is comfortable. Count the number of stitches used. Make sure that you have a plus stitch to use for sewing the ribbing.

Obviously this foolproof way of determining arm/wrist ribbing widths will not work if you are making the sleeves first. Likewise, it will not work if the intended wearer is unavailable.

The number of ribbing stitches decided upon for this sweater was 43.

$$\begin{array}{rl}
13'' & \text{(from \#7a, desired width of puff sleeves)} \\
\times \quad 4.75 & \text{(gauge: sts per inch)} \\
\hline
= 61.75 & \text{(approximate number of sts of width on puff sleeve)}
\end{array}$$

Round this number up to 62.

$$\begin{array}{rl}
62 & \text{(number of sts of width on puff sleeve)} \\
- \quad 43 & \text{(desired number of sts on arm ribbing)} \\
\hline
= 19 & \text{(number of sts to increase between ribbing and puff sleeve)}
\end{array}$$

Oops. That is a lot of increases to cram in across a small (nonresilient) area. It is almost 50 percent.

It is possible to write instructions to do anything; it is possible to write instructions to increase 50 percent of the stitches. Actually doing it may be very difficult or nearly impossible.

Because of the large number of stitches to be increased from the tight nonresilient ribbing to a puff sleeve, it was necessary to *spread that increase over 2 rows.* There was not enough slack in the yarn between the ribbing stitches to manufacture sufficient increases. Therefore we made half of the increases (9) on one row, and then the remaining half (10) on the next row.

18. Plan the shaping of set-in sleeve at underarms:

It is customary to exactly match the shaping of the set-in sleeve to the shaping of the set-in armhole on the body.

On the body we "BO 4 sts at beg of next 2 rows, then dec 1 st ea side EOR 4 ×." We will do exactly the same for this sweater.

It is not mandatory, nor is it always desirable, that the shaping of the armholes of set-in sleeves match the body shaping. People with large chests, narrow shoulders, and slender arms certainly wouldn't want the underarm shapings to match. People with large upper arms and small chests wouldn't want it either.

The beauty of designing your own sweater is knowing what the rules are and when and where and how to break them!

19. Shaping the top of puff sleeves:

Puff sleeves are the easiest thing in the world to design. After the underarm shaping, simply keep on working straight up until the sleeve is nearly as long as the armhole and then decrease and bind off as many stitches as you can as fast as you can.

We have already determined that (from the beginning of the armhole shaping) our body armhole will be 5″ long on the front and 6″ long on the back to allow for boatneck ribbing overlap at shoulders. (See #9.)

We can simply make our puff sleeves 1.5″ shorter than the armhole; that is, 4.5″ long from beginning of armhole shaping.

Next, we can decrease one-half of the stitches by knitting 2 together across the row. On the following row we can decrease and bind off the remaining stitches all at the same time. (To do this, bind off across by knitting 2 together as follows: Knit 2 together, *Knit 2 together, lift first stitch up and over 2nd stitch to bind off.* Repeat between *s across.) These 2 rows and the additional remaining stitches/width will

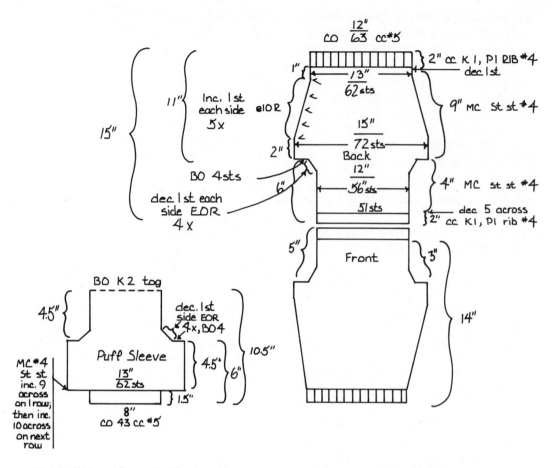

20.4 Puff-Sleeved Boatnecked Beauty with measurements, stitches, rows, and instructions

account for the necessary half-inch of additional length for the sleeve to fit the armhole.

Once all the arithmetic is complete, fill in the measurements, stitches, rows, etc., on the pattern layout. (See Figure 20.4.)

MAKING UP THE GARMENT

Measure as you go, but don't forget that because the working gauge has fewer stitches per inch than the finished/washed gauge, the measurements of widths as you knit will be smaller than your finished, washed, and worn garment will be.

FINISHING THE SWEATER

After the sleeves are woven in place, sew in a folded crescent of stiff nonwoven fabric (like Pellon®) to help puffed or tucked sleeves stand up, out and away from the body.

You may wish to permanently sew the triangular overlap area of the boatneck.

VARIATIONS

Pleat the top of the sleeves, either by knitting double on last (plain) knit row, or by folding tops in and forming when sewing.

Lengthen sleeves to elbow length if your upper arms are fleshy.

Add a bust dart for big-bosomed women. With this addition the Waist-Length Puff-Sleeved Boatneck Beauty makes a great and flattering sweater for women with a tiffany diamond figure.

Make long or leg-o-mutton sleeves.

Make a striped design with or without slipped stitches.

Make an intarsia design on the front with colorful geometric shapes or a spray of bright poppies.

Embroider a spray of flowers on sweater front.

Add back and front stitches together and work entire body in the round to the armholes. Also work sleeves in the round on a 16-inch needle.

Don't have enough yarn? Make a delightful half-and-half sweater: Make the right sleeve blue, the other white; then make a diagonal color change line across front and back. (See Figure 20.5.)

Do those color changes suggested above in plaids instead of all solid.

20.5 Two-color sweater

CONCLUSION

A boatneck sweater like this one flatters only those people whose neck bones are as high or higher than their shoulder bones. It is a quick-and-easy garment to both design and make. For triangular, bottom-heavy hourglass, and Tiffany diamond figures, it is a great style. It is *not* suitable for either "V" or rectangular figures; their shoulders need no attention drawn to them with puff sleeves.

21

A V-Necked Pullover Vest

In this chapter you will learn how to:

1. *Work with pattern stitches;*
2. *Shape shoulders;*
3. *Plan a V-neck, plotting diagonals where the numbers don't come out even;*
4. *Pick up stitches,*
   a. *horizontal,*
   b. *diagonal,*
   c. *vertical;*
5. *Design for a "V"-type body.*

In the previous chapter we learned how to shape armholes for set-in sleeves, and found that it was really very easy to do. We were not entirely pleased, however, with the straight-across boat neckline and the lack of shoulder shaping. Moreover we concluded that the Puff-Sleeved Beauty would look beautiful on sweet young girls and on lovely swan-necked women but hardly anyone else.

Most people's shoulders slope down from the neck and their neck bones are *lower* than the tips of the shoulders. They need a different shoulder and neck design. Therefore in this chapter we are going to learn how to shape shoulders so that they slope from neck to shoulder tip and how to plan a neck shaping for neck bones that are lower than shoulder tips.

THE IDEA

A very special man complains of the air conditioning in his office. It is too warm for a suit coat, too cool for shirtsleeves. What do you say? "I'll knit a vest for you."

FLOOR PLAN OF THE PIECES

21.1 Rough sketch of V-Necked Pullover Vest

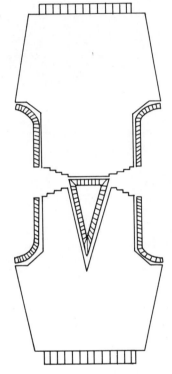

21.2 Layout of V-Necked Pullover Vest (this longer-than-waist-length vest will look best on a V-shaped body)

THE YARN, THE GAUGE, AND THE PATTERN STITCH

Patons Lady Gray "Kroy," a fingering-weight, machine-washable, classic worsted wool-nylon blend was chosen. There are 209 yards per 50-gram ball.

The following basketweave pattern stitch was chosen from *Vogue's Dictionary of Pattern Stitches* (New York: Conde Nast Publications, Ltd., 1984):

21.3 V-Necked Pullover (yarn supplied by Susan Bates, Inc., USA distributor for Paton; knitted by Melody Sowa; modeled by Pat Jamison)

Basketweave: A multiple of 6 stitches and a repeat of 8 rows.
Rows 1 & 3) *K 2, p 4, rep from * across.
Rows 2 & 4) *K 4, p 2, rep from * across.
Rows 5 & 7) P 3, *k 2, p 4, rep from * across, end k 2, p 1.
Rows 6 & 8) K 1, p 2, *k 4, p 2, rep from * across, end k 3.
Repeat these 8 rows for pattern stitch.

This basketweave pattern stitch is a multiple of 6 stitches and has a repeat of 8 rows. The finished stitch creates a somewhat stretchy fabric and care must be taken to ensure that the finished garment is not too large.

As you double-check width while you are knitting the pieces, remember that the finished sweater will be both wider and longer after the first wearing and washing.

GAUGE: Body: Basketweave—7.3 sts and 8 rows = 1″ on #4 needles

Because we are planning a V-neck, an accurate row gauge is needed.

For once, the "Pocket Yarn Yardage Guide" fails me in estimating how much yarn will be necessary. It does not include estimates for fingering-weight yarn. If I use the estimates for sport-weight yarn instead, I will need 960 yards or 4.59 balls for a man's Large sleeveless sweater. But in this fingering yarn there will be more stitches and rows per inch than in sports-weight yarn *and* the intended wearer is quite tall and broad-shouldered so 8 balls of yarn are purchased.

PLOTTING THE LENGTHS AND WIDTHS

As I start to design this V-neck vest, I go through the same plotting and planning of lengths and widths as in previous chapters for the other sweaters.

The intended wearer has wide shoulders and narrow hips. To accommodate his body, it is necessary to increase body width from bottom to underarm, and to decrease fewer stitches from underarm to shoulder tip.

But those are simple things that you already know how to handle. Figure 21.4 shows what should be done.

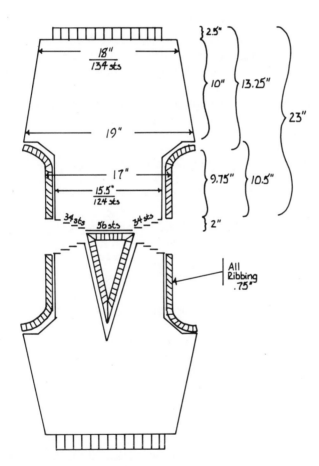

21.4 V-Necked Pullover Vest with measurements

DOING THE ARITHMETIC

Every sweater is different. This sweater is no exception. There are two special things to consider for this particular garment.

1. Ordinarily, V-neck sweaters with 1 × 1 ribbing trim at the neck need to be made over an ODD NUMBER of stitches so that when the front right and left sides of the V are separated, the center (odd) stitch can be placed on a holder to become the center stitch of the ribbing. However, with this particular sweater pattern stitch there is NO CENTER STITCH AVAILABLE. When we divide the front for the V-neck WE WILL HAVE TO INCREASE 1 STITCH (FRENCH MAKE-1) IN ORDER TO HAVE A CENTER V RIBBING STITCH. We will include this instruction in the written directions for shaping the V-neck.

2. One selvedge stitch should be added at each edge of the fabric to facilitate making increases and to make a smooth side seam. Therefore, we must call our pattern stitch a multiple of 6 stitches + 2 (selvedge stitches).

We have worked with multiples that had a *plus 1* before, and the process of working with a *plus 2* is basically the same.

ESTABLISHING THE NUMBER OF PATTERN REPEATS ACROSS

```
        18"    (desired width at bottom edge of sweater)
  ×    7.3  (gauge: sts per inch)
  =  131.4  (approximate number of sts)
  ÷     6   (number of sts in each multiple)
  =   21.9  (approximate number of pattern repeats across)
```

Round up to a whole number.

```
        22  (approximate number of patterns across)
  ×      6  (pattern st multiple)
  =    132  (number of sts necessary for 22 multiples)
  +      2  (selvedge sts—1 for each side)
  =    134  (Final number of sts of width across bottom)
```

SHAPING THE SHOULDERS

In order to plan for this vest to cover the armhole seams of the dress shirt that will be worn underneath, we measured the desired shoulder width to *include* a ribbing extending from the body fabric .75" (¾") on each side. The desired width of the body fabric at the shoulders is 124 stitches.

In order to allow room for the shirt collar and tie, we measured the back neck of our intended wearer *across the width of the body fabric stitch* knowing that .75″ ribbing trim on each side would fill in another 1.5″. The desired width of the back neck fabric is 56 stitches.

   124 (number of sts across back shoulders)
   − 56 (number of sts desired for back neck width)
   = 68 (total number of sts remaining for both shoulders)
   ÷ 2 (half for each shoulder)
   = 34 (sts available for sloping each shoulder)

The intended wearer's shoulders slope 2.5″ from the neck-shoulder joining to the spot where we want the back body fabric to end slightly beyond the shoulder-bone tips. We are going to let the "forgivingness" of the fabric take care of .5″ of that slope and round down the length of the shoulder slope to 2″.

   2″ (length of shoulder slope)
   × 8 (gauge: rows per inch)
   = 16 (total number of rows available for shoulder shaping)

But we can bind off only at the beginning of a row (never at the end of it), so we will have only half of this number of rows to make our stairstep bind-offs on each side.

   16 (total number of rows available for shoulder shaping)
   ÷ 2 (can bind off only at beginning of a row)
   = 8 (number of rows available on each side for making stairstep shoulder shaping)

Now we divide the number of stitches to be shaped on each side by the number of rows available to do the shaping.

   34 (sts available to be stairstepped on each side)
   ÷ 8 (number of rows available for making the stairsteps)
   = 4, with a remainder of 2

Because the numbers did not come out even and there is a remainder, we must go to the next whole number, which is 5. Now, suppose we were to bind off 5 stitches 8 times. We would have consumed 40 stitches, which is 6 stitches too many. Six of our 8 stairsteps will have to have 1 less stitch than the other 2 stairsteps.

Our shoulder stairsteps will be made: 4, 4, 4, 4, 4, 4, 5, 5. Add it up and verify that it works.

$$4 \text{ (number of sts to be bound off)}$$
$$\times \quad 6 \text{ (number of times to bind off)}$$
$$= 24 \text{ (number of sts used up at rate of ``BO 4 sts 6} \times \text{'')}$$

$$5 \text{ (number of sts to be bound off)}$$
$$\times \quad 2 \text{ (number of times to bind off)}$$
$$= 10 \text{ (number of sts used up at rate of ``BO 5 sts 2} \times \text{'')}$$

$$24 \text{ (number of sts used up at rate of ``BO 4 sts 6} \times \text{'')}$$
$$+ \quad 10 \text{ (number of sts used up at rate of ``BO 5 sts 2} \times \text{'')}$$
$$= 34 \text{ (total number of sts used up in shoulder stairstep BOs)}$$

WRITTEN INSTRUCTIONS FOR SHAPING SHOULDERS AND BACK NECK

When piece measures 10.5″ from UA-BO begin to shape shoulders. At each armhole edge, BO 4 sts 6 times then BO 5 sts 2 times. Transfer rem 56 sts to holder for back neck.

Or: Work even until back measures 10.5″ beyond beg of armhole shaping. At beg of next 12 rows BO 4. Then at beg of next 4 rows BO 5. Slip rem 56 sts to holder for back neck. (See Figure #21.5.)

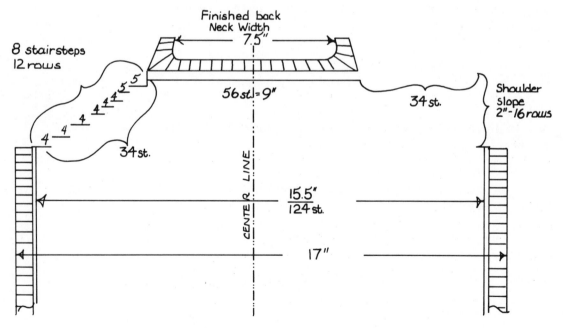

21.5 Close-up of shoulder shaping for V-Necked Pullover Vest

USING THE FORMULA FOR DIAGONALS THAT DO NOT COME OUT EVEN TO PLAN V-NECK DECREASES

In Chapter 4, I discussed the differences in designing for knit fabric and for woven cloth. Planning a V-neck sweater is one of those instances where the forgivingness of the knit fabric really becomes important. In cloth garments the V is usually begun at a higher point; for sweaters we usually begin to shape a V-neck *at the same time* we begin to shape the armholes. On this particular vest, we have 140 stitches of width at this point and will shape our armholes in the following way: BO 4 sts at the beg of next 2 rows, then dec one st each side EOR 4 times until 124 sts rem (we'll need to know this when we write up the instructions for dividing the stitches at the center).

Now we need to determine how much length is available to decrease the sides of our V-neck. From the section above we know that we will work even 10.5″ from the beginning of the armhole shaping and then we will use 2″ more of length to shape the shoulders.

$$
\begin{array}{rl}
10.5″ & \text{(inches of length from start of armhole } and \text{ V-neck)} \\
+\quad 2″ & \text{(inches of length in shoulder shaping)} \\
\hline
= 12.5″ & \text{(total number of inches in which to decrease sides of V-neck)}
\end{array}
$$

But V-necks always fit better if the V shaping ends before the shoulder seam. I like to leave anywhere from .75″ to 1.25″ even and plain after the final decrease has been made. *Always plan a little extra space at the end of the decreases in case the row gauge is slightly off.* Let's settle for .75 inch plain.

$$
\begin{array}{rl}
12.5″ & \text{(total number of inches in which to decrease sides of V-neck)} \\
-\quad .75″ & \text{(desired number of inches to be left plain at the top)} \\
\hline
= 11.75″ & \text{(final number of inches in which to decrease sides of V)} \\
\times\quad 8\quad & \text{(gauge: rows per inch)} \\
\hline
= 94 & \text{(number of rows in which to make V-neck decreases)}
\end{array}
$$

From your layout drawing, note that we will have a total of 56 (the number of stitches in the neck back) stitches to get rid of in shaping the V-neck. One-half of these stitches will be decreased on the right side and one-half on the left side of the V.

$$
\begin{array}{rl}
56 & \text{(total number of neck sts to decrease)} \\
\div\quad 2 & \text{(half on right side, half on left side)} \\
\hline
28 & \text{(number of sts to decrease on each side of V-neck)}
\end{array}
$$

         94   (number of rows in which to make V-neck decreases)
    ÷ 28   (number of sts to decrease each side of V)
    =   3.36 (frequency rate at which to decrease neck stitches)

Note that this number is not nice and clean and even.

Get out the equation and let's fill in what we know. (See pages 175–180.)

____ (Total Number of   ____ (Number of Rows
     Decreases)   Available for De-
                                        creases)

                        =   =

____ (Smaller Whole × ____ (Number of   = ____ (Number of Rows
     Even Number)   Times Made)   Used by Smaller
                                               Number)

                        +   +

____ (Larger Whole × ____ (Number of   = ____ (Number of Rows
     Even Number)   Times Made)   Used by Larger
                                               Number)

                        =   =

____ Total Number of   ____ Number of Rows
     Decreases   Available for De-
                                          creases

We know that *2 is the next lowest even whole number.*

We know that *4 is the next highest even whole number.*

We know that *we have 28 decreases to make.*

We know that *we have 94 rows available in which to make those decreases.*

With a pencil write in what we know. These are final numbers, so enter them without parentheses.

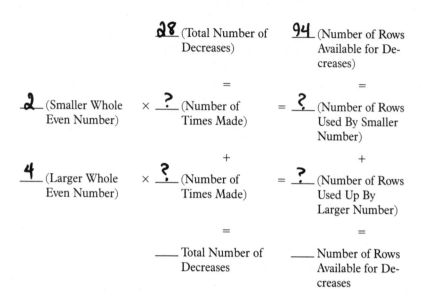

28 (Total Number of Decreases)

94 (Number of Rows Available for Decreases)

=

=

2 (Smaller Whole Even Number) × ? (Number of Times Made) = ? (Number of Rows Used By Smaller Number)

+

+

4 (Larger Whole Even Number) × ? (Number of Times Made) = ? (Number of Rows Used Up By Larger Number)

=

=

____ Total Number of Decreases

____ Number of Rows Available for Decreases

Now suppose that we were to make *all* the decreases at the rate of the lowest even whole number (every 2nd row). Multiply the number of rows that would be consumed (2 × 28 = 56) and subtract the number from the total number of rows available. Be sure to write in "temporary" numbers in parentheses for clarity. Divide the remainder (38, the "supposed" number of rows still available for decreases) by 2.

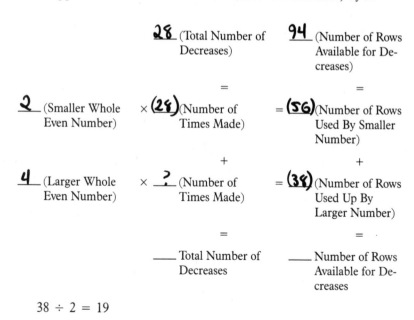

28 (Total Number of Decreases)

94 (Number of Rows Available for Decreases)

=

=

2 (Smaller Whole Even Number) × (28) (Number of Times Made) = (56) (Number of Rows Used By Smaller Number)

+

+

4 (Larger Whole Even Number) × ? (Number of Times Made) = (38) (Number of Rows Used Up By Larger Number)

=

=

____ Total Number of Decreases

____ Number of Rows Available for Decreases

38 ÷ 2 = 19

This is the number of times we will make our decreases at the higher even whole number (every 4th row). Fill in this final number; erase all temporary numbers in parentheses. Subtract the number of times the decreases will be made at the rate of the higher even whole number from the number of decreases. This is the number of times the decreases will be made at the lower even whole number.

28 − 19 = 9

Complete the formula.

<table>
<tr><td>**28** (Total Number of Decreases)</td><td>**94** (Number of Rows Available for Decreases)</td></tr>
<tr><td>=</td><td>=</td></tr>
<tr><td>**2** (Smaller Whole Even Number) × **9** (Number of Times Made)</td><td>= **18** (Number of Rows Used by Smaller Number)</td></tr>
<tr><td>+</td><td>+</td></tr>
<tr><td>**4** (Larger Whole Even Number) × **19** (Number of Times Made)</td><td>= **76** (Number of Rows Used Up by Larger Number)</td></tr>
<tr><td>=</td><td>=</td></tr>
<tr><td>**28** Total Number of Decreases</td><td>**94** Number of Rows Available for Decreases</td></tr>
</table>

WRITTEN INSTRUCTIONS FOR V-NECK SHAPING

Work even until piece measures 13″ long overall, ending after completing a private-side row.

At the beginning of the next row, BO 4 st. Work across 63 sts, k 2 tog, k 1, inc 1 st (French M-1). Attach a new ball of yarn, K 1, SSK, k across. At beg of next row BO 4 sts. Now work both sides at the same time with separate balls of yarn. Maintaining selvedge sts at all edges, dec 1 st ea armhole side EOR 4 x, *and at the same time* at ea neck edge dec 1 st alternately every 4th row and every 2nd row 9 ×, then dec 1 st every 4th row 10 × more until 28 neck edge sts have been dec'd ea side, *and at the same time* when armhole measures 10.5″ from UA BO shape shoulders same as back (i.e., 4, 4, 4, 4, 4, 4, 5, 5).

MAKING UP THE GARMENT

INCREASING ON THE EDGES OF A PATTERN STITCH

Some knitters are not familiar with making increases of width when working with a pattern stitch. They ask, "If I increase a stitch at the beginning of a row, won't it throw my pattern stitch off and move it over 1 stitch to the right? And if I add another stitch at the end of the row, how can I keep my pattern stitch running straight up and down?" I have a handy way of avoiding problems when increasing at the edges of a pattern stitch. At the beginning of a row, after you work the selvedge stitch and make the increase, slip a ring marker on the needle before the beginning of the first stitch of the first multiple. After you have made the last stitch of the last multiple, slip on another ring marker, now increase, and then work the final selvedge stitch. The markers will act like street signs. At the beginning of a row, on top of the newly increased stitch, work the *last* stitch of the multiple, slip the marker, and begin the multiple all over again exactly on top of where you began it on previous rows. At the end of a row, slip the marker and on top of the newly increased stitch, work the *first* stitch of the pattern multiple to begin a new repeat. When it is time to make another pair of increases, make them on the *same side* of the markers as the previous increases. Then, when you have increased 2 stitches at each end of the needle, your ring markers will still be there to show you where to begin the repeat, and to tell you how many of the stitches at the end of the sequence you must work before you can start fresh again at the ring marker. The ring markers will also tell you when you have enough stitches to begin a new multiple repeat.

DON'T BIND OFF NECK STITCHES

As a knitting instructor who has seen thousands of problem sweaters, I don't know how I can tell you strongly enough:

Do not bind off the back neck stitches. Slip them to a holder to wait until you are ready to complete the neck ribbing. More sweaters are killed by tightly bound off neck stitches than by any other cause. If the finished back neck or shoulders are too loose they can always be firmed up and reinforced with a bit of seam tape, or a row of crochet slip stitches on the underside. But if they are too tight (which is what usually happens when they are bound off), the wearer will have difficulty getting the sweater over his/her head.

FINISHING THE SWEATER

When picking up stitches around an opening such as the V-neck and the armholes that we have on this sweater, the knitter has two choices. She can work these ribbing edges flat or in the round. Her choice will depend upon whether or not she enjoys working with circular needles.

Whether you choose to work the ribbing flat or circular, remember to pick up the stitches with the public side of the garment facing you, and with a smaller-size needle than you intend to use for the ribbing.

After you have determined the number of stitches to be picked up along a particular area of fabric by following the instructions below, divide the number by 4.

Divide the corresponding area of the garment first in halves and then in quarters, marking the divisions with tiny safety pins. As you pick up the stitches, put in ring markers at the safety pin locations. It is easier to evenly space 25 stitches to be picked up over a 6″ area than it is to try to pick up 100 stitches over a 24″-long space.

MAKING THE RIBBING FLAT

Begin with the neckline first. Weave together one shoulder seam, leaving the other open. When picking up, be sure to *allow an extra stitch* in the ribbing to use later in sewing up the seam. From the public side the ribbing should begin and end with a knit stitch.

When the ribbing is finished and bound off, weave the remaining shoulder seam.

Now pick up the stitches around the armhole, again allowing 1 stitch for later when sewing to form the underarm seam. When the armhole trim is completed, weave the underarm seam.

MAKING THE RIBBING IN THE ROUND

Weave together all the seams, but don't conceal the tag ends of yarn at the edges. Work the ribbing on the shortest convenient-length circular needle. Since there is no seam to sew, no extra stitch is needed.

FORMULAS FOR PICKING UP STITCHES

Knitters can often get frantic trying to figure out *exactly* how many stitches they are supposed to pick up. The object of any finishing work, and that includes picking up stitches for ribbing, is to make the sweater fit, look good, and wear well. The point is: Never pick up *exactly* X number of stitches if that number makes your edge ripple or pucker. Keep this in mind as you learn the following formulas. Then if ever you have a problem with rippling or puckering, you can tell yourself, "The formula doesn't work for this sweater. Next time I'll pick up a few stitches less (or more)."

HORIZONTAL

Along a horizontal edge that has been bound off, pick up stitch for stitch.

Along a horizontal edge where the stitches have been placed on a holder, use each stitch.

DIAGONAL

There are two ways to determine how many stitches need to be picked up along a diagonal.

1. Place a tape measure along the finished diagonal edge. Measure the length of the area and multiply by the stitch gauge of the (slightly stretched) ribbing fabric.

Example:

12″	(actual finished measurement of one side of V-neck)
× 5	(ribbing gauge: sts per inch *slightly stretched)*
= 60	(number of sts to pick up along each side of diagonal V-neck edge)

2. Pick up 1 stitch in 3 rows out of 4. At the edge of your knitting, 1 row will look like a long loop and the next row will look like a knot, long loop, and knot, etc. So picking up in 3 rows out of 4 would be: *long loop, knot, long loop, and *skip the next knot**, repeat between *s along diagonal edge.

VERTICAL

To determine the number of stitches to be picked up along a vertical edge, go back to the numbers in your original gauge swatch. Make a fraction out of the number of stitches and the number of rows per inch.

Example:

Gauge: 6 stitches and 10 rows = 1 inch would be 6/10. Then reduce this fraction to its lowest terms. 6/10 = 3/5 This means: pick up 3 stitches in every 5 rows. Or, *long loop, knot, *skip long loop*, knot, *skip long loop**, repeat from * across.

VARIATIONS

You can form the shoulder shaping by making short rows instead of bind-offs, and then make the shoulder seam with a double bind-off.

Knit the sweater in the round using steeks at the armholes and V-neck.

Vary the pattern stitch.

Use an argyle (flat), Fair Isle (in the round), mosaic design, or stripes.

After you learn in later chapters how to plan cables, make them on the front or over the whole vest.

CONCLUSION

You are now learning to design real garments for real people and you may have come to realize why knitting magazines and pamphlets are full of Da Vinci Man and other simple designs even if they don't fit. It is much easier to design a couple of simple rectangles. Shaping for real bodies takes a lot more thought, planning, and juggling. It is more work, but if you're like most knitters I know, you're tired of making sweaters that are uncomfortable and do not fit, so it is worth the extra effort.

22

A Cabled, Classic, Crew-Necked Long-Sleeved Pullover

In this chapter you will learn how to:

1. Work with a multiple of 4 plus 1;
2. Shape a crew neck;
3. Plan a fitted sleeve cap;
4. Increase stitches for cable panels;
5. Design for a Big and Beautiful body type.

With this chapter, you will find a change in format. Since you have been carefully led through the laying out of the measurements and the working of the arithmetical processes in previous chapters, from here on I will skip these basic steps. We will spend our time instead working out both the special needs of special bodies and the peculiarities of particular designs.

THE IDEA

If there was ever one almost perfect sweater design for everyone, this is it. For toddlers, teenagers, adults, and grandparents this is a warm, very comfortable, always good-looking design. It has a realistically shaped neckline; the shoulders are properly sloped; the set-in sleeves allow for normal use of the arms without extra flapping fabric as in the Da Vinci Man sweater. (See Figure 22.2.)

22.1 Classic Crew-Necked Pullover ("Aries" yarn supplied by William Unger Co.; knitted by Jan Carmichel; modeled by Whit Robbins)

All this sweater design needs is customizing for any size and any body type. In this lesson we are going to learn to design for a "Big and Beautiful" woman.

FLOOR PLAN OF THE PIECES

Note the differences in these two layouts (Figures 22.3 and 22.4).

1. Big and Beautiful shoulders are *not* necessarily wider, but the sleeve caps are.
2. Big and Beautiful has more stitches taken off at the underarm in order to quickly reduce the circumference and avoid overly wide shoulders, which would make the wearer look broader.
3. Big and Beautiful has a bust dart.
4. Big and Beautiful may have wider hips.

THE YARN AND THE GAUGE

Unger's "Aries," a smooth classic worsted-weight (standard 4-ply, Class C) machine-washable blend of 55 percent acrylic and 45 percent wool, approximately 180 yards per 100-gram skein.

When making your gauge swatch, don't stop with just stockinette. Make a purl ridge row and continue with the cable pattern. You will

22.2 Rough sketch of Classic Crew-Necked Pullover

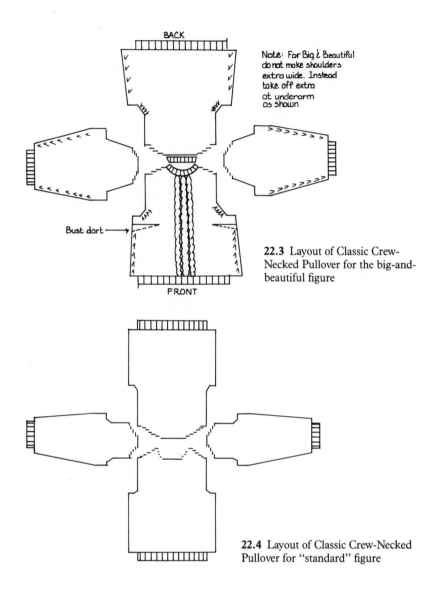

Note: For Big & Beautiful do not make shoulders extra wide. Instead take off extra at underarm as shown

Bust dart

BACK

FRONT

22.3 Layout of Classic Crew-Necked Pullover for the big-and-beautiful figure

22.4 Layout of Classic Crew-Necked Pullover for "standard" figure

need to know how many stitches of width those cables will use. Also make some 2 × 2 ribbing because you need to know the elasticity of the ribbing.

GAUGE: Body: Stockinette stitch—4 sts and 3 rows = 1″ on #8 needles
At this gauge, the fabric is loose and stretchy.
Ribbing: 2 × 2—4.5 sts = 1″ on #6 needles.
At this gauge, the ribbing is very elastic.

Cable pattern: Three 6-stitch-wide cables separated by single purl stitches, twisted every 8th row. The center cable is twisted on row 1, and the outside cables are twisted on row 5, making the cables cuddle up against one another. The pattern will be set off from the stockinette stitch background on each side by a twisted minicable and an extra purl stitch. This makes a total of 26 stitches, which will be important later. (Twist 2 k sts, [p 1, k 6] 3 times, p 1, twist 2 k sts.)

Center Cable Panel:

Row 1) (public side) *K in the 2nd st but do not remove from the needle, k the first st, remove both sts from needle (twist st made)*, p 1, #sl 3 sts to a cable needle and hold at back of work, k 3, k 3 from cable needle (cable twist made), p 1#, k 6, p 1, rep bet #s, rep bet *s.

Row 2 and all even-numbered rows) (private side) P 2, k 1, *p 6, k 1*, rep bet *s 3 times, p 2.

Row 3) twist st, p1, (k 6, p 1) 3 times, twist st.

Row 5) twist st, p 1, k 6, p 1, cable, p 1, k 6, p 1, twist st.

Row 7) same as row 3

Repeat these 8 rows for pattern stitch.

Make your swatch the complete width of this cable panel. The difference in width of this center panel and the stockinette stitch on either side of it must be taken into consideration.

MEASUREMENTS NEEDED

Note that both more and often different measurements are needed for sweaters for Big and Beautiful people than for other body types.

1. *Chest circumference.* If this were to be an outdoor sweater, extra ease would need to be added to cover undergarments.
2. *Circumference at bottom of sweater.*
3. *Length from nape of neck to bottom of sweater.* Extra ease length must be added to allow for the roundness of Big and Beautiful people.
4. a. *Actual body underarm depth.*
   b. *Desired sweater underarm depth.*
5. *Length from garment underarm to bottom of sweater.*
6. a. *Width of body between shoulder tips.*
   b. *Desired width of sweater at shoulders.* Some body types will look better with the shoulders artificially broadened by shoulder pads. If you plan to use shoulder pads, add width to allow for them—2″ to 4″.

7. *Back neck width.* Measure the person's back neck from fabric stitch edge to fabric stitch edge, allowing for ribbing to be filled in later. (If a collared cloth shirt will be worn under this sweater, the neck opening would be planned as much as 1″ or 1.5″ wider.)
8. *Slope of shoulders.*
9. *Distance from shoulder tip to shoulder tip across upper arm.* This measurement is needed whenever the intended wearer has heavy upper arms. Allow sufficient width to cover the upper arms, but that width needs to be put in the sleeves, not on the body!
10. *Sleeve width at underarm.*
11. *Sleeve width above wrist.* (This is necessary because of the Big and Beautiful body type.)
12. *Wrist.* (Again this is necessary because of the Big and Beautiful body type.)
13. *Sleeve length from underarm to wrist.*

Mark the layout in red as usual.

DOING THE ARITHMETIC

Remember that 2 × 2 ribbing is a multiple of 4 plus 1.

PLANNING THE BACK

Because this is a Big and Beautiful person, very tight bottom ribbing might look unattractive. Plan the ribbing to have about 10 percent fewer stitches than the body bottom edge.

If the hips are larger than the bust, decrease along the side seams to get rid of excess width.

If the bust is larger than the hips, increase along the side seams to add additional width.

Inexperienced designers often make the armhole depth much too long on sweaters for large people. It is true that the complete arm circumference of large people may be greater than that of slender people, but it is better to increase this circumference with bigger underarm bind-offs than with greater length.

Just as you have done with the two previous sweaters, subtract the width between the shoulders from the underarm width and divide in half to find how many stitches are to be gotten rid of on each side at the underarm. Do not be alarmed at the number. Start juggling. Calculate the number of stitches that would be consumed in 1.5″ of decreases made every other row. Subtract this amount from the total number of stitches to be gotten rid of. The underarm bind-off on each side of the back *can* be as wide as 2.5″ and the every-other-row decreases *can* extend 2.5″ toward the shoulder.

Plan the shoulder shaping just as you did for the vest.

Mark back neck stitches "To Holder" (TH).

PLANNING THE FRONT

Use the same *layout outline* that you made for the back.

Increase the same number of stitches across the row after the ribbing is completed as you did for the back.

We know that cables eat width and that we will have to increase extra stitches over the cable area so that our body front will be the same size as the body back. Now we have to figure out just how many stitches of width our particular cable pattern will eat, and in exactly what location to place the necessary increases.

Our stockinette stitch gauge is 4 sts = 1″.

The front should be 94 stitches wide at the hip to match the back.

Our cable panel is 4″ wide.

It contains a total of 26 stitches.

We need to subtract 4″ of stockinette stitch width from the total front width, and replace that area with our cable panel of 26 stitches.

$$
\begin{array}{rl}
 & 4″ \text{ (inches of width on center front)} \\
\times\ 4 & \text{(gauge: sts per inch)} \\
\hline
=\ 16 & \text{(sts of St st at center front to be replaced by cable panel)}
\end{array}
$$

$$
\begin{array}{rl}
 & 26 \text{ (number of sts in cable panel)} \\
-\ 16 & \text{(number of sts of St st that will be replaced)} \\
\hline
=\ 10 & \text{(sts to increase across area of cable panel)}
\end{array}
$$

Okay, this tells us that our cable panel will eat 10 stitches of width and we will need to add 10 stitches directly under the cable panel. Ah, but how will we know how many stitches to work across in plain stockinette stitch *before* we begin to make those increases? To find that number, we must go back to the total width again, subtract the number of stitches the cable panel will replace and divide the remainder by two, half for the right side and half for the left side.

$$
\begin{array}{rl}
 & 94 \text{ (total number of sts on front)} \\
-\ 16 & \text{(number of sts to be replaced by cable panel)} \\
\hline
=\ 78 & \text{(number of plain sts of St st to remain)} \\
\div\ 2 & \text{(half for right side, half for left side)} \\
\hline
=\ 39 & \text{(number of sts of St st each side)}
\end{array}
$$

This tells us that we work across 39 stitches, increase 10 stitches over the next 16 stitches, and then work across the remaining 39 stitches.

If you are knitting the sweater for yourself, you can count stitches to be worked in stockinette on each side of the front panel (39) and mark those areas with slip-on ring markers. On next row, between the markers, increase (10) for cable panel using the blind stockinette type of increase (see page 148). If you are writing the instructions for someone else, you will change the preceding bold paragraph to knitting shorthand.

In either case, it is nice to know how many stitches remain.

$$\begin{array}{rl} & 78 \quad \text{(number of plain sts of St st to remain)} \\ + & 26 \quad \text{(number of cable panel sts)} \\ \hline = & 104 \quad \text{(number of sts remaining)} \end{array}$$

BUST DART

In the next chapter I will go into detail about making bust darts for large-breasted women. But unless the bosom is quite large, often a short shallow bust dart is sufficient. For a woman's sweater, I almost always put one in as follows (see Figure 22.5):

Locate the bust darts 2″ below the beginning of the underarm shaping.

Make the darts 2.5″ long from each side seam toward the center.

$$\begin{array}{rl} & 2.5″ \quad \text{(length of bust dart)} \\ \times & 4 \quad \text{(gauge: sts per inch)} \\ \hline = & 10 \quad \text{(number of sts the bust dart will extend from each side edge)} \end{array}$$

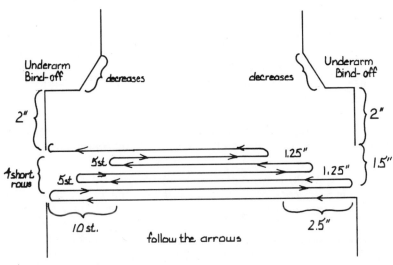

22.5 Layout of bust dart for Classic Crew-Necked Pullover

Make the bust dart 1″ or 1.5″ in depth.

$$
\begin{array}{r}
1.5''\ \text{(depth of bust dart)} \\
\times\ 3\ \quad \text{(gauge: rows per inch)} \\
\hline
=\ 4.5\ \ \text{(number of rows in bust dart)}
\end{array}
$$

Round this off to an even whole number, 4.

One short row consumes 2 regular rows so divide the number of rows in the bust dart by 2 to find out how many turns there will be on each side.

$$
\begin{array}{r}
4\ \text{(total number of short rows)} \\
\div\ 2 \\
\hline
=\ 2\ \text{(number of short rows on each side)}
\end{array}
$$

We need to make only 2 short-row turns over a length of 10 stitches.

$$
\begin{array}{r}
10\ \text{(number of sts the bust dart will extend from each side edge)} \\
\div\ 2\ \ \text{(number of short rows on each side front)} \\
\hline
=\ 5\ \ \text{(number of sts in each short row)}
\end{array}
$$

When front is 2″ shorter than back to armhole shaping, short-row 5 stitches 4 times.

ARMHOLE AND SHOULDER SHAPING

It is customary to shape the armholes and the shoulders the same on the front and the back. Only the neck shaping is different.

PLANNING A CREW NECKLINE

The front of the human neck is set at an angle into the torso at a spot about 1.5″ lower than the neck-shoulder joining. This depth varies according to body type, weight, and age.

A crew neck is a bite out of the sweater front that is as wide as the back neck and as low as the body neck/torso joining.

The depth at which we choose to begin shaping our crew neck will depend in part upon how we plan to finish the completed neckline. The deeper the planned ribbing, the deeper the neckline will have to be to accommodate it.

On this sweater, the wearer's neck is 1.75″ lower than the neck-shoulder joining and the ribbing will be .75″ deep. Let's make our neck 2.5″ deep.

The back neck of the sweater will be 7.5″ wide.

Therefore the "bite" out of this sweater front will be 7.5″ wide and 2.5″ deep.

Now we need to shape that bite (see Figure 22.6):

$$
\begin{array}{rl}
& 2.5″ \text{ (desired depth of front neck)} \\
\times\ 3 & \text{(gauge: rows per inch)} \\
\hline
=\ 7.5 & \text{(number of rows deep the front neck will be)}
\end{array}
$$

Round this up to a whole even number, 8.

That means that 4 stitches can be decreased at each side of the flat part of the crew neck at the rate of "dec 1 st each side every other row."

We have already decided to make the back (stockinette stitch) neck width 7.5″, or 30 stitches wide. If we did not have the extra center cable panel on the front we would figure the neck as follows:

$$
\begin{array}{rl}
& 30 \text{ (total number of sts on back neck)} \\
-\ 8 & \text{(number of sts that can be decreased at each side at the rate of 1 st each side every other row)} \\
\hline
=\ 22 & \text{(number of sts to be placed on holder for center front neck)}
\end{array}
$$

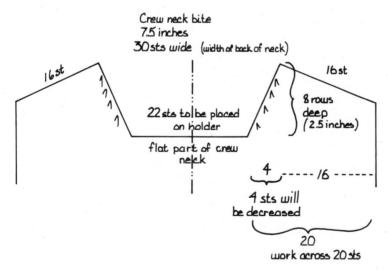

22.6 Close-up of neck area of Classic Crew-Necked Pullover

That would be 11 stitches on each side of an imaginary center line. But knitters don't usually have a center line running up and down the middle of their knitting, so we need to figure how many stitches to work across before "slipping the stitches to a holder."

> 16 (number of sts on *each* back shoulder)
> + 4 (sts to be decreased at *each* neck edge)
> = 20 (number of sts to work across before placing center sts on holder for flat part of front neck)

If the front were plain stockinette stitch we could say:

When front is 5.5″ long from the beginning of the armhole shaping (that is, 2.5″ shorter than back), work across 20 stitches, place center 22 stitches on holder for center front neck, add a new ball of yarn. Work across remaining 20 stitches. At each neck edge, decrease 1 stitch every other row 4 times, AND AT THE SAME TIME, when front measures same as back, shape shoulders same as back.

For this particular sweater, because of the increased stitches over the cable panel, there will be more stitches to place on the stitch holder at the center front. All that needs to be changed in the italicized paragraph above is the number of stitches that are slipped to the holder; that is, the extra 10 stitches we increased. *Place center 32 stitches on holder.*

PLANNING LONG SET-IN SLEEVES

A shaped/fitted sleeve cap differs in many respects from the puff sleeve described in Chapter 20. This sleeve is longer and it is tapered between wrist and underarm. At the underarm shaping it is similar to the puff sleeve but there the similarity ends. On the puff sleeve we just knit straight up until the sleeve is almost as long as the body armhole and then decrease stitches rapidly over just 2 rows.

The top of this sleeve is different, too. The shaped/fitted sleeve cap tapers in gradually; it is shorter in length than the gathered puff sleeve; and it has a rounded top. For the sake of learning, let's discuss each part separately. (Later, when you are more experienced, you'll be at ease with juggling them all at once.)

Tapered Long Sleeves   Calculate wrist ribbing stitches as follows:

1. Measure wrist.
2. Multiply by ribbing gauge.

3. Divide by pattern stitch multiple to determine number of complete patterns.
4. Round the number up or down.
5. Multiply again by pattern stitch multiple.
6. Add the plus number.

Plan width increase above wrist ribbing as follows:

7. Measure arm just above wrist.
8. Add an ease allowance factor of about .33.
9. Multiply by fabric stitch gauge.
10. From the number above, subtract the number of ribbing stitches. This will tell you exactly how many stitches to increase across the row as you change pattern stitch and needle size.

Widen at side seams to underarm width as follows:

11. Measure desired upper arm circumference.
12. Multiply by stitch gauge.
13. From the number above (#12) subtract the number of stitches on needle after completing the "increase across the row" just above the wrist (#9). This will tell you exactly how many stitches to increase from lower arm to upper arm.
14. Divide this number by 2 in order to make half the increases on the right edge and the other half on the left edge.
15. Measure the desired sleeve length and from this subtract the wrist ribbing length *and* approximately 2″ to work even (i.e., without increases) after the last span is completed. This will give you the length available for making increases.
16. Count the number of *spans* desired.
17. *Note:* You will want all of your increases to be made on the public side of the fabric.
18. If you can quickly divide the figures in your head, *do it.* If, for instance, you have 13 spans (each side) and 14 inches of length available to make increases, move that extra inch somewhere else. Either add it to the plain 2″ area near the top or put in an extra inch on the sleeve before you begin to increase and then increase 1 stitch each side every 1″.
19. If you cannot quickly decide what to do, multiply the length available for making increases by row gauge. Then divide this number of rows by the number of spans. If you will *cheat, juggle, and fudge,* it is usually not necessary to resort to "The Formula for Diagonals That Don't Come Out Even" (see pages 175–180).

SHAPING THE SLEEVE CAP

Before we can begin to discuss the sleeve armhole shaping, we need to detour to the top of the sleeve cap and talk about what shape we are trying to achieve. We are trying to make a round-topped, bell-shaped curve.

Note in Figure 22.7 that sleeves *must* be shorter than armhole by length of "flat" (i.e., bind-off) area at top of sleeve.

The width of the flat top of the sleeve is divided by 2. One-half of the flat top of the sleeve is subtracted from the length of each sleeve.

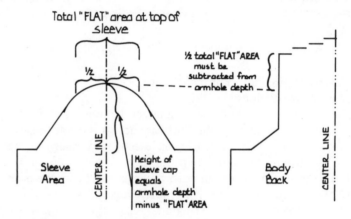

22.7 Difference in length between body and sleeve armholes

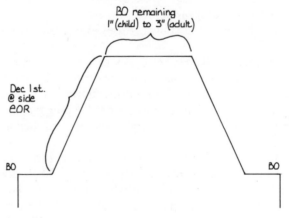

22.8 Standard (usual) sleeve cap

The traditional way to achieve this shape is shown in Figure 22.8.

The usual way of shaping a sleeve cap is to bind off on each side the same number of stitches that were bound off on the sweater back, and then "decrease 1 stitch each side every other row until 2″ (for children) or 3″ (for adults) of stitches remain. Bind off all stitches." There are a number of problems with this shaping system.

The first problem is with the ratio of the number of stitches per inch to the number of rows per inch. If there is a "bad" ratio, decrease of 1 stitch each side every other row can make the sleeve cap either much too short or much too long.

Even if the ratio of stitches and rows worked out perfectly and the sleeve cap was the desired length, there would still be a problem when sewing the sleeve in place. The "horns" of fabric at the beginning of the sleeve bind-off area must be tucked in underneath the armhole seam. This always leaves a triangle of unwanted fabric on the inside of the armhole.

A final problem is that "usual" sleeves are often not wide enough from shoulder tip to shoulder tip for Big and Beautiful people with heavy upper arms.

The round-top sleeve cap shown in Figure 22.9 solves all these problems.

It reserves 3″ of stitches of the width for the top bind off (adults). It keeps the sleeve cap length 1.5″ inches shorter than the corresponding body armhole length (adults). *In order to keep the sleeve cap as wide as possible as long as possible,* following the regular underarm shaping of "bind off/decrease every other row," it makes decreases every 4th (sometimes every 6th) row until about 8 or 10 rows short of the final desired length. To avoid the horns of the standard sleeve cap, it makes

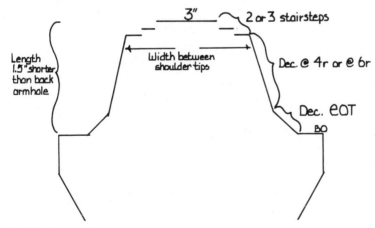

22.9 Round-top sleeve cap

wide stairstep bind-offs to get rid of unwanted stitches rapidly. Two stairsteps each side are commonly used; sometimes three each side are necessary.

I begin to design my sleeve caps by determining the number of rows available. To do this I subtract 1.5" inches from the length of the body back armhole and convert that figure to rows. Next I decide on the underarm bind-off and every-other-row decreases. Then I have to jump to the top of the sleeve and plan top down: stitches in the stairsteps, stitches for the final bind-off. What is left is the space in between to be decreased every 4th or every 6th row. It is not the easiest sleeve to design, *but it fits both the person and the armhole, it is comfortable, and it looks beautiful.*

SLEEVE ARMHOLE AND CAP SHAPING

For Big and Beautiful people with heavy upper arms:

1. Make a layout drawing and mark it with lengths and widths in inches.
2. Convert all lengths and widths to stitches and rows.
3. Decide the number of stitches to bind off at underarm (should be nearly the same as back armhole bind-offs).
4. Decide the number of stitches to "decrease 1 stitch each side every other row" at underarm. This will ordinarily match the body back underarm shape.
5. Calculate how many stitches and rows will be left on the sleeves at this point.

$$
\begin{array}{rl}
& 6 \text{ (sts each side bound off } in\ 2\ rows) \\
+ & 4 \text{ (sts each side decreased } in\ 8\ rows) \\
\hline
= & 10 \text{ (sts gotten rid of on each side)} \\
\times & 2 \text{ (right and left sides)} \\
\hline
= & 20 \text{ (total number of sts gotten rid of at underarm)} \\
\end{array}
$$

$$
\begin{array}{rl}
& 53 \text{ (number of sts existing before underarm shaping)} \\
- & 20 \text{ (total number of sts gotten rid of at underarm)} \\
\hline
= & 33 \text{ (sts remaining on sleeve cap)} \\
\end{array}
$$

$$
\begin{array}{rl}
& 26 \text{ (original number of rows)} \\
- & 10 \text{ (rows used up in underarm shaping)} \\
\hline
= & 16 \text{ (rows remaining on sleeve cap)} \\
\end{array}
$$

6. Find the approximate number of stitches to reserve for the flat area on the top: 3" (adult) times gauge (3" × 4 = 12 sts). We will have to add 1 stitch to this number so that an even number of stitches will

remain for identical shaping on the two shoulders. Because there is an odd number of stitches between the shoulder tips (see #7), it is necessary to subtract an odd number to yield an even number of stitches to divide between the right and left shoulders (see #8).

7. On your layout drawing note the width between shoulder tips across upper arm. (7.25" = 29 sts)
8. Find stitches for stairsteps. Subtract #6 from #7.

$$
\begin{array}{rl}
  & 29 \text{ (sts between shoulder tips, \#7)} \\
- & 13 \text{ (sts reserved for flat bind-off, \#6)} \\
\hline
= & 16 \text{ (total sts in stairsteps)} \\
\div & 2 \text{ (half for each side)} \\
\hline
= & 8 \text{ (sts to stairstep each side)}
\end{array}
$$

Make 2 stairsteps of 4 stitches each on each side. (Instructions would say, "Bind off 4 sts at beg of the next 4 rows. BO rem 13 sts.")
9. Now plan to get rid of the stitches in the middle. You will have used up both rows and stitches in the final finishing.

$$
\begin{array}{rl}
  & 1 \text{ (row consumed in final bind-off)} \\
+ & 4 \text{ (rows consumed in stairsteps, \#8)} \\
\hline
= & 5 \text{ (rows consumed in final cap finishing)}
\end{array}
$$

$$
\begin{array}{rl}
  & 16 \text{ (rows remaining on sleeve after underarm shaping, \#5)} \\
- & 5 \text{ (rows consumed in final cap finishing)} \\
\hline
= & 11 \text{ (rows to get rid of remaining [middle] stitches)}
\end{array}
$$

$$
\begin{array}{rl}
  & 33 \text{ (sts remaining after underarm shaping, \#5)} \\
- & 29 \text{ (sts consumed in final cap shaping, \#7)} \\
\hline
= & 4 \text{ (total sts to get rid of between underarm and cap)} \\
- & 2 \text{ (half on each side)} \\
\hline
= & 2 \text{ (sts to get rid of each side between underarm and cap)}
\end{array}
$$

You have 11 rows to get rid of 2 stitches. Fudge and make that number of rows 12 so that you can plan for 3 spans. Now you can say, "Work 4 rows even. Dec 1 stitch each side every 4th row 2 times." This will consume the 12 rows and get rid of the 4 stitches. You will now be ready to shape the cap that we have already planned. Now go back and put all these figures and things to do in their proper sequence.

At the beginning of the next _____ rows bind off _____ sts.
Decrease 1 st each side every other row _____ times.
Work _____ rows even (_____ sts remain).
Dec. 1 st each side every 4th row _____ times (_____ sts rem and sleeve cap measures _____ inches from beginning of armhole shaping).

At the beginning of the next _____ rows bind off _____ stitches.

Bind off _____ remaining stitches.

Finished sleeve measures _____ inches less than body armhole.

Mark the layout in green with the number of stitches, your notes about pattern stitches, and the needle size changes. (See Figure 22.10.)

MAKING THE SWEATER

If you are not sure you have sufficient yarn, make the sleeves first, because sleeves that are too short look ridiculous. So long as the back and front of the sweater cover the tummy, making the body a little bit shorter will not drastically affect the way the sweater looks. Of course, if you find that you have sufficient yarn, you can make the sweater any length you wish.

Do not bind off either the center back or the center front neck stitches; put them on a holder to be worked later for neck ribbing. This applies to all closed-neck designs, because a tight bind-off may prevent the wearer from getting the sweater over his or her head.

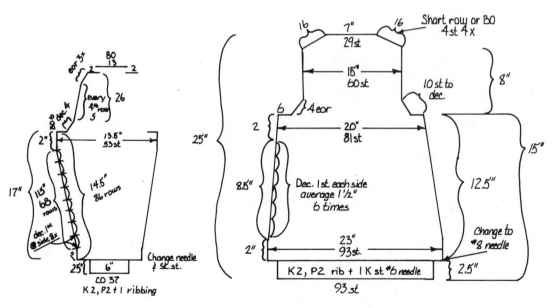

22.10 Sleeve armhole and cap with measurements, stitches, rows, and instructions

FINISHING THE SWEATER

All that was said in Chapter 21 ("A V-Neck Vested Pullover") about working the neck ribbing stitches flat or in the round applies to this crew neck as well.

I almost always make the neck ribbing of crew-necked sweaters double length to be folded to the inside and whip-stitched in place. Especially if you are working with an unfamiliar yarn, you cannot know how it will behave until the sweater is completed and worn several times. If the yarn stretches at the neckline, you will be prepared to insert a soft lingerie elastic into the tube of the fold-under ribbing.

After the neckline ribbing is completed and the shoulder seams are woven, weave the sleeves in place.

Finally weave the underarm seams. First, weave the sleeves working from the wrist to the underarm. Then weave the body from the bottom edge to the underarm. That way, if you are off a few rows between back and front you can cheat in your weaving of row to row near the underarm.

VARIATIONS

In warmer climates a sport-weight, Class B, or what the English call "double knitting weight" yarn might be desired.

For summer, try the sweater in cotton, linen, silk, or ramie.

Omit the center front cable pattern and make graphic intarsia designs instead (see Chapter 34).

Omit the center front cable pattern and work the whole garment in any pattern stitch or striping pattern desired.

Get as fancy as you wish and try intricate Aran fisherman cable stitches up the front, and perhaps up the center of the sleeves as well (see Chapter 30).

The front cable pattern could be worked in a different color (or colors) using bobbins. A lighter-color cable panel against a darker background would be slenderizing; a darker color cable with lighter-colored yarn for the rest of the sweater would add width and the appearance of extra weight. (Remember that bobbin work must be done flat, back and forth.) (See the note about colored cables on page 377.)

The body of this sweater can be worked in the round. At the underarm shaping you can then work flat, back and forth. If you are a

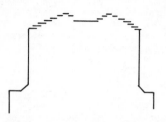

22.11 Close-up of sweater back, showing dropped neck

confirmed circular knitter, the body armhole openings can be allowed for with steeks and cut open.

Make the sleeves in the round to the underarm shaping.

Some knitters, especially Europeans, like to drop the center back neck down approximately 1″ from the inner tip of the shoulders. (See Figure 22.11.)

The shoulder slopes may be short-rowed instead of being formed with bound-off stairsteps. If you choose to short-row the shoulder steps, you can then form the shoulder seam with a double bind-off. (Following the completion of short-row shoulder shaping, place the stitches of the back and the front on separate circular needles. Hold the needles parallel with the outsides of the pieces facing each other. Insert your working needle through the first stitch on *each* of the other needles and bind off both pieces together at the same time.)

The sleeves don't have to be long. Make them any length you choose—short, elbow, or three-quarter (between elbow and wrist) length.

You can marry this crew neck to the vest in Chapter 21, or you can marry the V-neck of the previous chapter to this sweater.

To suit yourself (and the wearer) is the name of the game. Mix and match elements of different sweaters to get the effect you want.

CONCLUSION

Classic ideas are hard to beat. This crew-necked, long-sleeved pullover is not only flattering to all ages and most figures but is also variable, versatile, comfortable, and warm. Any fiber/type/weight/variety of yarn may be used. Endless modifications of the basic design are possible.

23

A Cardigan Jacket

THE IDEA

A sweater doesn't always have to be just a sweater. Sometimes it can be a jacket.

So far in Part II we have been designing only pullovers because I wanted to allow you to become familiar with the different elements that go into creating sweaters before I said, "Now cut the front in half and add some extra fabric to the front edges without disturbing the neck shaping." But the time has come for me to say exactly that to you. (See Figure 23.2.)

From the chapter lessons box you can see that we have many

23.1 Cardigan Jacket worn by Tiffany-diamond-shaped woman (yarn supplied by Bernat and DMC; knitted by Shirley Robb; modeled by Susan Bumbarger)

objectives in this chapter. Because there is so much material to be covered, I will not repeat the basics of plotting and multiplying lengths, widths, and stitches. But just because we go on to learn other things does not mean that the basics are forgotten.

FLOOR PLAN OF THE PIECES

Looking at Figure 23.3, notice the difference in the front pieces between the garment designed for the Tiffany diamond figure and for "ordinary" figures. If you need to, review pages 115–128 on some of the problems of designing for Tiffany diamond figures.

THE YARN AND THE GAUGE

Since this is to be a coat/jacket, we wouldn't be satisfied with an ordinary sweater-looking knitted fabric. We need to do something to the texture of our stitches to make the fabric both firmer and more interesting. There are several obvious choices available to us to achieve this end: using a combination of yarns, pattern stitch, and gauge that will give a firm fabric.

1. The yarn: For jackets and coats a favorite trick of mine is to combine one strand of standard 4-ply (worsted—Class C) with one strand of a similar color glossy, nubby, or boucle dress (sport—Class B) weight

23.2 Rough sketch of Cardigan Jacket

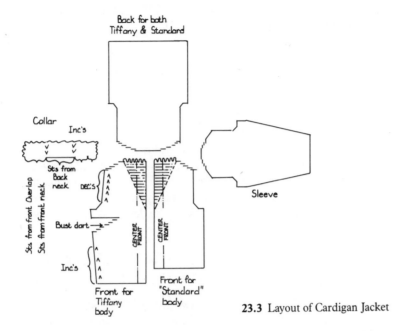

23.3 Layout of Cardigan Jacket

yarn in a slightly lighter or darker tone. Working the two strands together as if they were one makes a firmer fabric.

For this garment we have selected Bernat's "Glouster® Wool," a smooth, soft, high-quality 100 percent virgin wool, 47 grams and approximately 96 yards per skein. *And* DMC's "Brilliant Knitting/ Crochet Cotton," a glossy 100 percent cotton smooth classic thread. Each ball contains 50 grams and has approximately 218 yards.

As far as estimating how much yarn will be necessary, our handy little pocket guide stops at "Men's X-Large, 48"," saying 1,700 yards. That isn't the answer for this 56" garment. True, our jacket will be shorter in both body and sleeves than a man's X-Large, but to be certain, I'm going to order 2,000 yards.

2. *The pattern stitch:* Some pattern stitches are firmer, crisper, and less stretchy than stockinette stitch. The herringbone is such a pattern. It is a multiple of 5 stitches plus 2 (i.e., a selvedge stitch on each side), and a repeat of 10 rows. Over a base of stockinette in which the stitches on the public side are knitted and the stitches on the private side are purled, on every knit row 3 stitches are knitted and with the yarn at the front, the 4th and 5th stitches are slipped as if to purl. This pattern has an interesting diagonal effect because on every subsequent knit row the knitter moves the slipped stitches 1 stitch to the left.

Herringbone:

Note: All slipped stitches are made as if to purl with the yarn at the front of the work.

Row 1 and all odd-numbered rows) (private side) P across

Row 2) K 1, *k 3, sl 2*, rep bet *s across, end k 1.

Row 4) K 1, sl 1, *k 3, sl 2*, rep bet *s, end k 3, sl 1, k 1.

Row 6) K 1, sl 2, *k 3, sl 2*, rep bet *s, end k 4.

Row 8) K 2, sl 2, *k 3, sl 2*, rep bet *s, end k 3.

Row 10) *K 3, sl 2*, rep bet *s across, end k 2.

Of course there are many other pattern stitch options, but I have chosen for this learning lesson to use the herringbone partly because its multiple is 5 stitches (plus 2) and one part of this lesson is learning to work with multiples. The other task in this lesson is to learn to make short rows in a pattern stitch.

3. Work on smaller-than-ordinary needles to give a tighter, more substantial gauge. To give a tight gauge we have chosen to work on a #6 needle.

Be sure to double-check your row gauge! The slipped stitches shorten the fabric and it will take more rows to make the same number of inches than if you were simply doing stockinette stitch. This difference in row gauge becomes very important when planning the armholes, sleeve caps, and lapel turn-back.

GAUGE: Herringbone—4.6 sts and 8 rows = 1″ on #6 needles.

SPECIAL CONSIDERATION IN DESIGNING FOR A TIFFANY DIAMOND FIGURE

On all Tiffany diamonds there will be a big difference between circumference at bust and width of shoulders.

Do not be tempted to make extrawide shoulders for a Tiffany diamond figure. That will only make the bust look larger.

To accommodate the large bosom, the widths of the back and front are not the same; the front is wider. However, the back and front shoulders need to be *nearly the same* width. Getting rid of such a large number of stitches will take some special thought.

How do you get rid of the extra stitches to make the proportionately narrower shoulders on the front come out nearly equal to the back?

1. Use extrawide armhole bind-offs. Depending on the person, a total (back and front) of 4 or 5 or 6 or more inches is often used. And the bind-offs on the back do *not* have to be as wide as those on the front.

2. The "every-other-row" decreases on the armhole can continue up higher than normal. Don't stop at 1.5″. Go up farther, perhaps 3″. Again, what you do on the front does not have to match what happens on the back.

3. Don't stop decreasing and go straight up at the end of the every-other-row armhole decreases. Space decreases farther apart, perhaps every 4th or 6th or 8th row, and continue these decreases all the way up the armhole to shoulders.

4. Fudge the shoulder seams. Several paragraphs ago I used the phrase "nearly the same." The shoulder front can easily have a few more stitches than the back. The difference can be concealed by careful finishing work.

5. More stitches, up to 2″, can be allowed on the front neck opening than on the back neck opening.

On Tiffany diamond figures, the back and front are not only different widths but also different lengths. Your tape measure will tell you it is longer from the neck-shoulder joining on the front down to the bottom of the garment than it is from the nape of the back neck to the bottom. The front needs extra length, but not at the underarm—only at the center front. A bust dart the approximate length of the difference between back and front lengths makes up the discrepancy. (Planning and making bust darts is described in detail in Chapter 14.) Just make sure you draw the dart on your layout because it will affect the position of the collar and the buttonholes.

The sleeves for Tiffany diamonds can be quite ordinary.

Though underarm bind-offs need to be nearly equal in width to body underarm bind-offs, the subsequent decreases do not have to match.

Don't bother trying to make the two sides of the sleeve differently. When you sew them in place the sleeve underarm seam does not have to align with the body underarm seam.

SPECIAL CONSIDERATIONS IN DESIGNING A CARDIGAN

Unless you intend either to crochet front bands or pick up stitches along the vertical edge and make ribbing crosswise, you will need to plan a front overlap for your cardigan. The easiest way to do this is to begin by drawing a centerline on your front layout to keep you from

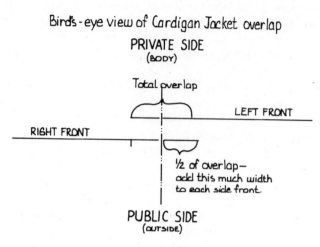

23.4 Bird's-eye view of Cardigan Jacket overlap

getting confused. Think of the overlap from a bird's-eye view. (See Figure 23.4.)

The width of the overlap depends on the size of the person and the size of the buttons. On each side of the front, unless otherwise dictated by the diameter of the chosen buttons, a baby will need only about .5″; a moderate-size adult will need an 1″; a large person will need 1.5″.

MEASUREMENTS NEEDED

1. Chest circumference: In this example, we will use 56″ as the measurement of the chest circumference. (The back measures 24″ from side seam to side seam; the front measure 32″.) This is to be an outdoor sweater made of a rather stiff fabric. Sufficient ease must be added to cover undergarments. I would suggest a total of about 3″: 1″ on the back, 2″ on the front.

    a. Back chest width side seam to side seam:

	24″	(back chest width at bustline)
+	1″	(allowance for ease)
=	25″	(total desired back width)
×	4.6	(gauge: sts per inch)
=	115	(approximate number of sts on back)
÷	5	(pattern st multiple)
=	23	(whole patterns across)

The number came out even on the first try! That means all we need to do is add the 2 selvedge stitches.

> 115 (approximate number of sts on back)
> + 2 (selvedge sts)
> = 117 (final number of sts on back)

> b. *Front chest width side seam to side seam:*

> 32" (front chest width at bustline)
> + 2" (allowance for ease)
> = 34" (total desired front width)
> ÷ 2 (half right side, half left side)
> = 17" (approximate width each side front *to center line*)
> + 1.5" (to allow overlap)
> = 18.5" (desired width each side front)
> × 4.6 (gauge: sts per inch)
> = 85.1 (approximate number of sts on each side front)

Round the number up or down.

> 85 (rounded approximate number of sts on each side front)
> ÷ 5 (pattern st multiple)
> = 17 (whole pattern multiples across)

> 85 (approximate sts)
> + 2 (selvedge sts)
> = 87 (final number of sts for each side front)

2. *Circumference at bottom of sweater: 57"* (body measure plus 3"). Ease already added will take care of the 1" difference between bust and hips for this person. However, many Tiffany diamond figures have much smaller hips and it might be necessary for the bottom circumference to be narrower than the chest.

3. *Length from nape of neck to bottom of sweater on back: 21". Length from side of front neck over bosom to bottom of sweater: 26".* This tells us how many inches of short rows are necessary for a bust dart.

> 26" (front length)
> − 21" (back length)
> = 5" (difference between front and back lengths/length of bust dart)

4. a. *Actual body underarm depth: 10"*
   b. *Desired sweater underarm depth: 11"*

5. *Length from garment underarm to bottom of sweater:* 10″
Do #4b and #5 add up to #3? Yes: 11″ + 10″ = 21″.

6. a. *Width of body between shoulder tips:* 15″.
b. *Desired width of sweater at shoulders:* 15.5″. Some body types will look better with the shoulders artificially broadened by shoulder pads. If you plan to use shoulder pads, add width to allow for them. Purchase pads; set them in place and measure. (This particular body did not need shoulders pads. The 15.5″ is a measurement from the body.)

7. *Back neck width:* 7.5″ Measure the person's back neck from fabric stitch edge to fabric stitch edge.

8. *Slope of shoulders:* 2.5″.

9. *Sleeve width at underarm:* 20″.

10. *Desired sleeve width at wrist:* 11.5″.

11. *Sleeve length from underarm to wrist:* 14″.

12. *Shoulder tip to shoulder tip across upper arm:* 12″.

13. *Distance between bust points (nipples):* 12″.

      12″ (total distance between bust points)
÷   2 (This is a cardigan; the front is made in two pieces; we need to know the distance to the center line)
=   6″ (distance from bust point to center line)

14. *Length down from armpit to height of bust point:*

      5″ (length down from armpit to height of bust)
− 1″ (allowance for underarm ease)
= 4″ (location on sweater of bust dart below underarm bind-off)

THE BACK

The back of this garment is made in the same way as most other backs so there is no need to go over it again here, except to say that for Tiffany, Big and Beautiful, and other large-breasted body types you will have a large number of stitches to get rid of between the underarm width and the desired shoulder width.

THE FRONT

WHERE TO PLACE BUTTONHOLES HORIZONTALLY

It is important to remember that when the garment is worn, the buttons will not rest in the center of the buttonholes. The outermost edge of the buttonhole will rest against the spot where the button is attached. Therefore

do not center the buttonholes along the center line of the garment.

For example, if you plan a buttonhole 4 stitches wide, from the centerline, make 1 of those stitches toward the front edge and the other 3 stitches toward the underarm. Likewise, if your buttonhole is to be 8 stitches wide, make 2 or 3 stitches toward the front and the remaining stitches toward the underarm. (See Figure 23.5.)

Another thing to remember about buttonholes is that their width is a function of the gauge. This becomes important when your garment has ribbing on both the bottom and the neck edge.

Buttonholes in ribbing need to contain more stitches of width than buttonholes on the same garment in the fabric stitch.

WHERE TO PLACE BUTTONHOLES VERTICALLY

Envisioning the diameter of the button, decide where you wish the bottommost button to be placed. The buttonhole for a button 2″ in diameter needs to be placed at least 1.5″ from the bottom so that some fabric will be visible below it. Of course more than .5″ can be allowed.

> 1″ (half the diameter of the button)
> + .5″ (of fabric to show at the bottom of button)
> = 1.5″ (location of center bottom button from bottom edge of finished sweater)

In the same manner, now decide where you wish the uppermost button to be placed. On a typical jacket with a fold-back lapel it will be at about the armhole bind-off, or however many inches you choose below the shoulder-neck joining.

Don't let the addition of a bust dart confuse you. You need to work with the numbers of the front edge length, not the numbers of the underarm seam length.

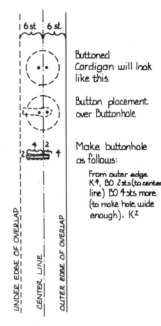

23.5 Centerline buttonhole placement for Cardigan Jacket

To plan the buttonhole spacing, from the total front length (shoulder-neck joining to bottom of garment, which includes the length added by the bust dart) subtract:

26″ (total front length)
− 1.5″ (desired distance from bottom edge)
− 10″ (desired distance from top edge)
= 14.5″ (available for placement of buttons)

Next you must decide how many buttons you wish to put in this length. In the days before women's lib, it used to be a rule that an even number of buttons were put on men's clothing and that an odd number were put on women's, odd numbers being considered more feminine. If you are a traditionalist, follow these rules; if you are not, do anything you want.

If you have the buttons or similar-sized ones on hand, spread them out over the 14.5″ length. Your eye will tell you how many are enough. You will have one less space than you will have buttonholes. Five buttons minus 1 equals 4 spaces. Divide the available space (either in inches or in rows) by the number of spaces needed. If it doesn't come out neat and even, fudge! (See Figure 23.6.)

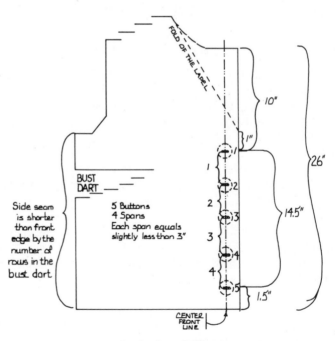

23.6 Button placement for Cardigan Jacket

PLOTTING A FOLD-BACK LAPEL

Looking through knitting publications, whenever I see a cardigan with the wrong side of the fabric showing on a lapel, I know that the garment was designed by an amateur. Such a mistake is easy to avoid. Simply plan a diagonal line from the shoulder-neck joining to a spot on the front edge about .5″ above the radius of the uppermost button. Plot it in the same way you would a V-neck. Reverse the pattern stitch from front to back along that line.

SLEEVES FOR LARGE PEOPLE

Many Tiffany diamonds have very small upper arm circumferences. However, the woman for whom we are making this particular sweater has large upper arms, as do many other body types.

In planning these special sleeves, we need to do two things:

1. Get rid of many stitches quickly at the underarm. To start with, make an extrawide underarm bind-off. So long as the amount is within a few stitches of the number of body underarm bind-off stitches, there can be *more* bind-offs at the sleeve underarm when necessary. Next,

   the number of decreases following the underarm bind-off DO NOT HAVE TO MATCH the number of decreases on either the back or the front. You are not looking for precision; you are looking for a good fit.

2. For people with wide distances from front to back between the shoulder tips, make the flat area at the top of the sleeve cap wider than usual in order to keep the sleeve as wide as possible as far up as possible. As much as 4″ is okay. Remember to subtract one-half of that bind-off width from the overall length of the sleeve cap.

COLLAR

The simplest of all collars is just an extension of the stitches of the back and front neck edge stitches. Obviously stockinette stitch is not an appropriate choice of fabric but, if we were not already making a fancy pattern stitch, seed or Irish moss would be.

The back neck stitches should already be waiting on holders. Slip the front lapel stitches to holders. Work across one lapel, work across the stitches from the back neck of garment, then work across final lapel.

An easy way to make the collar flare slightly so that it fits nicely across the upper shoulders is to CHANGE TO A NEEDLE ONE SIZE LARGER about every 1″ or 1.5″ to avoid making increases that would disrupt the look of a pattern stitch.

The length of the collar will depend on the stiffness of the fabric as well as the size of the person. If you have already completed the shoulder seams, it is an easy matter to judge how long to make that collar. Just look at it and decide when to quit.

Since the trim on this sweater will be crocheted, you don't have to bind off the stitches. You can crochet directly from your knitting needle.

PATCH POCKETS

The purpose of a pocket is either to be decorative or to hold things. If the pocket is not simply decorative, its size and shape will be determined by the objects you want it to hold. I plan to accommodate a purse pack of tissues and perhaps a pair of soft gloves. Lay the objects the pocket is to contain on a flat surface and measure them, adding a bit of ease; what could be simpler?

If you want pockets in which to thrust your hands on cold winter days, the size of the pocket opening and depth will be determined by the size of your hand.

A nondecorative pocket should be placed where it is easy for the hands to slip into. Often the best placement is decided after the garment fronts are finished.

MAKING THE SWEATER

If forming buttonholes causes you concern, you might find it helpful to refer to the chapter on buttonholes in *Knitting in Plain English* by Maggie Righetti (New York: St. Martin's Press, 1986).

I deliberately designed this garment with *both* a pattern stitch and a short-row bust dart to let you know that such a thing can be done, and to give you practice in doing it. You may be intimidated at the thought of doing the two things at the same time, but just dive in, juggle, and make it work.

Don't forget to begin to reverse the pattern stitch for the lapel turn-back when you reach the appropriate place. I find that slip-on ring markers are handy reminders when placed beside the change/fold line. I can quickly move them as the lapel needs to widen according to the layout diagram.

FINISHING THE SWEATER

I planned the edges of this coat/jacket (including the patch pockets) to be finished with a crochet edge. Bulky fabrics like the one used here don't take kindly to folded-back front bands and double collars. A row of single crochet followed by a row of crab stitch, which is single crochet worked from left to right, solves the problem of unfinished edges very nicely.

First crochet the sides and top edge of the pocket. Pin the pocket in place somewhat off-center between the front edge and the side seam, a bit nearer the side seam than the front. Form the bottom seam of the pocket at the same time as you finish the bottom edge of the jacket by working through the two layers of fabric at once.

VARIATIONS

You can go to any length with this simple idea. Quickly and easily this basic idea can become a coat.

If you plan for your coat/jacket to be longer than 7″ below the waistline, *do not taper in for a narrow hipline.*

There is a secret to designing coats so that they will not hang open in the front. The trick is to make a line of decreases up the center BACK of the coat from bottom to top.

Making a 2″- or 3″-wide vertical tapering/decreasing dart from the bottom of the *center back* to 2″ below the underarm bind-off point will keep the jacket *fronts* from spreading apart.

Plan this and also, if desired, a very slight side seam increase when drawing the layout diagram. From a point about 3″ below the bustline, gradually increase at each side seam (front and back) to the bottom edge until at least about 4″ in total width has been added (not including the back dart). (See Figure 23.7.)

Collar and pocket choice, of course, may be varied. How about a mandarin collar (with no folded-back lapel) and a vertical slash pocket? Consider a notched collar.

Using three or more strands, each of a different lightweight (finger-

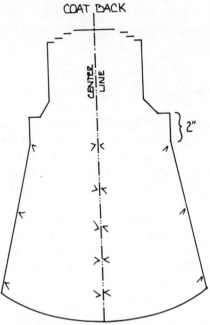

COAT BACK

CENTER LINE

} 2"

Increases at sides and center of back
will allow coat to hang straight
at the center front.

23.7 Layout of Cardigan Jacket back, showing increases at sides and center

ing—Class A) yarn, together with a firm pattern stitch can give a wonderfully effective fabric.

The basic plan works well for a knitted suit jacket over a knitted A-line skirt. You would probably choose a sport—Class B yarn. If that suit were for summer, you might want shorter sleeves and a silk or linen yarn.

CONCLUSION

Male and female, young and old of any body type look great in this classic style. Size it and vary it for the intended wearer, and you've got a winner.

24

A Child's Raglan Turtleneck

In this chapter you will learn how to:

1. Design for children;
2. Allow for pattern stitch multiples;
3. Plot raglans;
4. Plan turtlenecks.

SPECIAL NOTES ABOUT DESIGNING FOR CHILDREN

Infants and children are not miniature adults. There are several fundamental differences between the body shapes and proportions of infants and children and those of adults. If we don't take these differences into consideration, the garments we lovingly make for children are not going to fit.

Kids have big heads!

The heads of infants and children are much larger in proportion to the rest of their bodies than are the heads of adults. Sweaters for children need neck openings large enough to go over their big heads. For adults we often divide the width between the shoulder tips into thirds when planning garments: one third for the right shoulder, one third for the neck opening, and the final third for the left shoulder. This formula does not work when designing for children under twelve years of age.

24.1 Child's Raglan Turtleneck worn
by child (yarn supplied by Brunswick; knitted by Jane Burns; modeled
by Adam Newdow)

For newborns, we divide:
  2-inch shoulder, 3-inch neck, 2-inch shoulder.

For two-year-olds:
  2½-inch shoulder, 4-inch neck, 2½-inch shoulder.

For eight-year-olds:
  3-inch shoulder, 4½-inch neck, 3-inch shoulder.

For twelve-year-olds:
  3¼-inch shoulder, 5-inch neck, 3¼-inch shoulder.

(For complete sets of children's standard measurements, see Appendix
pages 388–390.)

**As children grow, their bodies quickly get longer, but not much
wider.**

There is very little difference between the chest measurement of a
newborn and that of a twelve-year-old, but there is a big difference in
the lengths. Do not be surprised by the numbers you will encounter in
designing for children.

**If you want to allow for growth room for children, make the
garment a bit longer, but not necessarily wider.**

Also, *children have no waistlines*. From shoulder to hips they are
straight up and down.

THE IDEA

The *American Heritage Dictionary* (Boston: Houghton Mifflin Co., 1982, Second College Edition) defines a raglan as "a loose garment with slanted shoulder seams and with the sleeves extending in one piece to the neckline."

Set-in sleeves for sweaters were a great improvement over the straight-out-at-a-right-angle-sleeves of the Da Vinci Man sweater. A further design improvement since set-in sleeves is the *raglan*. The raglan is a comparatively recent development, dating only to the middle of the last century. The concept was originated by a British field marshal, Baron Raglan, who wanted a coat for his men that would allow full movement of the arms but not be bulky or cumbersome like a cape. He solved the problem not only for his soldiers, but for many others of us as well, because raglan design avoids the problem of excess fabric under the arms, allows free use of the arms, and is very comfortable.

Raglan sleeves are not flattering to triangular and Tiffany diamond body types, but for the rest of us they are very desirable.

ABOUT KNITTED RAGLANS

To shape the diagonal seams from underarm to shoulders, traditional knitting design calls for one stitch to be decreased each side every other row from underarm to neck on the back, front, and sleeves. This formula fits infants, children between size 2 and size 12 (see Figure 24.2), and adults over size 42 *when working with knitting worsted*. For sizes between 12 and 42 or when working with other yarns that have different ratios of stitches to rows, this formula makes either the armholes too short or the body and sleeves too wide. (In the next chapter I'll tell you what to do about those in-between sizes and other yarns.)

24.2 Rough sketch of Child's Raglan Turtleneck

FLOOR PLAN OF THE PIECES

On all simple raglans, if the back chest (at underarm) starts out to be 6″ wider than a sleeve (at underarm), at the neckline the back will still be 6″ wider than the sleeve. A fancier way of saying this is: where the rate of decrease is the same on body and sleeves, the difference in proportional width between the parts will always remain the same.

The difference in the proportional width is usually established at the back neckline.

TURTLENECKS AREN'T TIGHT

The opening for a turtleneck needs to be WIDER than the opening for a regular crew neck.

The ribbing stitches of a turtleneck when folded over on themselves once or twice tend to compress against the wearer's neck. And even though the wearer wants to keep his neck warm, he will still need to swallow and talk. The designers rule of thumb is that an opening to be filled in with a turtleneck is usually made 2″ wider than for a crew neck. The number of ribbing stitches picked up around that wider neckline is also proportionately larger.

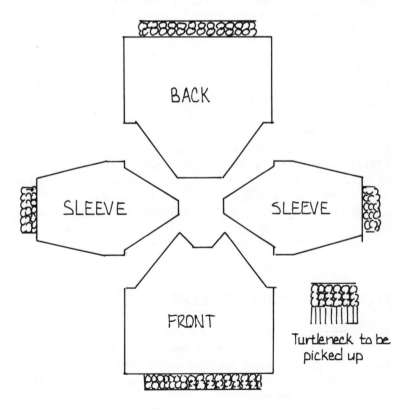

24.3 Layout of Child's Raglan Turtleneck

On a raglan the neck circumference comprises not only the back and front necks but also the tops of the sleeves. (See Figure 24.3, layout.)

THE YARN AND THE GAUGE

Brunswick's "Windrush", a machine-washable and -dryable 100 percent orlon acrylic—4-ply, knitting worsted weight, 100 grams, 230 yards per skein. Faded Denim Heather #9072 for cabled ribbing trim, and Denim Ombré* #9205 for body and sleeves.

It took a bit of swatch making, playing with both the stockinette and the cable ribbing, to work out a compatible set of gauges that would avoid making a *decrease* between the ribbing and the body stitches.

GAUGE: Stockinette stitch—5 sts and 7 rows = 1″ on #7 needles
GAUGE: Cable ribbing trim—5.5 sts and 8 rows = 1″ on #7 needles

Cable ribbing trim: 4-stitch-wide cables with 1 purl stitch in between. The cables are twisted every 4th row. (This is a multiple of 5 + 1 with a repeat of 4 rows.)

Cable Stitch Ribbing (Trim):
Row 1) (public side) *P 1, k 4*, rep bet *s, end p 1.
Row 2 and all even-numbered rows, private side) *K 1, p 4*, rep bet *s, end k 1.
Row 3) (public side) *P 1, sl 2 sts to cable needle and hold at back of work, k 2, k 2 sts from cable needle*, rep bet *s, end p 1.
Row 4) same as row 2.
Repeat these 4 rows.

It should take a total of about 600 yards to make this child's size 6–8 sweater. If the sweater were all one color, a purchase of 3 skeins would be sufficient. However, because the trim is a different color, it's best to buy 3 skeins of the ombré and 1 skein of the heather.

---

*The definition of ombré yarns is that they have colors or tones that shade into each other. Sometimes when knitting on a straight-sided piece, unwanted patterns of the colors will develop. The remedy is simple: Since it is unlikely that any two balls of yarn will begin at precisely the same place in the color sequence, 1) in the round, work each round with a different ball of yarn; 2) flat, i.e., back and forth, change balls of yarn after every 2nd row. In either case, it is not necessary to continually cut off and add the different balls of yarn. Leave them both attached to the work and alternate their use.

DESIRED FINISHED SWEATER MEASUREMENTS

Back neck width: 4.5"
Underarm (raglan) depth: 6"
Nape of neck to bottom edge: 19"
Length from underarm to bottom edge: 13"
Upper arm sleeve width: 10.5"
Finished sleeve length: 12"

The design process for a raglan sweater is unlike that for any other sweater. We do not start with the body circumference; this would only lead to grief and frustration. Instead, we begin designing our raglan sweaters with the key number, the desired underarm depth times the row gauge.

The key number in designing a raglan is the number of ROWS of sweater underarm depth. This figure tells us the number of rows available within which to decrease from underarm to neck at the rate of "1 stitch each side every other row." The key number will determine the number of stitches that can be gotten rid of between the chest and the neck. The number of raglan decreases on both the body back and the sleeves must be very close to the key number.

Cheating is allowed! The number of stitches on the back chest and at the neck and the number of rows of armhole depth can be manipulated to make things come out neat and even. If your numbers refuse to come out clean and tidy, juggle them. Add (or eliminate) an underarm bind-off. Add or subtract a few stitches from the neck width of the back and front or the tops of the sleeves. Often designers will make sleeve width at underarm a bit wider to allow the decrease rows to work out nicely.

At first the numbers arrived at by multiplying stitch and row gauge for back, back neck, sleeve width at underarm, underarm depth, and sleeve width at neck are *all only approximate*. In order to make the decreases from the underarm to the neck come out even with the number of rows available to make these decreases "1 stitch each side every other row" juggling and adjusting are usually necessary.

Let's go through the steps of designing this child's sweater, and then I'll explain when and where and how to cheat if necessary.

STEP #1: FINDING THE KEY NUMBER

The first measurement you need in designing a raglan is the key number, the desired underarm depth times the row gauge.

      5″ (actual body underarm depth)
  +   1″ (raglan ease allowance)
  =   6″ (approximate sweater underarm depth)
  ×   7 (gauge: rows per inch)
  = 42 (key number: approximate number of rows available for decreases)

STEP #2: COMPARE KEY NUMBER AND BACK WIDTH AND NECK

The number of stitches on the back to be decreased from the underarm to the neck must be approximately the same as the key number in order to make our decreases "1 stitch each side every other row."

Next we need to compare the key number with the desired back width. Of course we are going to have to find out the back chest width before we can do any comparing.

      26″ (body chest circumference)
  +   2″ (ease allowance)
  = 28″ (total desired chest circumference)
  ÷   2 (half for back, half for front)
  = 14″ (width each back and front)
  ×   5 (gauge: sts per inch)
  = 70 (approximate number of sts for back chest)
  − 42 (key number, number of decreases possible)
  = 28 (approximate number of sts remaining for back neck)

How does this check out with the *real* desired back neck? Well, let's divide the number of stitches remaining for the back neck by the stitch gauge.

      28 (number of sts remaining for back neck)
  ÷   5   (gauge: sts per inch)
  =   5.6″ (proposed width of back neck)

Does this sound about right? No, what we want for a back neck width is approximately 4.5″. 5.6″ is a little too wide, especially when we consider that we have to get the tops of the sleeves added into this neck opening, too.

STEP #3: JUGGLING REMAINING STITCHES AND BACK NECK

We could bind off some of those back chest stitches *before* we start our raglan decreases to get rid of some of that "remaining back neck width."

$$
\begin{array}{rl}
4.5'' & \text{(back neck width)} \\
\times \quad 5 & \text{(gauge: sts per inch)} \\
\hline
= \ 22.5 & \text{(approximate number of back neck sts)} \\
= \ 23 & \text{(round-off number of sts desired for back neck)} \\[6pt]
28 & \text{(original number of sts remaining for back neck derived from} \\
& \text{back chest minus key number)} \\
- \ 23 & \text{(desired number of sts for back neck)} \\
\hline
= \ 5 & \text{(approximate number of sts to bind off back at underarms)}
\end{array}
$$

Oops, 5 is an odd number; it cannot be evenly divided by 2 to split up the bind-offs between the right and left sides of the sweater back at underarm. Round it off.

$$
\begin{array}{rl}
4 & \text{(rounded-off number of sts to bind off at underarms)} \\
\div \ 2 & \text{(half for right side, half for left side)} \\
\hline
= \ 2 & \text{(final number of sts to bind off on each side of back at underarm)}
\end{array}
$$

We must now add back into the number of stitches remaining at the back neck the 1 stitch we lost when we rounded that odd-number 5 down to an even-number 4.

$$
\begin{array}{rl}
23 & \text{(desired number of sts for back neck)} \\
+ \ 1 & \text{(st lost in rounding off number)} \\
\hline
= \ 24 & \text{(final number of sts for back neck)}
\end{array}
$$

STEP #4: DESIGNING THE SLEEVES

Remembering that the proportional width difference between the body and the sleeves will always remain the same, let's figure out how wide we want the sleeves at the underarm to be.

$$
\begin{array}{rl}
8.5'' & \text{(body measurement at upper arm)} \\
+ \ 2.5'' & \text{(allowance for ease)} \\
\hline
= \ 11'' & \text{(approximate width of sleeve at underarm, may be adjusted to} \\
& \text{accommodate raglan decrease)} \\
\times \quad 5 & \text{(gauge: sts per inch)} \\
\hline
= \ 55 & \text{(approximate number of sts at underarm)}
\end{array}
$$

Round up to an even number.

    56 (approximate number of sts at underarm)
 − 42 (the key number, the number of sts that can be decreased to match raglan decreases of body)
= 14 (approximate number of sts to remain at sleeve neck)
 − 4 (sts to be bound off at underarm to match body back)
= 10 (approximate number of sts to remain at sleeve neck)
÷   5 (gauge: sts per inch)
=   2″ (approximate width to remain at sleeve neck)

Is this width of 2″ to remain at the top of the sleeve at the neck okay? Considering that we are designing for a child (with a large head), and for a turtleneck (that is not too tight), yes, it is okay!

Quickly, before you get confused, mark down on your layout drawing in green the number of stitches required. Mark in red the corresponding number of inches. (See Figure 24.4.)

STEP #5: DESIGNING THE REST OF THE SWEATER

Now it is a cinch to design the rest of the raglan sweater. All of the following things we have already gone over in previous chapters:

BODY

1. Plan front neck shaping (as if for a crew neck).
2. Decide on body length.
3. Double-check length from nape of neck and from underarm to bottom edge of sweater.
4. Compare chest width with hip circumference to find out if it is necessary to taper to hips or chest.
5. Plan ribbing for bottom body edge and adjust to fit cable pattern stitch multiple of 5 + 1.

SLEEVE

1. Decide on sleeve length.
2. Decide on wrist and lower arm circumference.
3. Decide on sleeve shaping from wrist to underarm.
4. Plan ribbing for bottom sleeve edge/wrist and adjust to fit cable pattern stitch multiple of 5 + 1.

TURTLENECK

1. Count existing number of stitches at neck edge and adjust to cable pattern stitch multiple. The first inch or two of the turtleneck nearest the neck edge of the sweater can be made in 1 × 1 rib if desired.
2. When all calculations are complete, transfer measurements, stitches, rows, and instructions to the pattern layout. (See Figure 24.4.)

ADJUSTING THE STITCHES FOR A RAGLAN

For this sweater/lesson I deliberately chose a size and a gauge that I knew would work out easily. It will not always be possible for you to deliberately choose a size and a gauge that will work, but don't let this keep you from designing raglan sweaters. The possibilities for juggling and cheating are endless.

1. If the number of stitches to decrease is *larger than* the key number/ raglan depth:
   • Bind off a lot more stitches at the underarm,
   • Make the neck wider (it can be tightened with ribbing trim later),

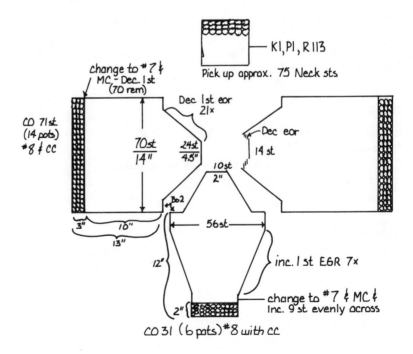

24.4 Child's Raglan Turtleneck with measurements, stitches, rows, and instructions

- Make the width of the body/sleeve narrower,
- In desperation you can make the depth of the raglan longer, but please read pages 291–294 first.

2. If the number of stitches to decrease is *smaller than* the key number/ raglan depth:
   - Eliminate any bound-off stitches at the underarm,
   - Make the key number less, that is, shorten the length of the raglan depth,
   - Enlarge the width of the body/sleeve.

The only option I forbid you to use is "the formula for decreases that do not come out even" to adjust your raglan decreases. If simple juggling will not work, read on to the next chapter about "compound-angle raglans." Please do not fall prey to spacing your decreases farther apart near either the neck or the underarm.

MAKING UP THE SWEATER

Never make the decreases in the edge stitch. If you do, you'll have a very messy raglan seam. Make the raglan decreases on the 3rd and 4th stitches in from each edge. That way you will have both a decorative design element and a good-looking seam.

Don't bind off the neck stitches. Slip the neck stitches to a stitch holder. You want to maintain the stretchiness of the neck opening.

FINISHING THE SWEATER

After three of the raglan seams are woven you can move the neck stitches from their holders to one needle and work the turtleneck flat. If you prefer, you can weave all four raglan seams and work the turtleneck in the round.

Remember that the turtleneck will *fold outward* and that the cables will appear on the *reverse side*. Still the stitches need to be picked up with the public side of the garment facing you so that there will be no unsightly mess along the pick-up line. But this does not mean that you have to make the whole turtleneck inside out if you are knitting in the round. On the first round after the pick-up, reverse the direction in which you are working.

I repeat that the first inch or so of the turtleneck next to the body can be made in 1×1 ribbing if you choose.

VARIATIONS

You can work the body and the sleeves in rounds and then join the whole thing together at the underarm and make the raglan yoke and decreases all in one piece with no seams to sew.

If you follow the suggestion above, you can adjust a few stitches and put cables into the "raglan seam" areas between the raglan decreases.

Make a plain rib and put cable panels up the center front and the centers of the sleeves.

Make an all-over cable or pattern stitch such as a fisherman (brioche) stitch.

Make stripes and/or wide bands of color.

Knit in the child's initials or nickname, or make intarsia animals or scenes.

Try other necklines such as crew neck or V-neck.

Make a raglan cardigan, shorten the turtleneck (which now opens in the front middle), and you have a fold-back collar.

CONCLUSION

I'm glad that raglan sleeves were invented, even if it was rather late in knitting history. Raglans are one of my favorite kinds of sweaters. They are a bit messy to plan and design *when creating them from the bottom up*. If you like the knitting of and the finished look of raglans, read on and in Chapter 26 you'll learn how to make them from the top down with only the back neck measurement to bother with.

25

A Timeless Adult Raglan Cardigan

In this chapter you will learn how to:

1. *Plan a sweater with a long length;*
2. *Set up compound angle raglan decreases;*
3. *Design fold-under front bands and lapel;*
4. *Plan a shawl collar;*
5. *Design set-in slit pockets;*
6. *Design for a top-heavy hourglass body type.*

THE IDEA

The idea for this sweater came from a British TV mystery series. While walking along high windy cliffs above a turbulent ocean, the heroine wore a sweater similar to this. Shawl collar turned up against the breeze, hands jammed in deep pockets of the fingertip length sweater, she looked calm and warm even though she was troubled about the murder. I liked the look of the sweater and decided to knit it up. (See Figure 25.2.)

COMPOUND-ANGLE RAGLANS

When we make a regular raglan sweater we are, in theory, trying to achieve a nearly perfect rectangle of fabric around the neck opening once all the raglan seams are woven. With most adult bodies and with

25.1 Adult Raglan Cardigan (yarn supplied by Reynolds; knitted by Victoria Kearney; modeled by Whit Robbins)

25.2 Rough sketch of Adult Raglan Cardigan

many sizes of yarn, there are two problems when regular raglan decreases are made in the traditional way, "1 stitch each side every other row," from underarm to neck.

The first problem is that *most human bodies do not need a perfect rectangle of fabric.* This problem is easier to visualize if we look at the body from the neck down. It is true that from the neck edge to the shoulder tip we do need a rectangle. But from the shoulder tip down to the actual body underarm, we do not. The body simply does not increase in width as fast as it does in length between these points. At the underarm we need *both* to add 1″ or 1.5″ of length for ease and movement, *and* to move at a 45° angle into the armpit area. Then we need a flat horizontal area to travel under the arm to the side seam.

The second problem of traditional raglan decreases made "1 stitch each side every other row" concerns the relationship of stitch gauge to row gauge. Unless the number of stitches per inch is very close to the number of rows per inch, a true rectangle is not achieved. In many yarns, traditional raglan decreases of "1 stitch each side every other row" cause the raglan to have either an armhole depth that is too short or, to get a sufficient depth to the armhole, bodies and sleeves that are too wide. *The angle you get with a standard regular raglan decrease of "1 stitch each side every other row" is a function of the relationship of row gauge to stitch gauge.* For most people and most yarns, in order to get a good fit we need to make our decreases *less often than* every other row. A decrease in every 3rd row would solve the length-width problem better, but other difficulties arise. Machine-knitters can make perfectly matching decreases spaced with 2 plain rows in between, but hand-knitters cannot. Hand-knitters can make perfectly matched decreases only on the knit side of the fabric, and every 3rd row for them would turn out to be "alternate decreases every other row with every 4th row." Even if this equivalent of decreases every 3rd row were made, it does not solve the problem that the human body does not slant from underarm seam to neck edge in a straight diagonal line.

The solution is to plan the raglan from the top down. (You don't have to knit it in that direction, but it is easier to visualize the problem and the solution from the neck down.) (See Figure 25.3.)

From the neck edge to the tip of the shoulder bones, decreases are spaced every other row (approximately a 45° angle).

From the shoulder tip to the actual body underarm depth, decreases are spaced every 4th row (approximately a 60° angle).

Down from the actual body underarm for 1″ (women and children) to 1.5″ (men), decreases are made every other row (approximately a 45° angle).

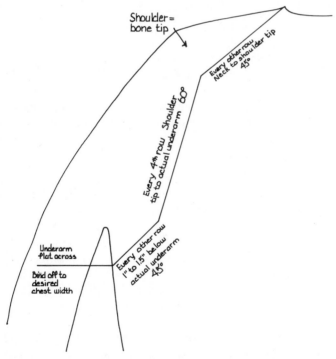

25.3 Right torso and arm showing compound angle for raglan sleeve

Any additional width (stitches) that it is necessary to get rid of is bound off at the underarm.

(Turn to page 302 to see how to lay this out on graph paper.)

AN IMPORTANT REMINDER

As I said in the last chapter on raglans, the difference in width of the body back (and front) and the sleeve remains the same from underarm to the neck. If the body back is 6″ wider than the sleeve at the beginning of the underarm shaping it will still be 6″ wider at the neck edge. If the sleeve is decreased down to 1 or 2 stitches of width at the neckline, the stitches remaining on the back will become the neck width.

In designing any raglan, subtracting the width of the sleeve at the underarm from the width of the back chest at the underarm will tell you the width that will remain at the back neck.

Example:

> 44″ (desired chest circumference)
> ÷ 2 (half for back, half for front)
> = 22″ (back chest width at underarm)
> − 17″ (desired sleeve width at underarm)
> = 5″ (remaining width at back neck)

If the "remaining width at back neck" is not wide enough for the wearer's neck, add the same amount of additional width to BOTH the sleeve and the back.

Example:

> 7″ (width of wearer's neck at back)
> − 5″ (remaining width at back neck)
> = 2″ (additional width needed on both the sleeve and the back)

Juggling and adjusting are allowed and encouraged in designing raglans. If you need 2″ of extra width at the back neck, but do not need it at the back chest underarm, you can alter the *rate* at which the decreases are made to get rid of the extra width.

If the "remaining width at the back neck" is too wide for the wearer's neck, get rid of the extra stitches at the underarm bind-off.

FLOOR PLAN OF THE PIECES

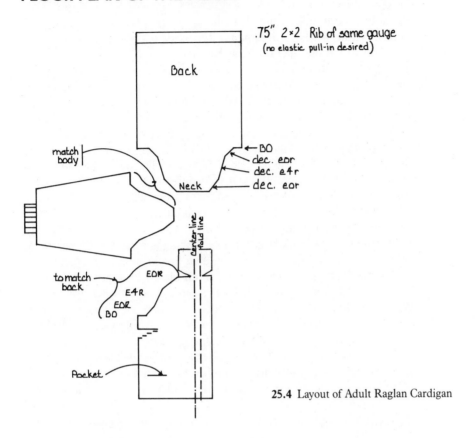

.75″ 2×2 Rib of same gauge
(no elastic pull-in desired)

Back

match body

← BO
dec. eor
dec. e4r
dec. eor

Neck

to match back

EOR
E4R
EOR
BO

center line
fold line

Pocket

25.4 Layout of Adult Raglan Cardigan

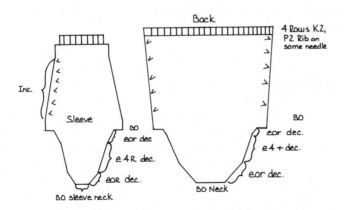

Back

4 Rows K2,
P2 Rib on
same needle

Inc.

Sleeve

BO
eor dec

e4R dec.

eor dec.

BO sleeve neck

BO

eor dec.

e4 + dec.

eor dec.

BO Neck

25.5 Layout of sleeve and back for Adult Raglan Cardigan

THE YARN AND THE GAUGE

Reynold's "Candide, Light Weight" a single-ply, sport-weight, 100 percent virgin wool, approximately 240 yards per 50-gram skein.

According to the "Pocket Yarn Yardage Guide," the estimate for the amount of yarn for a woman's size 44 long-sleeved sweater in sport weight would be 1,800 yards. But this garment has several differences from a standard pullover: it will be knitted on a knitting machine (which always uses more yarn than hand-knitting), it will be about 5″ longer than normal, it will have a tie belt (of the same yarn), it not only is a cardigan with a front overlap but also has fold-under front bands that extend up to become the fold-over shawl collar. Even the addition of two double-sided slit pockets will make a difference. *More yarn than normal will be needed.* (Twelve skeins—2,880 yards—were actually used.)

A 50-stitch by 50-stitch swatch was made and allowed to rest. It had a gauge of 6 stitches and 8 rows per inch. The swatch was steamed and remeasured and it looked gorgeous. When the swatch was washed in cold water and laid flat to dry, the swatch biased, that is, it developed a corkscrew twist. The once-square swatch biased in width 1.25″ over a 6″ length. No amount of additional steaming could force the swatch back into a square.

This problem took us completely by surprise. The yarn had neither "twisted back on itself" nor been in any way difficult to knit. After notifying the manufacturer, we went ahead and made up the sweater. It was steamed, Scotchgarded® to minimize moisture absorption, and we will enclose a note with the sweater, "Do Not Wash; Dry-Clean Only!"

STEAMED GAUGE: Stockinette stitch—6 sts and 8 rows = 1″

Because of the planning necessary for the raglan, row gauge will be very important.

MEASUREMENTS NEEDED

1. *Chest circumference.* Since this is to be an outdoor sweater, more ease allowance than normal must be added to cover undergarments.
2. *Circumference at bottom of sweater.* Because of the below-hip length, special care must be taken to make sure the sweater does not cup under the derrière.
3. *Length from nape of neck to bottom of sweater.*
4. a. *Actual body underarm depth.*
   b. *Desired sweater underarm depth.*

5. *Length from garment underarm to bottom of sweater.*
6. *Back neck width.* Measure the person's back neck from fabric-stitch edge to fabric-stitch edge.
7. *Width from sweater neck edge to shoulder tip.*
8. *Sleeve width at underarm.*
9. *Sleeve width above wrist.*
10. *Wrist.*
11. *Sleeve length from underarm to wrist.*
12. *Desired length of belt.* Wrap a tape measure around the waist and make a single tie. How long do you want the tail-ends to be?

SPECIAL MEASUREMENTS NEEDED FOR LARGE-CHESTED PEOPLE

13. *Total chest circumference.*
14. *Difference in back and front chest measurement* (to determine if there is significant difference in front and back because of a large chest).
15. *Length from back nape of neck to bottom of sweater, and front neck-shoulder joining to bottom of sweater* (to determine how many inches of short-rowing for a bust dart will be necessary).

NOTES ABOUT THE LONG-SHAWL-COLLAR CARDIGAN DESIGN

We know that the finished garment will stretch somewhat in length because there is no resting place for the bottom of the sweater. The fabric itself will also stretch because of the somewhat looser than normal gauge this slightly hairy yarn must be knitted at in order to show off its lovely fuzz. In planning the sweater to end between the hips and the knees we leave both ourselves and the sweater room for change.

When you design a garment that will be longer than the widest part of the hips (wherever that may be), it is important to plan the bottom of the sweater so that it will not cling to the body and pull in under the hips and cause a blimplike effect. One solution is to give the fabric firmness and weight by making a hem. A good-looking hem that will lay flat is made as follows:

1. Using needles one or two sizes smaller than used on the garment, work the underside of hem in K 1, P 1 ribbing for 1" to 2".
2. With the same smaller-sized needles, work a purl ridge turning row; that is, on the outside of the garment, purl one row.

3. Change to regular-size needles and complete the garment.
4. Whip-stitch the hem in place catching only the outer loop of every other cast-on stitch and the "bead" of every other purl stitch of the body.

There is however, another solution that will work out better for this particular style:

Make a bottom body ribbing of four rows of K 2, P 2. Do not change needle size; do not change the number of stitches. Work the four rows of ribbing on same-size needles with same number of stitches. It will keep the bottom from cupping under the derrière.

PLANNING A FOLD-UNDER FRONT BAND

If an ordinary knit stitch is slipped (as if to purl) on the public side of the fabric on every other row, it will form a natural fold line toward the private side of the fabric. On the private side of the fabric that slipped stitch will appear as a ladder.

These characteristics of a slipped stitch allow us to make neat and tidy double-faced fold-under front bands and shawl collars.

When learning to design the Cardigan Jacket in Chapter 23, we learned about planning center front lines and overlap allowance, and how buttons affect the way we figure our overlap width. On this sweater our "double-faced fold-under front band" is simply an ordinary overlap that is doubled in width with a slipped stitch added for a fold line between the front and back sides.

As a lazy person, I usually also add another slipped stitch on the front of the sweater. I want to utilize the ladder on the private side as a guide for sewing down the underside of the finished front band. The slipped-stitch sewing line is carefully placed along a line where the back side of the front band will need to be fastened down in the finishing process.

Notice in the photo at the beginning of this chapter that the knitter chose not to make any buttonholes. If you want this sweater to button up, you will plan the spacing and location of the buttons just as was done for the cardigan jacket (Chapter 23). The only difference is that you have two thicknesses of fabric on the fold-under front band. If you are going to knit in the buttonholes, I would suggest a "three-row buttonhole" (see page 157). Many knitters will prefer to wait and make sewing-machine buttonholes in the finished sweater.

PLANNING A SHAWL COLLAR AS AN EXTENSION OF THE FRONT BANDS

On this garment the shawl collar rises as an extension of the folded-under front bands. The V-neck-type shaping of the sweater front causes the collar to widen and begin to roll and curl around the neck. At the point where the front neck edge decreases are completed, a set of short rows widens the outer edge of the collar and gives it extra length to turn and flow across the back of the neck. (See Figure 25.6)

The slipped-stitch sewing line and the matching increases at the outer edge of the fold-under front band follow-V-neck-type shaping. In Chapter 21, "A V-necked Pullover Vest," you learned to design and shape V-necks. You know that V-necks are usually begun at the point

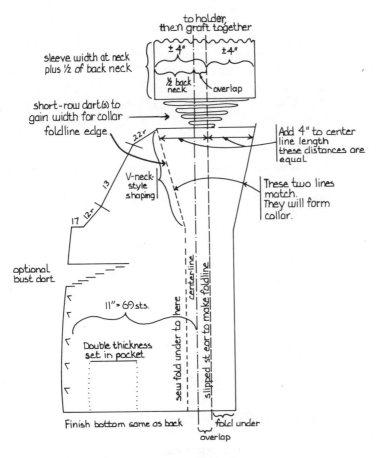

25.6 Layout of front/overlap for Adult Raglan Cardigan

of the beginning of the underarm shaping, which is what we will do on this sweater. You learned how to determine the number of rows available to shape the neck. You learned how to divide the number of stitches on the back neck by 2, and use one-half for the right and one-half for the left side. And you learned the "formula for diagonals that don't come out even" (see pages 175–180) to arrange the shaping of the V-neck-type lines. Note from the drawing (Figure 25.6) that on both the body front and the fold-under side of the front band, the bottom of the V shaping begins at the outer edges of the front band.

Note also the short rows going across the fold-line/outer-edge of the shawl collar ending short of the outer edge.

HORIZONTAL SLIT POCKETS

There are two kinds of slit pockets, double and single fabric thickness. Which type you choose will depend on the weight and thickness of the yarn you are using. Double-fabric slit pockets are a delight in fingering, sport, and sometimes worsted-weight yarns. They hang free and do not need to be stitched down to the sweater fabric. In thick or bulky-weight yarns double-fabric slit pockets are not advisable. They are too thick and too bulky. When using heavier-weight yarns the single-thickness pockets must be attached to the sweater body on the bottom and at the sides.

Double-fabric slit pockets are usually constructed all in one with the front of the garment. (See Figure 25.7.) When the knitter reaches the level of the top of the pocket, the stitches to each side are put on holders to wait while the length of the pocket is worked.

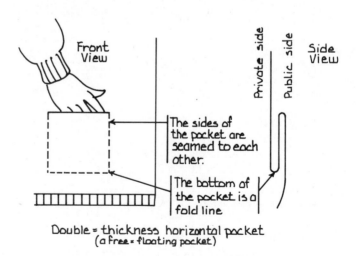

25.7 Double-thickness horizontal pocket (free-floating pocket)

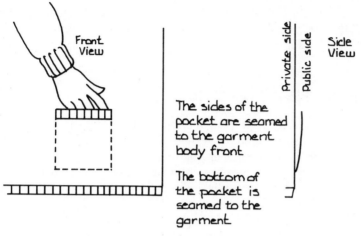

Single-thickness horizontal pocket

25.8 Single-thickness horizontal pocket

Single-thickness pockets are sometimes worked in advance and held on stitch holders. (See Figure 25.8.) Then, when the level of the top of the pocket is reached, the front stitches of the pocket are bound off and replaced by the already-prepared inside of the pocket.

When this sweater was completed, our knitter added a bit of ribbing along the top of the fold-to-the-inside line of the double-thickness pocket. She felt she wanted to add some definition at that spot. That is the joy of feeling free and knowing what you are doing—to change any element at whatever time.

BELT FABRIC PATTERN STITCH

I envisioned this garment with a knitted self-belt. All knitted belts need to be made of a very special fabric pattern stitch, one that will lie flat without curling or rolling, and be somewhat stretchy so that the belt can be tied with a simple flip-over that won't easily come undone. A pattern stitch that works very well for belts is seed stitch. (See page 00.) More adventuresome knitters may wish to make a "double-knitting tube" belt with either ribs or slipped stitches.

WIDTH OF BELT

Depending on the style of the garment, the thickness of the yarn, and the size of the person, a belt needs to be anywhere from 2" to 3.5" wide.

Occasionally knitted belts look great with buckles, but usually they have a better appearance when simply tied. If your design calls for a buckle, purchase the buckle before you make the belt to be sure of getting the right width.

DOING THE ARITHMETIC

When you are ready to plan the raglan decreases, get out standard graph paper and simply draw it out, square by square as follows: Convert the desired numbers of inches to the desired number of stitches. On the graph paper, each square horizontally across the paper represents 1 stitch. Vertically up and down the paper, each square represents 1 row. Begin with the back first. (I usually mark a center line and plot only one side. The other side will be a flip-flopped repeat. (See Figure 25.9.)

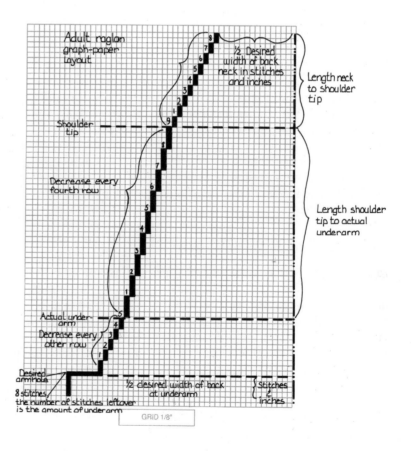

1. Mark off the desired armhole depth.
2. Mark off the width of the back neck.
3. Mark off the number of stitches of width to get rid of between the neck edge and the underarm seam.
4. Make horizontal lines at the shoulder tip depth, at the actual underarm depth, and the desired armhole depth.
5. Starting at the neck edge, draw a jagged pencil line moving over 1 square and down 2 squares, until you reach the horizontal shoulder tip width line.

   From the neck edge to the tip of the shoulder bones, decreases are spaced every other row (approximately a 45° angle).

6. Now change the jagged pencil line to over 1 square and down 4 squares until you reach the actual underarm depth.

   From the shoulder tip to the actual body underarm depth, decreases are spaced every 4th row (approximately a 60° angle).

7. Change the jagged pencil line back to over 1 square and down 2 squares until you reach the desired raglan depth.

   Down from the actual body underarm for 1″ (women and children) to 1.5″ (men), decreases are made every other row (approximately a 45° angle).

8. Make a horizontal line across the remainder of the width of the back to indicate the stitches to be bound off at the underarm.

   Any additional width (stitches) that it is necessary to get rid of is bound off at the underarm.

VARIATIONS

Now that you know how to design compound-angle raglans that *really* fit, you can use this formula to design pullovers as well as cardigans. With what you've already learned about designing sweaters, you can make V, turtle, or crew necks.

When using heavier-weight yarns in which a fold-under lapel and shawl collar would be too bulky and heavy, make the lapel and shawl collar of a single thickness of garter stitch.

Forget the buttons and create a wrap sweater by making each side of the front of the sweater extrawide.

Start the V shaping for the shawl collar higher up nearer the neck, or lower down nearer the waist.

You can make the sleeves long, midlength, or short.

For a raglan vest with small capped sleeves, begin the sleeves with ribbing at a point just below the underarm, i.e., the point of the body underarm bind-off.

By this time you should be aware that you can change pattern stitch, add stripes, etc.; in short, you can do anything you want to do.

CONCLUSION

Being a square-shouldered person, I like raglan sweaters because they flatter my shape. As a knitter it didn't take me long to discover that many raglans did not work out quite right, but I didn't know why. As a budding designer, I tried to figure out what was wrong, and stumbled onto the compound-angle raglan. I love the way these sweaters fit, but I just couldn't tolerate planning them, until one day I realized that *I could just draw the angles on graph paper.*

Now you know my secrets of both the compound-angle and the graph paper. I hope they simplify and perfect your plotting of raglan designs.

26

All-in-One-Piece-from-the-Neck-Down Pullover

> *In this chapter you will learn how to:*
>
> 1. *Make a sweater from the top down;*
> 2. *Work in a circle;*
> 3. *Fit as you go;*
> 4. *Design for a perfect hourglass body type.*

THE IDEA

Working from the top down solves the problem of the first great lie of knitters, "I always knit to gauge and I always stay on gauge." The neck is the smallest circumference of the body of a sweater. There is very little difference in neck sizes of adults. Unlike starting at the hipline of a garment, *when starting at the neck, gauge is not of critical importance.* If the neckline turns out to be too large, it is a simple matter to make a tight neck ribbing and pull the sweater in to fit the wearer. Moreover, minor variations of gauge are swallowed up in the garment as a whole. There can be no such thing as having knitted the back of the garment at a looser gauge than the front; both are knitted together at the same time. And since you stop and try on as you go along, you can easily adjust the number of stitches whenever you need to.

Garments made from the top down always fit. Since you are increasing from the smallest circumference—the neck—to the largest—the chest or the hips—when the sweater is as wide as it needs to be, you

just quit increasing. This gets around the second great lie of knitters, "I am a size 34. You don't need to put a tape measure on me." And no tape measure is put on the person, just the sweater-in-progress itself.

Moreover, working from the top down solves the problem of not knowing if you have enough yarn. Knit awhile on the sleeves, then knit awhile on the body, going from one area to the other until you run out of yarn. When you run out, bind off.

And after that final binding off, the garment is complete. *There are no seams to weave together!*

The one drawback to top-down sweaters is that as you approach completion, the work gets heavy. Some knitters object to all that weight in their laps; others don't mind at all.

The garment in this chapter is the simplest of all-in-one-piece-from-the-neck-down sweaters. It is a hip-length pullover with a crew neck, raglan shoulders, and long sleeves that are slightly gathered at the wrist. (See Figure 26.2.)

FLOOR PLAN OF THE PIECES

It is difficult to make a drawing of a set of three circular tubes that will be worked all in one piece. In Figure 26.3, the broken lines do not mean seams. They are indications of where the tubes join themselves.

26.2 Rough sketch of From-the-Neck-Down Pullover

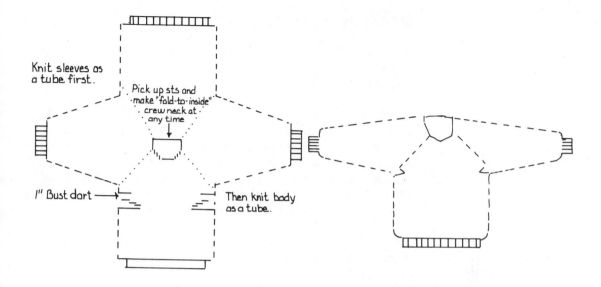

Knit sleeves as a tube first.

Pick up sts and make "fold-to-inside" crew neck at any time

1" Bust dart →

Then knit body as a tube.

26.3 Layout of From-the-Neck-Down Pullover

THE YARN AND THE GAUGE

We used Bernat "Kid Mohair." It is a bulky Class D yarn composed of 66 percent Kid Mohair, 26 percent wool, and 8 percent nylon, containing 95 yards per 40-gram ball. Three skeins each of three colors were used.

Remember that we will be working with *circular needles* to make top-down sweaters. Do not use straight needles to make your gauge.

GAUGE: Stockinette stitch—4 sts = 1″ on #9 needle

Do not block or apply steam to this mohair swatch; the fibers will mat. Lovingly hand-wash the swatch instead.

Remember: This sweater is going to be made of soft fuzzy yarn that will be knitted at a rather loose gauge. The knitted fabric will expand widthwise, therefore no added width ease is necessary. Moreover, it will stretch lengthwise, so "body resting places" are imperative. Firm ribbings at the neck, wrists, and hipline are necessary.

MEASUREMENTS NEEDED

If the intended wearer is handy for frequent fitting, few measurements are needed. In any case, to begin the sweater, *only* the widths of the back and sleeves at the neck are needed.

Recall from Chapter 24 (pages 285–286) how to plan the back neck width: Desired back width at chest minus the desired circumference of the upper arm equals the width that will occur at the back neck. If this number is satisfactory, each sleeve will require only 2 cast-on stitches. If this number is not wide enough, add width to both the back and the sleeve. If this number is too wide, you will have to juggle the proportional width of the sleeves.

Because the beginning of the sweater knits up so quickly, I like also to know the length from base of neck to shoulder tip, and the actual underarm depth measurement.

THE TRYING-ON PLACES

If the intended wearer is handy and obliging, instead of using other measurements, try the sweater on the intended wearer at the following progress points:

1. *When the shoulder tips are reached.* How are the color, the pattern stitch, and the gauge of the yarn working out? Is this sweater going to be what you thought it was?
2. *When the actual underarm is reached.* How are the widths working out? Was the measurement for the underarm depth correct?
3. *When you are ready to separate the sleeves from the body.* The sweater should now be longer than actual armpit depth (by 1″ for small women and children, up to 2″ or 2.5″ for large women and big men). Now it is time to ask:
   - Do you need to cast on extra width stitches for the body and sleeves?
   - How long should the sleeves be? How should they be tapered?
   - How long should the body be? Should it be decreased in to the waist or hips? Should it be increased in width?
4. *One inch after separating point.* Just to double-check width and determine if a bust dart is required.
5. *When you think that the sleeves and body are long enough.* Before you are ready to change to smaller needles and do the finishing trim, try it on one last time and decide if any changes are necessary.

INSTRUCTIONS FOR TRYING ON A SWEATER-IN-PROGRESS

Whenever desired, simply slip-as-if-to-purl some of the stitches to a smaller-size circular needle (or a ⅛"-wide piece of ribbon). Put rubber point protectors on both of the needles to prevent the stitches from falling off. Lay the garment over the shoulders of the intended wearer. Don't worry about *how many* stitches you have. You are after perfect fit, not numbers. When it is wide enough, stop making it any wider. When it is long enough, stop knitting.

If you cannot try the sweater-in-progress on the intended wearer, you will need the following measurements:

1. *Chest circumference.*
2. *Circumference at bottom of sweater.*
3. *Length from nape of neck to bottom of sweater.*
4. a. *Actual body underarm depth* (to know when to resume every-other-row increases).
   b. *Desired sweater underarm depth* (to know when to separate the sleeves from the body).
5. *Length from garment underarm to bottom of sweater.*
6. *Back neck width.*
7. *Sleeve width at underarm.*
8. *Sleeve length from underarm to wrist.*
9. *Length from neck edge to shoulder tip.*

SPECIAL CONSIDERATIONS FOR A PERFECT HOURGLASS FIGURE

1. *Chest circumference. Is a bust dart necessary?* Because of the forgiving-ness of *this* fabric, a bust dart will be necessary only for very large-bosomed women.
2. *Circumference at bottom of sweater. Is it necessary to increase for hips?* If the difference is less than 4", don't bother because of the forgivingness of *this* fabric.

INSTRUCTIONS FOR TOP-DOWN CREW-NECK RAGLAN PULLOVER

For clarity and brevity, the following instructions *suppose* you are working in stockinette stitch (see Figure 26.4). In reality, you can work any pattern stitch you choose. These instructions also assume you are using only one color/kind of yarn. In reality, you can change yarns whenever you choose. Using circular needles, cast on:

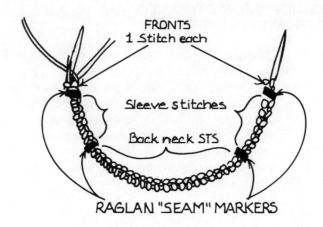

26.4 Circular needle with stitches and markers

1 stitch for front,
place a marker,
_____ stitches for sleeve width at neck,
place a marker,
_____ stitches for back neck width,
place a marker,
_____ stitches for sleeve width at neck,
place a marker,
1 stitch for front.

Work back and forth until the center front neck shaping is completed as follows (see Figure 26.5):

Row 1 and all odd-numbered rows (this is the private side): Purl.
Row 2 (this is the public side): *First increase row.*
In plain English: Slipping markers as you work, increase before and after each raglan marker.
In knitting jargon: Inc in first st, *sl M, inc in next st, work to within 1 st of next M, inc*. Rep bet *s 2 times, end sl M, inc in last st.
(8 raglan sts inc'd).
Row 4: *Begin to shape front neck and second increase row:*
In plain English: Slipping the markers as you go, increase in the first stitch, before and after every raglan marker, and in the last stitch.
In knitting jargon: Inc in first st, *k to within 1 st of next M, inc, sl M, inc*, rep bet *s 3 times ending k to within one st of end, inc in last st.
(10 sts inc'd, 8 raglan and 2 front neck edge sts).

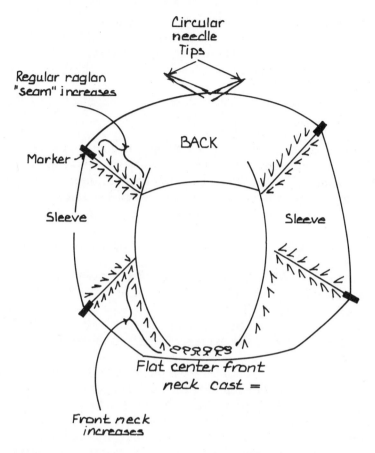

26.5 Circular front neck showing increases and flat cast-ons

Row 6: *Third Increase row:*
In plain English: Slipping the markers as you work, increase in first stitch, before and after each marker, and in the *next-to-last stitch.*
In knitting jargon: Inc, *k to within 1 st of next M, inc, sl M, inc*, rep bet *s 3 times ending inc, k to within 2 sts of end, inc in *next-to-last st*, k 1. (*This NEXT-TO-THE-LAST STITCH trick makes the right and left sides of the neck match exactly.*)
(10 sts inc'd, 8 raglan and 2 front neck edge sts).

In both plain English and knitting jargon: Repeat Row 6 *and* Row 1 until the center back length is the desired depth of the front neck. Count the number of stitches between the raglan markers on the center back;

count the number of stitches between the outermost markers and each front edge and add these stitches together;

subtract the total front stitches from the back stitches;

the remainder is the number of stitches to cast on for the flat part of the center front neck.

Cast on desired number of neck stitches. Join, work in circular rounds from here on.

How do you join to form a circle? When you come to the end of a knit (public side) row, push the stitches to the tips of the needle and, making sure that the piece is not twisted, insert your right-hand needle tip into the last stitch on the left-hand needle tip and keep on going. You now have a tube.

If necessary, continue to increase every other round until shoulder tips are reached. TRY ON THE SWEATER.

Increase every 4th round from shoulder tip to actual body underarm

Increase every other round from actual underarm to desired underarm: TRY ON THE SWEATER.

How many (if any) stitches of additional width need to be added (at the underarm) after the sleeves are separated from the body?

How do you divide the sleeves from the body? When you get to a raglan "seam" marker denoting the beginning of a body section, drop the yarn, pick up an extra circular needle, and, one at a time as if to purl, slip the body stitches to the extra needle. When you get to the next raglan marker denoting a sleeve, add a new ball of yarn. Work across the sleeve to the next raglan marker. Again slip as if to purl the body stitches to another extra circular needle. Secure the ends of the extra needles with rubber point protectors to keep the stitches from slipping off. These extra needles now serve as stitch holders. The sleeves and the body are now separated. Both sleeves are sitting on the same circular needle with separate balls of yarn attached to them.

After the division of the sleeves from the body, it is imperative to start the sleeves first.

You do not have to *finish* the sleeves before working on the body section, but you *must* work the sleeves for about 2". You can knit flat, working both sleeves at the same time using separate balls of yarn, *or* you can work each sleeve separately in the round.

If you plan to make stripes, you can begin them while you are still working back and forth shaping the front neck. Once you join the sweater into the round, *slip all of the stitches until you reach the back shoulder raglan marker. Flag this marker.* From here on, count this spot as the beginning of the rounds. (This is a less obvious place to join different colors/types yarns.)

Remember to make the bottom ribbing bind-offs in pattern stitch. Do not bind off all the stitches knitwise; the fabric will roll to the front if you do.

Be sure to make the bind-offs at the bottom of the ribbing of the sleeves and the body VERY LOOSE. Use a needle much larger in size to make that bind-off row.

FINISHING THE SWEATER

Finish as for any crew neck.

Neck-down sweaters almost always need one special finishing touch. The edge stitches at the raglan "seam" division points are usually stretched and need tightening. The best and quickest way I know to remedy the situation is to make a duplicate stitch over each of those offenders and simply cover them up (See *Knitting in Plain English,* page 118).

VARIATIONS

Change the type of neckline from a crew neck to one of the following:

V-neck: increase 1 stitch each side of front neck edge every *4th* row until the number of stitches on both fronts totals the number of stitches on the back. Cast on 1 stitch for center of V. Join. Continue, now working in the round.

Very deep V ("golf sweater neckline"); increase 1 stitch each side of front neck edge every *8th* row.

Pullover: When the number of stitches on both fronts totals the number of stitches on the back, cast on 1 stitch for the center of V. Join. Continue now working in the round.

Cardigan: If you plan to cut the sweater open later, make a steek or add 3 extra stitches (for sewing-machine stitching and cutting) and work in the round. If you don't like the idea of cutting knits, continue to work back and forth.

Turtleneck: Recall from the child's turtleneck, Chapter 24, that we need to plan all the neck areas, i.e., back, front, and sleeve tops, a bit wider than usual.

    a) Start the sweater with a *very loose* cast-on. Work the turtleneck ribbing. Then, when the turtleneck is finished, make short rows across the sleeve tops and back to shape the lowered front neckline. Or

    b) Make the original neck cast-on with waste yarn and, after working some on the body, go back and pick up the turtleneck to be worked from bottom up.

Boatneck: Recall Boatnecked Beauty from Chapter 20? You can make it from the top down! Measure the width between the tips of the shoulders. Cast on sufficient stitches for back neck-shoulder ribbing. Work two separate ribbing pieces, making the back section 1″ longer than the front. Do not bind off either ribbing piece. Place stitches on separate holders. Overlap ribbing sections as shown in Figure 26.6. Change to larger needle. Work across back stitches. Place a marker. Pick up desired number of stitches along right shoulder to become right sleeve. Place marker. Work across front neck stitches. Place marker. Pick up same number of stitches along left shoulder, place marker. Join. Work in the round increasing 1 stitch on each side of each sleeve every 4th round to actual underarm. Increase before and after every marker to desired underarm. Complete in usual way.

Square neck: This design looks good on every woman I have ever seen it on! Instead of making the two separate neck pieces described in the Boatneck above, begin by making a hollow square that is open at the center front. (See Figure 26.7.) To determine width of back neck,

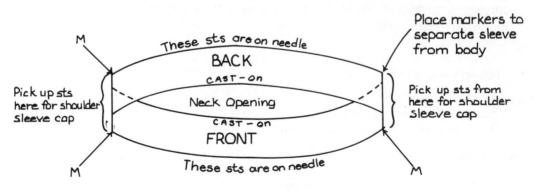

26.6 Close-up of overlapped neck area on boatnecked sweater

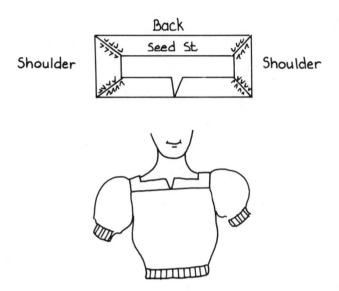

26.7 Close-up of top-down square yoke

measure between bra straps and subtract 1″. Divide this number by 2 for each side of the front neck. For shoulder/sleeves, allow 1″ for small sizes, 2″ for medium sizes, 2.5″ for large sizes. Round the results up or down to get all odd numbers of stitches. Placing a marker between each area, and increasing before and after each marker, work in seed stitch until the back is the desired width between the shoulder tips. Complete as for the boatneck sweater above.

After you learn about *circular yokes* in Chapter 29, you can make them from the top down also.

CONCLUSION

I hope this chapter has opened a new world of sweater design to you. The concept of knitting from the top down certainly changed my knitting habits!

27

A Coat of Many Colors

A Cardigan of Leftover Yarn Made in One Piece from the Neck Down

In this chapter you will learn how to:

1. *Use up leftover yarn, and wing it as you go;*
2. *Plan vertical slit pockets;*
3. *Make crochet trim on sweaters;*
4. *Design for a bottom-heavy hourglass body type.*

27.1 Rough sketch of Coat of Many Colors

THE IDEA

"What can I do with all this leftover yarn? There isn't enough of any one color or kind to make anything. Well, maybe there is enough of this green to make a hat, and enough of the blue to make some mittens, *but I hate making hats and mittens!* So what do I do?"

You make a "coat of many colors"—a little of this, a smidgen of that, and one thin strand of something else to tie all the colors and yarns together. You begin at the neck, making a steek (see page 149) at the center front so that you can cut the garment open to become a cardigan. And you just knit away until all those oddball bits of yarn are used up. (See Figure 27.1.)

27.2 Coat of Many Colors worn by somewhat wide-hipped woman (yarn supplied by Brunswick, Plymouth, Caron, Reynolds, and Spinnerin; knitted by Joyce Culpepper; modeled by Joyce Culpepper)

THE YARN AND THE GAUGE

Sort the yarn into piles according to weight—thin, medium, and heavy. Aim for a combined weight equal to a bulky, Class D yarn, which will have a gauge of about 3 stitches per inch. Take out a #9 or #10 needle and start plying and playing.

It is doubtful that anyone else would have on hand or want to purchase exactly the same yarns that were used for our sample garment. However, so that you get an idea of the great diversity and the surprisingly small quantities of yarns that were used, they are listed below:

Brunswick's "Pomfret," a smooth classic sport-weight worsted 100 percent wool yarn, was used as a "run-along" to tie all the other colors and weights together. Each 50-gram skein holds 175 yards; 7 skeins used.

Plymouth "Puff," a bulky-weight 100 percent wool slubbed boucle. Each 100-gram skein holds 110 yards; 2 each of three colors.

Caron's "Highland Spice," a soft fluffy blend of acrylic, polyester, wool, and angora. Each 40-gram skein holds 52 yards; 6 balls used.

Reynolds "Candide, Light Weight," a sport-weight, single-ply 100 percent wool yarn. Each 2-ounce skein holds 275 yards; 1 each of three colors used.

Spinnerin "Illustra" was added for sparkle and glitter. It is a fingering-weight blend of viscose and metalized fiber. Each 20-gram ball holds 87 yards; 1 ball used.

MEASUREMENTS AND ARITHMETIC

To start, all you need to know is the difference in desired width of the back chest and the upper arm width, how wide the back of your neck is, and, of course, the gauge of the yarn. Use the compound-angle raglan formula of increases to the underarm (see pages 291–294). After that, continue trying it on and adjust as you go.

If your hips are bigger than your chest, increase at the imaginary side seams to gain width for your hips. Because this will be an open-down-the-front coat, increase also at the center back in order to make the front edges hang straight up and down.

Slit pockets work well on this sweater, placed at a handy spot to dig into for car keys. When you're almost finished, decide how to trim it, with ribbing or crochet or maybe a collar. The finishing will depend on how much of what yarn you have left over.

MAKING UP THE SWEATER

Try on the sweater at the progress points mentioned in the previous chapter (see page 308)—the shoulder tips, the actual underarm, the division point, about 1″ past the division point, and when you think body and sleeves are long enough.

When the sleeves are almost as long as you want them to be, try on the coat and decide how the bottoms of the sleeves should be ended. How would you both look best *and* be most comfortable? With ribbing? A lightweight hem? Crochet trim? (Fold-back cuffs would probably be too heavy for this bulky garment.) On the sweater shown here, we decreased 20 percent of the stitches and made 3″ of a K 1, P 1 ribbing.

FINISHING THE SWEATER

When the garment is as long as you wish it to be, take an inventory of what yarns (if any) are left over.

Decide how the bottom edge of the sweater should be finished. *It does not have to be finished in the same manner as the sleeves!* Do what looks good *and* feels comfortable to you. On the sweater shown here, we worked 4 rows of 2 × 2 ribbing on a needle one size smaller than the body.

Before you cut open the steek, try on the sweater one more time. Hold a handful of strands vertically down the center front to get an idea of how much of which color would best accentuate the desired effect. Think about how many of what kind of buttons you want. This will affect both the type and the width of the add-on front bands.

On this sweater, we decided to make rows of single crochet for the front bands, making appropriate-size buttonholes as we worked. We used one strand of each of the three colors of "Candide, Light Weight" plus one strand of the "Pomfret." (After the crocheting was complete, though, we loved the effect but vowed never to do it again. Trying to crochet evenly with four strands of sport-weight yarn was very difficult.)

While you're standing in front of the mirror, hold those strands of remaining yarn around your neck. What kind and what color collar would look best? (If you prefer, you can wait for this decision until the front bands are completed.) We decided to crochet a 2"-wide mandarin collar.

Now place the strands where you want to insert the pockets to both locate the exact spot to cut, and to decide what color you want to trim them with. (See Figure 27.3.) If you don't know where you want those pockets, wait until the front bands are completed. Then, wearing the jacket, stand in front of a mirror holding the things you wish to carry

Locate pocket where hand will easily fit into it.

Neck

SIDE SEAM

slightly less than half

slightly more than half

center front

END POCKET ABOUT 1.5" ABOVE BOTTOM OF JACKET

Bottom

27.3 Shape and placement of pockets

in the pocket. Don't locate the pockets at the imaginary side seams; that is too far back. Make them low enough to accommodate your hands without cramping your elbows. The outside trim on the pockets does not have to match the front bands of the coat either in color or in outside trim! We decided to make a couple of rows of the same crochet as on the front edges. Make the underside of pocket of cloth, or knit of one thin yarn. (There is no reason to add extra bulk.)

Do the machine-sewing and prepare to cut open the steeks as described on page 149.

Before you cut the steek, measure the length of the finished garment at the point of the steek. Write down the number. As you crochet, MEASURE, MEASURE, MEASURE. Make sure that both sides are the same length and that they are the length they are supposed to be.

A PROBLEM WITH ONE-PIECE JACKETS

There is one problem with making such large garments in one piece from the top down. They do get heavy once you are past the waist; it may not be convenient to carry with you everywhere you go the large work basket that will be required to hold all the yarn and the in-process garment. Such a garment may be an "at home only" project.

VARIATIONS

Instead of a steek, plan a front overlap just as you did on the cardigan jacket (see Chapter 23). Make the front bands of either seed or garter stitch and work the garment back and forth instead of in the round.

CONCLUSION

Yarn-aholics of the world, rejoice! Thrifty knitters, take note! Bargain hunters, be glad! You now have a foolproof way to use up all kinds of odds and ends. It works; I know because I was once a yarn-aholic and thrifty bargain hunter too. Now my yarn closet is clean—well, at least cleaner.

28

The True Batwing Sweater

In this chapter you will learn how to:

1. Design a crosswise sweater;
2. Plan a true batwing sweater;
3. Plan the modified batwing sweater.

THE IDEA

A crosswise-knit true batwing sweater is not my favorite type of garment. But examples of it appear so frequently in needlework magazines and pattern books that I feel I must not only comment on it, but also tell you how to design one. Batwing sweaters are very easy to design, can quickly and easily be made on a knitting machine, and, since most batwing sweaters are knitted crosswise from wrist to wrist, they offer an easy way to achieve vertical stripes without the bother of bobbins. Like the Coat of Many Colors, they offer an excellent opportunity for striping that allows the knitter to use up odd lots of yarn. (See Figure 28.2.)

On the smiling models in the photographs, these sweaters look exquisite. If the model were to move and start to live a real life, she might stop smiling. Let me explain why I am not fond of them. A few of my objections are:

On a true batwing sweater, the waistline depth is the underarm depth.

28.1 Modified Batwing Sweater (knitted by Victoria Kearney; modeled by Betty Wallace)

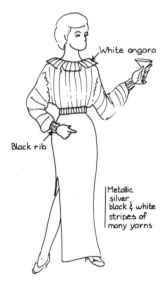

White angora

Black rib

Metallic silver black & white stripes of many yarns

28.2 Rough sketch of Batwing Sweater with split cowl neck

If it is cold enough *inside* to wear a sweater that covers the body from wrist to wrist, it is going to be much colder *outside*. The armholes of most coats aren't large enough to stuff in all that extra fabric and still allow room for a human arm. The only outer garment that I know of that will fit over an armhole/cum/waistline sweater is a cape.

And don't plan to eat while you are wearing a true batwing sweater; at least don't reach for any food. The armhole/cum/waistline sleeves fall into any plate or platter that you reach across.

Finally, knit fabrics used crosswise can behave in unpredictable ways. I took a survey of Atlanta knitters about their experiences with stockinette stitch used crosswise on batwing sweaters:

Three knitters (one using silk, one wool, one novelty blend) found their fabric stretched lengthwise; because the sleeves were too long, two knitters had to go back, remove wrist ribbing, rip back the sleeve endings, and redo ribbing. One knitter gave the sweater away.

Two knitters (one using cotton, one wool) found their fabric stretched crosswise and caused a big saggy bulge just above the waistline. One knitter salvaged her sweater by machine-stitching, cutting off excess, and remaking the bottom ribbing. One knitter stopped wearing the sweater.

Two knitters had no problems at all, except for the overcoat problem. A third knitter said, "I made my cowl-neck, batwing sweater of the wool-mohair blend called for by the magazine. Inside a building I absolutely roast; outside I freeze to death."

FLOOR PLAN OF THE PIECES

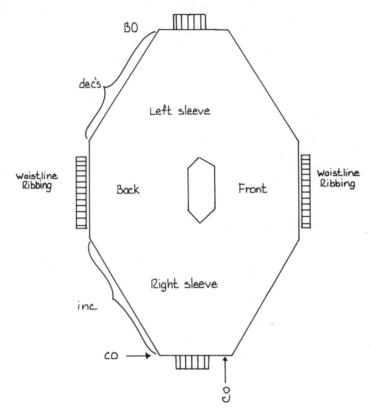

28.3 Layout of true Batwing Sweater

THE YARN AND THE GAUGE

Any type of yarn *can* be used to knit a batwing sweater. However, it is safer to stay with a sport-weight resilient (wool) yarn worked at a rather firm gauge. Though fuzzy animal fiber such as mohair or angora would make a gorgeous garment, I'd be a bit afraid of both the excessive warmth and the loose gauge at which those fibers must be worked. Loose gauge can mean stretch problems.

Regardless of what yarn you use, row gauge is critical because total width as well as increases and decreases along the diagonal lines are spaced and calculated according to row gauge.

MEASUREMENTS NEEDED

You don't need any measurements; a true batwing sweater comes close to being a one-size-fits-all sweater.

1. *Nape of neck to bottom of garment.* Be sure to allow added length for a blousing effect (see Figure 28.2).
2. *Circumference at bottom of garment, that is, the waistline.* You need two different numbers here: the fabric circumference and the bottom ribbing circumference.
3. *Center back nape of neck down arm to wrist.* (See Figure 28.4.)
4. *Wrist circumference.*
5. *Desired width of back neck.*

DOING THE ARITHMETIC

You won't have any trouble plotting this sweater. Just keep in mind the sweater is knitted crosswise from wrist to wrist and the numbers that would ordinarily be multiplied by stitch gauge are multiplied by row gauge and vice versa.

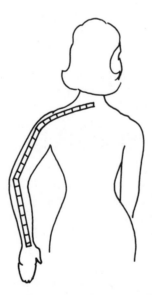

28.4 Correct placement of measuring tape for center-back-nape-of-neck-down-to-waist measurement for Batwing Sweater

THE MODIFIED BATWING SWEATER

After I had planned this garment and started to write this chapter I had second thoughts. "Maggie, why teach your students to make a dubious project just because they see it in all the magazines? Is there an improved version? Could you teach the students how to design *it?*"

"Well, yes, there is an improved version. Instead of having a true diagonal line from wrist to waistline, you limit the sleeve width to about 20″ and have an area the width of the body go straight up and down. But it doesn't really solve the whole problem, so why bother?"

Then one day, I came up with the solution. (See Figure 28.5.)

Start the sweater at the center front with a removable cast-on. (That way you can watch the stretch as you go instead of measuring a swatch,

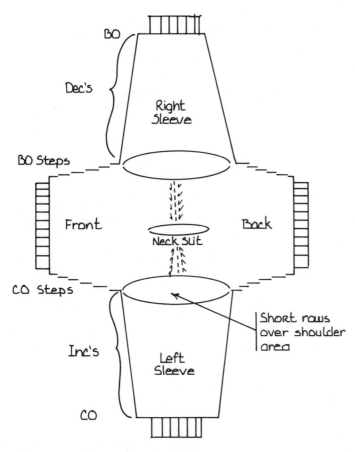

28.5 Layout for Modified Batwing Sweater

multiplying rows, and praying.) When the garment is partially completed, take out the cast-on and use a Kitchner stitch graft* to join the two sides together. (If you work both sides of the front at the same time on separate needles, this technique also allows you to knit a little way on first one side and then on the other, and to use up little bits of leftover yarn while keeping the two sides identical. However, it is not necessary to make the stripes on both sides match.)

Make a slit neck. Simply do not weave the two sides together in the area of the head! The neckline can be finished with a row or two of simple single crochet.

Let the "sleeves" slide down on the shoulder. Make pairs of matching decreases along the top of the shoulder to act like shoulder shaping. (This will eliminate some of the saggy-baggy fabric at the underarm.)

Limit the width of the sleeves to 20″.

At the time the shoulder decreases are completed and before the extra width is bound off to complete the "body," make a couple of inches of short rows on the "sleeves." (This will eliminate some more of the saggy-baggy fabric at the underarm.)

Look at the photo at the beginning of this chapter. Victoria Kearney was the knitter. I simply gave her my scribbled notes and described my idea. I handed her a bag full of all kinds of yarns in black and white. The odd lots included metallics, eyelash, angora, thick-and-thin chenille, slubbed and boucle wools, and glossy nubbed and smooth matte-finish cottons. And look what she came up with! She made the sweater all in a combination of stockinette stitch and reverse stockinette stitch. That is to say some of the stripes are reverse side out. She did not increase or decrease the number of stitches across the row when she changed from a worsted weight to lighter or heavier weights of yarn, but she did sometimes change needle sizes.

Both the sweater and the knitter are a marvel!

(It is a shame that most knitting magazines are not comfortable with

---

*The Kitchner stitch graft involves making a row of knitting "in thin air" to invisibly join two pieces of knitted fabric together. (The pieces must be free of cast-on or bound-off edges.)

On a flat surface, lay the pieces to be joined as shown in Figure 28.6.

Thread yarn on a tapestry needle and bring it up in the base of the last stitch on the right-hand side of the lower piece. Go across the gap to the upper piece. Put the needle down in the first loop and up in the next one, *across the gap. Down in the spot we came out of before, up in the base of the next stitch. Across the gap and down in the stitch we were in before and up in the next one.* Repeat between the asterisks.

28.6 Kitchner stitch graft

"start and see what happens and wing it" sweater-making directions. Because these kinds of instructions are rarely printed, knitters are deprived of learning to trust their own creativity.)

VARIATIONS

Make a cardigan of a true batwing design. Start at the wrist, increase to waist, work even to edge of neck. Begin shaping neckline (let the back stitches wait). Work to within ½" of front center line. On the front, change to ribbing and smaller needles. Work 1" ribbing. Bind off. Cast on same number of stitches on smaller needles. Work 1" ribbing. Change back to larger needles. (You are now ½" *beyond* the front center line.) Resume knitting on the back and catch up to the same row as the front. Complete sweater.

Make a cardigan of the modified batwing sweater. Weave the center back together, but add strips of ribbing front bands to the front sections.

In the same way that you design a cardigan, you can make a front-opening placket or slit combined with a regular (or wide) crew-shaped neck.

CONCLUSION

Once I made a true batwing sweater. Once was enough; I have never made another. If you feel you must make one, go ahead, but if you do not feel you must make a true batwing, give the modified version a try.

The intention of this book is to give the reader the necessary tools to select and design enjoyable knitted garments, to enable the reader to know in advance how each garment will look and feel on the intended wearer before making any investment of time or money.

Therefore it is crucial to include sweater styles and configurations that, though routinely presented in knitting publications, are complete failures. To simply ignore these styles that are less than satisfactory does not prepare the reader to avoid them. Moreover, when designs such as the batwing are augmented/modified/improved, they can become attractive and wearable garments.

29

Icelandic Yoke Pullover

In this chapter you will learn how to:

1. *Formulate a circle or yoke;*
2. *Customize and adapt printed patterns;*
3. *Design for an oval body type.*

THE IDEA

Ethnic designs in clothing rarely go out of style. You can wear them for a year or two, clean and carefully store them, and then bring them out again a few years later for another round of use. Created over generations of trial and error, many ethnic designs have reached a state of near perfection and timeless quality. The Yoked Icelandic Pullover is a fine example. (See Figure 29.1.) The whole family of Icelandic designs with their radiating, overlapping, and concentric diamonds is flattering to almost all types of figures.

For body types that do not desire emphasis at the hips, simply leave out the repetition of the charted design pattern around the bottom of the sweater and make the bottom ribbing the same color as the body. Also make sure that the skirts or slacks will be the same color as the sweater so as not to draw attention to the hipline.

Special fitting aids can easily be put in Icelandic sweaters as

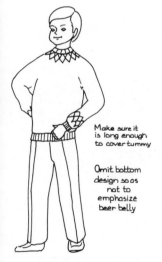

Make sure it is long enough to cover tummy

Omit bottom design so as not to emphasize beer belly

29.1 Rough sketch of Icelandic Yoked Pullover

needed. **These could include bust darts, wide or narrower hip shaping, longer or shorter sleeve lengths, or the special helps for oval figures that we are going to discuss here.**

By including this chapter I am not suggesting that you *must* or even *should* design your own yoked ethnic sweaters. If someone else has already worked out the charted designs and the arithmetic, why tamper with perfection? Rather, I have included this sweater so that you will understand the principle of designing yoked garments. Also, I hope, with a few quick tips, to lead you to modify and adapt existing sweater instructions when you do not choose to modify the ethnic yoke.

The Reynolds Yarn Company has kindly allowed me to use their pattern number 2704 from volume number 27.

FLOOR PLAN OF THE PIECES

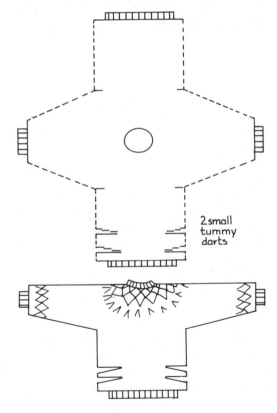

2 small
tummy
darts

29.2 Layout of Icelandic Yoked Pullover

29.3 Icelandic Yoked Pullover (yarn supplied by Reynolds; pattern and charts used with permission of Reynolds; knitted by Yvonne Morris; modeled by Gordon Robbins)

THE YARN AND THE GAUGE

The Icelandic people knit their garments of a bulky-weight, somewhat fleecy yarn in naturally occurring colors of sheep's wool. Tones of black and off-white, differing grays, and all shades of brown from near-ebony to off-white are commonly used. Because the colors are natural ones does not mean that the finished sweaters are in any way dull or uninteresting. Quite the contrary, they are real eye-stoppers.

For this garment we are using Reynolds "Lopi®," 100 percent Icelandic wool, water-repellent, approximately 110 yards per 100-gram skein.

GAUGE: Stockinette stitch—(solid color) 3.5 sts and 4.5 rows = 1″ on USA #10 needles

Because the wearer had an oval figure we did not choose to emphasize the hipline and so left off the charted design at the bottom of the sweater, making the body all one color from the yoke down. Also, to accommodate the tummy and provide extra length we added horizontal darts over the tummy area. Therefore it was necessary to order one extra skein of the main-color yarn.

MAKING CHANGES IN PRINTED PATTERNS

Now that you know how to *write* instuctions for knitting, you should have no trouble understanding someone else's printed directions. When you find a pattern you want to make, choose the size pattern nearest the chest size you desire. Go through the pattern until you find the total number of stitches at the chest and at the hip. Divide the number of stitches at each location by the stitch gauge to find the actual circumferences (in inches) of the finished garment.

Do these circumferences of the garment suit your desires? If they don't, change them.

Cast on more stitches to accommodate wide hips and gradually decrease at the side seams to the width you desire at the chest. Cast on fewer stitches for narrow hips and gradually increase at the side seams for the chest.

Do you need a bust dart for better fit? Put one in!

Since you already know how to plan bust darts (see Making Darts, pages 150–156) it is a simple matter to add them to existing instructions. So long as you end up with the proper number of stitches at the beginning of the charted designs for the yoke, you can use someone else's arithmetic and planning.

If the shoulders are too wide (and many pre-designed sweaters with set-in sleeves have shoulders that would fit a weight lifter), narrow them.

Increase the number of "every-other-row" decreases at the armhole shaping until you get the shoulder width you desire. Refigure the shoulder bind-offs according to the number of stitches you have remaining.

Changing sleeve lengths and shapes should be no problem. You know what you want and you know how to figure them.

SPECIAL CONSIDERATIONS IN DESIGNING FOR OVAL BODY TYPES

Oval bodies are unlike other nonpregnant body types in that, both male and female, they have a large pouch in the front. The "forgivingness" of the knitted fabric will cover a lot of situations, but it does have its limits. There comes a time in knitting for oval body types when you must plan extra width and length to cover the front pouch.

MEASUREMENTS NEEDED TO MAKE CHANGES FOR OVAL FIGURES

If you cannot readily see it with the eye, find out where the largest protuberance is located (barrel chest?, tummy paunch?, sagging belly?) and if more width is needed on the front than on the back:

How much of the total *chest* circumference belongs in the front and how much in the back?

How much of the total *tummy* circumference belongs in the front and how much in the back?

How much of the total *hip/belly* circumference belongs in the front and how much in the back?

Where is the largest circumference located—chest, tummy, or belly?

How much is the difference between the largest and the smallest of the three areas?

PLANNING INCREASES FOR THE FRONT

If the difference between any of the above front/back measurements is more than 4″, you'll have to make changes in the printed pattern:

For barrel chests and tummy paunches, increase the width of the front over the protruding area and then decrease it back again before the yoke pattern begins. (See Figure 29.4.)

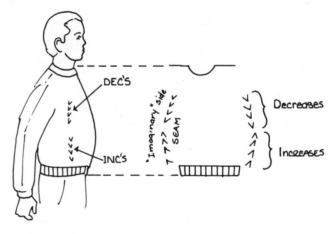

29.4 Front of Icelandic Yoked Pullover, showing increases and decreases to accommodate protruding stomach

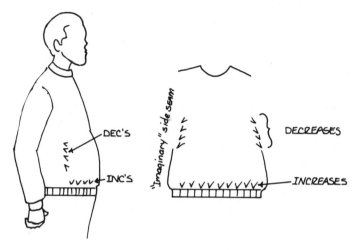

29.5 Front of Icelandic Yoked Pullover, showing added width and compensating decreases

Use the French Make-1 or blind stockinette type of increase (see page 333), and be sure to alternate your decreases between SSK and K 2 tog to keep the grain of the fabric running straight up and down.

For sagging bellies, increase the width of the front along the bottom. Gradually decrease that width along the imaginary side seams. (See Figure 29.5.)

Find out if the front length is longer than the back length and if short-row darts are necessary. (Your eye cannot tell you this; you'll need a tape measure.) What is the difference between front neck-shoulder joining to bottom length and back nape of neck to bottom length? If this difference is more than 1.5″ you will have to make darts. Comparing the front and back lengths will also tell you the length to make the darts.

PLANNING THE TUMMY DARTS

Tummy darts are unlike bust darts because the protuberance is rounded and does not come to a point. Instead of making one large dart on each side, make two smaller ones separated by several inches. (See Figure 29.6.)

Divide front stitches into four equal areas. Each dart will extend from the (imaginary) side seam one-fourth of the way toward the center. The half portion of stitches at the center will not be used for the dart.

Multiply the number of inches of length to be added by the row

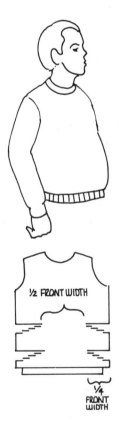

29.6 Front of Icelandic Yoked Pullover showing matching darts

gauge, and then divide the number of rows by 2. On each side make two matching short-row darts one-fourth of the way from the (imaginary) side seam toward the center.

PRINCIPLES OF CONSTRUCTING A CIRCULAR YOKE

There may be times when you wish to create your own ethniclike designs. Therefore, this section contains the formula for designing circular yokes.

Because I am more comfortable thinking in terms of working from the neck down, I am going to describe the process that way, as we did in understanding compound-angle raglans. Though it is easier to create the design from the top down, once the planning is complete you do not have to make them that way if you prefer knitting from bottom up.

Remember from Chapter 26 (see pages 313–314) that to make the more or less square-yoked raglan we increased 1 stitch before and after each of the four raglan markers on every other row. Moreover, we grouped these increases in pairs and made them over and over again along the same diagonal line. We increased 8 stitches every other row to make a fabric that would lie flat. That is the equivalent of making 4 increases every row.

If we had wanted a circular instead of a rectangle yoke, we could have increased 4 stitches every row, scattering the increases across the round of knitting so that none of them ever fell one on top of another.

The key to forming a circular yoke is to increase the equivalent of 4 stitches every round and never let those increases fall on top of one another.

In the area between the neck and shoulder tips, where we need an almost perfect circle, the equivalent of 4 stitches per round should be strictly maintained.

In the area between the shoulder tips and the actual underarm, where we need less width than a perfect circle, we change our increase formula to 4 stitches *every other round*. Then, after the final charted design is completed, circular-yoked sweaters usually revert to raglan-increase-type shaping at the underarm for a better fit. Often there will also be a number of cast-on stitches at the underarm.

It is not necessary to make increases on each and every row. That would wreak havoc with making multicolored graphed designs such as snowflakes. Instead, because knitted fabric is so forgiving, we can work a number of rounds even, without increases, to complete a graphed design, and then cram in many increases on one round. Often that increase round is a solid color and marks the change from one design to another.

For the areas between the neck and the shoulder tips and between the actual underarm and the sweater underarm, these are the equivalents of "4 stitches every round":

Work 2 rounds even, then increase 8 stitches on the next.
Work 4 rounds even, then increase 16 stitches on the next.
Work 6 rounds even, then increase 24 stitches on the next.
Work 8 rounds even, then increase 32 stitches on the next.
Work 10 rounds even, then increase 40 stitches on the next.

It is doubtful that at the neck area you would want to knit even much more than 10 rounds before making the next increase row.

For the area between the shoulder tips and the actual underarm, these are the equivalents of "4 stitches *every other* round":

Work 2 rounds even, then increase 4 stitches on the next.
Work 4 rounds even, then increase 8 stitches on the next.
Work 6 rounds even, then increase 12 stitches on the next.
Work 8 rounds even, then increase 16 stitches on the next.
Work 10 rounds even, then increase 20 stitches on the next.
Work 12 rounds even, then increase 24 stitches on the next.
Work 14 rounds even, then increase 28 stitches on the next.

The charted designs are usually discontinued at a point about 4″ above the underarm. This is because, where the garment begins to move down and into the armpit, the continuity of the design would be lost.

STEPS TO DESIGN YOUR OWN YOKED SWEATER

1. Measure the circumference of the neck where the finished sweater will rest. Remember that ribbing will be added to this.
2. Measure a diagonal raglanlike armhole length.
3. In the usual way, mark layout drawing with inches and stitches and rows.
4. Multiply neck circumference by stitch gauge. Add an ease factor of at least 2″. Adjust number of stitches to accommodate charted multicolor design multiple.

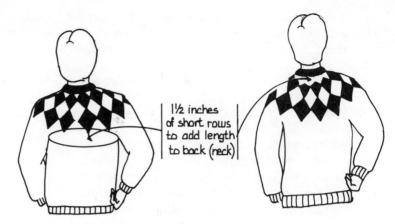

29.7 Short rows can be added below the graphed design (A) or at the neck (B) to allow the front neck to hang lower than the back neck

5. From the neck down plan the yoke placement of designs and increases.
6. From the armhole up, plan several inches of raglan shaping.
7. Adjust and juggle to make the numbers of rows and stitches correspond.

VARIATIONS

Some knitters like to add 1.5″ of short rows across the back, either just before the lowest graphed design of the yoke or at the neck just before the ribbing, to allow the front neck to hang lower than the back neck. (See Figure 29.7.)

CONCLUSION

Now that you know the principles of sweater design, if you see a printed pattern you like, you can alter it for a better fit without reconstructing the whole thing.

30

Traditional Aran Fisherman Sweaters

In this chapter you will learn how to:

1. *Work with multiple pattern stitches that have different gauges;*
2. *Check the shaping of a sleeve cap.*

THE IDEA

Traditional Aran fisherman sweaters can be made as pullovers or as cardigans. (See Figure 30.1.) Smooth classic worsted yarn in either sport or worsted weight can be used. Though the true ethnic color is off-white, some knitters like to make them in other light and/or heather colors. (Dark colors will swallow up the light-and-shadow patterns of the cables, ribs, and twists that give these garments their everlasting beauty.)

Originally these sweaters, made for working on fishing boats, were knit of unscoured wool yarn, meaning that the yarn was not washed and cleansed to remove the lanolin, the natural sheep oil. Leaving the oil in the fiber made these sweaters not only spray- and rain-proof but also unsinkable life jackets that helped to keep a sailor afloat in the water. *It also made him smell like a wet, dirty sheep.* Today our sweaters can be made water repellent with unsmelly Scotchgard®, and most knitters prefer not to use unscoured yarn.

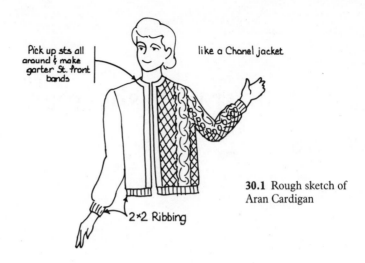

Pick up sts all
around & make
garter St. front
bands

like a Chanel jacket

2×2 Ribbing

30.1 Rough sketch of
Aran Cardigan

FLOOR PLAN OF THE PIECES

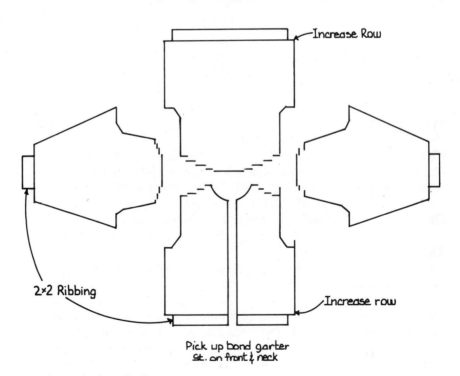

Increase Row

2×2 Ribbing

Increase row

Pick up band garter
St. on front & neck

30.2 Layout for Aran Cardigan

30.3 Aran Cardigan (yarn supplied by Brunswick; knitted by Shirley Robb; modeled by Maggie Righetti)

THE YARN, THE GAUGE, AND MAKING UP THE DIRECTIONS

Brunswick's "Pomfret" sport-weight (Class B) smooth classic worsted wool in an off-white color was selected. It contains approximately 175 yards per 50-gram ball. The reference table says that, in sport weight, a woman's large "ordinary, nonpatterned," long-sleeved, crew-necked sweater would require approximately 1,600 yards. Dividing that amount by our figure of 175 yards per skein, we would need 9.14 skeins. But richly embossed and encrusted Aran sweaters are hardly ordinary. We ordered instead 11 skeins, making a total of 1,925 yards, and we just barely had sufficient yarn.

DESIGNING MULTIPATTERNED SWEATERS

The big problem in designing an Aran sweater is that you are working with many different pattern stitches, each of which may have a different gauge.

The cables and twists will certainly eat width; blackberry stitch may have many fewer stitches per inch; Irish moss will be expansive.

The gauge of each and every pattern's stitch must be considered separately.

Before beginning an Aran sweater, it's a good idea to obtain several books containing Aran pattern stitches and to make swatch strips of various pattern stitches. You will likely discard some because they are more work than the effect warrants. Some ideas may be discarded because their design is not compatible with other stitch patterns.

When you have selected your desired pattern stitches, try this clever trick, thought of by Atlanta knitter Shirley Robb, to help calculate the number of stitches you'll need. (See Figure 30.4.)

Put the selected swatches face down on a photocopy machine and make actual-size "photos" of them, reproducing several times the stitches that are to be repeated on different areas. Next, tape together pieces of plain paper until they are the combined width of the back and the front. Put this paper, which is the desired width of the finished sweater, down on the table. Onto this actual-sized floor plan, cut and paste 3″-long photocopies of the pattern stitches where you think you want them to be. It will take some arranging and rearranging to make the pasted-up floor plan look just the way you want the finished sweater to look.

This method tells you not only how much *area* will be used up by each pattern but also how many *stitches* will be necessary for each of the differing designs.

It is just a matter of counting the total number of stitches in each swatch and adding them together. After you complete the ribbing and increases for the number of stitches for the body, put in ring

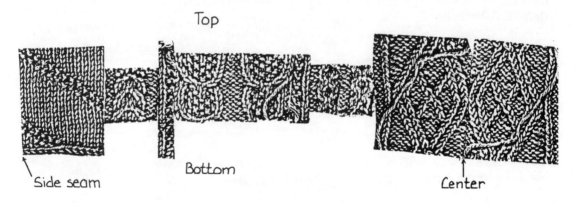

Top

Side seam

Bottom

Center

30.4 Experiment with taping together photocopies of the desired stitch patterns until you achieve the look you want.

markers separating the patterns from each other so that you won't get confused.

Shirley Robb has opened the door for all of us who do not like intricate arithmetic to a new and ingenious way of designing *any* kind of multipatterned sweater.

Make and prepare your swatches. Make an actual-sized paper layout pattern of the widths you want your various parts to be. Make a number of photocopies of the pattern stitches you want to use. Arrange and rearrange these "photos" until you are pleased with the look of the completed design. Count the number of stitches in each photo panel. Add up the stitches necessary for each layout pattern piece. (If you desire, make a chart of the stitches as arranged.) Plan the number of ribbing stitches as a percentage of the total number of stitches.

Shirley did what every good teacher hopes all students will do. She assessed her own problem, figured out a unique and simple way to solve it, and did her own thing just the way she wanted it (leaving her admiring teacher in the dust).

MAKING UP THE GARMENT

I taught Shirley the mechanics of designing a well-fitting sleeve shoulder cap as discussed in Chapter 22 (see pages 258–260). Recall that the sleeve is shorter than the armhole of the back of the sweater. The amount it is shorter is one-half the width of the flat area on the top of the sleeve. This amount must be subtracted from the length of the sleeve. "But then it will be too short," she said.

"No," I reaffirmed, "it will work beautifully."

When she brought the finished sweater back, she said, "You were right about the shaping of the sleeve cap. But as I was working it, I didn't believe you, so, when I got to the end of the every-other-row decreases on the sleeves, I sewed the underarm seams on both the body and sleeves and basted the sleeves in place. That way I could check on the fit of the sleeve cap as I worked it. To my surprise, you were absolutely correct."

Again Shirley Robb came up with a unique solution to a problem. She doesn't like to make a mistake and rip out any more than the rest of us do. She invented a way to check the finished fit as she went along.

If you are ever worried about the fit of a sleeve cap, try Shirley's method of checking as you go.

FINISHING THE SWEATER

We discussed how to finish the neck and front edges. Because we have both had disasters using the ethnic method of making Knit 1, Purl 1 ribbing bands, that was not even considered. Instead, Shirley chose to pick up stitches along those edges and make a 1" wide continuous garter stitch front/neck band. "I never intend to button this sweater, so I will not bother making buttonholes."

I agreed that leaving out buttonholes was okay. I reminded her to put a ring marker at the right-angle corner where the front and front neck join so that she would remember to make increases before and after the corner on every other row to ensure that the band would lie flat.

VARIATIONS

Now that the trick of using twentieth-century technology to plan a centuries-old design is out in the open, you can use a photocopy machine when designing any sort of garment with multiple pattern stitches and gauges. This simple idea can be expanded and put to use when planning garments of two or more different yarns with different gauges.

31

Diagonal Sweaters

Sweaters knitted on the diagonal with rows running catty-corner instead of across or up and down can look oh, so appealing, but beware!

BEWARE #1

Before you design or make any type of sweater that uses the finished stitches diagonally, be aware that

knitted stitches are not square. Usually there are more rows per inch than there are stitches per inch (for instance, "7 stitches and 10 rows = 1 inch"). This directly affects how our diagonally made sweaters are going to be shaped with increases and decreases.

When knitting on the diagonal, whether you get a usable square or an unwanted elongated triangle and/or diamond is a function of the relationship between the diameter of the yarn and the circumference of the needle used. If that sounds like an unintelligible mouthful, let me say it another way. *You will have to fiddle with the weight and loft of the yarn and the size of the needle until you get a gauge that is truly square with the same number of stitches and rows per inch.* If your gauge is not square, your piece cannot be square; an "increase 1 stitch each side every other row" will cause your work to become that unwanted triangle and/or diamond. If your gauge is not square, you will have to fiddle endlessly with the sequence of increases (and/or decreases) making perhaps "1 stitch every row twice, then 1 stitch every row once, then 1 stitch every other row twice more, then every row three times."

BEWARE #2

Diagonally knitted fabric can hang in peculiar ways!

Though it is true that ordinary knitted fabric does not have a true bias as does woven cloth, if the fabric is knitted so loosely that the stitch gauge and the row gauge are approximately the same, the completed catty-corner garment can drape over the human body in a very strange and unpredictable manner. Sometimes it looks great; sometimes it looks lousy; and I don't know how to tell ahead of time just what it will look like.

DIAGONAL KNITTING PUT TO GOOD USE

With those "Bewares" in mind, we can talk about situations in which diagonal knitting is used, often with wonderful visual effects:

Making On-the-Bias Rectangular or Triangular Pieces. The easiest diagonal piece is a "granny shawl." It is begun with one or two or three stitches and increased at each edge to the desired size (or until the yarn or the knitter's patience runs out) and then bound off. Usually a long fringe is added.

Another easy piece is the diagonally striped square-cut or "Chinese menu" sweater. It is a rectangle that the knitter starts in one corner and increases at each edge until the sides are as long as she wishes the front of the sweater to be wide. Then decreases are made along the sides until there are no stitches left. (See Figures 31.1 and 31.2).

"V" or Poncho-type Sweaters. Fads come and go in knitting just as much as they do in foods. One year beef Wellington is *in,* the next year it is steak tartare, and then it is roast beef with raspberry purée. One year oversized pullovers are *in,* the next year it is capes, and then it is ponchos. When the ponchos have died, knitters remember how lovely the V-neck hung and how prettily the stripes moved diagonally up the shoulders. And they incorporate the poncho shaping into other types of sweaters.

Because these sweaters are usually made of soft, lightweight yarns and because they are usually made from the top down, they almost always work out well. (See Figure 31.3.)

Right-angle Designs. Though they are not truly "diagonal," I have included right-angle designs here because the above warning about knitted stitches not usually being perfect squares applies. To get the

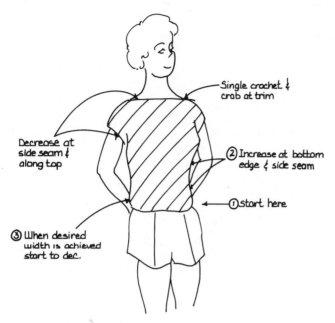

Single crochet & crab at trim

Decrease at side seam & along top

② Increase at bottom edge & side seam

① start here

③ When desired width is achieved start to dec.

31.1 Rough sketch of a square-cut sweater knit on the diagonal

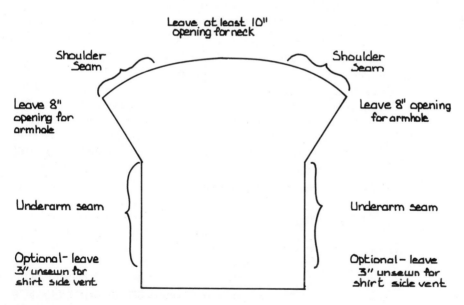

Leave at least 10" opening for neck

Shoulder Seam

Shoulder Seam

Leave 8" opening for armhole

Leave 8" opening for armhole

Underarm seam

Underarm seam

Optional – leave 3" unsewn for shirt side vent

Optional – leave 3" unsewn for shirt side vent

31.2 Layout of square-cut sweater knit on the diagonal

31.3 Rough sketch of a poncho-type sweater

true right-angle effect you either must be very careful about the gauge or watch your increases (decreases) very carefully. (See Figure 31.4.)

Pretzel Sweaters. The pretzel sweater is a further development of the right-angle sweater. Made all in one piece, the right and left sides mirror each other, as do the back and the front. (See Figure 31.5.) They are lots of fun to make and because they are usually multicolor and multitexture they can consume gobs of oddball yarn. Whether or not the decreases form perfect 45° angles is again a function of the ratio of the number of stitches to the number of rows. However, because of the way the pretzel sweater form-fits the body, often it does not matter whether or not the decrease angles are perfect.

Pretzel Sweater Instructions:

1. Cast on and work bottom ribbing.
2. Work approximately 2″ of body.
3. At one "seam" place a marker. Cast on sufficient stitches to go up and over shoulder and back to beginning (this will become the side seam and the armhole). Place a marker. Work across front, place a

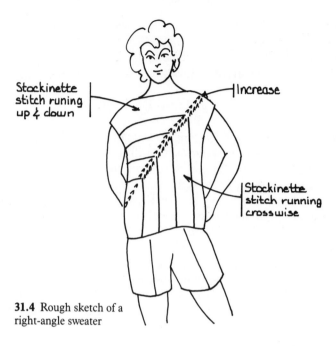

Stockinette stitch runing up & down

Increase

Stockinette stitch running crosswise

31.4 Rough sketch of a right-angle sweater

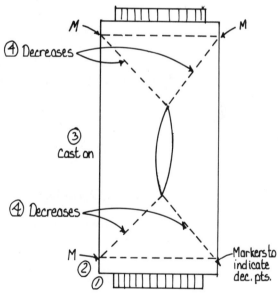

M   M

④ Decreases

③ Cast on

④ Decreases

M
②
①

Markers to indicate dec. pts.

Cast on enough sts to go up & over shoulder & back to here.

Bind off

Pick up sleeve ribbing

Decrease

Weave seam

31.5 Rough sketch and layout of a pretzel sweater

marker. Cast on same number of stitches as before, place a marker. Work across back.
4. Work round and round the rectangle, decreasing every other row at markers until all the front and back stitches have been used up.
5. Rib and bind off neck edge.
6. Weave side seams. Pick up and rib armhole stitches.

Crazy Quilt Designs with a Patch of This and a Patch of That. Every once in a while a needlework magazine will feature a truly marvelous-looking jacket or coat assembled of squares and swatches of different pattern stitches including diagonal ones. I think that this idea works better as an afghan or a throw, and since you have read the "Bewares" in this chapter and also Chapter 9 about the differences in behavior of pattern stitches, you probably will think so too.

31.6 Rough sketch of a diagonal basketweave sweater

Basketweave Effects. Begun with a series of diagonally knitted triangles of different colors, squares are then added to each valley between the triangles and the entire garment is constructed of small squares set at right angles to resemble a catty-corner woven basket. (See Figure 31.6.)

BEWARE #3

If you are following someone else's instructions for, or modifying, a basketweave sweater, be sure your gauge accurately matches the gauge of the designer. After the first row of triangles is completed, you pick up stitches along the row edge to make the next set of squares at a 90° angle to the first row. If your stitch and row gauge are not a perfect match to the designer's, your new squares will not be square.

CONCLUSION

When you try to make any kind of garment other than an ordinary sweater out of knitted fabric, some problems occur. Sometimes the problems are easily solved, sometimes they are not, *but if you are not aware of the problems, you cannot solve them.*

32

Designing Your Own Sleeves

In previous chapters, we learned how to design flat-top sleeves for dropped shoulders, puff sleeves, smooth capped set-in sleeves, simple and compound-angle raglan sleeves, and batwing sleeves. These are the most commonly used types of sleeves, but there are lots of other ways to cover the arms. Let's explore some of them.

THREE KINDS OF CAP SLEEVES

Though many designers and printed sweater instructions would lead you to believe otherwise, good-looking short capped sleeves *are not made* by simply avoiding armhole and shoulder shaping. Though artful photography may disguise the fact, the results of avoiding armhole shaping are usually exceedingly ugly. If the yarn is stiff and the stitches are firm, you will get a pair of wings instead of cap sleeves. If the fiber is soft, you get a droopy, saggy underarm pouch. There are better ways to make cap sleeves.

CAP SLEEVES AS AN EXTENSION OF THE BODY

I'm fond of these. I've never seen them *not* look great. On the body front and back, at the point where you would usually begin to reduce the number of stitches with underarm shaping, begin instead to widen the garment. For 1″ of rows, *on every row*, either cast on or increase 1 stitch at each side edge. Next, along these outer edges, increase 1 stitch each side every ½″ until sufficient width has been increased so that the garment will reach halfway across the upper arm between the shoulder

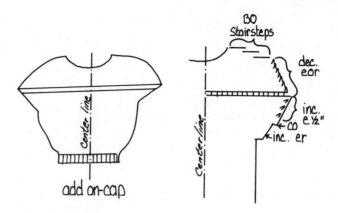

32.1 Sketch and layout for add-on cap sleeve

tips. Now begin to rapidly shape the shoulders by decreasing (or short-rowing or binding off) 1 stitch each side every row until the desired armhole depth is reached. Finally, shape the remaining shoulder stitches in the ordinary stairstep way. (See Figure 32.1.)

SHORT SET-IN CAP SLEEVES

Set-in sleeves that begin an inch or so below the armhole bind-off shaping and that are much, much shorter than the body underarm length make wonderful cap sleeves.

On ordinary set-in sleeves (described in Chapter 22 pages 256–257) we decide on and then subtract from the body armhole length the width of the flat area at the top of the sleeve cap. We do that also for short cap sleeves. But we then shape the rest of the top of the sleeve much more abruptly, binding off on each side of the flat top area, at least ½" (up to 1") of stitches on each row for at least 4". This cause the overall length of the sleeve cap to be much shorter than for regular sleeves. (See Figure 32.2.)

The bottom edge of the sleeve can be finished in any way you choose. Either a short length of ribbing or a crocheted edging can be very effective.

ULTRASHORT RAGLAN SLEEVES

Many times I have made capped-sleeve vests in the raglan top-down method. Women who must live and work in chilly atmospheres appreciate the extra few inches of added fabric over the tips of their shoulders

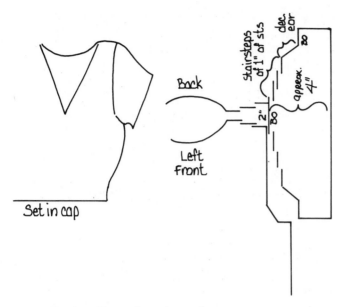

Text inside the figure: Back, Left Front, Set in cap, Stairsteps of 1" of sts, dec. eor, BO, approx. 4", 2", BO

32.2 Sketch and layout for set-in cap sleeve

that they would not get with ordinary sleeveless vests. Begun at the neck, the sleeves are ended and finished off at the underarm division point. If extra stitches are to be cast on for the body at the body/sleeve separation point, I also cast them on for the cap sleeves, and then immediately finish off the sleeves with a short ribbing.

LEG-O'-MUTTON SLEEVES

A leg-o'-mutton sleeve is nothing more than a puff sleeve married to elongated ribbing. The puff sleeve (described in Chapter 20) can be of any pattern stitch, width, or length ending above the elbow. (See Figure 32.3.)

Since the circumference of the arm just above the elbow is greater than the circumference of the wrist, the width of the ribbing will need to be increased. The number of stitches can be added to at an underarm seam. An easier way to increase the width, however, is to change needle sizes. Starting at the wrist use small needles; change to the next larger size after about 4″, and then to still larger ones as the elbow length is reached.

Wide-shouldered and heavy-breasted body types should avoid leg-o'-

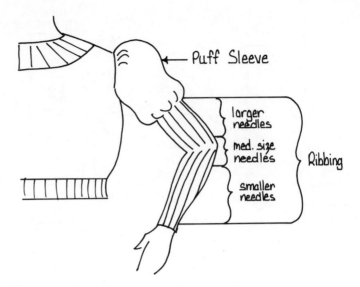

32.3 Leg-o'-mutton sleeve

mutton sleeves, which accentuate apparent shoulder and chest width. On narrow-shouldered and small-breasted people, they are wonderfully flattering.

DOLMAN SLEEVES

A dolman sleeve is similar in appearance to a batwing sleeve. The difference is that a dolman sleeve is usually a separate piece whereas the batwing is all-in-one with the body. In the batwing, the armhole depth is to the waistline; in the dolman, the armhole depth is usually somewhat shorter than the waist, but still longer than for capped-top, set-in sleeves.

A traditional dolman sleeve is somewhat like the flat-topped Da Vinci Man sleeve, but instead of being attached to a dropped shoulder, it is set into an indented square armhole opening.

Traditional dolman, Da Vinci, and batwing sleeves all have the same problem of great gobs of fabric hanging loose at the underarm. They are all grossly unflattering to square-shouldered and large-breasted body types who do not need added visual width in the chest area.

A few simple adjustments can modify the traditional dolman to make it hang better as well as eliminate some of the excess fabric (see Figure 32.4):

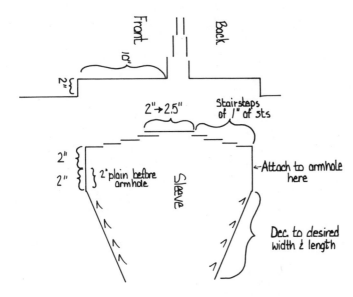

32.4 Layout for modified dolman sleeve

1. Limit the armhole depth to approximately 10″.
2. When planning the body, inset the square armhole into the body to a depth of 2″ or 2.5″.
3. On the sleeves, make sure that you add the same amount of length that you inset the armholes. Now, instead of binding off the top of the sleeve flat across, which would be traditional, shape the top of it. Bind off 1″ of stitches at the beginning of each row until only the center 2″ to 4″ remain. Then bind off the center stitches.

These modifications will give a bit of extra length from neck to wrist to cause the sweater to hang nicely at the shoulders and still avoid extra underarm fabric.

MODIFIED DA VINCI MAN SLEEVES

On Da Vinci Man sweaters, instead of making a flat-across bind-off, you can bind off the sleeves as follows: 1″ of stitches at the beginning of each row until only the center 2″ remain. Then bind off the center 2″. This will allow the tops of the sleeves to fall lower on the arm and you can then shorten the (unshaped) armhole depth and narrow the corresponding upper arm sleeve width. Lots of excess fabric at the underarms will disappear and the sweater will be more comfortable to wear.

The layout drawing for this sleeve now looks exactly like the layout for the modified dolman sleeve, Figure 32.4.

SADDLE SLEEVES

Saddle sleeves are really raglan sleeves married to a body that has standard-shaped armholes.

The sleeves are decreased from the armhole in raglan style (1 stitch each side every other row) until only 2″ to 4″ of stitches remain. These remaining stitches form the saddle, which continues up across the shoulder all the way to the neckline. To make allowance for the saddle shaping, half of the width of the saddle is subtracted from the armhole depth of both the back and the front. (See Figure 32.5.)

Often an Aran-like cable design runs up the center of the sleeve and saddle to end at the neck. A compatible but wider design can be centered on the front of the sweater. This gives a sweater the embellished look of an Irish fisherman sweater without having to work with time-consuming pattern stitches all over the body of the garment.

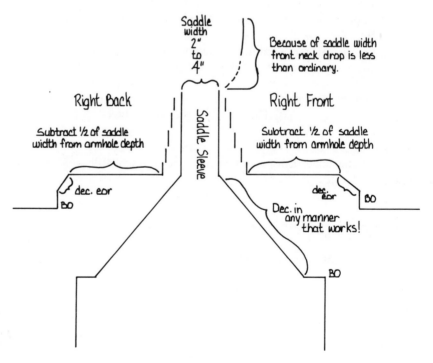

32.5 Layout for back, front, and saddle sleeve

Saddle sleeves, especially cabled ones, tend to make wide- and/or square-shouldered people look like they are wearing football-sized shoulder pads, but on narrow- or slopping-shouldered people they are very flattering.

PEAKED SLEEVES

We know that shoulders that are not stairstepped with bind-offs do not fit most human bodies. But it is not necessary to stairstep *both* the back and the front in order to get a well-fitting garment. If we were to bind off the front shoulder straight across, and then compensate for it by making twice as many stairsteps on the back shoulder, our sweater would conform to the shape of the human body. Of course we would end up with a rather strangely shaped armhole, but we could compensate for that by making an off-center peak on the top of our sleeves. (See Figure 32.6.)

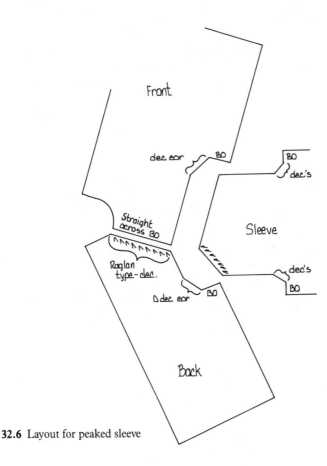

32.6 Layout for peaked sleeve

Frequently on peaked-sleeve sweaters the stairstep bind offs on the body back are changed to full-fashioned decreases, making it easy to sew the shoulders into place. The whole effect can be very handsome, making a statement of elegance and timeless taste.

HALTER-STYLE TOPS

The front arm edge of a halter-style sweater is a straight/diagonal raglan without sleeves. The neck edge can be anything you want it to be: turtle, scoop, or even a flat, narrow boatneck. You can slant the raglan so that there is an inch or two of shoulder, or just a few stitches.

According to your preference, the back of the sweater can be the same as the front or, if you have not added a collar, it can have crisscrossing straps. (See Figure 32.7.)

SLEEVE LENGTHS

Sleeve lengths can be as long or as short as you wish them to be. When I was young and my upper arms were firm and slender, I loved wearing tank tops, sweaters with short cap sleeves, open halter types, or simply no sleeves at all. Now that I am no longer young and slender, I almost always plan my sleeves to be long enough to rest just above the elbow.

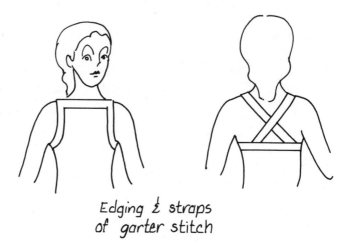

Edging & straps of garter stitch

32.7 Rough sketch of halter with flat, narrow boatneck and crisscross straps

Remember that the purpose in designing your own sweaters is not only to get a better fit but also to flatter the figure of the intended wearer.

If arms and elbows are unattractive, cover them up!

Another purpose in desiging sweaters is to solve our own problems. For example, people whose jobs cause them to wash their hands frequently during the day may prefer three-quarter-length sleeves that end between the elbow and the wrist.

You know the basics of measuring bodies and multiplying stitches. Make sleeves any length you choose.

SLEEVE BOTTOMS

Though hems are sometimes very effective on sweaters, a traditional wrist ribbing treatment gives knitted fabric a "resting place" against the body and keeps long sleeves out of the soup. Without a ribbing resting place, any knitted sleeve will stretch and lengthen somewhat.

Never forget the characteristics of knitted fabric!

MANY SLEEVES CAN BE KNITTED FROM THE TOP DOWN!

Until I learned to machine-knit in the late 1960s, I had never heard of sewing the back and front shoulder seams together, picking up stitches around the armhole edges, and working the sleeve from the top down to the wrist. I'm sorry that it was so late in my knitting career that I encountered the idea, because it is a great one. By using short rows to shape the sleeve cap, the sleeves always fit, and there is never a malfitting armhole seam to weave.

When you knit sleeves from the top down, you are not restricted to making set-in sleeves. Almost any sleeve that can be made from the bottom up can also be made from the top down, with perhaps the exception of peaked sleeves.

I first spoke of making sleeves from the top down when we discussed variations of the Da Vinci Man sweater. And, because it is such a simple garment, let me use a modified Da Vinci Man sleeve as an example in explaining the technique of top-down sleeve making (see Figure 19.7). Even if you don't have a Da Vinci Man sweater in progress, even if you never intend to make one, read through the following instructions. If you can "get" the concept with this easy example, you will have no trouble comprehending the directions for shaped-armhole set-in sleeves that will follow.

LEARN HOW TO SHORT-ROW

In order to make a nice-looking sleeve from the top down, you must know the "short-row" technique of turning around in the middle of a row without leaving a hole. (See pages 150–152.) A complete chapter in *Knitting in Plain English* is devoted to carefully explaining how to make short rows. In the instructions that follow, it is assumed that you know how to make short rows and to place ring markers at each turning point.

INSTRUCTIONS FOR KNITTING A MODIFIED DA VINCI MAN SLEEVE FROM THE TOP DOWN

Complete the back and the front of the sweater. Weave the shoulder seams together. DO NOT SEW THE UNDERARM SEAM.

With the public side of the garment facing you, from underarm shaping flag marker to underarm shaping flag marker, pick up the required number of stitches for the sleeve width at underarm. Turn the work around to begin a new row.

Purl back across those picked-up stitches to a point 1" BEYOND the shoulder seam. Turn.

Knit to the shoulder seam, and then 1" beyond it. Turn.

Continue in the same manner working 1" beyond the previous marker-turn on every following row until all the stitches at both ends of the work are incorporated.

Your knitting should look like the diagram in Figure 32.8.

Complete the sleeve, working either flat or in the round, making decreases along the underarm "seam."

A modified dolman sleeve would be knit from the top down in the same way. The only difference would be to pick up the first row of stitches from within the set-in area. (See Figure 32.4.)

INSTRUCTIONS FOR MAKING SET-IN SLEEVES FROM THE TOP DOWN

Making sleeves from the top down works well even if:

1. You worked flat, either by hand or machine, and the pieces have (or do not have) shaped armholes,

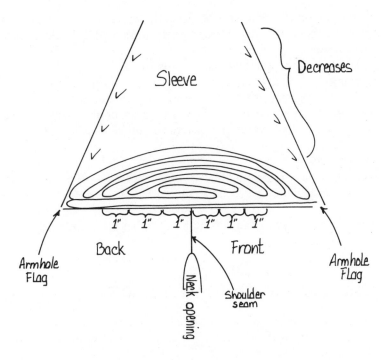

32.8 Diagram of modified Da Vinci Man sleeve worked from the top down

2. You worked the body in the round *a)* to the armhole and then flat thereafter, *b)* all the way to the shoulder, having shaped the armhole, made a steek, and cut the steek open.

Regardless of how you have made your sweater body, the following *general* instructions apply (see Figure 32.9):

- Complete the back and the front of the sweater.
- Weave the shoulder seam (and perhaps the underarm seam).
- Determine the number of stitches you wish the sleeve upper arm width to be.
- If the body armhole has been shaped with either bind-offs or by placing stitches on holders, subtract this number of stitches from the total desired number of sleeve stitches. We will call this new number *Q*. Write it down. Divide the *Q* number by 6. Call it 1/6 *Q*.
- With the public side of the garment facing you, carefully pick up stitch for stitch along any bound-off stitches. Place a marker on the needle. Then pick up the *Q* number of stitches evenly spaced around the armhole until you reach the other bound-off stitches. Place another marker, again pick up any bound-off stitches stitch for stitch.

- Place a slip-on ring marker at the shoulder seam.
- Either in the round, or back and forth, work to the shoulder seam marker plus 1/6 Q. Turn.
- Again work to the shoulder marker plus 1/6 Q. Turn.
- Working back and forth going 1 stitch past the previous turning stitch on each row, making short rows, incorporate more and more stitches on each side of the first two turns until all stitches are incorporated or you reach the underarm bound-off stitches (if there were any).
- Stop the short-rowing.
- Work across any remaining bound-off stitches all at once. The sleeve cap is formed!

After the short-rowed cap is completed, finish the sleeve in any way you choose.

SADDLE SLEEVES ON ARAN SWEATERS

Some authorities insist that originally all Irish fisherman sweaters were made with saddle sleeves in one piece from the top down. It really is possible to do it.

If you make the neck-to-shoulder strips of a saddle sleeve sweater

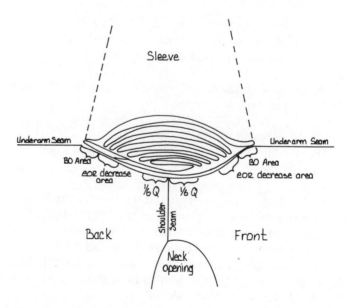

32.9 Short-rowed sleeve cap in progress

first, you can place markers to define the different areas as you pick up shoulder stitches, cast on for the back and front necks, and then make the whole garment from the top down.

I have tried it, and I have a couple of problems executing the technique. First of all, I have difficulty in making a clean and neat pick-up-the-stitches line on the saddle strips. (That problem can be solved by covering up the pick-up line of the completed garment with a single row of decorative crocheted chain stitch.)

Secondly, in order to cause the shoulders to slope down from neck to shoulder tip and the front neck to drop lower in front than in the back, some very fancy short-rowing must be done. If there is any commotion going on in the house or if anything interrupts me, I get thoroughly confused on my short-rowing. (I can't solve that problem.)

If you live in a quiet place (with no phone, neighbors, or delivery people) and if you are not easily rattled, give it a try.*

---

*Dixie Falls has perfected this technique and written the instructions for it. Her (self-published) booklet called "Aran from the Neck Down" sells for $16.50 including postage and handling (10955 Parrish Gap Road, Turner, OR 97392).

33

Designing Your Own Necklines and Collars

In previous chapters we learned to make the following necklines and collars: boatneck, V-neck, crew neck, turtleneck, vertical slit neck, classic shawl collar for cardigans, and a jacket/coat that is an extension of the front lapels. These are the most common types used, but there are other kinds to consider so that our repertoire is complete.

In designing all of the following necklines, I use a simple technique that makes the planning much easier. Add it to your bag of tricks.

1. Measure the desired width of the neckline EXCLUDING THE FINAL TRIM. Remember to cover bra straps. Convert to stitch gauge.
2. Measure the desired depth EXCLUDING THE FINAL TRIM from the corner where the shoulder joins the neck. Convert to row gauge.
3. Plan the layout of the back and front of the sweater as if you were going to make a crew neck. Be sure to include center lines on the back and front.
4. Mark out the desired neckline, that is, multiply the number of rows down from the top of the shoulder and the stitches from center front out toward the shoulders.
5. Subtract the neckline stitches from the stitches of total width at the desired height to know how many stitches to work across before beginning the neck shaping.

If you are concerned about the details of shaping any of the following necklines, feel free to lay them out on knitter's graph paper to determine the exact number of center bind-off stitches and the bind-off stairsteps and decreases on the curved sides. Usually I just squint my eyes and say, "Oh, about one-third of the stitches flat across on the center front, one-sixth of the stitches in stairsteps on each side, and the final sixth in every-other-row decreases." Of course my fractions never come out perfect when translated into stitches and *necklines are always a juggling act.*

SQUARE NECKS

Recall the forgivingness of knitted fabric and remember its saggy-baggy characteristics. Recall the straight-across boatneck of the Da Vinci Man sweater and remember how it had a tendency to sag in the middle. A square neck, though it isn't as wide as a boatneck, will also sag in the middle and resemble a *U* more than a straight line. For this reason, I don't make it, but Figure 33.1 shows how it is done.

The neckline can be finished with either ribbing or crocheting. Whichever you choose, be sure to make right-angle decreases at the corners so that the trim will lay flat. *Garter stitch is not advised as a neckline trim because it is expansive.*

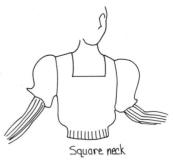

Square neck

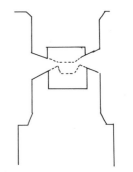

33.1 Square neckline overlaid on a crew neck

SWEETHEART NECKLINE

The sweetheart is a square neck with filled-in corners. It doesn't sag or bag. Often it is a flattering way to finish summer or evening sweaters. The diagonals are formed by decreasing raglan style on every other row. (See Figure 33.2.)

A simple crocheted picot edging is often very effective on a sweetheart neckline. Ribbing needs decreases at *all* of the corners and can look a mess.

U-NECK

If you widen and broaden the shaping for a crew neck and then marry it to the width and depth of a square neck, you have a U-neck. (See Figure 33.3.)

Ribbing trim for a U-neck requires a decrease in width horizontally across the row. However, any decreases other than at right angles will mess up ribbing patterns. Instead of making ordinary decreases, try *changing needle size* as you work toward the neck, getting smaller with every row.

I have often used crocheting on U-necks with lovely results.

Sweetheart neck

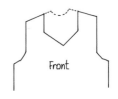

Front

33.2 Sweetheart neckline overlaid on a crew neck

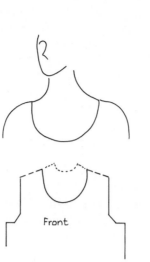

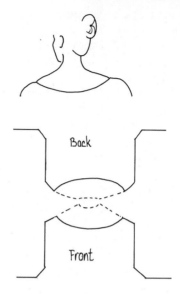

33.3 U-neckline overlaid on a crew neck

33.4 Portrait neckline overlaid on a crew neck

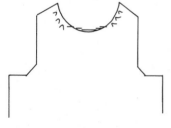

33.5 Scoop neckline overlaid on a crew neck

PORTRAIT AND SCOOP NECKLINES

Both portrait (broader and more shallow) and scoop (narrower and deeper) necklines are just widened and deepened versions of a crew neck. The portrait neck (see Figure 33.4) flatters women with broad/straight shoulders; the scoop neck (see Figure 33.5) flatters women with narrow/sloping shoulders.

After picking up stitches and making a purl ridge row, I have successfully finished portrait necklines with fold-under bands in both ribbing and stockinette. I have tried to finish scooped necklines in the same manner, but the stockinette had to be decreased to fit the curve and then expanded again for the underside. Ribbing did not work at all because "secret" decreases could not be made in it.

PLACKETED OVERLAPPED SHAWL FOR PULLOVERS

If you plan a square neckline with the back neck width just an inch or two wider than normal and then fill in the opening with ribbing, you get a wonderful placketed opening and a rolled shawl collar. (See Figure 33.6. The collar does not sag like a plain square neck does; the ribbing holds it in place.)

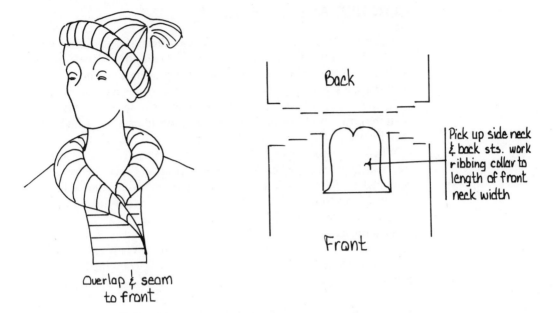

33.6 Sketch and layout for placketed neckline with ribbed shawl collar

The stitches for the ribbing are picked up along the vertical neck edge on the fronts and horizontally across the back. The ribbing, which is made as deep as the front opening is wide, can be of any reversible pattern. Overlap and stitch the vertical edges of the ribbing in place across the front of the placket and you are prepared for the coldest winds that may blow your way.

ONE-SHOULDER-STYLE NECKLINES

One-shouldered sweaters (see Figure 33.7) could have been discussed in the chapter about sleeves. However, I have included them here with necklines because if you plan a neckline that goes from upper left shoulder to right armpit you have a one-shouldered sweater. The other, the left shoulder/armhole side, is usually planned as a set-in armhole. I'd advise you *not* to put a sleeve into the armhole; doing so will move the center of gravity of the sweater to the left shoulder tip.

A friend made such a sweater once. It slithered and slid and wouldn't stay put so she lined the sweater, and the single sleeve still kept sliding down. She couldn't rip the sweater because it was made of a fuzzy mohair so she threw it away.

33.7 One-shouldered sweater

NOTCHED ADD-ON COLLAR

In Chapter 23 we learned how to make a cardigan jacket with a fold-to-the-outside collar that was a continuation of the front lapels and the back neck. We could just as well have put a crew neck on the jacket and then made a separate collar. That collar could be sewn on or picked up (with the *private side facing*). If we made that separate collar a bit shorter than the entire neckline of the sweater, we would have a notched collar. (See Figure 33.8.)

When designing a collar like this, try to envision the recipient wearing the sweater/jacket. Will the wearer always keep the top button buttoned? Will the back side of the knitted fabric be exposed? If so, you will have to use a reversible fabric or plan a fold-line and reverse the pattern stitch as we did in Chapter 23.

Sometimes, in order to lie flat, the collar will need to be wider at the outer edge than where it is attached to the neck. This can be accomplished in a number of ways, sometimes using a combination of these techniques.

1. Make increases at the front edge about every 4th row,
2. Make increases directly above the shoulder seams,
3. Widen by changing to larger-size needles at intervals.

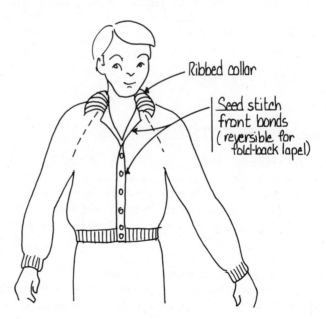

33.8 Sweater with fold-back collar

COWL COLLAR

A cowl is a low wide turtleneck placed over a portrait or scoop neckline. (See Figure 33.9.) It can be made as a separate piece with increases placed horizontally along every few rows. I prefer to pick up stitches around the neck and change to larger-size needles as I need to add width to the cowl.

MANDARIN COLLAR

A mandarin collar is *not* a straight horizontal band attached to the neckline of a sweater. It more nearly resembles three-quarters of a circle. (See Figure 33.10.)

A mandarin collar can be knitted (preferably in seed stitch) or crocheted (usually in single crochet). It can be made as a separate piece to be sewn on later, but I usually prefer to make it directly on the sweater. That way I know it will fit, and I can space and adjust my decreases according to the way the collar wants to lie. (To maintain pattern in seed stitch, see page 00, make double decreases getting rid of 2 stitches at once.)

33.9 Sweater with cowl collar over a portrait neckline

Mandarin Collar showing decreases from neck pick-up line

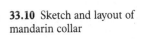

Child with Mandarin Collar on zippered jacket

33.10 Sketch and layout of mandarin collar

Crosswise knit
Purl cotton lace
collar gathered
onto sweater

I-Cord Trim
for neck edge,
placket & tie

33.11 Sweater with lace collar
on round neckline

Make an extrawide,
extradeep slinky V-neck
sweater to wear over
a slinky slit skirt.
Add a silver metallic
tied collar (let the
cleavage show!).
Add silver slippers.

33.12 Sweater with tied
collar on a V-neckline

GATHERED LACE COLLARS

Fine yarn worked up into frothy, fluffy lace can decorate any rounded or V-neckline. Usually the neckline itself must be finished off firmly, either with ribbing, I-cord, or crocheting, before the lace can be attached. The lace, often of a contrasting color, can be made crosswise as a long strip and gathered onto the sweater. Or it can be made horizontally on picked-up stitches, increasing in width from the top down. (See Figure 33.11.)

TIED COLLARS

Make a long narrow belt. Drape it around any kind of neckline. Place the tie in any location you choose. Fasten in place. What could be simpler? (See Figure 33.12.)

Try K4, P4 ribbing-
add eyelets & drawstrings
if desired. Bust dart
will add front length.

33.13 Tube top

THE NO-NECKLINE TUBE TOP

It is possible to make a sweater with no neckline at all. No shoulders either! It is called a "tube top." It is just an extratight ribbed circle of knitting (sometimes with a bust dart). Lithe young girls look great in them. (See Figure 33.13.)

Just be sure that you make the tube narrow enough that it will not slide down to the waistline.

CONCLUSION

There are other styles of neckline treatments that you sometimes see in "fashion" knitting magazines: draped front, tulip, off-center diagonal, etc. *They rarely hang well in knitted garments or look flattering on anyone over a size 8.* My opinion is that these necklines are created by inexperienced designers trying to duplicate a woven-cloth garment in knitting without realizing that knitted fabric is not woven cloth. What's wrong with letting a sweater be a sweater? If you want a woven-cloth garment there's nothing to stop you from getting one. Just beware when these types of necklines show up in magazines and pattern books.

34

Creating Your Own Interesting Effects: Stripes, Intarsia, Different-Colored Cables

All kinds of interesting multicolor additions can be made to our simple garments once we have learned how to shape them. We can stripe, form intarsia patterns, make stranded designs, or embroider over our knits.

In making the above-mentioned interesting effects, remember that:

Color changes apparent size. Know that the colors you choose for any of these designs will change the apparent size and shape of both the garment as a whole and the different colored areas.

HORIZONTAL COLORED STRIPE PATTERNS

It takes almost no preplanning to throw stripes into made-from-the-neck-down-in-one-piece sweaters. Making stripes in these garments is almost as easy as changing color whenever the knitter feels like doing so.

It is a very different story, however, when making sweaters in separate pieces from the bottom up. Not only must the stripes for these sweaters be preplanned just as soon as the bottom ribbing (of either the sleeves or the back) is completed, but an *accurate row gauge* must be calculated and maintained.

PLANNING BODY STRIPE PATTERNS FOR GARMENTS MADE IN PIECES

34.1 Da Vinci Man sweater with stripes

For this lesson, let's use the example of the Da Vinci Man sweater that we designed in Chapter 19. Let's use 6 colors of yarn, 1 for the ribbing and the other 5 for the stripes. Let's call the colors A (ribbing), B, C, D, E, F.

We have already determined that there would be 23″ of stockinette stitch on the body between the top of the bottom ribbing and the bottom of the top ribbing. We have 5 remaining colors of yarn with which to make 5 even-width stripes over this space of 23″. We need to find out how many rows of each color there will be.

To do this it is necessary to change the number of inches to the number of rows by multiplying inches (23) by row gauge (6).

$$\begin{array}{rl} 23″ & \text{(of St st length)} \\ \times \quad 6 & \text{(gauge: rows per inch)} \\ \hline = \; 138 & \text{(number of rows to divide equally among 5 colors)} \end{array}$$

To determine how many rows of each color will be worked, divide the total number of rows by the number of colors.

$$\begin{array}{rl} 138 & \text{(total number of rows)} \\ \div \quad 5 & \text{(colors)} \\ \hline = \; 27.6 & \text{(approximate number of rows of each color)} \end{array}$$

Oops! We don't want to make six-tenths of a row of a color, so we need to change that approximate number of rows of each color; round 27.6 up to 28. Now let's check what the total number of rows would be if we were to make 28 rows of each of 5 colors.

$$\begin{array}{rl} 28 & \text{(number of rows of each color)} \\ \times \quad 5 & \text{(number of colors)} \\ \hline = \; 140 & \text{(proposed total number of rows used)} \end{array}$$

Let's compare this new total number of rows (140) to our old number (138):

$$\begin{array}{rl} 140 & \text{(proposed total number of rows used } [5 \times 28]) \\ - \; 138 & \text{(approximate total number of rows available)} \\ \hline = \quad 2 & \text{(difference in the approximate number of rows and the proposed number of rows)} \end{array}$$

Hallelujah! These numbers are only 2 rows apart. Two rows more or less never killed any knitter. We will simply make 2 rows more than we originally intended in order to accommodate equal areas of each of the 5 colors.

The following instructions would be inserted in our instructions for the Da Vinci Man sweater after completing the body bottom ribbing:

Changing color after every 28 rows, work even in St st until piece measures 15″ from beg of St st (17.5″ overall). Place flag markers on each side edge of the work to note bottom edge of sleeve joining. Work even in pattern stitch as established until stripes of all 5 colors have been completed. Piece measures 23″ from beginning of St st (25.5″ overall).

Note that the underarm shaping begins after 15″ of working the color stripes. Figure out what row number of which color of the stockinette stitch this point is.

$$
\begin{array}{rl}
& 15''\ \text{(length)} \\
\times & 6\ \text{(gauge rows per inch)} \\
\hline
= & 90\text{th row}
\end{array}
$$

Each color has used 28 rows. On the body back,
color B began at row 1,
color C began at row 29,
color D began at row 56,
color E began at row 87,
row 90 is the 3rd row of color E.

MAKING SLEEVE STRIPES MATCH BODY STRIPES

The striping pattern on the sleeves must be planned both up and down from the underarm, because it is imperative that the stripes match across from body to sleeve at the underarm. If they don't, the wearer's arms may look disjointed and distorted. In the Da Vinci Man sweater there is no underarm shaping, only a flag marker. On other kinds of sleeves—set-in, raglan, and saddle—it will still be at the underarm that the stripe patterns must match exactly.

In planning stripes I find it helpful to redraw and adjust my piece

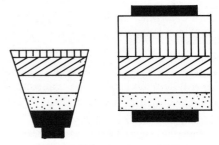

34.2 Adjusted layout for matching back and sleeve armholes at same level

Side-by-Side placement of DaVinci Man sweater

layout so that the back and the sleeve sit side by side with the armholes shaping in a straight-across line. (See Figure 34.2.)

Note that the sleeve is longer from underarm to bottom of stockinette stitch than is the body back.

On the drawing mark that the body underarm shaping begins at the 3rd row of color E (90th row).

PLANNING THE SLEEVE FROM THE ARMHOLE DOWN

From your layout drawing take the number of inches of sleeve length from the underarm shaping down to the top of the bottom ribbing to find out how many rows difference there is in length. On the Da Vinci Man sweater this length is 17.5″. Multiply that length by the row gauge:

	17.5″	(inches of length from top of ribbing to underarm shaping)
×	6	(gauge: rows per inch)
=	105	(number of rows available for stripes on sleeves between ribbing and underarm)

	105	(number of rows available for stripes on sleeves between ribbing and underarm)
−	90	(row number *of the body* on which the sleeve striping must match the body)
=	15	(more rows on sleeve to underarm than on body to underarm)

We will have to work 15 rows of another color (probably A, the bottom ribbing color) before we can begin the same color striping pattern as is on the body.

INSTRUCTIONS FOR STARTING THE SLEEVE FROM THE BOTTOM

The instructions for the Da Vinci Man sweater sleeves following the completion of the wrist ribbing would say:

Continuing in color A work 15 rows of St st, inc'ing on the 6th row and every 6th row thereafter AND AT THE SAME TIME changing color on row 16 to follow same sequence as on back. After row 3 of color E (piece measures 17.5″ of St st, 20″ overall, 90 sts rem), BO all sts.

Please notice that on this sweater the whole problem of matching the sleeve and body stripes could have been averted by starting on row 4 of color E and MAKING THE SLEEVE FROM THE TOP DOWN!

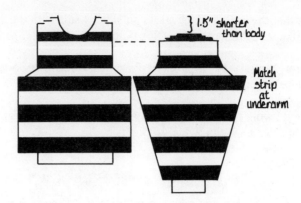

34.3 Back and sleeve armholes should be at the same level when matching stripes on sweaters with set-in sleeves.

PLANNING THE STRIPED CAPS OF OTHER TYPES OF SLEEVES

Raglan, saddle-sleeved, and circular-yoked sweaters offer no problems in planning the sleeve tops above the beginning of the underarm shaping *because from underarm shaping to shoulder tip both the body and the sleeve caps have the same number of rows.*

Standard set-in sleeves, however, can be quite a problem, because the sleeve caps are several inches shorter than the body armhole. Remember that there is a flat area on the top of standard set-in sleeves, half of the length of which must be subtracted from the body armhole depth of each the back and the front. (See Figure 34.3.) *Sometimes you must make the stripes on the sleeve cap a few rows narrower than the body stripes so that when sewn in place they will APPEAR to be the same width.*★

If you are designing and making the garment yourself, simply use Shirley Robb's technique of basting the sleeves in place as you go (see Chapter 30) and altering the widths of the stripes as seems appropriate.

If, however, you are designing the sweater for someone else to knit without ever having made it yourself, you may have to do some fancy arithmetic depending upon the widths of the body stripes.

INTARSIA PATTERNS

Once upon a time, years and years ago when all furniture was made with hand tools, some fine craftsmen decorated the flat surfaces of these

★If the stripes on the body are numerous and/or very narrow, it may not be possible to make the sleeves match the body.

chests and tables with designs of animals and flowers and landscapes using different colors and textures of wood. The finished effect was called "intarsia." Some years ago, the word *intarsia* was taken over by knitters who liked to make similar designs on the flat surfaces of their knitted fabric.

Intarsia patterns are always worked flat, that is, back and forth, never in the round. Usually bobbins are used to hold the various colors of yarn that will be used across a row.

FREEHAND AND STYLIZED GRAPHICS

In the Atlanta Knitting Guild, some of the knitters just "wing it" and make up designs as they go along. I see no problem with this so long as you do not have to produce some design that resembles a real object, like rabbits or kittens or houses.

If you want a design that resembles a real object, invest in knitters' graph paper with the same gauge that you are getting on your trial swatch. You can use a drawing of your own, or one from any other source.

Using carbon paper, the design can be traced and copied onto the knitters' graph paper. Once the outline of the design has been transferred, take colored pencils and "clean up" the edges of each different-colored area so that they will match actual stitches. Color in the various areas approximating the colors of yarn you intend to use. *Be sure both your layout drawing and your graphed design have vertical and horizontal center lines so that you can accurately locate your design on your layout drawing.*

Use bobbins when knitting up the design.

DIAGONALS AND GEOMETRIC SHAPES

Multicolored and multitoned squares and triangles, circles and stars, hexagons and octagons, snowflakes and streaks of lightning, arches and rainbows—overlapping, interlocking, endlessly intriguing and playing with the eye—can be wonderful fun to knit and spectacular to wear. Any and all of the above are possible to design and to knit.

Now that you are armed with the knowledge that knit stitches are not square, that desired width/length times stitches/rows equals number of stitches/rows necessary, that there are formulas for diagonals that do not come out even, and that knitters' graph paper can cure many headaches, I expect you to design special and unique sweaters.

The only limiting factors will be the types and colors of yarns available and the time to knit them up. Neither lack of courage nor fear of criticism and failure should deter you.

ARGYLES

Argyle socks! Many a happy hour riding home from high school on the bus has been spent knitting argyle socks. A form of intarsia with an old Scottish history, the interlocking diamonds and diagonals are endlessly fun to knit.

They are not, however, endless joy to create. They can cause a real headache trying to correlate the size of the person with the size of the diamonds with the gauge of the yarn with all the diagonals coming out even and matching at the seams.

I feel about argyles as I feel about Icelandic designs. If somebody else has already sweat blood over designing the thing to perfection, why bother re-creating their toil and redoing their design?

And since it is difficult to change the number of stitches to accommodate wide hips, why not change needle size and gauge. No one will notice and I won't tell if you make the hip-tummy part of a gorgeous argyle on a size 6 needle and the chest part on a size 5.

A dear friend of mine, Anne Macdonald, has done a lot of work designing and planning argyles. She has carefully plotted each of her patterns so that it has a multiple of an even number of stitches and a repeat of an even number of rows. Each row is repeated twice. This allows the colors that cross over on a knit row to uncross on the following purl row. Moreover, she has invented and patented a device so that the yarns will return to their parallel positions on each subsequent row.*

If you do not follow Anne's scheme of things, you must work your argyles with bobbins.

STRANDED DESIGNS

We discussed the pros and cons of knitting Fair Isle and mosaic types of pattern stitches in Chapter 9. Only a few things need be said here about incorporating them into your designs.

---

*The special yarn holder and complete patterns in many sizes may be ordered from Anne Macdonald. For more information and prices, write Great Scot, 5606 Mohican Road, Bethesda, MD 20816.

Be sure to proportion the size of the design to the size of the intended wearer, dainty little things for small folk, big splashy designs for big people.

Be careful to center the design. Our eyes expect symmetry, so a V-neck that begins on one side of a snowflake instead of in the center can be upsetting.

Recall that any stranded multicolor pattern stitch will be firmer than plain stockinette stitch fabric and it may be necessary both to add more ease allowance and to make openings for heads and arms a bit larger.

CABLES OF DIFFERENT COLORS

A delightful way to add color and form to otherwise plain sweaters is to intersperse cables of different colors up sleeves and bodies of sweaters.

When planning cables of one color against a background of another color, dispense with the purl stitches that usually sit at each side of the cable. The differences in color will be sufficient to visually set off the cables. You must wrap the yarn as you change from one color to another, and the purl stitches make that wrapping process much more difficult.

You do not have to limit yourself to just one color of cables against the background yarn. You can have many different cables, each of a different color. You can have bicolor cables with half of the stitches a different color. You can even have a basketweave cable with six or more colors interplaying with each other.

One can visualize a single center-front cable to be split by a V-neck opening, but it is difficult to execute. You are much better off to plan a *pair* of center front cables separated by about 4 or 5 stitches of background color. Make your split in the background color rather than trying to split the cable itself. Compared to the full one, the split cable will look underfed and spindly.

EMBROIDERY

If you wish to embellish your finished knitted garments with hand-stitching, I heartily endorse the idea. Be warned though:

Don't use a lot of duplicate stitch. It changes the texture of the knitted fabric over which it is made, causing it to be inelastic, cast-iron firm, and bulky.

Woven fabric appliqués are not usually a good idea, either. It is difficult to attach woven cloth to knitted fabric without either one stretching or puckering.

Casual, freehand embroidery is another matter all together. Simple embroidery such as lazy-daisy flowers, satin-stitch leaves, and chain-stitch stems can be an exquisite way to decorate plain sweaters. Around the neckline of a pale pink matte-finish nubby cotton sweater I once embroidered a garland of brightly colored glossy perle cotton flowers. It looked really spectacular.

A few words of advice about embroidering on knitted fabric follow:

- Don't stretch or overload the knitted fabric. The wonderful "forgiving" quality of knitted fabric can distort intricate embroidered designs.
- Keep the stitches large, simple, and lightweight.
- Stay away from fuzzy yarn such as angora for either the background or the added-on design. Fuzz will detract from the effect and be very difficult to stitch with or on.

CONCLUSION/THE FINAL BINDING OFF

Now you know. I've told you my secrets, the secrets of color and line and light and shadow that I learned in art classes, the secrets of using those lessons to flatter the human body. I've shared my secrets of the equation for diagonal decreases when the numbers don't come out even, the sleeve cap that really fits, and the foolproof compound-angle raglan. And you now know that the fiber you choose will determine the fabric you get and may well dictate the fashion you can achieve. You have it all; you are ready to take control of your knitting realizing that if you don't make changes things can never get any better.

Whether you put to use what you have learned here to be more selective in choosing commercial sweater designs, to modify the designs and instructions of others for your purposes, or whether you choose to start from scratch, there is nothing to it but to do it.

Sweater designing is like any other project. The first time is always the hardest. After that it gets easier every time. Just remember to have fun while you knit. Laugh at your mistakes; take pride in your successes. Enjoy yourself and your creations.

PART III

Appendices

APPENDIX A

Conversion Charts

Conversion chart—ounces and grams:

OUNCES TO GRAMS	YARDS TO METERS	GRAMS TO OUNCES	METERS TO YARDS
1 = 28.4	1 = .91	25 = ⅞	25 = 27.34
2 = 56.7	10 = 9.14	40 = 1⅖	50 = 54.68
3 = 85.0	50 = 45.5	50 = 1¾	75 = 82.02
4 = 113.4	75 = 68.25	100 = 3½	100 = 109.36
	100 = 91.44		

Conversion chart of knitting needle sizes:

United States (US)	0	1	2	3	4	5	6	7	8	9	10	10½	11	13	15
Great Britain (GB)	14	13	12	11	10	9	8	7	6	5	4	2	1	00	0000
Metric (MM)	2	2¼	2¾	3	3¼	3¾	4	4½	5	5½	6	7	7½	9	11

Metric Conversion Table: Inches to Centimeters

		INCHES PLUS FRACTIONS							
WHOLE INCHES	CENTIMETER EQUIVALENTS	1/16" 0.16	1/8" 0.32	1/4" 0.64	3/8" 0.95	1/2" 1.27	5/8" 1.59	3/4" 1.91	7/8" 2.22
1 =	2.54	2.70	2.86	3.18	3.49	3.81	4.13	4.45	4.76
2	5.08	5.24	5.40	5.72	6.03	6.35	6.67	6.99	7.30
3	7.62	7.78	7.94	8.26	8.57	8.89	9.21	9.53	9.84
4	10.16	10.32	10.48	10.80	11.11	11.43	11.75	12.07	12.38
5	12.70	12.86	13.02	13.34	13.65	13.97	14.29	14.61	14.92
6	15.24	15.40	15.56	15.88	16.19	16.51	16.83	17.15	17.46
7	17.78	17.94	18.10	18.42	18.73	19.05	19.37	19.69	20.00
8	20.32	20.48	20.64	20.96	21.27	21.59	21.91	22.23	22.54
9	22.86	23.02	23.18	23.50	23.81	24.13	24.45	24.77	25.08
10	25.40	25.56	25.72	26.04	26.35	26.67	26.99	27.31	27.62
11	27.94	28.10	28.26	28.58	28.89	29.21	29.53	29.85	30.16
12	30.48	30.64	30.80	31.12	31.43	31.75	32.02	32.39	32.70
13	33.02	33.18	33.34	33.66	33.97	34.29	34.61	34.93	35.24
14	35.56	35.72	35.88	36.20	36.51	36.83	37.15	37.47	37.78
15	38.10	38.26	38.42	38.74	39.05	39.37	36.69	40.01	40.32
16	40.64	40.80	40.96	41.28	41.59	41.91	42.23	42.55	42.86
17	43.18	43.34	43.50	43.82	44.13	44.45	44.77	45.09	45.40
18	45.72	45.88	46.04	46.36	46.67	46.99	47.31	47.63	47.94
19	48.26	48.42	48.58	48.90	49.21	49.53	49.85	50.17	50.48
20	50.80	50.96	51.12	51.44	51.75	52.07	52.39	52.71	53.02
21	53.34	53.50	53.66	53.98	54.29	54.61	54.93	55.25	55.56
22	55.88	56.04	56.20	56.52	56.83	57.15	57.47	57.79	58.10
23	58.42	58.58	58.74	59.06	59.37	59.69	60.01	60.33	60.64
24	60.96	61.12	61.28	61.60	61.91	62.23	62.55	62.87	63.18
25	63.50	63.66	63.82	64.14	64.45	64.77	65.09	65.41	65.72
26	66.04	66.20	66.36	66.68	66.99	67.31	67.63	67.95	68.26
27	68.58	68.74	68.90	69.22	69.53	69.85	70.17	70.49	70.80
28	71.12	71.28	71.44	71.76	72.07	72.39	72.71	73.03	73.34
29	73.66	73.82	73.98	74.30	74.61	74.93	75.25	75.57	75.88
30	76.20	76.36	76.52	76.84	77.15	77.47	77.79	78.11	78.42

WHOLE INCHES	CENTIMETER EQUIVALENTS	1/16" 0.16	1/8" 0.32	1/4" 0.64	3/8" 0.95	1/2" 1.27	5/8" 1.59	3/4" 1.91	7/8" 2.22
31 =	78.74	78.90	79.06	79.38	79.69	80.01	80.33	80.65	80.96
32	81.28	81.44	81.60	81.92	82.23	82.55	82.87	83.19	83.50
33	83.82	83.98	84.14	84.46	84.77	85.09	85.41	85.73	86.04
34	86.36	86.52	86.68	87.00	84.31	87.63	87.95	88.27	88.58
35	88.90	89.06	89.22	89.54	89.85	90.17	90.49	90.81	91.12
36	91.44	91.60	91.76	92.08	92.39	92.71	93.03	93.35	93.66
37	93.98	94.14	94.30	94.62	94.93	95.25	95.57	95.89	96.20
38	96.52	96.68	96.84	97.16	97.47	97.79	98.11	98.43	98.74
39	99.06	99.22	99.38	99.70	100.01	100.33	100.65	100.97	101.28
40	101.60	101.76	101.92	102.24	102.55	102.87	103.19	103.51	103.82
41	104.14	104.30	104.46	104.78	105.09	105.41	105.73	106.05	106.36
42	106.68	106.84	107.00	107.32	107.63	107.95	108.27	108.59	108.90
43	109.22	109.38	109.54	109.86	110.17	110.49	110.81	111.13	111.44
44	111.76	111.92	112.08	112.40	112.71	113.03	113.35	113.67	113.98
45	114.30	114.46	114.62	114.94	115.25	115.57	115.89	116.21	116.52
46	116.84	117.00	117.16	117.48	117.79	118.11	118.43	118.75	119.06
47	119.38	119.54	119.70	120.02	120.33	120.65	120.97	121.29	121.60
48	121.92	122.08	122.24	122.56	122.87	123.19	123.51	123.83	124.14
49	124.46	124.62	124.78	125.10	125.41	125.73	126.05	126.37	126.68
50	127.00	127.16	127.32	127.64	127.95	128.27	128.59	128.91	129.22
51	129.54	129.70	129.86	130.18	130.49	130.81	131.13	131.45	131.76
52	132.08	132.24	132.40	132.72	133.03	133.35	133.67	133.99	134.30
53	134.62	134.78	134.94	135.26	135.57	135.89	136.21	136.53	136.84
54	137.16	137.32	137.48	137.80	138.11	138.43	138.75	139.07	139.38
55	139.70	139.86	140.02	140.34	140.65	140.97	141.29	141.61	141.92
56	142.24	142.40	142.56	142.88	143.19	143.51	143.83	144.15	144.46
57	144.78	144.94	145.10	145.42	145.73	146.05	146.37	146.69	147.00
58	147.32	147.48	147.64	147.96	148.27	148.59	148.91	149.23	149.54
59	149.86	150.02	150.18	150.50	150.81	151.13	151.45	151.77	152.09
60	152.40	152.56	152.72	153.04	153.35	153.67	153.99	154.31	154.62

APPENDIX B

National Knit and Crochet Standards

Chest Sizes for Instructions

BABY

AGE	CHEST	WEIGHT
Newborn	to 18"	5–10 lbs.
6 months	to 20"	11–18 lbs.
12 months	to 22"	19–24 lbs.

CHILDREN

Size	C-2	C-3	C-4	C-5	C-6	C-7	C-8	C-10
Chest	21"	22"	23"	24"	25"	26"	27"	28"

Size	C-12	C-14	C-16
Chest	30"	32"	34"

Note: at C-14 Girl's size may change to a Misses' 6 or 8, at C-16 Boy's size may change to a Man's 34.

MISSES

Size	6	8	10	12	14	16	18
Bust	30½"	31½"	32½"	34"	36"	38"	40"

WOMEN

Size	38	40	42	44	46	48	50
Bust	42"	44"	46"	48"	50"	52"	54"

MEN

Size	34	36	38	40	42	44	46	48
Chest	34"	36"	38"	40"	42"	44"	46"	48"

Neckband sizes will not be used.

BODY MEASUREMENTS FOR THE DEVELOPMENT OF PATTERNS

These are minimum BODY measurements to be used as guidelines for sizing knit and crochet garments. They are not meant, in all cases, to be used as is. Ease for fit and design characteristics must be added. They are based on the voluntary standards of the National Bureau of Standards and are "average." It is still advisable to include in instructions the words "or to length desired" to allow for individual fit.

Body Measurements for Babies

	NEWBORN 5 TO 10 LBS.	6 MONTHS 11 TO 18 LBS.	12 MONTHS 19 TO 24 LBS.
Chest	to 18″	to 20″	to 22″
Waist	18″	19″	20″
Hip	19″	20″	21″
Back Waist Length	6⅛″	6⅞″	7½″
Across Back	7¼″	7¾″	8¼″
Shoulder	2″	2¼″	2½″
Neck	3¼″	3¼″	3¼″
Sleeve Length to Underarm	6″	6½″	7½″
Armhole Depth	3¼″	3½″	3¾″
Upper Arm Circumference	6½″	7″	7¼″
Wrist Circumference	5″	5⅛″	5⅛″
Head	15″	15″	16″

Body Measurements for Children

	SIZE:								
	C-2	C-3	C-4	C-5	C-6	C-7	C-8	C-10	C-12
Chest	21″	22″	23″	24″	25″	26″	27″	28½″	30″
Waist	20″	20½″	21″	21½″	22″	22½″	23″	24″	25″
Hip	22″	23″	24″	25″	26″	27″	28″	30″	32″
Back Waist Length	8½″	9″	9½″	10″	10½″	11½″	12½″	14″	15″
Across Back	8¾″	9¼″	9½″	9¾″	10¼″	10¾″	11″	11½″	12″
Shoulder	2¾″	3″	3″	3⅛″	3⅜″	3½″	3⅝″	3¾″	4″
Neck	3¼″	3¼″	3½″	3½″	3½″	3¾″	3¾″	4″	4″
Sleeve Length to Underarm	8½″	9½″	10½″	11″	11½″	12″	12½″	13½″	15″
Armhole Depth	4¼″	4¾″	5½″	5½″	6″	6″	6¼″	6½″	7″
Upper Arm Circumference	7½″	7¾″	8″	8¼″	8½″	8¾″	9″	9⅜″	9¾″
Wrist Circumference	5¼″	5¼″	5½″	5½″	5½″	5¾″	5¾″	6″	6″
Head	17″	18″							

Body Measurements for Misses

				SIZE:			
	6	8	10	12	14	16	18
Bust	30½"	31½"	32½"	34"	36"	38"	40"
Waist	23"	24"	25"	26½"	28"	30"	32"
Hip	32½"	33½"	34½"	36"	38"	40"	42"
Back Waist Length	15½"	15¾"	16"	16¼"	16½"	16¾"	17"
Across Back	13½"	13½"	14"	14½"	15"	15½"	16"
Shoulder	4¾"	4¾"	5"	5"	5"	5¼"	5¼"
Neck	4"	4"	4"	4½"	5"	5"	5½"
Sleeve Length to Underarm	16¾"	16¾"	17"	17½"	17¾"	18"	18¼"
Armhole Depth	7"	7"	7½"	7½"	7½"	8"	8"
Upper Arm Circumference	9¾"	9¾"	10¼"	10½"	11"	11½"	12"
Wrist Circumference	6"	6"	6¼"	6¼"	6½"	6½"	6½"

Body Measurements for Women

				SIZE:			
	38	40	42	44	46	48	50
Bust	42"	44"	46"	48"	50"	52"	54"
Waist	35"	37"	39"	41½"	44"	46½"	49"
Hip	44"	46"	48"	50"	52"	54"	56"
Back Waist Length	17¼"	17⅜"	17½"	17⅝"	17¾"	17⅞"	18"
Across Back	16½"	17"	17½"	18"	18"	18½"	18½"
Shoulder	5½"	5½"	5¾"	5¾"	6"	6¼"	6¼"
Neck	5½"	6"	6"	6"	6"	6"	6"
Sleeve Length to Underarm	18¼"	18¼"	18¼"	18¼"	18¼"	18¼"	18¼"
Armhole Depth	8¼"	8¼"	8¼"	8½"	8½"	8¾"	8¾"
Upper Arm Circumference	13"	13½"	14"	15"	15¾"	16½"	17"
Wrist Circumference	6¾"	7"	7¼"	7½"	7¾"	8"	8"

Special Addition: Maggie's Measurements for Big and Beautiful Women

	SIZE:						
	38	40	42	44	46	48	50
Finished Width at Underarm	39"	41"	43"	45"	47"	49"	51"
Back Inches at Underarm	19.5"	20.5"	21.5"	22.5"	23.5"	24.5"	25.5"
Back Stitches	—	—	—	—	—	—	—
Length to Underarm	15"	15"	15"	15"	15"	15"	15"
Underarm Bind-off	—	—	—	—	—	—	—
Underarm Decrease	—	—	—	—	—	—	—
Shoulder Width	14"	14"	14.5"	15"	15"	15.5"	16"
Shoulder Inches	—	—	—	—	—	—	—
Armhole Depth	8"	8"	8"	8"	8"	8"	8"
Sweater Depth	—	—	—	—	—	—	—
Neck Inches	6.5"	6.5"	7"	7.5"	7.5"	7.5"	8"
Neck Stitches	—	—	—	—	—	—	—
Each Shoulder Inches	3.75"	3.75"	3.75"	3.75"	3.75"	3.75"	3.75"
Each Shoulder Stitches	—	—	—	—	—	—	—
Wrist Inches	6.5"	7"	7"	7.5"	7.5"	8"	8.5"
Wrist Stitches	—	—	—	—	—	—	—
Lower Arm Inches	11.5"	12"	12.5"	13"	13.5"	14"	14.5"
Lower Arm Stitches	—	—	—	—	—	—	—
Upper Arm Inches	13.5"	14"	16"	16.5"	17"	17.5"	18"
Upper Arm Stitches	—	—	—	—	—	—	—
Finished Length from Back Neck	—	—	—	—	—	—	—

Body Measurements for Men

	SIZE:							
	34	36	38	40	42	44	46	48
Chest	34"	36"	38"	40"	42"	44"	46"	48"
Waist	28"	30"	32"	34"	36"	39"	42"	44"
Hip	35"	37"	39"	41"	43"	45"	47"	49"
Across Back	15½"	16"	16½"	17"	17½"	18"	18½"	19"
Shoulder	5"	5¼"	5½"	5½"	5½"	6"	6"	6"
Neck: Shirt Size	14"	14½"	15"	15½"	16"	16½"	17"	17½"
Length to Armhole	14"	14½"	15"	15½"	16"	16"	16½"	17"
Armhole Depth	8"	8½"	9"	9½"	10"	10½"	11"	11½"
Sleeve to Underarm	17½"	18"	18½"	19"	19½"	20"	20"	20½"
Back Length	22"	23"	24"	25"	26"	26½"	27½"	28½"

Leisure Arts' Standards (Finished Sizes)

Body Measurements for Children

	SIZE:					
	4	6	8	10	12	14
Actual Chest Measurement	22″	23½″	25″	27″	29″	31″
Chest:						
Pullover	23″	24½″	26″	28″	30″	32″
Cardigan	24″	25½″	27″	29″	31″	33″
Waist (both)	21″	22½″	24″	25½″	27″	28″
Armhole Depth (for set-in sleeve; add 1″ for raglan sleeve):						
Pullover	5¼″	5¾″	6¼″	6¾″	7″	7¼″
Cardigan	5¾″	6¼″	6¾″	7¼″	7½″	7¾″
Body Length to Underarm★:						
Pullover	9″	10″	11″	11½″	12″	13″
Cardigan	9½″	10½″	11½″	12″	12½″	13½″
Sleeve Length (both)★	10½″	11¾″	13″	14¼″	15½″	17″
Body Width at Shoulder:						
Pullover	9½″	10″	10½″	11″	11½″	12″
Cardigan	10″	10½″	11″	11½″	12″	12½″
Neck (both)	4″	4″	4½″	4½″	5″	5″
Each Shoulder:						
Pullover	2¾″	3″	3″	3¼″	3¼″	3½″
Cardigan	3″	3¼″	3¼″	3½″	3½″	3¾″
Sleeve Width at Upper Arm:						
Pullover	9″	9½″	10″	10½″	11″	11½″
Cardigan	9½″	10″	10½″	11″	11½″	12″
Sleeve Width at Lower Arm:						
Pullover	7½″	8″	8″	8½″	9″	9½″
Cardigan	8″	8½″	8½″	9″	9½″	10″

★Or, to desired length.

Body Measurements for Toddlers

	SIZE: 3 MOS.	6 MOS.	12 MOS.	18 MOS.	24 MOS.
Actual Chest Measurement	17"	19"	20"	20½"	21"
Finished Chest:					
Pullover	18"	20"	21"	21½"	22"
Cardigan	19"	21"	22"	22½"	23"
Waist*	16"	18"	19"	19½"	20"
Hip*	18"	20"	21"	22"	23"
Armhole Depth (for set-in sleeve; add ½" for raglan sleeve):					
Pullover	3¾"	4"	4¼"	4½"	5"
Cardigan	4"	4¼"	4½"	4¾"	5¼"
Body Length to Underarm:					
Pullover	5½"	6½"	7"	7½"	8"
Cardigan	6"	7"	7½"	8"	8½"
Sleeve Length (both)	5"	6"	7"	8"	9"
Body Width at Shoulders (both)	7"	7½"	8"	8½"	9"
Neck (both)	3"	3½"	3½"	3½"	4"
Each Shoulder (both)	2"	2"	2¼"	2½"	2½"
Sleeve Width at Underarm:					
Pullover	6"	7"	8"	8¼"	8½"
Cardigan	6¼"	7¼"	8¼"	8½"	8¾
Crotch Length*	6"	7"	8"	8½"	9"
Leg Length to Crotch	6"	7"	8"	9"	10"
Head Circumference	15"	16"	16"	16½"	17"
Wrist	4½"	5"	5¼"	5¼"	5¼"
Total Height	25"	28"	31"	32½"	34"

*Measurements allow for diapers.

Addition to Toddler Standards

	SIZE:				
	3 MOS.	6 MOS.	12 MOS.	18 MOS.	24 MOS.
Close Fitting Bonnet:					
Neck	8″	9″	10″	10½″	11″
Widest part	11″	12″	13″	13½″	14″
Height	6″	7″	7½″	7¾″	8″

Hood

Sizing should reflect appropriate increases to the above measurements allowing for a looser fit especially adding extra height to allow for joining at shoulder level, rather than where a bonnet would tie at the neck.

Hand length—					
wrist to fingertip	3¼″	3½″	3¾″	3¾″	4″
Wrist	4½″	5″	5¼″	5¼″	5¼″
Foot length—					
heel to toe (Booties)	3¾″	4″	4½″		
Ankle	4¾″	5″	5½″		

Body Measurements for Women

	32"	34"	36"	38"	40"
BUST MEASUREMENT:					

Finished Measurements

Bust:

	32"	34"	36"	38"	40"
Pullover	33"	35"	37"	39"	41"
Cardigan	34"	36"	38"	40"	42"

Armhole Depth (for set-in sleeve; add 1" for raglan sleeve):

	32"	34"	36"	38"	40"
Pullover	8¼"	8½"	8¾"	9"	9¼"
Cardigan	8½"	8¾"	9"	9¼"	

Body Length to Underarm:

Pullover	15" or desired	
Cardigan	16" or desired	

Sleeve Length (both):

	32"	34"	36"	38"	40"
	17¼"	17½"	17¾"	18"	18¼"

Body Width at Shoulder:

	32"	34"	36"	38"	40"
Pullover	12½"	13"	13½"	14"	14½"
Cardigan	13"	13½"	14"	14½"	15"

Neck (both):

	32"	34"	36"	38"	40"
	5½"	5½"	6"	6½"	6½"

Each Shoulder:

	32"	34"	36"	38"	40"
Pullover	3½"	3¾"	3¾"	3¾"	4"
Cardigan	3¾"	4"	4"	4"	4¼"

Sleeve Width at Upper Arm:

	32"	34"	36"	38"	40"
Pullover	11½"	12"	12½"	13"	13½"
Cardigan	12"	12½"	13"	13½"	14"

Sleeve Width at Lower Arm:

	32"	34"	36"	38"	40"
Pullover	10"	10½"	11"	11"	11½"
Cardigan	10½"	11"	11½"	11½"	12"

Body Measurements for Men

	CHEST MEASUREMENT:				
	36"	38"	40"	42"	44"
Finished Measurements					
Chest:					
Pullover	37"	39"	41"	43"	45"
Cardigan	38"	40"	42"	44"	46"
Armhole Depth (for set-in sleeve; add 1" for raglan sleeve):					
Pullover	9¼"	9½"	9¾"	10"	10¼"
Cardigan	9¾"	10"	10¼"	10½"	10¾"
Body Length to Underarm:					
Pullover	16" or desired				
Cardigan	17" or desired				
Sleeve Length (both)	18"	18½"	19"	19½"	20"
Body Width at Shoulder:					
Pullover	15"	15½"	16"	16½"	17"
Cardigan	15½"	16"	16½"	17"	17½"
Neck (both)	6"	6½"	6½"	7"	7½"
Each Shoulder:					
Pullover	4½"	4½"	4¾"	4¾"	4¾"
Cardigan	4¾"	4¾"	5"	5"	5"
Sleeve Width at Upper Arm:					
Pullover	14"	14½"	15"	16"	16½"
Cardigan	14½"	15"	15½"	16½"	17"
Sleeve Width at Lower Arm:					
Pullover	12½"	13"	13½"	14"	14½"
Cardigan	13"	13½"	14"	14½"	15"

APPENDIX D

Personal Measurement Charts and Records

Body Measurement Record

NAME   DATE   WEIGHT   BODY TYPE

GARMENT STYLE   TYPE OF YARN

ACTUAL BODY MEASUREMENT   DESIRED GARMENT MEASUREMENT

_____ . . . . Back Neck Width . . . . _____

_____ . . . . Slope of Shoulder . . . . . . _____

_____ . . . . . Width Between Shoulder Bone Tips. . . . . . _____

_____ . . . . Chest/Bust . . . . _____

_____ . . . . Armhole Depth . . . . _____

_____ . . . . Desired Back Length of Garment from Nape of Neck . . . _____

_____ Desired Front Length of Garment from Neck-Shoulder Joining _____

_____ . . . . . . Length from Armhole to Desired Length . . . . _____

_____ . . . . . . Circumference at Desired Length . . . . . _____

_____ . . . . Upper Arm Width . . . . _____

_____ . . . . Desired Sleeve Length . . . . . . _____

_____ . . . . Wrist . . . . _____

_____ . . . . Waist . . . . _____

_____ . . . . Tummy . . . . _____

_____ . . . . Length from Waist to Tummy . . . . . _____

_____ . . . . . . Hip, Measured at Widest Circumference . . . . _____

_____ . . . . Length from Waist to Hip . . . . . _____

_____ . . . . Length from Waist to Skirt Bottom . . . . _____

Horizontal darts necessary _____ Vertical darts necessary _____

Additional notes: _____

Body Measurement Record

NAME   DATE   WEIGHT   BODY TYPE

GARMENT STYLE   TYPE OF YARN

**ACTUAL BODY
MEASUREMENT**
                                     **DESIRED GARMENT
MEASUREMENT**

—— . . . . Back Neck Width . . . . ——

—— . . . . Slope of Shoulder . . . . ——

—— . . . . . Width Between Shoulder Bone Tips. . . . . . ——

—— . . . . Chest/Bust . . . . ——

—— . . . . Armhole Depth . . . . ——

—— . . . Desired Back Length of Garment from Nape of Neck . . . ——

—— Desired Front Length of Garment from Neck-Shoulder Joining ——

—— . . . . . Length from Armhole to Desired Length . . . . . ——

—— . . . . . Circumference at Desired Length . . . . . ——

—— . . . . . . Upper Arm Width . . . . . . ——

—— . . . . . . Desired Sleeve Length . . . . . . ——

—— . . . . Wrist . . . . ——

—— . . . . Waist . . . . ——

—— . . . . Tummy . . . . ——

—— . . . . . Length from Waist to Tummy . . . . . ——

—— . . . . Hip, Measured at Widest Circumference . . . . ——

—— . . . . . Length from Waist to Hip . . . . . ——

—— . . . . . Length from Waist to Skirt Bottom . . . . . ——

Horizontal darts necessary _____ Vertical darts necessary _____

Additional notes: _____

Project Record Form

MADE BY (NAME)

ADDRESS

TOWN   STATE   ZIP CODE

PHONE (HOME)   (WORK)

MADE FOR (NAME)

ADDRESS

TOWN   STATE   ZIP CODE

PHONE (HOME)   (WORK)

WEIGHT OF PERSON MADE FOR

DATE PROJECT BEGUN

IDEA AND/OR PATTERN FROM (BOOKLET OR INSTRUCTOR)

TYPE OF ARTICLE

STYLE

YARN: BRAND

AMOUNT

COLOR

DYE LOT

FIBER CONTENT

NEEDLE OR HOOK SIZE (GARMENT)

(TRIM)

GAUGE: STITCHES

ROWS

BODY MEASUREMENTS		GARMENT MEASUREMENTS
_____	. . . . . Bust	_____
_____	. . . . . Hips	_____
_____	. . . . . Waist	_____
_____	. . . . Neck (back) . . .	_____
_____	. . . Armhole depth . . .	_____
_____	. . . . Upper chest . . .	_____
_____	. . . Shoulder length . .	_____
_____	. . . Sleeve length . . .	_____
_____	. . . . . Wrist	_____
_____	. . . . UA to waist	_____
_____	. . . . . Tummy	_____
_____	. . Length to tummy . .	_____
_____	. . . . . Hip	_____
_____	. . . Length to hip . . .	_____
_____	. . . Finished length . . .	_____

Special Techniques and/or Pattern St:

Sketch:

Index